Journal of
Camus Studies

2012

www.camus-society.com

www.camus-us.com

Journal of Camus Studies

The purpose of the *Journal of Camus Studies* is to further understanding of the work and thought of Albert Camus.

The material contained in this journal represents the opinions of the authors and not necessarily those of the Albert Camus Society or anyone affiliated with the Society.

Authors – paper submissions

In the first instance email an abstract of no more than 300 words to secretary@camus-society.com

For more information on submissions we refer you to the guidelines printed at the end of this journal.

Copyright

ISBN: 978-1-291-37497-1

Table of Contents

Introductions by Peter Francev and Simon Lea

2012 was a banner year for the Albert Camus societies of the USA and UK. At the annual meeting, in November, in London, we had our largest turnout—twenty-three members present, with twelve scholars presenting. Essays were presented on a wide variety of Camus' texts, and demonstrated the importance (and need) of our societies in the field of Camus studies. Unfortunately, however, we did run out of time, and the consensus among attendees was that for 2013, the meeting be held over two days. This way, each paper presented will have adequate time for its presentation and ample time for follow-up questions and answers.

The fact that there are seventeen essays in this edition is, I believe, a testament to Camus' relevance in the twenty-first century. I hope that they prove to be a catalyst for your own thinking and research in Camus studies.

In mid-2013, there will be a Call for Papers for the 2013 London meeting and the journal, which will be held in Bloomsbury, London, England in mid-November. For submission guidelines, please reference the Submission Guidelines which are found the end of the journal. For 2013, the Journal will be requiring authors to strictly follow the guidelines; otherwise their essay will be returned without publication. A more detailed submission outline booklet will be made available later this year. Also, feel free to check out the "updates" section of the Society's Academia.edu profile page, as well as the UK society's Facebook page.

In closing, while I cannot and will not take all of the credit, the number of thanks that are indebted to Simon and Helen Lea, for their work as copy editors before the journal went to press, as well as to the Journal's Associate Editors: Dr. Brent Sleasman and Dr. Matthew Bowker cannot be quantified. Without your help, this journal would have never come to fruition.

Sincerely yours,

Peter Francev
Editor, *Journal of Camus Studies*

The Albert Camus Society is growing. From our beginnings in 2005 it took four years to get together the first journal and from then on each year this journal has grown in size, both in terms of readership and the number of articles contained inside. There have been five annual conferences with delegates attending from around the world. This year we will hold our first two-day conference in London. The Camus Society is active on Facebook and Twitter and we operate three websites, camus-society.com, camus-us.com, and albertcamus.info. In 2013 we look to publish other works on Camus in addition to the journal. Members of the UK and US societies are also in the process of publishing works on Camus with other publishers: academic monographs, collected essays and books for general public. We also hope to play a role in bringing Camus to the London stage later this year.

It would be wrong, however, to forget that we are still a small Society. There is a lot more room to grow. My thanks go out to everyone who has helped us, and who continues to help us, in taking the Albert Camus Society from strength to strength.

Warmest regards,

Simon Lea
President, *Albert Camus Society*

Paneloux's Turn: An Analysis of the Sermons of *The Plague*

By Eric Berg

I'd rather succeed in doing what we can than fail to do what we can't.[1]

18. The acts of men are worthy of neither fire nor heaven.[2]

In this essay I will argue that Camus presents two possible Christian answers for a classic theodicy. The first is an Augustinian answer and the second is from Tertullian (a second century Christian theologian from North Africa.) in the end both fail and theodicy yields absurdity.

In an essay titled "A Tribute to Albert Camus", Jean-Paul Sartre remarked that "One had to avoid him or fight him—he was indispensable to that tension which makes intellectual life what it is."[3] This is the fate of Father Paneloux in *The Plague*. Camus sets forth a classic theodicy dilemma, and the Roman priest must face the horns of the bull; much like Sartre's observation of Camus, Paneloux was caught in that terrible intellectual tension and dies a "doubtful case."

Father Paneloux delivers two sermons to the inhabitants of Oran during their year of plague. *The Plague,* as a novel, is carefully constructed in five sections; positioned within parts one and four, like twin pillars, are the two sermons of Father Paneloux. Camus very obviously draws attention to elements in and around the sermons that set the two apart. What is most clear is that Father Paneloux has changed between the two sermons he

---

[1] Richard Adams, *Watership Down* (New York: Scribner, 1972)

[2] Jorge Luis Borges, "Fragments from an Apocryphal Gospel", *Selected Poems*, edited by Alexander Coleman (New York: Penguin Books, 1999).

[3] Jean-Paul Sartre, "A Tribute to Albert Camus", *Camus: a Collection of Essays*, edited by Germaine Bree. Engelwood Cliffs: Prentice Hall, 1962. P.174

delivers. The direct cause of the change is not in question, it is the death of a child, but several questions do remain unanswered. What does Camus say to the reader with the tension between the two sermons? What are the underlying theological changes in Paneloux's sermon, and how do they attempt to answer the dilemma raised by Camus? Are they successful?

The first question formulated above is answered by saying that Camus demonstrated to the reader that there is no successful Christian resolution to the theodicy dilemma presented in *The Plague*. Paneloux holds to a firm Augustinian line based upon the supreme will of God as an answer to the plague in the first sermon. In the second sermon, he shifts to a position closer to Tertullian's *credo quia absurdum est*[4] (I believe because it is absurd) or a move to the mystery of God. In the face of the death of the child, both attempts to avoid the horns fail, and what finally can be said is said by Rieux in the closing of the novel. Camus'/Rieux's answer is that "...we learn in times of pestilence: that there are more things to admire in men than to despise."[5]

Who is Father Paneloux? We know from Camus that he is a Jesuit priest who serves the Roman church in Oran, Algeria. He is an expert on Augustine as Camus himself was.[6] Paneloux is introduced to the reader in part one of the novel by attending to a parishioner (apparently), and Dr. Rieux is about to see the parishioner in question. The narrator describes the Father as a "...learned and militant Jesuit... who was very highly thought of in our town, even in circles quite indifferent to religion."[7] This introduction of Paneloux serves to dismiss any charges of Camus creating a straw-man out of the Christian position. As a "learned and militant Jesuit" Paneloux would be extremely well equipped in any theological or philosophical debate. The Jesuit order of the Roman Church should immediately bring considerable academic credibility to Paneloux, and I would presume that "militant" could be read as "orthodox" as well as an attitudinal disposition. The effect is that the reader cannot impeach his credentials to deal with the

---

[4] *Early Latin Theology* edited by S.L. Greenshade, (Louisville: The Westminster Press, 1986)

[5] Albert Camus, *The Plague* (New York: Vintage International, 1991) p. 308

[6] Camus' level of expertise is that of Paneloux's because Paneloux is a fictional character and his level of knowledge is derivative from the author.

[7] Albert Camus, *The Plague*, p. 17

theological issues that plague will bring. Furthermore, it should not be overlooked that, in this scene, it is Paneloux who makes the first correct assessment of the situation in Oran. He tells the doctor that this business of the rats has to do with "..an epidemic they are having." [8] This effectively demonstrates to the reader that Paneloux is aware of the concrete situation around him. Paneloux is used as a "stock" representative of the French Catholic church at the time of the German invasion or, as Camus dates the novel, "194-." Paneloux's views will accurately represent the views of French clergy at the time in France. Clearly Paneloux is a "cut above" the average French cleric in terms of education alone, not to mention other possible categories. What Paneloux represents is the intellectual leadership that will actually do the academic formulation of the theological responses to the German invasion. What men like Paneloux decide will work its way into the pulpits all around France through official channels. Paneloux is also employed to explore the question of evil, and his attempt is restrained by the size of the novel, and the fact that the Christian response is only one reaction that Camus intended to cover. Camus cannot represent every Christian position, so he must select one, and he does a fine job by selecting a Jesuit Augustine scholar.

Concerning the selection of Paneloux, Thomas Hanna makes an accurate observation about Christianity and Camus. Hanna wrote:

> It is a curious thing about the thought of Albert Camus that he has not estranged himself from Christian readers…when Christians pick up the works of Camus, it is with a mind to learn. It is encouraging and admirable that there continues to be a healthy dialogue between Camus and Christian thinkers. [9]

This is reflected in his careful choice of, and categorical character development of Paneloux. It has been speculated that Paneloux could be modeled after a priest named Pain whom Camus knew in Oran, but Jean Grenier thinks that Camus borrowed his name from the town of Le

---

[8] ibid. p.18

[9] Thomas L. Hanna, "Albert Camus and the Christian Faith", from *Camus: A Collection of Critical Essays*, edited by Germaine Bree (Engelwood Cliffs: Prentice Hall, 1962) p.56.

Panelier.[10] Prototypes aside, Paneloux is an extremely interesting character in the novel whom one cannot help but look to for answers.

James Woelfel, in his book *Camus: A Theological Perspective*, points to the direction of the questions I raise in this paper. Woelfel argues that Paneloux's second sermon is the "...only satisfactory rationale that can be constructed for the Christian resolution of the problem of evil given the divine omnipotence." [11] I agree with the claim in that it is an attempted resolution of the dilemma by Paneloux after the first attempt fails. However, it is my position that Camus demonstrates that both attempts by Paneloux end in failure; that there is no satisfactory answer for Paneloux given the dilemma and his theological commitments.

What this paper focuses upon is the classic theological dilemma set upon father Paneloux and the reader in *The Plague*. The dilemma is presented in the standard format.[12] The Christian God has the attributes of being both omnipotent and wholly good.[13] Being omnipotent entails having unchecked

---

[10] Jene Grenier, *Albert Camus: Sun and Shade: An Intellectual Biography* (Paris: Gallimard, 1987) P.155

[11] James Woelfel, *Camus: A Theological Perspective*. (New York: Abingdon Press, 1975) P.86

[12] This dilemma has been set forth in innumerable ways. For several examples see the following: Dostovesky's *Rebellion* from *The Brothers Karamazov*; J.L. Mackie, *Evil and Omnipotence*; and Peter Van Inwagen, *The Magnitude, Duration and Distribution of Evil: A Theodicy*.

[13] When considering the attributes of God for this dilemma it is important to consider omniscience. Typically I have collapsed this into omnipotence. What is a God that is all powerful but has limited knowledge? By separating out God's knowledge it seems to also eliminate the power of God. Without knowledge God is limited and looses some of his power, any loss of power makes God less than omnipotent. However, it is important to note that there are already limitations placed upon God. First are logical limitations. Does omnipotence mean God can create a round square? Furthermore, time seems to have a limiting factor of God. Can He change what has been? It is helpful to look at this from the Augustinian perspective as Paneloux and Camus might. God sees every moment as one. He has a special vision, and this does make some modification upon the theodicy problem. However, this paper as I see it is concerned with the arguments as I find them in *The Plague*. The categories of God's power are set forth in the three fold format that I argue for. A modern response may incorporate temporal consideration to the question, but as I see Paneloux's position, he recognizes God as Omnipotent and completely good, and any considerations of God's knowledge will be included in His power. For example this could be the very best state of

power and being wholly good entails having the will to do good at all times. The final component of the dilemma is not a trait of God, but an ontological claim that evil exists. The dilemma quickly moves to contradiction. Either God's power is limited in contradiction to being omnipotent, or he has not done the good thing that is within his power, a failure of the divine will. The last move available to save the attributes of God is to deny the existence of evil. In the face of the plague, and particularly the death of the innocent child this is also a move to contradiction. This is Paneloux's situation.

Camus intentionally draws the reader's attention to the differences between the two sermons. There are differences of style, the weather, the congregation, and Paneloux's shift in pronoun use. These differences should be considered when separating the two sermons from one another.

The first clear difference is the style of delivery between the two sermons. The narrator describes Paneloux as "..a man of passionate and fiery temperament...who flung himself wholeheartedly into the task assigned him."[14] He is described as being a "stocky man with a massive torso." The reader can picture an imposing figure with a bass voice perhaps. The first sermon is delivered with a "powerful and emotional delivery...with clear emphatic tones." As Paneloux delivers the sermon, he actually gains intensity as it matches the thunderstorm outside. Toward the end of the delivery, he is physically worn out, "his hair was straggling over his forehead...his body shaken with tremors."[15] and he speaks in a lower voice that is described as "matter-of-fact." At the very end, it is reported that he pauses enough to give the impression he is done, and then launches into a final assault. This is a widely used tactic employed in public speaking and preaching that draws attention to the conclusion. In terms of form, the sermon is passionate, dramatic and above all authoritative. The first sermon is delivered by a scholar who also demonstrates an ability to preach.

The second sermon is delivered in a much more personal way, less intentional. Paneloux shows the characteristics of a person who has been

---

affaires possible for Oran in 194_. However, it does not make the dilemma dissipate or help with the death of the child.

[14] Albert Camus, *The Plague*.

[15] Albert Camus, *The Plague*.

through a plague not of a professional orator, but Camus still describes it as a "performance." Paneloux now delivers his sermon in a "...gentler, more thoughtful tone...and several times stumbled over his words." His voice only grows firmer as he proceeds, and then he finally manages a dramatic gesture. As the sermon comes to an end, he recaptures the spirit from the first sermon, slams his fist on the pulpit and ends in a voice that is "ringing." After the sermon, two priests describe the sermon as more "uneasy" than powerful. This uneasiness can be attributed to his shift in theological position. The first sermon is delivered in a powerful self-assured form. Paneloux has Augustine figuratively standing right behind him in the pulpit; he is sure of all his claims. The uneasiness of the second delivery demonstrates a lack of confidence, and it marks a shift in theology. It is a shift from the sure-footed and familiar terrain of Hippo (Augustine) to the treacherous and foreign terrain of Carthage (Tertullian).

Next, is the congregation that hears the sermon. The attendance is considered high for Oran, but Camus is quick to qualify this. It is because the beaches are closed, and the anxiety of plague setting in draws the curious. Camus also hints that many of the congregation have adopted the seductive Pascalian position of believing "it can't do any harm." In this time of great crisis, the inhabitants of Oran have turned toward religion as opposed to their lives during a more normal time when there is no immediate crisis. It has quickly been calculated by some parts of the general population that going to church can operate as an insurance policy.

For one reason or another people come to hear Paneloux and the cathedral is full for the first sermon; people are spilling out onto the street to hear him preach. It is haunting that Paneloux himself calls attention to St. Roch, a Roman Catholic Saint invoked during a time of plague, in the first sermon, and when the plague is raging in full force many of his congregation turn to St. Roch in almost idolatry. For the second sermon, Paneloux is delivering his message to a designated crowd. Paneloux preaches his second sermon at a "Mass for men", which sets it apart curiously from the first sermon. The narrator reports that the congregation is "sparser...three quarters full" as St.

Roch has attracted his following, and the women are missing.[16] Dr Rieux is present at both sermons and provides the highly observant reporting of each.

Camus also uses extraordinary weather conditions to support the sermons and distinguish them. The first sermon is occasioned by a tremendous rainstorm. The rain sets the tone in the church by way of "heavy" fumes of incense and wet clothes. The narrator notes that "… these words, striking through a silence intensified by the drumming of raindrops on the chancel windows…"[17] When the sermon is done, we are informed that the sun has broken out and the rain is gone. Paneloux has outlasted the thunderstorm. This will not be the case in the second sermon. During the second sermon, there is a great wind blowing, and it is described as "filling the church with sudden drafts." The rain seems to work in favor of the first sermon, and the wind against the second. As Paneloux begins to finally gather some steam in his delivery the wind begins to "thump" the cathedral door, and it draws attention away from the sermon at the critical moment that Paneloux is gaining some momentum on his situation. The wind blown door leaves the reader feeling distracted when reading the sermon, and places the reader into the equally distracted mind of someone in the cathedral. When the congregation of men leave, the second sermon the wind is still raging and Paneloux is done, his words and those of his critics seem to be lost in the African wind. Camus is clear to point out that the wind is from inland, and not the sea. When the wind begins to blow in from the Mediterranean the plague will break.

The final and most telling difference is the shift in pronoun use. Paneloux shifts from "you" to the all inclusive "we." The narrator calls direct attention to this difference, so it should not be taken lightly. Camus remarks, "A yet more noteworthy change was that instead of saying 'you' he now said 'we'." Paneloux from the first sermon: "Calamity has come upon you, my brethren." [18] Paneloux from the second sermon: "We must believe everything, or deny everything." [19] The focus on God's judgment separated

---

[16] This description of the congregation is similar to the reports in the rest of the novel by the fact that there is no mention of any Arabs.

[17] Albert Camus, *The Plague* p.93

[18] Albert Camus, *The Plague* p. 94

[19] Ibid. p. 224

Paneloux from the other inhabitants of Oran; he does not see himself as part of the chain of cause and effect that has brought plague to the city. In the second sermon, he is one of the indicted, and the guilt becomes corporate, as does the struggle.

As the novel should be considered operating on three levels, the story of Oran itself, of Nazi occupation of France, and of the human condition, the analysis of Paneloux's sermons must be investigated from all three perspectives. [20] The three levels are: first as a particular city gripped by the plague, second as a metaphor for the German invasion of France, and, third as a commentary on the universal human condition.

I shall consider the second level first, or the German invasion of France. Considering the sermons as a metaphor for the German occupation of France, Germaine Brée made an interesting observation in her book titled *Camus*. In a foot-note (unfortunately unsupported by any citation), she reported that the first sermon of Paneloux recalls Catholic sermons delivered in France in 1940. These sermons called for the French to "...consider the defeat and occupation of France as the natural punishment for its sins and to accept it therefore as such, to repent and trust in God." [21] Thomas Merton follows the lead of Brée, and also makes a direct connection to the sermons delivered in France in the 1940's. Merton reported: "The theme of plague as punishment for sin echoes the preaching of many French Catholic priests and bishops after the fall of France during the 'great penitence of Vichy.'" [22] Unfortunately this represents, with a few exceptions, the reaction of the

---

[20] An interesting fourth option has been put forth by Lulu M. Haroutunian. Haroutunian also sees Camus' *Plague* operating as a metaphor for those who suffer from tuberculosis during this time, as Camus did. In the article titled *Albert Camus and the White Plague* (MLN, Vol. 79, Issue 3, French Issue, May 1964) Haroutunian makes a compelling argument that Camus is also talking from experience and relating the novel to his time in the sanatorium. Haroutunian argues that the word "Plague" can be read as "Tuberculosis" and "Plague bacillus" for "tubercle bacillis". By contrast Theodore Ziolkowski in his article titled *Camus in Germany, or the Return of the Prodigal* Son (Theodore Ziolkowski, *Yale French Studies, Volume 0*, Issue 25, 1960) argues that Germans have only read *The Plague* on one or two levels. He stated that Germans have "...consistently ignored this interpretation (Oran as France)...And Germany, whose solicitous paternity he firmly declined, is left holding the calf—which has grown remarkable fat."

[21] Germaine Bree, *Camus,* (p.126

[22] Thomas Merton, *Albert Camus' The Plague* (New York: The Seabury Press, 1968) p.12

Church as a whole to the war and the holocaust in Europe. The move from Augustine to Tertullian that Paneloux makes is representative of the Church in Europe at the time. Both the Roman Church and the various Protestant denominations were in a fight for survival, being divided like the populations of Europe. Some served their homes in exile, and others served fascist governments. When we consider Paneloux as a character on this level, he begins as a passive force, giving no direction and extolling only judgment. His next sermon only adds confusion to judgment with the move to absurdity. Finally, he seems to resist by joining the sanitation squads, bringing forth memories of people like Simone Weil and Dietrich Bonhoeffer.

It is also worth noting that both Augustine and Tertullian attack Marcion (first century Christian bishop eventually excommunicated by the Chruch) in their work, particularly the work that I attribute to Camus for the formulation of the sermons in *The Plague*. Marcion attempted to eliminate the Old Testament from the canon, and traces of Judaism from the New Testament. His canon became the Gospel of Luke and the letters of Paul. For these reasons he became an important theological instrument in the hands of the Third Reich. The selection of Augustine and Tertullian in light of their criticism of Marcion is an important connection to keep in mind when reading *The Plague* as a metaphor for Christian reactions to the Nazi invasion of France. The theologians that I propose Camus makes use of to advance his theological arguments in the text both attack Marcion, thus representing positive Christian elements in Europe during the time of Nazi dominance.

Paneloux's sermons work as a commentary on the first and third level reading[23] of *The Plague* at the same time. The sermons are employed to represent the Christian reaction to natural evil given their particular ontological belief. Each character in the novel has a different set of beliefs that are brought to bear on the question of natural evil. Dr. Rieux has no transcendent being to contend with, but he does have special knowledge of the evil, and with this knowledge comes an ability and responsibility to fight it. Cottard sees it as a reprieve from the normal human system that haunts

---

[23] The first level being a story about a city gripped in plague, or a particular human condition. The second level as the German occupation of France during World War Two. The third level being about the universal human condition.

him. He takes it as an opportunity. The other citizens of Oran have found themselves in his position. They are now all under indictment and arrest, awaiting judgment. In some ways he has a special theological vision, that of Barrabas, the one set free. Paneloux is placed in a unique position; he has a transcendent being that has taken an active hand in the plague, but one that he will not blame. This presents a very special set of circumstances to work out regarding the question of natural evil, and transforms itself into a theodicy dilemma.

Augustinian Elements of the First Sermon

It is clear that Paneloux functions as a theological voice for Camus. He wants to address the question of universal human suffering in the face of evil from several perspectives, and Paneloux's is the religious perspective. As I have argued in this paper, the selection of a Jesuit Augustine scholar is not by accident. Camus knew the theological position of Augustine very well. He did his graduate work in philosophy on Augustine, and this allows Camus to work competently from a theological position for the construction of the sermons. Furthermore, it also represents what Camus may see as the best Christian theologian to work with: an African from the Mediterranean region who knew Greek philosophy. This would suit Camus' taste and background much better than a theologian from northern Europe who called Aristotle "a whore and worse" for example.

In this section, I will reconstruct Paneloux's first sermon from the theological works of Augustine. In the following section, I will do the same with Paneloux's second sermon and Tertullian.

Augustine argues in his *Enchiridion*: "It is enough for the Christian to believe that the only cause of all created things, whether heavenly or earthly...is the goodness of God; and that nothing exists...that does not derive its existence from Him".[24] Paneloux reflected this belief when he preached: "Today the truth is a command. It is a red spear pointing to the narrow path, the one of salvation...the divine compassion which has ordained good and evil in everything; wrath and pity; the plague and your

---

[24] St. Augustine, *Enchiridion on Faith Hope and Love*, Translated by Thomas S. Hibbs, (Washington: Regnery Publishing, 1996.) P. 10

salvation. This same pestilence which is slaying you works for your good and points your path…"[25] All things work for the good for Augustine and Paneloux. The plague that has visited Oran is there to deliver them to a higher good, it comes to change their path and judge them. It is from God, it appears evil but ultimately it is good. This is a complicated theological position that Paneloux must work out, it traces the path of evil and sets it into the created order. This functions as a necessary condition to set in motion the contradiction. This formulation will attempt to shift the blame from God to the human agent, but it moves quickly to contradiction. The evil is derivative from God, and the dilemma of being omnipotent and willing the good quickly corners Paneloux.

The following passages set forth the classic theodicy dilemma for Augustine. Augustine commits himself (and Paneloux) to the classic threefold form of the dilemma. In it he claims the omnipotence of God, along with his entire goodness, and the existence of evil. The elements are presented clearly and completely when Augustine argues, "…If he were not so omnipotent and good that He can bring good even out of evil."[26] All the necessary conditions are present in this formulation from Augustine. He claims the omnipotence of God, his goodness, and that evil exists. Paneloux echoes this when he preaches, "It (plague) reveals the will of God in action, unfailingly transforming evil into good." [27] The two are theologically linked, and committed to arguing the theodicy dilemma from the classical Augustine position.

With the necessary conditions of the theodicy dilemma in place, Augustine's move is to God's judgment. Augustine argued, "Nor can we doubt that God does well even in the permission of what is evil. For He permits it only in the justice of His judgment." [28] Paneloux confidently follows his master: "And this is why, wearied of waiting for you to come to him, He loosed on you this visitation; as he has visited all the cities that offended against Him since the dawn of history." [29] The blame stands with the community, and the plague

---

[25] Albert Camus, *The Plague*, p. 96.

[26] St. Augustine, *Enchiridion* p.11

[27] Albert Camus, *The Plague*, p. 99.

[28] St. Augustine, *Enchiridion*, p. 110

[29] Albert Camus, *The Plague*, p. 97

that has been sent by God is a necessary consequence of their actions. The problem with this is that it checks God's power. The actions of Oran logically (or metaphysically) entail that a plague be set loose, or at the least judgment be delivered. God had no other choice but to deliver the plague to Oran. When the emphasis is placed upon the judgment of God, God cannot overlook a city that calls for plague. It seems that God could have set loose some other form of judgment upon Oran. What is critical to realize is with the necessity of judgment in place God has to deliver. God has delivered judgment upon all the other cities in history that are like Oran.[30] Now, as time dictates, he judges Oran. The form has been set in holy history (*Heilsgeschichte*), judgment of the human from God. Similar to the famous sermon by Jonathan Edwards, *Sinners in the Hands of an Angry God*, now the consequences of their actions have come forth like the rats, and act as the first link in a deadly and tragic chain of events.

Augustine argues his point further in the *Enchiridion*: "The omnipotent God, then, whether in mercy He pitieth whom He will, or in judgment hardeneth whom He will, is never unjust in what he does..."[31] Paneloux exegetes Exodus to make his point: "Pharaoh set himself up against the divine will, and the plague beat him to his knees...Now, at last, you know the hour has struck to bend your thoughts to first and last things." [32] This part of the sermon functions to bring some Biblical clarity to the situation. Apparently, the citizens of Oran are guilty; as was the Pharaoh. The Pharaoh set himself up against God, and the result is plague. It is interesting to note that a close reading of the Exodus text shows that the Pharaoh had his heart hardened by God,[33] without any agency on his part. Exodus 4:21 reads, "And the Lord said to Moses, 'When you go back to Egypt, see that you perform before Pharaoh all the wonders that I have put in your power; but I will harden his heart, so that he will not let the people go.'"[34] He did not "set himself up against God," it seems that he was set up against, and by God. Is this a mistake by Camus or Paneloux? I blame the former. Regardless of the

---

[30] It is not clear to anyone in the novel what exactly the city has done. It could be a general attitude, or a build up of past sins that has reached a breaking point in the 1940's. Whatever it is, God has now judged.

[31] St. Augustine, *Enchiridion*, p. 118

[32] Albert Camus, *The Plague*, pp. 96-97

[33] See also Matthew 19:8.

[34] NRSV *The Harper Collins Study Bible*.

exegetical error, this demonstrates an act of necessity that is set into the holy history of the world, and has a precedent in Biblical narrative.

Paneloux is cornered by the horns of the bull. It is the will of God that has brought about this evil. To deny that is to check God's power or bind His will. The plague must originate somewhere, either from God or elsewhere. Take your pick, either move hangs Paneloux on a horn. If he denies that God sent plague then it came from somewhere else, and God did not have the power to stop it. If it came from God, then God is responsible for the evil. He does not deny that it is from God, in fact he asserts that it is an instrument of judgment wielded by God. If Paneloux denies that it is evil, he either denies that God is wholly good, or denies that plague is evil. All roads lead to contradiction for Father Paneloux. Upon reflection, and the death of the child, he delivers a second sermon.

The Second Sermon and Tertullian

Paneloux's theological position has significantly changed from the first sermon to the second. This change has come over time, and it is reasonable to assume that he has delivered only two sermons thus far during the plague. The narrator draws the reader's attention to the fact that it is a remarkable event for Paneloux to deliver these sermons. It is the death of the child that Paneloux observes that has the direct effect on his theological position. The narrator reports, "He had rubbed shoulders with death." [35] Paneloux cannot hold to the doctrine of plague as judgment after the death of the innocent child and the death of the child, Paneloux is under great pressure to abandon his master, Augustine. After deconstructing Paneloux's second sermon, and reading all the relevant secondary material on this sermon, I have concluded that Paneloux makes a move toward another early church father from Africa, Tertullian. [36] It is not as clear as his reliance on Augustine to formulate the first sermon, however the evidence points to Tertullian as the inspiration for the second sermon. At the very least if Camus is not familiar with Tertulian's work, the sermon is very close to Tertullian's theological formulation of "I believe because it is absurd." I do not believe that Camus

---

[35] *The Plague*, p. 222

[36] The word "absurd" appearing as a central theme of a theological position developed in North Africa was very attractive to Camus no doubt.

intend to, nor did he, break any new theological ground with this sermon. If he did not intend it to be formulated from Tertullian, it ends up there.

Like Augustine, it is not surprising that Camus would select Tertullian as the theological father of the second sermon. Tertullian, who is from the North African city of Carthage, was a convert to Christianity in his thirties, and is a prime candidate for Camus theologically, geographically, and historically. Tertullian concerned himself with the attributes of God, employing the first theological use of the terms *Trinitas, Persona*,[37] and *Substantia*. Tertullian's work on the Trinity comes through clearly in Paneloux's second sermon. Tertullian taught that God is one; nevertheless, God cannot be regarded as something or someone totally isolated from the created order as God is active in the created order. For Tertullian the three persons of the Trinity are distinct, yet not divided. What we experience is the complex action of such a being in human history, and thus the mystery. Paneloux seems to grab hold of this notion in the second sermon. In it he said, "...that there were some things we could grasp as touching God, and others we could not."[38]

What may have attracted Camus to his work is that Tertullian concerns himself with "fever" in a very intriguing way. Tertullian employs "fever" as a metaphor for heresy in his text titled *The Prescription Against The Heretics*.[39] Tertullian wrote:

> Fever, for example, we are not surprised to find in its appointed place among the fatal and excruciating issues which destroy human life, since it does in fact exist; and we are not surprised to find it destroying life, since that is why it exists. Similarly, if we are alarmed that

---

[37] *Persona* literally means "a mask" for the Romans. When considering the attributes of God it is the concept of *deus absconditus* that helps many Protestant theologians with theodicy dilemmas. The hiddenness of God and our inability to look behind the masks of God to reveal any clear meaning.

[38] Camus, The Plague, p.223

[39] *Early Latin Theology* edited by S.L. Greenshade, (Louisville: The Westminister Press, 1986) There is little doubt in my mind that Camus was very familiar with this work. His Masters Thesis on Augustine was focused on Marcion's heresy as is Tertullian's work cited above. Camus, Augustine and Tertullian all engage Marcion on the origin and function of evil in the world.

heresies which have been produced in order to weaken and kill the faith can actually do so… [40]

Plague and heresy are linked, and the same judgment follows from each naturally. After delivering his second sermon, Father Paneloux is considered by some of the priests to be in the early grip of heresy. As the two priests leave the second sermon, the comment that the sermon was "bold" in thought. This boldness made him uneasy and a priest Paneloux's age had no business being uneasy. This probable means a "uneasiness" with church doctrine and a "boldness" to venture beyond what is established, or what has come to be expected from Paneloux, the "militant" Jesuit. The Priests believe that his forthcoming essay (on the question of a priest seeking a doctor) will be bolder still, and will be refused imprimatur. The early signs of straying too far off the doctrinal path. As the readers of *The Plague* know at the time he delivers his second sermon, Paneloux is probably already infected with plague, or whatever strange fever he dies of in the end. Camus like Tertullian links fever and heresy.

The most common point of connection cited among Camus scholars is Tertullian's famous (albeit rather difficult to attribute) "I believe because it is absurd." Both Thomas Merton and Steven G. Kellman in their books titled respectively Albert Camus' *The Plague*,[41] and *The Plague: Fiction and Resistance*[42] attribute this passage from Tertullian as the inspiration for Paneloux's second sermon. After analysis of both Tertullian and the second sermon, I agree with this argument. The actual citation from Tertullian is as follows: "The Son of God was crucified; I am not ashamed just because men feel ashamed of it. And the Son of God died; it is by all means to be believed, because it is absurd. And he was buried, and rose again; the fact is certain, because it is impossible". [43] This famous passage serves as the magnet that attracts both Paneloux and Camus. It is a logical move from the unforgiving position of Augustine to the mystery and absurdity of Tertullian.

---

[40] Tertullian, *The Prescriptions Against Heretics*. P. 31

[41] Tomas Merton, *Albert Camus' The Plague*, p. 37

[42] Steven Kellman, *The Plague: Fiction and Resistance*, (New York, Twain Publishers, 1993) p.58

[43] E.Evans, *Tertullian's Treatise on the Incarnation*, (London: S.P.C.K., 1956) p. 197.

The centerpiece of Paneloux's second sermon is the "hard " either/or that he presents the congregation of Oran. Paneloux preaches: "My Brothers, a time of testing has come for us all. We must believe in everything or deny everything." [44] This hard either/or can clearly be developed from Tertullian. Tertullian sets forth his position, "When we come to believe, we have no desire to believe anything else; for when we begin by believing that there is nothing else which we have to believe."[45] Paneloux echoes Tertullian when he preaches, "Thus today God has vouchsafed to His creatures an ordeal such that they must acquire and practice the greatest of all virtues: that of the All or Nothing." [46] The development of the "virtue" of belief implies a correct content of belief with everything else standing outside this. For Paneloux, if we hold the virtue of belief then we have no desire to believe anything else. For example, this can be compared to the virtue of truth telling. If we have developed the virtue of truth telling, and we are faced with a situation in which we may lie, we are compelled to tell the truth. The use of virtue also shows Paneloux's Roman allegiance to Aristotle and to Aquinas, the "Angelic Doctor" of the Church. There are boundaries on what can be held as a belief and what cannot in the Roman system. There is an established order of beliefs to be held to that Tertullian stands within. Tertullian made his position clear when he wrote:

> My first principle is this. Christ laid down one definite system of truth which the world must believe without qualification, and which we must seek precisely in order to believe it when we find it…You must seek until you find, and when you find, you must believe. Then you have simply to keep what you have come to believe, since you also believe there is nothing else to believe…[47]

The characteristic of "active fatalism" is employed with this either/or in the second sermon. In his second sermon the term "active fatalism" is raised for the first time. He says that the people of Oran must be the ones who stay on and fight the Plague, but to trust in the divine goodness, even with the death

---

[44] Albert Camus, *The Plague*, p. 224

[45] Tertullian, "Prescriptions Against the Heretics", From *Early Latin Theology*, Edited by S.L. Greenshade.

[46] Ibid. P. 225

[47] Tertullian, "Prescriptions Against the Heretics", From *Early Latin Theology*, Edited by S.L. Greenshade.

of the children. It means holding to the absolute of God and being active among your neighbors. Understanding that the plague is here, not committing suicide or ignoring it, but working to do what you can in Oran. Paneloux recognizes the position he has found himself in, and attempts to modify the position. This is the strong move to faith that Tertullian offers Paneloux. Paneloux now teaches that the Christian must either believe all or believe nothing. Camus sees this as a move to an absolute or a leap of faith that is the trademark of the Christian in this situation.

The Turn

The value of Augustine for the first sermon is the strength of his position. He has an uncompromising position, and it is often attractive to defend such a systematic position. Paneloux cannot hold this position in light of the death of the child. The value of Tertullian is the ability to avoid the harsh judgment and the strong move to faith. Tertullian softens the blow of the death of the child by not demanding that it is part of the judgment of God. With Augustine Paneloux must hold that somehow in the large scheme of things that the child is guilty. The child may have been indicted by virtue of being a citizen of Oran, or due to original sin. Either way, the child is under the judgment of God and has been sentenced to immediate death by plague. Upon a direct viewing of this Paneloux cannot hold that the child was guilty of anything. How can God do this? How can he make the innocent child suffer and die a horrible long death? Even if it is the corporate guilt of original sin, it is wrong. He can have no part of it. Much like Dostovesky in *The Brothers Karamazov*, the death of one innocent child is too much. Even if justice will be served in a later life, the wait is too much. This traumatic event cannot by overlooked by Paneloux. Paneloux changes theologically. To move to the mystery of God takes away the judgment aspect or can at least delay its explanation. He still fights to maintain his belief in God, so he must find an accommodating position in light of the death of the child. Tertullian's *credo quia absurdum est* seems to accommodate Paneloux. There is absurdity and mystery in God, apparently enough to hold the death of a child. The mystery of the birth, death and resurrection of Christ is held by God, why not this? The weakness of Tertullian's position is the fatalistic component lurking in the background. Paneloux is quick to recognize this, and he does not hide from it. The narrator reports, "Well, he would not boggle at the word, fatalism, provided he were allowed to qualify it with the adjective 'active.'"[48] As Camus indicates, he calls direct attention to it and qualifies it with the modifier "active." As most people know who have at least a basic knowledge of the free will debate this qualifier does not help. The two philosophical terms, active and fatalism, are mutually exclusive; it comes down to either agency or fate. It is clear that Paneloux recognizes this situation, and he works with the term. Paneloux is trained to know the danger of a fatalistic position, and must modify the obvious meaning of the term. Not turning the entire content of his belief over to fate, but a certain level of understanding. Thus, the term active must be understood in light of the Mercy Monastery story. Paneloux will not resign himself or the human condition to fate after seeing the child die; as a believer, he is compelled to take an active role in saving others. We must be the one who stays. Paneloux, like Camus, knows the history of the plague from the Bible forward. He has studied the reactions of generations of people and clergy to the plague. From this study he has separated the reactions into those to admire, and those who either tempt God or reject him. What Paneloux finally means is "active" toward the neighbor and the community; not active in an outright attempt to beat judgment. However, I will demonstrate that it does function in this capacity for Paneloux despite his intentions. For Paneloux we still must hold to God, but reach out to the neighbor. Paneloux frames this choice as either "hate God or love God." This attempted theological solution is rejected by Camus. There are several problems with the Tertullian like theological position of the second sermon. What Paneloux inherits from Tertullian is a potentially fatal fallacy in his argument. The fallacy is commonly called the "death by a thousand qualifications," or the fallacy of "unfalsisifiable dogma."

Anthony Flew introduces the fallacy of "death by a thousand qualifications" clearly in the book he co-edited titled *New Essays in Philosophical Theology*.[49] In it Flew shows that the conclusion of such a position is that anything can count as evidence. The fallacy of a "death by a thousand qualifications" goes something like the following. If a theologian takes the position that "God is love, "for example, and is asked to defend the position. The protagonist points to the death of a person. The theologian responds that there is some good brought about by the death, thus God is still love. The

---

[48] Albert Camus, *The Plague*, P.226

[49] James Woelfel, *Camus: A Theological Perspective*. (New York: Abingdon Press, 1975) P.86

protagonist continues to point out situations that seem to be counter to a loving act. The theologian continues to qualify the example or the position. So many amendments are added to the original position that it is unrecognizable, even to the theologian. Any possible set of events can demonstrate God's love. What set of events could ever count against God's love if the death of a child qualifies? When the fallacy is named as "unfalsifiable dogma" it operates essentially the same way as the fallacy of "death by a thousand qualifications." When the theologian is asked, Where is the good in this situation? He or she responds that it is there-you just have not looked deeply enough yet. As the investigation proceeds, an infinite regress is set up, and the theologian keeps retreating behind this regress until the opponent gives up. Camus challenges theological thought in this way. How can the death of the innocent child possibly demonstrate the love of God? Panloux is faced with another difficult challenge to the plague and is starting to recognize the difficulty of any theological position to explain this death in particular.

Neither the Augustinian nor the Tertullian position is a sufficient answer in light of the death of the innocent child. More dangerous for Camus, they are both a leap to an absolute. The answer that the suffering of the child can and will be answered in an afterlife is why Camus rejects both attempts by Paneloux to come to grips with the question of evil in *The Plague*. As Thody wrote about Camus, he is attacking the two great escapes of the French middle class of his time, Marxism and Catholicism. Paneloux is seen as the advocate and defender of French Catholicism.[50] Woelfel compares "Evil as a part of a larger good" in Christian terms to "Evil as irreconcilable" in Camus' terms. This distinction between the two represents the critical split between Paneloux and Camus (Rieux). By holding to the Christian belief that evil is part of a larger good, Paneloux is committed to a metaphysical principle that separates him and Camus infinitely. Paneloux is given two chances by Camus to work with the question of evil, and fails both times. This makes the move to Rieux's solution of "original goodness" in humans much more attractive than the Panlouixian position that contains a

---

[50] Theodore Ziolkowski makes an interesting observation in his essay titled *Camus in Germany, or the Return of the Prodigal Son.* (*Yale French Studies*, Volume 0, Issue 25, Albert Camus 1960). In it he records that the French Catholic Church printed the following along with its obituary notice for Camus: "And even if the Christian reader misses in Camus the consoling prospects of which he, the Christian, may be assured, he would do well, for this very reason, to give Camus, the sincere ponderer (Grubler), the respect that he deserves."

doctrine of original sin.   Even with a form of "active" fatalism or "active" faith the jump to the absolute for an answer to the death of an innocent child is still the final outcome. Paneloux has put up a very hard fight, but lost.

What Camus clearly demonstrated in *The Plague* is that there is no solution for Paneloux to the theodicy dilemma.   Paneloux has moved between two positions in an attempt to solve the dilemma and it has not worked.   The move to the will of God turns out to be an impossible position for Paneloux after the-first hand experience of the death of a child.   The Augustinian position held in the first sermon fails on the third point of the theodicy dilemma, the existence of evil.   This turns Paneloux to the mystery of God or absurdity with Tertullian.   This fails because it contains an internal fallacy and it is a leap to religious abstraction which does not help in times of plague.   The horns of the dilemma cannot be avoided by Paneloux, and his attempt fails.   Furthermore, it has driven him to a death that is a "doubtful case."   Taken as a metaphorical statement on Paneloux's death, it represents the complete failure of his theological attempt to understand the plague. Camus has a note in his notebook from April, 1942 that is insightful regarding Paneloux's fate. Camus wrote, "People live according to different systems.   The Plague, abolishes all systems.   But they die all the same."[51] Some die of plague, others of heresy.

---

[51] Albert Camus, *Notebooks 1935-1942*, (New York: Paragon House, 1991)

Death in Oran: *The Plague* as Counter to Thomas Mann's *Death in Venice*

By Braden Cannon

Since its initial publication in 1947, Albert Camus' novel *The Plague* has been the subject of a curious lack of wide-ranging critical engagement and analysis. The consensus interpretation of the novel has decided that the origins of the work, its subject matter, and its perspective can all be understood rather simplistically through the lens of Camus' experiences during the Second World War and more broadly as an allegory of the occupation of France during that conflict. In particular, little attention has been given to the novel's inter-textual relationships and its place within the evolution of 20th century literature. Rather than reading the text as a response to or growth from earlier works by other authors, most critics have approached *The Plague* as a specific response to a highly singular event and is therefore firmly rooted in its time and place, albeit with universal themes.[1]

Thomas Mann's 1912 novella *Death in Venice*, on the other hand, has been subjected to a host of critical interpretations since its initial publication. These analyses have focused on themes of: homosexuality, the Other, inter-textual relationships to classical Greek mythology, and the role of the artist in society among many other interpretations. However, Mann's novella has not often been situated within its time and place; its critics have been inclined to interpret the work more universally or in relation to the Greek sources that it draws so heavily upon.[2]

---

[1] For a discussion of the critical reception of *The Plague*, see Colin Davis' *Interpreting* La Peste.

[2] For an in-depth history of the critical reception of *Death in Venice*, see Ellis Shookman's *Death in Venice: A Novella and its Critics*.

The goal of this paper is to turn these critical assumptions on their head by describing *Death in Venice* as a text very much rooted in its pre-First World War era and by situating *The Plague* as partially a direct counter to the pre-war tones and their implications found in the earlier work. In addition to the socio-historical influences of each work, this paper will also compare the attention given by each author to the relation of his characters with the natural world, the role of the Other, and the continuum between solidarity and solitude.

The Plague and *Death in Venice* have an immediately recognized link in that they both chronicle an outbreak of plague; however, the thematic substance of each text has many more similarities than the appearance of a plague. In *Death in Venice*, Mann creates a situation in which nationalism, xenophobia, and a lack of solidarity that leads to a full embrace of solitude, results in death and decay. Contrarily, in *The Plague* Camus counters these attitudes (which I will portray as being of their era) by expressly depicting how they must be overcome through solidarity and mutual aid.

Death in Venice makes immediate reference to the political climate of its day in the opening line: "Gustav Aschenbach (or von Aschenbach, as his name read officially since his fiftieth birthday), on a spring afternoon of that year 19-- which for months posed such a threat to our continent, had left his apartment in the Prinzregentenstrasse in Munich and had gone for a rather long walk all alone" (Mann 1). Editor Stanley Appelbaum identifies the continental threat mentioned in this line as the Second Moroccan Affair or Agadir Crisis of 1911, an incident that saw Germany deploying a warship to the Mediterranean in response to the French occupation of the cities of Fez and Rabat (Mann 65). This incident was just one of several, both major and minor, that led to an increasingly hostile and belligerent atmosphere in Europe, ultimately culminating in the First World War.

Although Mann, who wrote the novella in 1912, could not have known how the European situation would unfold, he was very much working in an environment of growing nationalism, jingoism, and xenophobia that was typical of the era and is now seen as a cause of the war.[3] This becomes

---

[3] For more information on the rather thorny topic of the causes of the First World War, see *The Outbreak of World War I*, edited by Holger H. Herwig.

apparent through the protagonist of *Death in Venice*, Gustav Aschenbach, who is keenly aware of the nationalities of those around him as soon as he arrives at his hotel in Venice from Germany, noting that "[h]ere were to be seen the dry, long face of the American, the large Russian family, English ladies, German children with French *bonnes*. The Slavic element seemed to prevail. In the immediate vicinity Polish was being spoken" (Mann 20). Interestingly, representatives of most of the major belligerents of the First World War are immediately identified in the Venice hotel.

The nationality of various characters that Aschenbach comes across during his trip to Venice from Germany is avidly noted by the character, often because he is ill at ease around foreigners or those who seem out of place or anomalous. Aschenbach is both fascinated and repulsed by the Other.

The conceptualization of the Other in *Death in Venice* has often been framed in terms of sexuality, with some critics noting that Aschenbach's homosexual desire for Tadzio, a young Polish boy who is staying at the same hotel as Aschenbach, makes the protagonist the Other within a hetero-normative society (Tobin). However, the embodiment of otherness found throughout the novella is defined in terms of ethno-nationalism at least as often as sexuality. Even before Aschenbach leaves his home in Munich, he catches sight of a man at the gates of a cemetery and observes him closely. The man is "clearly not of Bavarian ancestry: at least, the broad, straight-rimmed bast hat that covered his head lent his appearance the stamp of foreignness, of having come from far away" (Mann 2). The sense of foreignness that Aschenbach receives from this man is so intense that when the man returns the gaze, Aschenbach is filled with an overwhelming urge to travel to distant, exotic places. This sudden urge for dislocation experienced by Aschenbach would ironically place him in the role of the Other; however, Aschenbach has no sense of his own otherness as will be discussed below.

Aschenbach ultimately decides to travel but does not wish to go too far, "...not all the way to the tigers. One night in a sleeper and a siesta of three or four weeks at some well-known holiday resort in the charming south of Europe" (Mann 5). To Aschenbach, southern Europe is a "charming" and somewhat exotic locale, a half-Orient that is accessible on only one day's journey, just foreign enough to quench the desire inspired by the strange, non-Bavarian man encountered in Munich. Nearly upon his arrival in Venice, Aschenbach almost immediately encounters yet another strange, out-of-place, capped man.

While traveling by boat to Venice from the Italian mainland, Aschenbach observes a group of young, boisterous men. While watching them, one member of the group stands out from the rest. This one is wearing a bright, yellow suit with a red tie and Panama hat.

> But scarcely had Aschenbach taken a closer look at him, when with a sort of terror he realized that the youthful impression was spurious. This was an old man, there could be no doubt. Wrinkles surrounded his eyes and mouth. The faint crimson of his cheeks was rouge; the brown hair beneath the straw hat with its colorful band was a wig; his neck was scraggy and sinewy...and his hands, with signet rings on both index fingers, were those of an old, old man. With a feeling of horror Aschenbach watched him and his intercourse with his friends. Didn't they know, didn't they notice, that he was old, that it was wrong for him to be playing the part of one of them?...He felt as if things were not going normally, as if a dreamlike alienation, a deformation of the world into oddness, was beginning to gain ground[.] (Mann 13)

The urge to seek out foreignness inspired by the man in Munich brought Aschenbach to Venice and, upon his arrival he is horrified when confronted with an image of oddness and incongruity. The spectacle of the old man masquerading with men much younger than he brings about a sudden feeling of alienation; Aschenbach has taken his first step toward solitude and isolation.

This feeling of alienation is reinforced by Aschenbach's impressions of Venice, which he does not find charming at all but menacing and derelict:

> The narrow streets were unpleasantly sultry; the air was so thick that the odors emanating from homes, stores, and cookshops...hung like wisps of smoke without being dispersed. Cigarette smoke remained in place and drifted away only slowly. The jostling in narrow passages annoyed him instead of amusing him as he strolled. The longer he walked, the more tormented he became by the horrible state of health that the sea air can cause...He broke out into a distressing sweat. His eyes no longer performed their duty, he felt a tightness in his chest, he was feverish, the blood pounded in his head. He fled from the crowded shopping streets across bridges into the haunts of the poor. There he was importuned by beggars, and the foul effluvia of the canals made breathing a torture. (Mann 28)

Aschenbach is literally sickened by his surroundings in this foreign city. The scents are unfamiliar and therefore too "sultry;" the locals who he thought would provide him with amusement instead jostle and harangue him; and the defining trait of Venice, its canals, disgust him to the point of breathlessness. This unexpected reaction to the environs of Venice leads to Aschenbach spending most of his time on the grounds of his hotel, which is physically isolated from the rest of Venice and situated on the Lido and there Aschenbach succumbs to solitude.

Ensconced in his hotel, Aschenbach falls into the idle life as practiced by the denizens of the resort. Whatever their nationality, each of the hotel guests is accustomed to a high standard of living and the days are spent lounging in the sun, eating fine food, and playing on the beach. Aschenbach, who is a writer, is accustomed to solitude and finds his new surroundings pleasurable while recognizing the unsettling intensity of perpetual solitude. He recognizes that "[s]olitude produces originality, bold and astonishing beauty, poetry. But solitude also produces perverseness, the disproportionate, the absurd and the forbidden" (Mann 19).

For Aschenbach, the perversity begins to take shape as a form of nihilism in that he is drawn to empty nothingness and feels a growing "proclivity-- forbidden, directly counter to his life's work, and seductive for that very reason--for the unorganized, immoderate, eternal: for nothingness" (Mann 24). This gradually awakening desire for unorganized, meaningless nothing is very much a destructive tendency, despite its emergence in a resort setting wherein idle relaxation is the sole aspiration of the guests. The slow surrender to inactive solitude is noted as being counter to Aschenbach's work, which is to write and reach an audience in some form. But the decadence of the resort pulls away at his very nature:

> The comfortable regularity of this existence had already cast its spell over him; the soft, bright gentleness of this way of life had quickly bewitched him. Indeed what a fine place this was to stay...Aschenbach did not like pleasure. Whenever and wherever he had to leave off work, to take a rest, to have a good time, he soon felt the restless and reluctant desire--and this had been the case in his younger years especially--to return to his noble labors, the sober, hallowed servitude of his normal routine. Only this one spot enchanted him, relaxed his willpower, made him happy. (Mann 33- 34)

Having removed himself from his native element and been disgusted by his foreign surroundings, he succumbs to apathy for those around him and finds comfort and happiness in doing nothing in the warm environs.

There is still one person who arouses his interest, however, and that is Tadzio. As soon as he sees Tadzio on the resort beach, Aschenbach is smitten with him and takes great pleasure in watching him with his friends, on the beach, and eating with his family. To Aschenbach, Tadzio is a Greek god, Eros, and the very personification of the natural beauty found in the sun, beach, and sea. Aschenbach spends his hours lounging in the sun, gazing at the sea, and admiring Tadzio from afar. The elements and the boy become intertwined and inseparable. But in the world created in this novella, natural beauty is not invigorating so much as it acts "to numb and bewitch the understanding and the memory in such a way that, from sheer pleasure, the soul totally forgets its true condition and attaches itself with awestruck admiration to the most beautiful of the objects that the sun shines on" (Mann 36).

In this state of solitary decay, Aschenbach is particularly unprepared to cope with a humanitarian crisis, as are his fellow guests of the resort, tourists who pump large sums of money into the local economy. The crisis emerges during Aschenbach's fourth week at the resort when he notices less German being spoken around him until finally "in the dining room and on the beach, only foreign words met his ear." Aschenbach finds this odd but does not dwell on it until visiting a barber who mentioned another German family that had just departed and tells Aschenbach that "'you stay on, Sir; you have no fear of the disease'" (Mann 42-43).

Aschenbach then observes groups of Italians in the street intently reading notices posted to walls. His status as a foreigner himself and not just a German surrounded by foreigners finally made apparent, Aschenbach can only observe from without as "[g]roups of people were standing silently together on bridges and squares; and the foreigner stood among them, searching and pondering" (Mann 43). Aschenbach has no affinity, no solidarity with these groups of locals who stand together and understand the situation better than he. His withdrawal from the city based on xenophobic disgust has isolated him and made him susceptible to calamity.

Upon his return to the resort, Aschenbach discovers the nationalistic origin of the German exodus as German newspapers that are available in the hotel for tourists have been reporting on the outbreak of plague in Venice. Rather than sharing this information, the German guests have instead left en masse with the exception of Aschenbach, who senses that the local authorities are trying to downplay the dangers of the plague in order to maintain a healthy tourist industry:

> "They want people to cover this up!" But at the same time his heart was filled with the contentment about the adventure into which the outside world was about to enter. For passion, like crime, is not a friend of routine law and order or of the public welfare, and must welcome every weakening of the framework of society, every confusion and affliction of the world, because it can detect a remote chance to profit by it...this criminal secret of the city...coincided with his own dark secret...For, deeply in love, he worried only that Tadzio might go away. (Mann 44)

Aschenbach's isolation is total; it is symbolized in his lust for Tadzio, which was incubated in the idle hours spent separate from society, lounging in the sun and removing himself from the great, unwashed masses of Venice and Europe as a whole.

Aschenbach briefly considers an action that would be "cleansing and decent" (Mann 54), which would be to warn Tadzio's family of the danger and advise them to depart. However, forsaking even his own safety, he remains in Venice and ultimately becomes complicit in the cover-up: "'They want people to keep quiet!' he whispered violently. And added: 'I *will* keep quiet!' The consciousness that he was an accessory to the secret, and equally guilty, intoxicated him...What were art and virtue to him any longer in contrast to the advantages of chaos? He kept silent and he stayed on" (Mann 55). He does not even take the simple and effortless action of warning the family of his one remaining link to the wider world, Tadzio. Rather, he has become "incapable of resistance" (Mann 58) to his circumstances and falls victim to attacks of dizziness that are accompanied by "a feeling of inescapability and hopelessness; and it was not clear whether that feeling related to the outside world or to his own existence" (Mann 60).

Finally, Aschenbach is left entirely alone when Tadzio's family leaves the resort of their own volition. Then Aschenbach heads out to the beach one last time, "[s]eparated from the mainland by wide waters, separated from his companions by a caprice of his pride...completely isolated and devoid of human ties" (Mann 62). There on the beach, Aschenbach slumps into a chair and dies from the plague. By the end of the day, "a respectfully shocked world received the news of his death" (Mann 62); a pallid, bourgeois death for a man who had turned his back on his companions.

In *Death in Venice*, Mann creates a narrative in which the nationalist and increasingly militarist zeitgeist of the years leading up to the First World War are typified through the xenophobic alienation and detachment displayed by Aschenbach on his sojourn to Venice. Seduced into idleness by pleasant weather and surroundings, he becomes fixated on a young boy. This fixation becomes a monomania and when a plague breaks out in Venice, Aschenbach decides to remain solitary at the expense of his health and that of his fellows. For a relatively minor personal gain (being in the presence of Tadzio for a bit longer), Aschenbach not only ignores a looming disaster but is complicit in its cover-up in order to take personal advantage of a public health threat. Because of his actions Aschenbach ultimately contracts the disease and dies, but his death has no meaning nor did it come in the course of resistance to an oppressive force. His death is nothing more than the result of a full embrace of complete solitude and hedonistic inertia.

The Plague is the complete antithesis of the narrative found in the Mann novella; the works exist at extreme antipodes, both moral and social. But from the first line of *The Plague*, Camus establishes an inter-textual connection to the earlier work, as follows: "The unusual events described in this chronicle occurred in 194-, at Oran. Everyone agreed that, considering their somewhat extraordinary character, they were out of place there. For its ordinariness is what strikes one first about the town of Oran, which is merely a large French port on the Algerian coast" (Camus 5).

Not only does the inexact, ambiguous date of "194-" recall the same device found in *Death in Venice* (which occurs in the year "19--," as noted above), but Camus also sets his narrative in a strikingly ordinary town on the southern edge of the Mediterranean. The setting is like a mirror image of Venice, which is famed as an extraordinary city at the northern edge of the Adriatic, a sub-body of the Mediterranean. And as in *Death in Venice*, *The Plague* is populated by several main characters who, like Aschenbach, are not from the city at the heart of their narrative.

Indeed, the concept of the Other is as central to *The Plague* as it is to the Mann novella. Of the four main characters that this paper will discuss, all of them are somehow detached from their native element, otherwise ostracized from civil society, or existing in a state of solitude as found at the beginning of the text. Two of the characters, Tarrou and Rambert, are literally outsiders who find themselves in Oran at the start of the plague for separate reasons and are then unable to leave due to the imposition of the quarantine. Rambert is a journalist from France on assignment in Oran while Tarrou is a truly perplexing outsider in that his specific presence in Oran is never completely explained and he seems to have absolutely no ties to the city or any community within. A third character, Dr. Rieux, has been separated from his wife who had left Oran for convalescence prior to the quarantine. The fourth character, Cottard, is very much in his native element throughout the narrative but that element is located in the criminal underworld, outside the purview of civil society. Cottard is ostracized from society and as the novel opens, actually attempts suicide in reaction to some unknown crime that occurred prior to the start of the chronicle, for which he fears he will be arrested and executed.

At the beginning of the narrative, each of the four is nearly as solitary (or perhaps more so) as Aschenbach became by the end of *Death in Venice*. Solitude and alienation are the starting point, the point at which Mann ended in the earlier work and where Aschenbach succumbed to a lonely death. Dr. Rieux, despite his physical separation from his wife, never strays from acting in the name of solidarity, though. From the outset of the chronicle, he is central to the anti-plague efforts in his role as a public health official. He represents the pole of solidarity on the continuum and other characters' efforts can be gauged in relation to Rieux.

Rambert, like Tarrou, does not have any personal connection to Oran and professes to Rieux that he "doesn't know a soul here" (Camus 71) when trying to enlist the doctor's help in securing permission to leave the quarantined city. Not knowing that Rieux is in a similar situation, Rambert explains to the doctor that the quarantine has separated him from his wife in Paris but that argument fell on deaf ears at the city prefecture. Rambert pleads his case: "'But confound it!' Rambert exclaimed, 'I don't belong here!'" (Camus 72).

Rieux goes on to explain that even if he could be absolutely certain that Rambert does not carry the plague, it does not matter:

> "[b]ecause there are thousands of people placed as you are in this town and there can't be any question of allowing them to leave it.'

> "'Even supposing they haven't got the plague?'
>
> "'That's not a sufficient reason. Oh, I know it's an absurd situation, but we're all involved in it, and we've got to accept it as it is.'
>
> "'But I don't belong here.'
>
> "Unfortunately from now on you'll belong here, like everybody else.'" (Camus 73)

Even in his alienation, Rambert has common cause with everyone else in Oran because they are all equally alienated from the rest of the world. Some have a further alienation, including Rieux who is isolated from his wife exactly as Rambert. Though the reporter does not initially see his solidarity with the citizens of Oran, he has joined a community through common experience. In this way, Camus pushes the characters along the solitary-solidarity continuum closer to common purpose. This is an obvious contrast to the actions of the resort guests in *Death in Venice*; those who were first made aware of the plague chose not to inform the others and instead fled with their compatriots along nationalist lines. Common purpose was ignored for the sake of personal gain.

Unlike the resort denizens in Venice, Rambert does not remain in a state of solitude. He spends the bulk of the narrative trying to find a way out of Oran, legally or illegally, and finally arranges to slip out of town with the complicity of two sentries who are on the take. After the arrangement has been made, though, he speaks with Dr. Rieux and asks why the doctor does not try to stop him. "Rambert had elected for happiness, and he, Rieux, had no argument to put up against him" (Camus 165).

On the night of Rambert's planned escape, he comes to see Rieux again and explains that he wants to stay in Oran because if he were to leave, he would be embarrassed and ashamed to face the person for whom he wants to leave.

> Rieux told him that was sheer nonsense; there was nothing shameful in preferring happiness.
>
> "Certainly," Rambert replied. "But it may be shameful to be happy by oneself...Until now I always felt a stranger in this town, and that I'd no concern with you people. But now that I've seen what I have seen, I know that I belong here whether I want it or not. This business is everybody's business." (Camus 170)

In the face of a collective threat, personal happiness in a solitary state is a matter of shame to Rambert. This is the diametrically opposite position taken by Aschenbach, who willfully refused cooperative action in the face of a public threat for the sole purpose of achieving a fleeting and superficial sense of personal enjoyment. On the verge of pursuing such a course, Rambert blinks and opts to participate in collective action instead. He has shifted from a completely solitary outlook to one informed by solidarity.

As noted, Tarrou's solitude is less easily understood at first. He seemingly has no connections in Oran or elsewhere, does not appear to have work, and is very inscrutable to Rieux when he crosses paths with him. After Rieux gets to know Tarrou better, the latter's isolation becomes even more defined when he confesses to Rieux that he is estranged from his family because of his utter disgust at his father's complicity, in his role as a state prosecutor, in the execution of condemned men (Camus 203-204). In essence, Tarrou's solitude was brought about as an act of solidarity with those condemned to die by the state, though this act of solidarity finds Tarrou drifting through communities and never actively participating in common life. At the beginning of the chronicle his solitude, though more shaped by collective outlook, is just as total as Rambert's.

When the plague reaches pandemic proportions, though, Tarrou's reluctance to participate normally in civic life is given further nuance. His state of isolation is not defined by misanthropy or hedonism; rather, it is derived from a fundamental distrust of hierarchical authority structures, most especially those embodied in the state. He truly believes in cooperative, non-compulsory models of society and approaches Rieux with a plan to engage committed volunteers into "sanitary squads" that will operate outside of officialdom and allow common citizens to help alleviate suffering in the quarantined city without need of conscription, compulsory service, or the authoritarian hand of the state (Camus 104-105). Finding a way to participate in the struggle without collaborating with what he sees as an oppressive force, Tarrou fully engages in solidarity.

The fourth isolated character, the shady Cottard, is similar to Rieux in that he does not undergo a shift along the solitary-solidarity continuum. Whereas Rieux is in a partial state of isolation due to his separation from his wife but still acts in solidarity with his fellows and represents the solidarity pole of the continuum, Cottard exists firmly on the solitary pole and never shifts away from it. Of all of the characters, Cottard is the most like Aschenbach in his outlook and actions. Cottard's defining trait is "his aloofness, not to say his mistrust of everyone he met" (Camus 48).

As noted above, Cottard attempts suicide at the beginning of the narrative because he believes that he is on the verge of arrest for a crime that will lead to execution, though we do not know what that crime is. The unexpected arrival of the plague and its concomitant breakdown of social order, therefore, is greeted by Cottard as a reprieve to be taken advantage of fully. The plague not only alleviates the possibility of arrest due to the police being overwhelmed with other concerns, but it also gives Cottard the opportunity to enrich himself at the expense of the suffering brought on by the outbreak: "The truth was the Cottard, who had been beginning to live above his means, was now involved in smuggling ventures concerned with rationed goods. Selling contraband cigarettes and inferior spirits at steadily rising prices, he was on the way to building up a small fortune." (Camus 118)

He does not see his personal, solitary happiness as immoral or shameful as Rambert would have. Much like Aschenbach's decision to take advantage of the plague in Venice for personal gain, Cottard exists in a state that requires the suffering of others to meet his expectation of happiness. He starts in a solitary state and remains there for the entirety of the narrative. When the plague finally abates, without Cottard having taken any action whatsoever to help alleviate it, Cottard is once again distraught by the prospect of possible arrest and the return of the normal social order. Disconsolate, he ultimately opens fire on a public street and is subsequently captured by police; it is an ending as anti-social and useless as Aschenbach's.

The arcs of the various characters within *The Plague* are not the only counter to *Death in Venice*. The role of weather plays a significant role in both texts; Mann portrays the sunny, pleasant weather in Venice as conducive to Aschenbach's descent into idleness and isolation while Camus has an altogether different portrayal of the elements. One does not wish to lazily sun-bathe in the weather described by Camus:

> On the day following the unseasonable downpour of that Sunday, summer blazed out above the housetops. First a strong, scorching wind blew steadily for a whole day, drying up the walls. And then the sun took charge, incessant waves of heat and light swept the town daylong...The sun stalked our townsfolk along every byway, into every nook, and when they paused it struck. (Camus 94)

This is not weather for a summer idyll, this is weather that is actively stalking and striking down the citizenry. It is oppressive, sickening, and directly linked to the plague and growing numbers of deaths associated with the outbreak:

> For our fellow-citizens that summer sky, and the streets thick in dust, grey as their present lives, had the same ominous import as the hundred deaths now weighing daily on the town. That incessant sunlight and those bright hours associated with siesta or holidays no longer invited, as in the past, to frolics and flirtations on the beaches. Now they rang hollow in the silence of the closed town, they had lost the golden spell of happier summers. Plague had killed all colors, vetoed pleasure. (Camus 95)

Whereas Aschenbach's sun induced him to lounge about and appreciate Tadzio's young body, carrying "the bright assurance of a new sunshiny day of casually organized leisure" (Mann 33), the sun of Oran brings nothing but misery, death, and perfect conditions for the spread of disease. It makes pleasure impossible and bright colors dull and lackluster. This is no place for lust-filled observation of god-like bodies in a heavenly playground; this is a place to resist or be killed (or even to resist and be killed).

The natural elements of Oran are not entirely devoid to their pleasures, however. In one notable instance, Tarrou and Rieux gain succor from a quick swim in the moon-lit harbor of the city, though the purpose of this brief interlude from the struggle is not aimless revelry but instead re-invigoration before re-entering the fight against the omnipresent plague. After the swim, Tarrou and Rieux were "thinking that the disease had given them a respite, and this was good, but now they must set their shoulders to the wheel again" (Camus 210). They do not have the luxury of endless hours spent sun-bathing and walking barefoot through the sand; their trip to the beach comes at night, so as better to escape both the watchful eye of the sentries responsible for maintaining the quarantine and the relentless heat of the sun, and is only long enough to boost their morale for continued action against a public threat.

For one last example of the inter-textual counter of *The Plague* to *Death in Venice*, there is the very singular and unsettling appearance of performers in each of the texts. Each section in which the performers appear serves the plot of its respective text but also firmly underscores the thematic concerns, subtly engaging the reader in an unmasking of the fictive performance s/he is reading.

A troupe of street performers arrives at Aschenbach's hotel one evening and sets up in the garden terrace where the guests are congregated. The troupe is led by an obstreperous guitarist who makes up for his lack of talent with histrionic buffoonery. Aschenbach barely tolerates the music, which he deems as "vulgar" and "trashy," and is mildly repulsed by the "southern animation" of the lead buffoon, who strikes him as a "Neapolitan comedian, half pimp and half entertainer, brutal and feckless, dangerous and amusing" (Man 48-49). Once again, Aschenbach is discomfited by foreignness, even as a foreigner in the performer's native country. He is drawn toward the buffoon and simultaneously unnerved by such a close encounter. But the performer knows his audience and as soon as it is time to collect money, he drops the boisterous routine for a humble, obsequious mien. Moving among the guests' tables to receive tips:

> ...he was humble. Arching his back in low bows, he slinked between the tables, and a smile of cunning obsequiousness bared his large teeth...The guests surveyed the foreign-looking fellow with curiosity and with some repugnance as he collected his livelihood; they threw coins into his felt hat with the tips of their fingers, taking care not to touch him. Elimination of the physical distance between an actor and his respectable onlookers, no matter how much the latter enjoyed the performance, always produces a certain embarrassment. He felt this and tried to excuse himself by means of groveling. (Mann 50)

The performer is inescapably an Other, unworthy of meaningful interaction. The performance creates a distance between himself and the hotel guests and allows the latter a chance to feel as if they are taking in some local color and culture without the dangers of actually mixing with the locals nor entering their neighborhoods. Once the performance is over, however, and the mask is dropped, the audience is repulsed by the Other in their midst; there can be no solidarity here, no mutual understanding or aid. There is only the distasteful flicking of coins into the performer's hat in the hopes that he will be appeased and disappear back into the murky canals of Venice.

When the performer comes to Aschenbach, Aschenbach takes the opportunity to ask the man about a possible outbreak of disease. The performer desperately pleads ignorance, though clearly knows more than he lets on, and makes his way back to the makeshift stage area for a second round of songs:

> Now that the artistic distance between him and his distinguished public was restored, all of his impudence had returned, and his artificial laughter, brazenly directed upward at the terrace, was one of mockery. When approaching the end of the words in each stanza, he already seemed to be struggling with an uncontrollable urge to laugh. He sobbed, his voice wavered, he pressed his hand to his mouth, he twisted his shoulders, and, at the proper moment, the unruly laughter broke forth from him, howling and explosively, with such verisimilitude that it had a contagious effect...he was no longer laughing but screaming; he pointed upward as if there were nothing funnier than the laughing audience up there. (Mann 51)

The roles are reversed as the performer openly mocks his audience for their ignorance. Just as they have "caught" the contagious laughter emanating from the "foreign-looking" buffoon on stage, they stand to catch a much more serious contagion from the alien surroundings to which they have come to relax and idly enjoy themselves. The performer knows this and cannot help but laugh at their situation, at their passivity, at their detachment and isolation. The guests alone remain ignorant of the threat of plague (though Aschenbach at this point has figured out roughly what is happening) while the performers that they look down upon are aware of it and can take preventative measures. The mask of performance is removed right on stage to reveal contempt and isolation.

In *The Plague*, Cottard invites Tarrou to the opera one evening, which is performed weekly by the touring opera company, who are stranded in Oran for the length of the plague. Like several of the lead characters, they too are alienated and isolated.

The opera that they see is *Orpheus*, based on the Greek legend in which the title character journeys to the underworld to rescue his lover from death. The audience is mostly made up of the cream of Oran society in their finest evening wear as they try to carry on with their rituals and entertainments from before the outbreak of plague. In the second act of the opera, some of the audience members begin to notice that the actor portraying Orpheus is becoming rather jerky in his movement. In the third act, the actor

> ...stagger[s] grotesquely to the footlights, his arms and legs splayed out under his antique robe, and fall[s] down...appallingly so...[T]he audience rose and began to leave the auditorium, slowly and silently at first, like worshippers leaving church when the service ends, or a

> death-chamber after a farewell visit to the dead…But gradually their movements quickened, whispers rose to exclamations, and finally the crowd stampeded towards the exits, wedged together in the bottle-necks, and poured out into the street in a confused mass, with shrill cries of dismay. (Camus 162)

Once again, we see the mask of the performer drop in front of his audience, who are disturbed by the phenomenon. However, this time the unsettling aspect is not due to foreignness or otherness, but from a sense of warped, twisted solidarity; the audience is horrified because they just witnessed a man collapse on stage from plague and are keenly aware that the same fate could be in store for them. Even the character of Orpheus, who legendarily defeats death, succumbs to plague in the end. The audience tries to maintain a sense of decorum but as the full realization of the actor's collapse dawns on them, decorum turns to dismay.

In *The Plague*, the performers are not Others in the sense that the Italian troupe was in *Death in Venice*. Though the opera company is not from Oran, they perform weekly in an attempt to bring some kind of relief to the city while simultaneously being exposed to the same risks as the citizenry. These performers neither mock nor are subjected to mockery. There is a communal sense of shared risk that becomes all too apparent with the collapse and presumed death of the headlining actor.

When these two scenes are compared, the mask falls from the texts. We see the sense of hopeless alienation at the heart of *Death in Venice*, its merciless dividing of people from each other, its lure of solitude and the very pitfalls of same. Conversely, we see the hope beneath the seemingly unstoppable oppression of disease in *The Plague*, the shared risk taken by all of Oran's inhabitants and the decision made by many of them to affirm solidarity even in the face of such horrific onslaught. Plague lures Aschenbach to solitude but lures Rieux, Tarrou, and Rambert to solidarity.

Death in Venice was published at the precipice of a global conflict the scale of which was previously unimagined and depicts the nationalist, divisive, and xenophobic attitudes that partially contributed to the outbreak of the First World War. *The Plague* was published after the culmination of a second, even more horrific global conflict and has the benefit of synthesizing the lessons that could be learned from the two world wars. By the publication of *The Plague* in 1947, Camus was keenly aware of the destructive potential of humanity and the imperative need to resist such destructive tendencies. For him, the passive urges and nationalistic fears typified by Aschenbach were emblematic of pre-war attitudes and needed to be countered with a call to solidarity as issued in his novel. Whereas Aschenbach finally and perhaps willfully succumbs to plague in complete solitude, Camus provides a "record of what had had to be done, and what assuredly would have to be done again in the never-ending fight against terror and its relentless onslaughts, despite their personal afflictions, by all who, while unable to be saints but refusing to bow down to pestilences, strive their utmost to be healers" (Camus 251-252). Everything that Aschenbach and those who marched blindly into two world wars were not.

Works Cited

Camus, Albert. *The Plague.* Trans. Stuart Gilbert. London: Penguin Books, 1960. Print.

Davis, Colin. "Interpreting *La Peste.*" *The Romantic Review* 85:1 (1994) : 125-143. Print.

Herwig, Holger H. *The Outbreak of World War I.* Stamford, CT: Wadsworth Publishing, 1996. Print.

Mann, Thomas. *Death in Venice.* Trans. Stanley Appelbaum. New York: Dover Publications, 1995. Print.

Shookman, Ellis. *Death in Venice: A Novella and Its Critics.* Rochester, NY: Camden House, 2003. Print.

Tobin, Robert. "The Life and Work of Thomas Mann: A Gay Perspective." *Thomas Mann: Death in Venice.* Ed. Naomi Ritter. Boston: Bedford Books, 1998. Print.

Neoconservatism in the Political Thought of Albert Camus: A Preliminary Inquiry

By Jackson Doughart

This wretched state of being
Is the fate of those sad souls who lived a life but lived it with no blame
and with no praise.
They are mixed with that repulsive choir of angels neither faithful nor
unfaithful to their God
but undecided in neutrality.

— Dante Alighieri, *Inferno*[1]

I knew a pure-hearted man who rejected distrust. He was a pacifist, a
libertarian, and held an equal love for humans and animals. An elite
soul, that's for sure. . . He had written on the doorway of his house:
'Wherever you come from, come in and be welcome.' Who do you
think took up this nice invitation? The militiamen, who made
themselves at home and disemboweled him.

— Albert Camus, *The Fall*[2]

---

[1] Dante Alighieri (trans. Mark Musa), Dante's Inferno: The Indiana Critical Edition
(Bloomington, IN: Indiana University Press, 1995), pp. 35. The employed by President John
F. Kennedy in a 24 June 1963 speech: "Dante once said that the hottest places in hell are
reserved for those who in a period of moral crisis maintain their neutrality." In Public Papers
of the Presidents of the United States: John F. Kennedy, 1963, pp. 503

[2] Albert Camus, La Chute (Édition Numérique) (Saguenay, PQ: L'Université du Québec à
Chicoutimi, 2010), pp. 11-12
:http://classiques.uqac.ca/classiques/camus_albert/chute/Camus_la_chute.pdf. Unless
otherwise noted, all translations of Camus quotations are my own

Much of Albert Camus' journalistic and literary output was dedicated to the issues of his era, which makes the reading of his work a fruitful exercise in the study of 20th-century European history. However, several of Camus' best-known works are deeply philosophical and transcendent of his own time period, creating a fertile ground for discussion about the contemporary relevance and application of his ideas. In the spirit of these debates, I wish to examine the related themes of neutrality and allegiance, particularly as espoused by the Anglo-American tradition of neo-conservatism. This group of thinkers, whose intellectual roots are largely found in the revolutionary leftist movement of Trotskyism (also referred to as the "left opposition" to Stalinism), came of age as anti-communists who despised the moral equation of the United States with the Soviet Union, notwithstanding their own reservations about American capitalism. This position led to a rethinking and reformulation of political principles, resulting in a marked shift to the right that was nevertheless distinct from traditional conservatism. And when militant Islam revealed itself as a permanent and serious enemy of the West, a new generation of neo-conservatives underscored the incoherence of neutrality in matters of such importance.

I argue that several neo-conservative ideas, such as opposition to neutrality, insight into allegiance, and disdain for relativism, especially as articulated by Irving Kristol, find convincing expression in the philosophy of Albert Camus. To illustrate this, I examine Camus' 1957 short story "The Guest"[3] and explain the congruence between its themes and the neoconservative ideas that Kristol and others have espoused.

One should be conscious of a danger involved in this enterprise, which is worth dealing with at the outset. This danger involves the temptation to misconstrue the efforts of an author in order to falsely portray him as a partisan of one's own ideological perspective. One obvious victim of this practice is George Orwell, who has been invoked posthumously by both the political left and right, especially during the Cold War, based on selective interpretation. In fact, Camus shares with Orwell certain characteristics that make him attractive to various sides of the political spectrum. Both were men of the left, yet quarreled within their own schools of thought as a result of independent reflection, producing a series of political views, such as

---

[3] Albert Camus, "L'hôte" in L'exil et le royaume (Paris: Gallimard, 2010), pp. 79-99. Originally published in 1957. From here on I will refer to the story as "The Guest."

fervent anti-totalitarianism, which cross traditional ideological lines. In Camus' case, his disbelief in God and fierce opposition to capital punishment have clear appeal to the left, while his anti-communism and anti-nihilism have appealed to the right. To use Orwell's formulation about Charles Dickens, it may be said that Camus is an author well worth stealing. Another complicating factor is that Camus is notoriously difficult to pin down, intellectually speaking, and his views on many issues were constantly evolving, including his philosophical views. Nevertheless, I defend my ambition by noting that I am not attempting to contort Camus' endorsement of a specific policy held by contemporary neo-conservatives, such as the American war in Iraq in 2003. Nor am I suggesting that Camus was himself a neo-con. Such a claim would be anachronistic, since neo-conservatism was in its infancy and confined to a small group in the United States when Camus was killed in 1960. And it had not been identified by its current name until more than a decade later. Rather, I argue that there is an observable congruence between the disposition of Camus' philosophy and the persuasion of neo-conservatism.

It may be helpful to begin by sketching the elements of neoconservative thought under evaluation,[4] especially from the perspective of Irving Kristol, the founder of The Public Interest and The National Interest magazines, author of several non-fiction books, and "godfather of neo-conservatism." Broadly speaking, neoconservatives believe that the biggest problem of Western society is relativism, both in its moral and cultural forms. Kristol himself usually referred to this as non-judgmentalism, especially when referring to the left's insistence that the state not legislate morality or prefer certain lifestyles over others. Kristol was particularly hostile to multiculturalism, which he believed was "as much a 'war against the West' as Nazism and Stalinism ever were."[5] In a similar vein, Samuel Huntington claimed that multiculturalism was "in its essence anti-European civilization."[6] The anti-relativist sentiment is articulated in a more complete

---

[4] Please note that I will not discuss economic arguments, such as neoconservative support for capitalism or opposition to large state-financed social programs, as these have no impact on my thesis regarding Camus.

[5] Irving Kristol, "The Tragedy of Multiculturalism," in Irving Kristol (ed.), Neoconservatism: The Autobiography of an Idea (Chicago, IL: Elephant Paperbacks,1999), pp. 52, as quoted in Douglas Murray, Neoconservatism (New York, NY: Encounter Books, 2006), pp. 192.

[6] Samuel Huntington, Who Are We? (London, UK: Free Press, 2004), pp. 171, as quoted in Douglas Murray, Neoconservatism, pp. 192.

form in Allan Bloom's 1987 book *The Closing of the American Mind*, which the critic Patrick J. Deneen has identified as "a major touchstone in the development of 'neo-conservatism.'"[7] Bloom reproaches American culture for inculcating in youth the primary virtue of unqualified tolerance, replacing the superior and virtuous natural rights conception that preceded it. The result, according to Bloom, is a society without cultural roots or substantive foundations for identity, rendering the project of higher education meaningless. Kristol's fears about the consequences of non-judgmentalism were even more barbed. For him, rampant social problems such as rising crime rates, a growing rate of out-of-wedlock births, and greater dependence on the welfare state were not the fruit borne of poverty or inadequate state intervention, as suggested by his opponents on the left, but instead the result of a society committed to value neutrality and a refusal to actively shape the character of its citizens.

A related but separate point involves a belief in human nature. This belief can be contrasted with the historicist views associated with Hegel and Marx, which were critiqued by Professor Leo Strauss, whom Kristol admired and who is often cited as an influence among neo-conservatives. The essence of Strauss's critique is a call to return to the classical Platonic conception of natural right, which is not culturally or historically bound, and to reject the historicist and positivist approaches that, in Strauss's opinion, plague modernity. Their rejection of historicism brought them into conflict not only with cultural Marxists on the left, but also with paleo-conservatives on the right who preferred to view American society in ethno-cultural or ethno-religious terms. In the latter respect, neoconservatives were usually not themselves religious, though Kristol, while not an atheist, despised the conflation of theology with morality[8] and seemed to share Leo Strauss's view of religion as primarily salutary instead of revealed truth.[9]

---

[7] Patrick J. Deneen, "Who Closed the American Mind?" The American Conservative, 1 October 2012. Hyperlink: http://www.theamericanconservative.com/articles/who-closed-the-american-mind/.

[8] Irving Kristol, "A Note on Religious Tolerance," in Gertrude Himmelfarb (ed) The Neoconservative Persuasion (New York, NY: Basic Books, 2011), pp. 296-300.

[9] Christopher Hitchens, "Farewell to the Godfather: Irving Kristol, 1920-2009)," Slate Magazine. 20 September 2009. Hyperlink:
http://www.slate.com/articles/news_and_politics/fighting_words/2009/09/farewell_to_the_god father.html. ("Kristol was one of those who never minded saying that he was a Straussian, and

The extreme conclusion of the historicist failing was the Soviet Union, which Kristol and his fellow neo-conservatives staunchly opposed. But even more trenchant than this opposition was their abhorrence at the moral equation of the Soviet Union and the United States. On this point, they found themselves on common ground with the political right, even if they disagreed with some of its tactics, such as McCarthyism in the 1950s. This led to neo-conservative opposition to the policy of détente with the U.S.S.R. and fervent support for the foreign policy of Ronald Reagan, which was itself informed by the writings of Jeanne Kirkpatrick, a neo-conservative academic who rose to prominence as a critic of Jimmy Carter. After the fall of the Soviet Union, a new generation of neo-conservatives including William Kristol, Joshua Muravchik, Charles Krauthammer, and Paul Wolfowitz extended their attitude toward the evil empire into an ideology of conservative internationalism, which viewed the promotion of democracy and protection of human rights as vital parts of the American national interest. This stance came to particular light during the Balkan Wars that followed the breakup of Yugoslavia, where neo-conservatives, then out of power during the presidency of Bill Clinton, urged the American government to intervene militarily in defense of Bosnia and Herzegovina. One might note that the neo-conservatives of this era held a diametrically opposite view to that of other conservatives, who saw the Balkan conflict as undeserving of military attention due to the absence of any American material or geopolitical interest. And on the point of allegiance, neoconservative opposition to neutrality was no sharper than in the aftermath of the 11 September 2001 attacks, as encapsulated by President Bush's rather coarse assertion that Americans had to be either with him or with Islamic terrorists. All of this is to say that within their commitment to a form of internationalism, neo-conservatives remain convinced of a need for allegiance on crucial matters of principle.

If there is a single adjective that one might use to describe neo-conservatives, it would probably be "heretical." Neo-cons began as bad communists, being drawn to the Trotskyist opposition movement, and have since ended up as bad conservatives, accused by libertarians and traditionalists on the right of

---

Strauss is unusual among the pillars of American conservatism in having been decidedly skeptical about religious faith... Kristol appears to have been contradictory between an abstruse, elite intellectual and the popular will: If I understood him correctly, he believed that religion was a useful tool for making people behave well, quite independent of whether it was true or not.")

damaging the conservative movement through advocacy of "foreign adventures" in the Middle East and elsewhere. Some have even suggested that on a wide array of issues, including both domestic and foreign policies, neo-conservatives are actually disguised liberals who advance a neo-Wilsonian internationalism at the expense of the American republic. To an extent, it is accurate to observe a deep contrast between the philosophies of neo-conservatives and other variants of right-wing politics in America. But it would be incorrect to view the neo-cons as liberals, a label from which Irving Kristol expressly distanced himself in the earliest expressions of neo-conservatism.

Having provided this brief sketch, I next propose a few ways in which these principles are shared by both neo-conservatives and Camus. The most obvious similarity is a kind of love-hate relationship with the political left, whence both the neoconservatives and Camus came, but which also provided a ground for rebellion. Indeed, though Camus was unmistakably a leftist, having for a time been a member of the Algerian Communist Party (stating that communism was "a springboard and asceticism that prepares the ground for more spiritual activities" before being denounced as a Trotskyist)[10], his major philosophical disagreements took place with other leftists in much the same way as the Henry Jackson Democrats did in their transition to the political right. And skepticism about the inherent truth in the doctrines of organized religion is another similarity.

A more substantial point would be internationalism. I have explained the variety of conservative internationalism espoused by neo-conservatives, most explicitly in the post-Soviet era, which defined American national interest as allegiance to pro-democracy foundations instead of the mere material interest of American citizens and government. Camus makes the same point in a different way, in the context of his allegiance to anti-totalitarianism during the Second World War. In the preface to his *Letters to a German Friend*, he issued the following disclaimer indicating that his allegiance could only be understood in an internationalist sense:

> I want to avoid a misunderstanding. When the author writes "you," he does not mean "you Germans" but rather "you Nazis." When he writes

---

[10] Olivier Todd, Albert Camus: A Life (New York, NY: Alfred A. Knopf, 1998), pps. 37, 250

"we," he does not mean "we Frenchmen" but rather "we Free Europeans." I contrast two attitudes, not two nations, even if at this moment in history, these two nations could embody these two enemy attitudes. To repeat a phrase that is not my own, I love my country too much to be a nationalist.[11]

Similarly, Camus lampoons the concept of nationality, or at least its relationship to justice, in *The Stranger*, when Meursault reacts to being accused of murder— a crime against "the French people." Why not the German people, or the Chinese people? Meursault asks.[12]   Indeed, the very notion of legal jurisdiction seems inconsistent with any appeal to universal principles of justice. This is not to suggest that either Camus or the neo-cons pined for a state of affairs beyond the nation state or beyond nationality, but simply that their conception of allegiance was broader and more nuanced than either national or state borders alone could offer on their own.

A further illustration of Camus' view of neutrality and allegiance is found in his writings on the Algerian crisis, contained in the posthumous collection *Resistance, Rebellion, and Death*. These commentaries clarify a nuanced view of allegiance that, far from being neutral, admonishes non-alignment without resort to fighting on ethnic lines alone. He was particularly contemptuous of French apologists for Le Front de Libération Nationale (F.L.N.), who believed that the sordid history of French colonialism meant that "the Arabs [had] in a way earned a right to slaughter and mutilate," while Frenchmen of particular nationalist stripe were "willing to justify in a way all excesses" in repressing the revolt.[13] Camus disclosed that he was far from an impartial observer, being an Algerian of European descent who was determined to fight against knee-jerk calls for full independence for the Algerian Arabs, a state of affairs that would involve capitulating to the barbaric tactics of the F.L.N. and the turning of Algeria into a "mass of

---

[11] Albert Camus, Lettres à un ami allemand (Édition Numérique) (Saguenay, PQ: L'Université du Québec à Chicoutimi, 2010), pp. 14-15. Hyperlink: http://classiques.uqac.ca/classiques/camus_albert/lettres_ami_allemand/lettres_ami_allemand.pdf

[12] Albert Camus, L'Étranger (Édition Numérique) (Saguenay, PQ: L'Université du Québec à Chicoutimi, 2010), pp. 88. Hyperlink: http://classiques.uqac.ca/classiques/camus_albert/etranger/camus_etranger.pdf.

[13] Albert Camus, "Preface to Algerian Reports," Resistance, Rebellion, and Death (trans. Justin O'Brien) (New York: Alfred A. Knopf, 1961), pp. 116

ruins,"[14] where the various peoples of Algeria would be divorced from their homeland. Instead of advocating the status quo or outright independence, he endorsed a form of federalist sovereignty-association that would address the injustices committed by the French government while ensuring the permanent safety of all ethnic groups. But he knew that there was nothing neutral about this position, and that it was indeed something worth fighting for. Arguing against the impotence of French nationals who preferred to adopt a submissive attitude in the Algerian Crisis, and were thus willing to abandon non-Muslims living in North Africa, Camus offered the following commentary from his "Appeal for a Civilian Truce":

> I know that the great tragedies of history often fascinate men with approaching horror. Paralyzed, they cannot make up their minds to do anything but wait. So they wait, and one day the Gorgon devours them. But I should like to convince you that the spell can be broken, that there is only an illusion of impotence, that strength of heart, intelligence, and courage are enough to stop fate and sometimes reverse it. One has merely to will this, not blindly, but with a firm and reasoned will... The task of men of culture and faith, in any case, is not to desert historical struggles nor to serve the cruel and inhuman elements in those struggles. It is rather to remain what they are, to help man against what is oppressing him, to favor freedom against the fatalities that close in upon it.[15]

Furthermore, both Camus and the neoconservatives despised nihilism and the relativistic attitudes that inevitably lead thereto. Once again, the influence of Leo Strauss is worth underscoring. Writing in his book *Neoconservatism*, Douglas Murray summarized the Straussian and neoconservative view as follows:

> For Strauss, in *Natural Right and History*, the cause is clear: "The contemporary rejection of natural right leads to nihilism—nay, it is identical with nihilism."[16] In this, and similar passages, Strauss clearly and repeatedly stands with the American fathers, and against the

---

[14] Albert Camus, "Appeal for a Civilian Truce," Resistance, Rebellion, and Death, pp. 140.

[15] Albert Camus, "Appeal for a Civilian Truce," Resistance, Rebellion, and Death, pp. 141

[16] Leo Strauss, Natural Right and History (Chicago: University of Chicago Press, 1999), pp. 93, as quoted in Douglas Murray, Neoconservatism, pp. 16.

historical trend that he had seen develop towards relativism once before [in the Weimar Republic]. It is relativism that is identified by Strauss as the opening that leads to nihilism.

Relativism rejects the notion that any principle can be entirely and rationally justified, leaving itself ultimately mute before the excesses of which man is capable: it is the disintegrating component in democracy.[17]

From Camus' point of view, these excesses of which man is capable were clearly expressed in the nihilism of totalitarian rule. In fact, he wrote in his introduction to *The Rebel* that "one cannot be a half-way nihilist,"[18] and that he had dedicated his life to opposing such a philosophy. But what to do in opposition to this philosophy? Here too we see revealed a possible commonality between Camus and neo-conservatives, rooted in their shared admiration for Greek philosophy. In a 1952 essay entitled "The Philosopher's Hidden Truth," Irving Kristol identified himself as a supporter of Strauss's effort to reapply Ancient ideas to contemporary political philosophy, which Kristol presciently noted as the beginning of "nothing less than a revolution in intellectual history."[19] None of these Ancient ideas was more vital than a return to natural right and a rejection of historicism. Ron Srigley believes that a similar effort is afoot in the work of Camus, arguing that for Camus, the ancient Greeks bring to light things that had been distorted over the course 'of twenty centuries of Christianity and modernity.'[20] ... The Greeks did not take the path toward totalitarianism and technology that we moderns have taken. For those of us like Camus with reservations about our decision to do so and the long years necessary to complete it, thinking about why the Greeks chose not to is a potentially illuminating inquiry. That inquiry turns

---

[17] Douglas Murray, Neoconservatism, pp.16-17.

[18] Albert Camus, L'Homme Révolté. (Édition Numérique) (Saguenay, PQ: L'Université du Québec à Chicoutimi, 2010), pp. 16. Hyperlink: http://classiques.uqac.ca/classiques/camus_albert/homme_revolte/camus_homme_revolte.pdf

[19] Irving Kristol, "The Philosopher's Hidden Truth," in Gertrude Himmelfarb (ed) The Neoconservative Persuasion (New York, NY: Basic Books, 2011), pp. 32

[20] Albert Camus, Notebooks, 1942-1951, pp. 263, as quoted in Ronald D. Srigley, Albert Camus' Critique of Modernity (University of Missouri Press, 2011), pp. 14-15.

on the non-historicist assumption that the Greeks' choice was a real one… In such a view culture is not absolute, nor is it reducible to history.[21]

Through their identification with Leo Strauss's critique of historicism, neo-conservatives have identified anti-relativism, based on natural right, as the antidote to nihilism. If my analysis of Camus is correct, these themes are also present in his work. I turn briefly, then, to "The Guest," which I submit as a reliable and convincing expression of the aforementioned shared principles regarding relativism, neutrality, and allegiance. It is important to state that this claim hinges on my interpretation of the story, which views the protagonist as a character determined to maintain his neutrality in a conflict that will not allow it. This is not only a descriptive observation but also a normative one, which is directly related to the unfolding of the narrative and to Daru's fall.

To take the commonalities of relativism, neutrality, and allegiance in order, there are admonitions against both cultural and moral relativism in the story, particularly in Daru's attitude toward the Arab prisoner for whom he has become responsible. Specifically, Daru is reluctant to form a judgment about the prisoner's character, apparently for the sake of non-judgmentalism. This is evident when Daru learns that the Arab prisoner killed his cousin as a retribution for failing to repay a debt. There is no suggestion that Daru infers anything about the individual or the community whence he comes, indicating either a general disposition of amoralism or a refusal to judge the prisoner because of his different culture and background. And Camus' decision to describe Arabs in sparse detail and without names, as he did in The Stranger and in "The Adulteress Woman," indicates a similar desire to remain at enough of a distance from the Arabs for his protagonist to avoid the responsibility of judgment. One knows that these elements of the story are a rebuke on the part of Camus because Daru's non-judgmentalism is central to his eventual downfall. He simply underestimates the degree to which his amorality is consequential and how unmoved his enemies are by his generous reluctance to judge.

While some readings of "The Guest" may support an existentialist interpretation, as Daru's fate might indicate that one is "damned if he does,

---

[21] Ronald D. Srigley, Albert Camus' Critique of Modernity, pp. 14-15.

damned if he does not" and that the attachment of transcendental meaning to human actions is therefore erroneous, I think there is a more serious critique at hand about Daru's position of non-alignment or neutrality. This neutrality applies to both the affair of the individual Arab prisoner and the greater conflict in which Daru, as a Pied-Noir, finds himself. He attempts neutrality or non-alignment in three ways: First, in point of action, by allowing the Arab prisoner to take his own decision between exile and incarceration, when the interest of justice could only be served by the prisoner being delivered to Tinguit. Second, in point of judgment, by withholding appraisal of the prisoner's character for the reasons explained above. And third, in point of allegiance, by failing to recognize not only that a morally neutral position was unattainable, but that his own identity as a Pied-Noir was inescapable. Whether or not he would accept it, his own relationship to the conflict involving the Arab prisoner and his broader community was infinitely coloured by the fact that he was already a combatant. So the kind of distant objectivity that would allow Daru to take up a neutral position was itself a myth. And though his attempt to transcend race and culture is deserving of admiration, his inability to see a basic goodness in his own side and an basic badness in the other, along the lines of allegiance that I suggested earlier, is integral to his downfall.

Both the case of the individual prisoner and that of the wider conflict present the same problem: that Daru is abdicating a responsibility not only to judge but to enlist himself for one side. His desire to be neutral is apparent from the outset: he wishes that the whole thing had never come up, that he'd never had to take a position, and that he could go back to a state of affairs that did not confront his moral evasion. Yet the upshot of the story is that despite his repeated and relentless attempts to find it, the neutral position in this case was simply non-existent. By pushing away the responsibility foisted upon him and delegating it to the Arab prisoner, he simply invited the forces of barbarism to take the decision for him, and one should scarcely be surprised by the result. In short, Daru fully deserved his fate, and given their own attitude toward neutrality, neo-conservatives of past and present would overwhelmingly agree.

To conclude, I hope that this examination of "The Guest" may provide a starting point for further research about a neo-conservative disposition in the work of Albert Camus. Of particular interest would be the finding of any connections between the thesis advanced here and Camus' cyclical works. While it is certainly true that anti-relativism and anti-neutrality are not the sole province of neo-conservative thinkers, their insistence upon these themes as fundamental critiques of the contemporary Western psyche and culture are of supreme value to our political discourse. I have attempted to expose a measure of congruence between this persuasion and that of Camus, as expressed in "The Guest," which may be summed up in the following way: the concepts of neutrality and non-alignment are illusory, their pursuit cowardly, and as we learn from Daru's ultimate fate, the decision not to act is itself an action with predictable, inevitable, and unsavory consequences.

Of Dogs and Men: Empathy and Emotion in Camus' *The Stranger*

By Ingrid Fernandez

Introduction

In "Commentary on *The Stranger*," Jean-Paul Sartre remarks on the enigmatic title of Camus' novel, explaining, "The 'stranger' is man confronting the world...The stranger is also a man among men...The stranger is, finally, myself in relation to myself--that is, natural man in relation to mind: 'The stranger who, at certain moments, confronts us in a mirror'" (Sartre 77-78). Sartre heavily borrows from Camus' theory of the absurd expounded in *The Myth of Sisyphus*, a text published only a few months after the release of *The Stranger* and for many, serving as a manual for understanding the novel. However, the organic nature of the novel points to an even more fundamental concept: man's uneasiness in his own skin and the constant struggle between individual and authoritarian will and a body that refuses to hide its primordial essence—a body in constant eruption, a flesh that withers and decays, leaving man a vulnerable pariah of tissue and nerves standing on a precipice where he is ravaged by the forces of nature and the impositions of social institutions seeking to subject and control him. Camus follows the phenomenological tradition that seeks to explore the condition of embodiment. Here, the subject awakens to the world rather than viewing it as a mere spectator (Merleau-Ponty 8). However, he breaks with phenomenology by privileging the absurd. The absurd constitutes the ultimate negation of universal meaning and transcendence. It forces the subject to revel in the irrationality of the world with complete lucidity. In short, it is the very fabric of life itself and everyday experience. Embracing the absurd consists of a prime investment in physical confrontation and ultimately dissolution with the natural elements. Camus eloquently expresses it: "The absurd depends as much on man as on the world. For the moment it is all that links them together. It binds them on to the other as only hatred can weld two creatures together" (Camus, *MOS* 21). In some ways, partaking in the absurd is analogous to Deleuze and Guatari's notions of becoming animal or becoming earth, which emphasizes the alliance between distinct bodies at the molecular level (Deleuze and Guatari 11). The motif of a wounded common body as the essence of life recurs throughout *The Stranger* in the relationship between the human and the animal and the human and the landscape. It serves as the underlying law of interchange between bodies. Camus utilizes the figure of Salamano and his dog as a metaphor for the condemnation that forms the condition of living under the yoke of the body. Further, the pair serves to explicate the author's vision of the interaction between the subject and social authority as well as the nature of relationships of love and dependence.

Breaking with the Phenomenological Tradition

The Stranger exemplifies the emblematic tenets of the phenomenological tradition and underscores its pervading influence on mid twentieth century existentialism. According to Merleau-Ponty, the subject is not constituted by a static identity, but rather "we are experiences" (Merleau-Ponty 114-115). In *The Stranger*, Meursault constructs his life around this concept, not

...hold[ing] under [his] gaze a serial space and time nor the pure idea of series, but hav(ing) about [himself] a time and space that exist by piling up, by proliferation, by encroachment, by promiscuity—a perpetual pregnancy, perpetual parturition, generativity and generality, brute essence and brute existence, which are the nodes and antinodes of the same ontological vibration. (115)

Camus saw phenomenology as akin to his concept of the absurd. Husserl's philosophy initially declines to provide a unifying explanation of the world, only asserting the existence of an infinite multiplicity of truths beyond the human capacity to grasp. The main struggle behind the absurd is likewise the acceptance of the futility of explanation. The fragmented nature of the universe in which the only assurance rests on contradiction refutes the mind's desire for unity. He faults Husserl for succumbing, in the end, to a unifying principle of Eternal Reason in the form of the "concrete universe." This principle, something beyond individual human understanding but at the core of all life form, restores the comfort of the eternal and the illusion of hope in the belief of human transcendence. In contrast, for Camus, belonging to the world implies lucid contemplation in "the total absence of hope (which has nothing to do with despair), a continual rejection (which must not be confused with renunciation), and a conscious dissatisfaction (which must not be compared to immature unrest)" (Camus, *MOS* 31).

The Stranger revises the principles of phenomenology to underscore the primacy of the absurd as the only genuine way of life. The novel's individually-centered nature radiates through the use of first-person narrative as well as placing Meursault as the locus of sensation. As the embodiment of the Absurd man, Meursault approaches the world through an utter lack of desire to draw explanations and conclusions, instead "[aiming] to enumerate what [he] cannot transcend" and taking delight in his project (44). Replete and almost obsessed with physical description, Meursault's narrative captures the simultaneous confrontation and communion between man and his surrounding environment. Camus thus stands as a figure in between existentialism and phenomenology, much like Georges Bataille in his preference for intense experiences that find "the source of an abundant surge of life" in the very decomposition marking life's inevitable precariousness.

Following Deleuze and Guattari, the structure of *The Stranger* depends on its very rupture. Meursault emerges as the agent of discontinuity. Although the story has a chronological narrative, Meursault's detailed perceptions and descriptions interject to frustrate the forward drive of the story and any insights into his history. As a result, his presence obscures rather than elucidate. Abandoning the classical style, the story-teller relies on an assemblage of short-term memories and intensities, constantly departing from structures of long-term memory presented in the unit of the family, the social contract and the civilized state. For instance, during the burial of his mother, he describes the landscape *ad nauseam*, noticing the hills that separate Marengo from the sea, the sky streaked with red and the wind coming over the hill with the smell of salt. However, he exhibits great anxiety in social interaction and its regulated structures of memory and propriety. He cannot remember his mother's age, refuses to see the body inside the casket, and has forgotten all the technicalities leading to the murder of the Arab. Although his very life is on the line, during his trial, he feels: "...they seemed to be arguing the case as if it had nothing to do with me. Everything was happening without my participation. My fate was being decided without anyone so much as asking my opinion" (Camus, *S* 98). His passionate interaction with the landscape becomes mute in the face of the law, for the law attempts to classify and normalize human experience. In fact, the hero's insistent anti-authoritarian position can be best summed up in his decline to utilize language as a method of creating an identity or personal history. Refuting accusations of being taciturn and withdrawn, he matter-of-factly replies, "It's just that I don't have much to say. So I keep quiet" (66). Meursault finds himself precisely in the fragments of a life cut short. Much like Camus, he resists the social apparatus of power by maintaining his revolt, his freedom, and his passion (Camus, *MOS* 64).

Salamano and his Dog

The Condition of Having a Body

One of the most fascinating pairs in Camus' lifelong tradition of manly solidarity appears in the form of Salamano and his dog. The relationship between the two figures often takes the form of a complex metaphor of the human struggle to seek identification within the condition of exile. Camus relates this at both a social and physical level that reaches an allegorical form in Meursault's imagination. Like Meursault, Salamano and his dog belong to a population of eccentric outsiders deviating from normative social structures of kinship. Meursault describes old Salamano as an ill-humored Spanish widower barely getting through a scanty, threadbare existence in Algeria. Due to his age and non-salubrious exterior, Salamano falls into a category of citizens deemed unfit to care for themselves and taken into state welfare programs for the elderly. Similarly, his dog--coincidentally a spaniel--is infected with crusted scabies, a severe skin condition marking him as repulsive and unfit to live in a society that strongly adheres to the cleanliness of the body. Moreover, the type of mange the dog exhibits is not only debilitating, but contagious. If found by authorities regulating animal control, the dog would be a primary candidate for euthanasia. In this sense, their journeys possess a similar origin. Both represent a burden to the state, but silently mark their presence and rebel through a daily routine consisting of an uncouth and bizarre public spectacle. The reader first encounters the pair in a lengthy and somewhat intriguing description by Meursault, who cannot hide his fascination over the relation:

On my way upstairs, in the dark, I ran into Salamano, my neighbor across the landing. He was with his dog. The two of them have been inseparable for eight years. The spaniel has a skin disease—mange, I think—which makes almost all its hair fall out and leaves it covered with brown sores and scabs. After living together for so long, the two of them alone in one tiny room, they've ended up looking like each other. Salamano has reddish scabs of his face and wispy yellow hair. As for the dog, he's sort of taken on his master's stooped look, muzzle down, neck straining. They look as if they belong to the same species, and yet they hate each other. Twice a day, at eleven and six, the old man takes the dog out for a walk. They haven't changed their route in eight years. You can see them in the rue de Lyon, the dog pulling the man along until old Salamano stumbles. Then he beats the dog and swears at it. The dog cowers and trails behind. Then it's the old man who pulls the dog. Once the dog has forgotten, it starts dragging its master along again, and again gets beaten and sworn at. Then they both stand there on the sidewalk and stare at each other, the dog in terror, the man in hatred. (Camus, *S* 26-27)

For Deleuze and Guattari, the concept of becoming animal strives to break from the categorical classification of series-structures in natural history as well as analogies of proportion creating equivalents between nature and culture. Becoming transcends mimetic correspondence between subjects, allowing for a fusion outside of a system of imitation and classification. The reality of becoming displaces subject-object relations, as it emphasizes the alliance of two distinct beings outside a hierarchy of power and orders of filiation. Becoming finally asserts contagion and involution as a creative form of communication constantly expanding the limits of bio-experience and occurring within a multiplicity of forces. Salamano and his dog represent this fusion, placing them as anomalies within social constructs. They have transcended the exclusive categories of species, and now belong to a new species characterized by "confunctioning by contagion" and the ephemeral establishment of an assemblage (Deleuze and Guattari, 233-240). This assemblage can only exist on the fringes of society, thus, Salamano and his dog are marginal figures facing a double exile--one grounded in their biological category and the other expressing their lack of adherence to social structures. The concept of exile can be further developed if we analyze the etiology of their disease and its relation to leprosy. Mange, like leprosy, negates the concept of a clean and proper body, becoming an omnipresence state of abjection. The diseased body brings inevitable mortality back into the eyes of the world. In pre-modern medicine, being a leper became symbolic of a system of exclusion relying on observed characteristics involving the "grammar of difference" used to legitimize the dichotomizing economy of segregation based on race, gender and physical health (Edmond 58). Moreover, leprosy was viewed as a disease breaking down the sacred division between humans and animals. As a result of this ambivalence, the law appropriates the disease as an instrument of power enforced through the fear of the Other, echoing its biblical origins of the exclusion of difference through the language of sanitization and sin. In *The Stranger*, scabs override the sanctity of inside/outside divisions, even spreading to the landscape. The ruthless heat of the land invades the landscape, doubling the condition of human embodiment. Camus utilizes the language of wounding to describe the state of all matter in a world without appeal, this time highlighting the fusion of human and earth. While following the procession during the burial of his mother, Meursault characterizes the precariousness of all matter and the indifference of the world:

> All around me there was still the same glowing countryside flooded with sunlight. The glare from the sky was unbearable. At one point, we went over s a section of the road that had just been repaved. The tar had burst open in the sun. Our feet sank into it, leaving its shiny pulp exposed. (Camus, *S* 16-17)

Physical illness also externalizes the internal state of unrest. It is interesting to note that in the original French text, Camus utilizes the term *maladie* to describe the dog's condition. *Maladie* at one level implies bodily appearance associated with disease, but at another level it pertains to "an unwholesome or disordered condition," akin to Sartre's notion of nausea as existential anguish (Howard vi). In this sense, illness simultaneously extends to all that is human and natural and represents the fatal organic bond to the indifferent universe. In addition, it poses the physical being as the prime target of the absurdity of the world.

Finally, the human-animal-earth union--the common body-- reappears throughout the novel as a victim of the merciless persistence of the natural elements, in particular the sun's heat. The sun's radiance hurts Meursault's eyes in the morning after the wake, it renders the landscape "inhuman and oppressive" (Camus, *S* 15), it reaches apocalyptic proportions in the murder that leads to Meursault's downfall, "the scorching blade slashed at my eyelashes and stabbed at my stinging eyes...The sea carried up a thick, fiery breath. It seemed to me as if the sky split open from one end to the other to rain down fire (59)," and the morning heat prolongs the unbearable proceedings of the trial (101). This is consistent with Camus' observations in his diary of a collective invasion of vulnerable bodies exposed to the landscape. Camus depicts existence in Algeria during the first hot days of the year with solemn renouncement, "Stifling. All the animals are lying on their side...Trees and men stand motionless...An hour of tenderness and despair with nothing to embrace, nothing at whose feet to throw oneself, overcome with gratitude" (Camus, *Notebooks 1935-1942*, 22-23).

Nature of Relationship to Authority

The intricate bond between Salamano and his dog provides two models present in the symbiotic relationship of the subject to authority. Both models heavily rely on the body as the object where punishment is meted onto and marked. On one hand, Salamano and the dog re-enact the struggle between master and slave through physical depravation. Meursault tells us, "When the dog wants to urinate, the old man won't give him enough time and yanks at him, so that the spaniel leaves behind a trail of little drops. If the dog has an accident in the room, it gets beaten again" (Camus, *S* 27). Salamano's authority over the dog is not unlike the law's punishment of the criminal. Later in the story, Meursault contemplates justice's methods of chastising and marking the criminal through the denial of bodily desire and needs. Taking away one's freedom translates into strict sexual abstinence and the systematic removal of simple pleasures such as cigarettes. In *Discipline and Punish*, Foucault traces the origin of the modern prison system, finding its zenith in the manipulation of the individual as the point of application of the penalty (Foucault 128). The prohibitions work on a system of depravation that curtails the basic activities and gestures of everyday life. He demonstrates this system of operation, claiming:

> ...In the project for a prison institution that was then developing, punishment was seen as a technique for the coercion of individuals; it operated methods of training the body—not signs—by the traces it leaves, in the form of habits, in behavior; and it presupposed the setting up of a specific power for the administration of the penalty. (131)

The law relies on the invasion and surveillance of the private sphere of the subject. Punishment reconfigures the subject under a normative regime. It makes the body strange to oneself and utilizes the precariousness of the flesh as its formidable target of torture and coercion. Punishment indexes pain. Pain, whether physical or psychological, characterizes the weapons of authority. As Elaine Scarry points out, pain's etymology originates in the word "*poena*" or punishment (Scarry 16). Pain makes interiority visible and transforms the body into an enemy. According to her argument:

> Pain is a pure physical experience of negation, an immediate sensory rendering of "against," of something being against one, and of something one must be against. Even though it occurs within oneself,

it is at once identified as "not oneself," "not me," as something so alien that it must right now be gotten rid of. (52)

Pain, especially during interrogation, devaluates and extinguishes human will and individual identity through its totality. Justice wreaks vengeance on disorder by compromising the dignity of the subject through physical detriment. Meursault's narrative captures such moments with terms relating to disorientation and illness. Throughout the trial, the protagonist complains of dizziness, illness and a noise that "was getting painful" (Camus, *S* 73,75). He considers the relentless bureaucratic machinery and its plethora of officials and formalities as a form of denaturalization of the human subject. He feels his speech appropriated by his lawyer when the latter utilizes a first person narrative in his arguments for the defense. To Meursault, this constitutes "a way to exclude me even further from the case, reduce me to nothing, and, in a sense, substitute himself for me" (103). In a sense, apart from his inner dialogue, Meursault stands as a ghost in front of the law, unable to comprehend a system of signification foreign from his own experience. In a state from which there is no exit, Meursault identifies with Salamano's dog as a creature that chooses to live without appeal and indulges in constant memory lapses to make life tolerable. After being imprisoned and thrown naked under the iron wheels of authority, he engages in a performance of animal docility. Viewing his performance as a point of resistance, he dupes the authorities into believing they have mastered him. He finds happiness in the theatricality of this procedure, which elicits a pat on the head by his master, "those rare moments when the judge would lead me to the door of his office, slap me on the shoulder, and say to me cordially, 'That's all for today, Monsieur Antichrist'" (71).

The relation between Salamano and his dog also unravels a flaw within the apparatus of the law. Both the old man and the dog as well as Meursault and the patriarchs he scorns, rely on the interdependence of subject and object. Although Salamano's behavior toward the dog can sometimes present itself as cruel, the old man's purpose in life comes about precisely because of the existence of the canine. When the dog runs away, Salamano is thrown into despair. "What is going to happen to me?" he exclaims. Here, Salamano becomes as much a victim as the dog he victimizes, invalidating his possible link to other figures of authority in the novel. The reader is then introduced to a physical bond between the pair that heavily asserts a mutual condition of exile that rests on the marking of their bodies. Once a handsome spaniel, the dog has lost its coat due to mange. Salamano relishes early memories of the relationship when he fed the dog from a bottle. At this point in time, they both suffer a similar malady, one that appears in physical form through the scabs but also presents itself in the dilapidation of the self through old age. Meursault, also surprised by this discovery, remarks, "Every night and every morning after the dog had gotten the skin disease, Salamano rubbed him with ointment. But according to him, the dog's real sickness was old age, and there's no cure for old age" (45). Like old age, and the precariousness of having a body, the absurdity of the world is inescapable.

During Meursault's encounters with authorities, both legal and religious, a certain interdependence between the law and the criminal manifests itself. Both his attorney and the priest desire to reform Meursault, utilizing him as the object that gives their profession meaning. After a failed attempt at persuading Meursault to believe in God, his attorney exclaims, "Do you want my life to become meaningless?"(69). Meursault represents man's inner doubt and anxiety, a condition of being that the majority of people prefer to disavow. In his confrontation with the priest, the ambiguity of belief proves almost fatal. He snaps at the man, grabs him by the collar of his cassock and demonstrates the inner anguish that takes place in the here and now, in the burden of a body and the uncertainty at the basis of all life. In fact, what angers Meursault lies in the priest's frantic effort to ignore the world around him in search of abstract redemption. He fails his duty to life. Meursault's defiance takes the form of a struggle for identity. He accuses the priest because:

> He seemed so certain about everything, didn't he? And yet none of his certainties was worth one hair of a woman's head. He wasn't even sure he was alive, because he was living like a dead man...what did his God or the lives people choose or the fate they think they elect matter to me when we're all elected, me and billions of people like him who also called themselves my brothers? (120-121)

To Camus, Meursault's heroism stems from his ability to bluntly expose the "...'custom and 'diversion' [that] conceal from man his nothingness, his forlornness, his inadequacy, his impotence, and his emptiness..." (Sartre 75)

In the end, *The Stranger* amounts to a deep meditation on the construction of the abject. Meursault is subjected to a triple exile. He is born to an underclass of Western culture stubbornly subsisting on the deserts of Algeria. But, even within this group, he remains a stranger. He is sentenced to death because he represents a threat to the pillars of the social order. The law marks and excludes him by pathologizing his natural being. He belongs to the historical class of lepers, individuals populating colonies regulated through the systemic branding of rejection and exclusion. Interestingly enough, the leper colony would later lead to the evolution of the mental hospital and the modern prison system, both dedicated to the regulation and suppression of difference.

Nature of Relationships of Love and Dependence

Throughout the novel, the figures of Salamano and his dog accentuate the tension between unions of love regulated by a legal contract and the existence of affective relationships not bound to law. The strange interdependence between man and animal functions to enable Meursault's cathartic mourning as well as presenting the ideal condition in which bodies merge within the totality of the absurd. In the *Myth of Sisyphus*, Camus favors the fervent, but short-lived passions of Don Juan over the destructive, imperialistic and tyrannical coupling regulating desire under the law:

> We call love what binds us to certain creatures only by reference to a collective way of seeing for which books and legends are responsible. But of love I know only that mixture of desire, affection, and intelligence that binds me to this or that creature. That compound is not the same for another person. I do not have the right to cover all these experiences with the same name…There is no noble love but that which recognizes itself to be both short-lived and exceptional. (Camus, *MOS* 73-74)

In the majority of his work, Camus characterizes relationships with women as dangerous and debilitating. In *The Stranger*, he refers to the male-female interaction and the unit of the family by alluding to predatory activities. During his mother's vigil, he describes the women present as having bulging stomachs. In contrast, the men are "skinny and carry canes" (Camus, *S* 9-10). Maman's paramour, Monsieur Pérez, embodies the collapse of manhood under the coded eroticism allowed to breathe in the space of the law. After a long procession to the burial ground, he faints, "big tears of frustration and exhaustion" streaming down his cheeks (18). Camus treats the casket holding his lover's body in a completely different way, utilizing violent images to portray the final consolidation between the female body and nature in death. While Pérez collapses, "the blood-red earth [spills] over Maman's casket, the white flesh of the roots mixed in with it" (18). The burgeoning of the earth emphasizes Pérez's impotence and sterility. Later in the novel, Meursault once again reflects on the menacing aspect of relationships under the social contract, this time focusing on the fate of manhood within the structure of the heterosexual family unit. Perched at his window watching passer-bys, the protagonist observes "an enormous mother, in a brown silk dress, and the father, a rather frail little man I know by sight" (22). He sketches an image of the woman as cannibal, sapping manly strength and leaving behind nothing but devastation. Meursault's fear expresses itself in his skepticism towards marrying Marie and his refusal to show signs of grief and emotion towards his mother.

Meursault views unions in a much different light than the rest of society. He uses sexual pleasure as a way to transcend the human through intense experiences. He thus evades the legacy of the original sin and the ramifications of a flesh perpetually reproducing its own mortality (Rizzuto 50). Here, Camus follows Bataille's conception of eroticism and inevitable life. For Bataille, human existence poses a condition based on discontinuity, only reversed by the profound continuity of two bodies breaking physical and social boundaries during the pursuit of pleasure in the act of coitus. In *The Stranger*, Camus reveals a similar strategy. Meursault's loves is mediated through the intense experience of the natural world as when, for instance, "Together again, Marie and I swam out a ways, and we felt a closeness as we moved in unison and were happy" (Camus, *S* 50). The physical nature of the relationship comes full term when, separated from Marie while in prison, Meursault realizes a union not based on the primal instincts of the body is of no use to him. Although, he feels affection for Marie, the absence of her body annuls the union. Thus, Meursault coldly analyzes that once their bodies were separated, there was nothing that would keep the lovers together or remind them of each other (115).

However, Meursault is not entirely without emotion. During the trial, he feels profound love for Celeste, the restaurant owner who testifies in his defense. The relation between the two men rests on a fraternal solidarity, not imposed or prescribed, but subtly floating in the background. Further, Meursault alludes to the union between Salamano and his dog, which he views as an ideal relationship, as a stand-in for his deepest and true emotions. For instance, when Marie asks Meursault if he loves her and desires to marry, the latter diffuses the situation by introducing an alternative, telling Marie about the unusual pair (35). This remains consistent with Camus privileging of unions outside the social contract. In his notebooks, the author states: "Coupling with animals suppresses consciousness of the other. It represents 'freedom'" (Rizzuto 74). Fusion with the animal transcends the boundaries of the body and multiples points of identification. In the story, Salamano's dog literally symbolizes a particular love outside the social construct. We learn Salamano adopts the dog following the death of his wife because he found himself lonely. Interestingly enough, this social union was far from a happy one. Salamano, to Meursault's approval, explicates his love for his wife depended on habit and that "he'd pretty much gotten used to her" (Camus, *S* 44). This can serve as the rationale for Meursault's relationships. When he encounters Salamano, Meursault's mind comes back to the memory of his mother and a form of latent mourning. Meursault's co-existence with Maman relied on their interdependence and most importantly, habit and silence. Meursault places his mother in the home because, as Salamano claims at the trial, "he had run out of things to say" (94). Perhaps the most fascinating part of the dynamics between Meursault and the pair lies in the fact that Salamano allows the protagonist catharsis by expressing the very words Meursault's nature prevents him from uttering. Discussing Maman's fondness for the dog, Salamano assures Meursault that he knows he loved his mother and justifies his decision to place her in the home, where she could be better cared for and make friends. Once this guilt is resolved or at least explored, Meursault can move one. Part of Meursault's salvation derives from his meditation on Maman, his acceptance of her death, and his return to the symbolic womb present in nature. The end of the novel recalls the beginning. Meursault delineates an almost exact experience to that he felt after the burial: "Sounds of the countryside were drifting in. Smells of the night, earth, and salt air were cooling my temples. The wondrous peace of that sleeping summer flowed through me like a tide" (122). This marks the precise moment of identification with his mother. Resigned for death, Meursault for the first time opens himself to "the gentle indifference of the world" and finds a solution to the meaning of life as well as a way to connect with others (122).

Works Cited

Bataille, Georges. *Eroticism: Death and Sensuality.* Trans.Mary Dalwood. San Francisco: City Lights Books, 1986. Print.

Camus, Albert. *The Myth of Sisyphus and Other Essays.* Trans. Justin O'Brien. New York: Vintage International, 1991. Print.

Camus, Albert. *Notebooks 1935-1942.* Trans. Justin O'Brien. New York: Marlowe & Company, 1996. Print.

Camus, Albert. *The Stranger.* Trans. Matthew Ward. New York: Vintage International, 1989. Print.

Deleuze, Gilles and Félix Guatari. *A Thousand Plateaus: Capitalism and Schizophrenia.* Trans. Brian Massumi. Minneapolis: University of Minnesota Press, 1987. Print.

Demaitre, Luke. *Leprosy in Premodern Medicine: A Malady of the Whole Body.* Baltimore: John Hopkins UP, 2007. Print.

Edmond, Rod. *Leprosy and Empire: A Medical and Cultural History.* Cambridge: Cambridge UP, 2006. Print.

Foucault, Michel. *Discipline and Punish: The Birth of the Prison.* Trans. Alan Sheridan. New York: Vintage Books, 1995. Print.

Howard, Richard. "A Foreword to *Nausea.*" *Nausea.* New York: New Directions Books, 2007. Print.

Merleau-Ponty, Maurice. *The Visible and the Invisible.* Trans. Alphonso Lingis. Evaston: Northwestern UP, 1968. Print.

Rizzuto, Anthony. *Camus: Love and Sexuality.* Gainesville: University Press of Florida, 1998. Print.

Sartre, Jean-Paul. "A Commentary on *The Stranger*." *Existentialism is a Humanism*. Trans. Carol Macomber. New Haven: Yale UP, 2007. Print.

Scarry, Elaine. *The Body in Pain: The Making and Unmaking of the World*. New York: Oxford UP, 1985. Print.

Homo-Social Eroticness in "The Guest"

By Peter Francev

Following World War II, academics across North America and Europe began to look at literature in a variety of compelling and different ways. They shifted the focus of literary analysis away from a deep understanding of the text-at-hand and began to create a multitude of avenues in which to pursue an understanding of literature. "Literature" no longer meant: poems, plays or works of fiction—both short and long—but, rather it constituted the aforementioned as well as different perspectives in which to examine the writing. These perspectives, as they are now taught in universities around the world, include: psychological, social, historical, structural and post-structural, colonial and post-colonial, and queer, to name just a few. Each of these literary theories, with its own philosophical and theoretical bases, enables the reader to deconstruct literature in such a way that in the de-construction the essence of the work is all-at-once exposed and revealed and the literature is reduced to simply a "text."

As such, I plan to present findings and thoughts on the idea of homo-eroticism in Camus' short story "The Guest". The idea of an unspoken bond between individuals of the same sex creates a(n) (un)necessary tension within the confines of the homo-social boundaries of the relationships between Daru and the prisoner. While Camus never explicitly means for the characters to be considered homosexual (nor could he have written about such frankness is in time), I argue that the tension and the desire are evident, if only just below the surface.

What I call homo-social eroticness has its roots in two terms: homo-social and homo-erotic which stem from the queer theory branch of post-structuralism that was prevalent in the 1980s. I define homo-social, in the vocabulary of queer theory, as an instance where two individuals of the same sex—not necessarily homosexual—are situated together in the social setting. (As a side-note, D.H. Lawrence's novels are notorious for homo-social settings.). Homo-eroticness, on the other hand, is where the qualities and characteristics of a sexual tension between two people of the same sex occur only without the physical act of copulation. The characters may not act out upon their desires, and these desires maybe purely subconscious, but they are evident nonetheless. Therefore, if we combine homo-social and homo-erotic, we have a homo-social eroticness in which characters in a given text are of the same sex, possibly of the same social class or in the same social setting (but not a prerequisite), and an underlying sexual tension that is "waiting" to be discovered and released.

The plot summary of "The Guest" is quite simple: Daru is a school-teacher who is out-posted on the Algerian "frontier" and is forced into a predicament by the unapologetic and unsympathetic *gendarme*, Balducci, by passing off an Arab prisoner to the authorities in the local village of Tinguit. Daru, perfectly content to the environs of the school-house, is more than annoyed when Balducci presents the prisoner (wanted for murdering his cousin over a petty dispute). According to Balducci, Daru is supposed to take the prisoner into the village, where the authorities are expecting both men. Daru tries to refuse Balducci's orders, but when the latter threatens with arrest, Daru simply and resentfully complies.

After Balducci leaves Daru with his "guest", the homo-social bonding begins. Daru is hungry and asks the prisoner if he is as well. He responds "Yes".[1] At this point, Daru exhibits the old notion of the feminine qualities of setting the table for two. Camus notes the minute details of methodically baking a cake for the guest. The baking of a cake, specifically, is quite interesting. On the one hand, it tells the reader that Daru is the "prefect host", in that he is willing to go to great lengths to make his guest feel "at home" in the schoolhouse. This could illustrate the idea that Daru is domesticated, thereby playing the role of the housekeeper while the Arab is the guest and is waited on hand and foot. Yet, we can also take Daru's generosity for merely that—friendliness from someone who, apart from his students, who attend class irregularly, longs for human contact. And, one could make the argument further and claim that since Daru does not seem to be as disgusted with the Arab as he is with Balducci, then he is more at ease with the prisoner than with the old gendarme.

---

[1] Camus "The Guest", pg. 419.

When the Arab asks Daru: "Why do you eat with me?" Daru responds: "I'm hungry." The simplicity of Daru's answer is a bit disconcerting because he really could just mean that he is hungry and just would like to eat his dinner. Or, the straightforwardness of his answer could signify that he is trying to cover for his own insecurities and inadequacies because, in the immediately following paragraph, Daru states: "There was nothing more to do or to get ready. He had to look at this man. He looked at him, therefore, trying to imagine his face bursting with rage. He couldn't do so. He could see nothing but the dark yet shining eyes and the animal mouth."[2]

Again, Camus presents readers with the question: "What does it (the passage) mean?" Well, for starters, one could take the superficial perspective that Daru is disgusted by this animalistic man—this sub-human of a man—who killed his cousin over a sack of grain. Yet if we choose to accept this assertion, then Daru imposes his will of in hierarchy of goodness, since he has not committed the grievous sin of murder. Of course, such a simplistic interpretation has its consequences: the most obvious is one that the reader fails to take into account, or realize, that the Arab prisoner is part of a nomadic culture who do not adhere or recognize the rules of their imperialist overlords, but, rather, follow their own laws of governance on the plains and plateaus of Algeria. However, the other interpretation is one that Daru's face burns with rage not because he cannot stand to look at this man—this murderer, but rather in him he sees a companion, a stranger, someone alienated from the world around him through the repression of sexuality; and here, in front of Daru, is a man who, like himself, is outcast from society— both geographically and socially, especially if they share the homo-sexual desires. Thus, his face burns with the rage of desire.

The "bursting with rage" that Daru feels is one that essentially frames the homo-social eroticness of the plot; after the beds are set up, the men go to bed. At some point:

> In the middle of the night, Daru was still not asleep. He had gone to bed after undressing completely; he generally slept naked. But when he suddenly realized that he had nothing on, he hesitated. He felt vulnerable and the temptation came to him to put on his clothes again.

---

[2] *Ibid.*, pg. 420.

> Then he shrugged his shoulders; after all, he wasn't a child and, if need be, he could break his adversary in two.[3]

In what I call the "first stage" of Daru and the Arab prisoner's homo-erotic socialness, Daru realizes that he is: naked, vulnerable, tempted and accepting. In the first instance, Daru is, quite literally, naked. He has stripped off his clothes and is naked to the world—at least the world of himself and the Arab. He is also figuratively naked. And it is this figurative nakedness that immediately leads to his vulnerability; for Daru is never more vulnerable than when he is naked. He is exposed to the elements of the outside world— including the vulnerability of exposure to the Arab. Daru is neither clothed, nor protected for the (un)wanted advances of his guest.

His secret, subconscious desires are wanted and his vulnerabilities lead Daru into the arena of temptation; except rather than feeling vulnerable and tempted in a shameful sense, where he would want to cover his nakedness in order to protect himself. One could make the argument that Daru is in a state of denial and, as such, he *claims* that he wants to be clothed, whereas he really wants to remain naked with the hopes that the Arab in as sexually curious as he. In order to support this claim, Daru justifies his subconscious desire with a very conscious rationalization: "if need be, he could break his adversary in two."

In the next stage, we find Daru observing the Arab in night:

> From his bed he could observe him, lying on his back, still motionless with his eyes closed under the harsh light. When Daru turned out the light, the darkness seemed to coagulate all of a sudden. Little by little, the night came back to life in the window where the starless sky was stirring gently. The schoolmaster soon made out the body lying at his feet. The Arab still did not move, but his eyes seemed open.[4]

Now that Daru has accepted his position with the Arab, the night comes to life with an infinite number of unspoken possibilities between the two men. With eyes closed, the night begins to swirl and coagulate in the confines of

---

[3] *Ibid.*, pg. 421.

[4] *Ibid.*, pg. 421.

limitless choices, wants and desires. While it is certainly possible, probable even, that the Arab is asleep, Daru creates in his mind the image of a sleeping guest, who lays feet from Daru, waiting with batted breath and open eyes secretly hoping that his "master" will make the first move towards unison. Waiting is, indeed, the hardest part.

The third stage is one in which we find Daru observing:

> The Arab turned over on his side with his back to Daru, who thought that he heard him moan. Then he listened for his guest's breathing, become heavier and more regular. He listened to that breath so close to him and mused without being able to go to sleep. In this room where he had been sleeping alone for a year, this presence bothered him.[5]

Here, we find the Arab making the first move towards receiving Daru. He (in)advertently turns onto his side, presenting Daru with his backside, in a moment of (sub)conscious submissiveness. If Daru perceives the Arab in this sense, then the latter is ready to receive the former in a kind of passive sexual offering. This is supplemented by the fact that Daru thought that he heard the Arab moan. Could the turning onto one's side and moaning be an unspoken sexual offering of one's self? I believe it so.

Next, no sooner does the Arab moan than readers are told that Daru "listened for his guest's breathing." What is so striking, is that in each of Camus' three novels—*The Stranger*, *The Plague*, and *The Fall*—we find the protagonists concerned with the "Other's" breathing as a sign of life: after swimming with Marie, Meursault puts his head on her stomach and listens to her heartbeat and her breathing; Rieux, more so than any one, is confronted with breathing as he deals with his wife's tuberculosis and the countless Oranians who have become afflicted with the plague; and then there is Clamence, who slows down the pace of his walk to hear the screams and cries for help of the mysterious woman who jumps into the Seine—until they cease to exist. In any event, Daru joins the ranks of Camus' protagonists in that breathing is not just a sign of life, but an affirmation of wanting—Meursault sexually wants Marie, and so he is attentive to her breathing; Rieux wants his patients to survive (especially, Jacques Othon), and so he listens for the life still

---

[5] *Ibid.*

within their lungs; and Clamence wants to not hear the woman's cries and screams. Daru's wants are slightly different in that unlike the overt desires of the other protagonists; he sees breathing-not as an affirmation of life, but one in which there is the moaning of sexual longing…much in the same sense as Meursault.

Finally, Daru "muses" about what exactly-the possibility of a sexual encounter with his prisoner? Yes. He muses at the possibilities of a connection—both sexual and spiritual—since "he had been sleeping alone for a year." The guest affords Daru the possibilities of limitless connections and because Daru has had no contact in the last year, "this presence bothered him."

Why does the presence bother Daru? Is it because he is not used to other adults? Is it because his guest is accused of murder? Or is it because he is sexually attracted to the Arab? The answer cannot be within the first two queries because: one would imagine that he has become comfortable with his loneliness; and, he acknowledges, more than once, that he is physically bigger than the Arab. Therefore, if it can be none of the first two assertions, then his uncomfortableness must stem from his repressed sexual desires for his guest as to express them openly would have been taboo, especially in 1950s French-controlled Algeria.

Lastly, we come to the fourth stage of the homo-social eroticness: justification. It is as if Daru tries to justify his sexual attraction towards the Arab by stating that:

> …it bothered him also by imposing on him a sort of brotherhood he knew well but refused to accept in the present circumstances. Men who share the same rooms, soldiers or prisoners, develop a strange alliance as if, having cast off their armour with their clothing, they fraternized every evening, over and above their differences, in the ancient community of dream and   fatigue. But Daru shook himself; he didn't like such musings, and it was essential to sleep.[6]

---

[6] *Ibid.* pg. 421-22.

Daru justifies his compelling feelings by comparing them to that of soldiers *and prisoners*; these are the same men who, in their respective situations, seem to come to terms with their feelings and desires. It is as if Daru does the same: requesting that we, his audience, support his choice at homo-social eroticness—the same homo-social eroticness that is brought upon by people of the same sex in situations in which they feel free and compelled to "cast off their armour with their clothing,' in yet another vivid description of blatant nakedness. However, Daru shakes himself and represses "such musings" because sleep will afford him the opportunity to slip into unconsciousness and forget such entertaining thoughts.

As Daru tries to forget his secretive desires, the Arab wakes and goes outside to relieve himself. As he slips outside, Daru states "'He is running away,' (....) 'Good riddance!'"[7] Daru's moment of overcompensation does not fool anyone.

The following morning, both men share breakfast together, on the same bed, in what can be seen as their final moment of togetherness. Daru, "...without knowing why, ... felt strangely empty and vulnerable."[8] Despite still being unsure of which course of action to take, he is certain of one thing: that the time spent with his guest is slowly slipping away.

As the Arab is washing his face, out by the shed, Daru looks out over the desert plain (which seems to stretch out into infiniteness—much like when Jeanine, in "The Adulterous Woman," looks out onto the desert from the rampart of the fort.); he tries to figure what, exactly, he is going to do with the prisoner.

In a moment of humanity, Daru gives the Arab "dates, bread, and sugar" and 'a thousand francs"[9] and two crucial choices: first, at the top of the plateau, where the road comes to a fork, the Arab can go east, for two-hours ,towards the village of Tinguit where he will "find the administration and the police."[10] Otherwise, he can head "roughly towards the south"[11] and "In a

---

[7] *Ibid.* pg. 422.

[8] *Ibid.*, pg. 423.

[9] *Ibid.*, pg. 424.

[10] *Ibid.*, pg. 425.

day's walk from here... find pasture lands and the first nomads."[12] Daru gives the Arab a choice of either being responsible and turning himself into the authorities, or hiding amongst the nomadic shepherds. Either way Daru, who did not want to be placed in this situation to begin with, allows the Arab to choose his own fate.

At that moment, as if not wanting to prolong the goodbye, Daru states "'Listen,' ... "'No, be quiet. Now I'm leaving you.'"[13] As if taken from Hollywood, this is how Camus chooses to end their "one-night stand." And in true cinematic fashion, the Arab turns around slowly and chooses the path towards Tinguit, but not before "Daru felt something rise in his throat."[14]

Of course, Daru will not have long to dwell on thoughts of losing the Arab, because when he returns to the classroom there "sprawled the clumsily chalked-up words he just read: 'You handed over our brother. You will pay for this.'"[15] Never more poignant, "Daru.... In this vast landscape he had loved so much, he was alone."[16]

In "The Guest", Camus does what he does best: and that is, he portrays his protagonists as isolated—be it geographically, ethically, morally, physically, or spiritually—not just from society, but from the rest of the world, and Daru is no exception. Here, just as in his novels and other short stories, do we find a story come full-circle, as it were, with regards to Daru's situation and placement in the world. He begins the story alone, as it were, only to have a guest forced upon him by Balducci. Somewhat apathetic, but still bothered by Balducci's imposition nonetheless, he agrees, reluctantly, to take care of the Arab before handing him over to the authorities. However, over the course of the evening and into the night, an unspoken bond seems to develop between the two men as they grow ever closer. There seems to be a perceived but unspoken sexual tension, and perhaps desire, between Daru and the Arab

---

[11] *Ibid.*

[12] *Ibid.*

[13] *Ibid.*

[14] *Ibid.*

[15] *Ibid.*, pg. 426.

[16] *Ibid.*

which is never resolved. And because the moment passes by all-too-quickly, Daru is left standing alone on the plateau watching his companion walk towards his death. Rather symbolically speaking, it is not just the Arab who walks towards death, but it is the death of desire and of homo-social eroticness that will perish when both men meet their fates.

'The Eternal Return of Sisyphus': Camus Interpreting Nietzsche

By Giovanni Gaetani

> Si l'on prend soin de définir le nietzschéen non pas comme celui qui fait de Nietzsche un fin à dupliquer mais un commencement à dépasser, alors Albert Camus fut l'un des grands philosophes nietzschéens du XXe siècle – peut-être même le plus grand.

> — Michel Onfray, *L'ordre libertaire.*

> Es hilft Nichts: Jeder Meister hat nur Einen Schüler – und der wird ihm untreu, – denn er ist zur Meisterschaft auch bestimmt.

> — Friedrich Nietzsche, *Menschliches, Allzumenschliches II*

Every careful reader of Albert Camus' works should be aware of the fundamental relationship that exists between him and the German philosopher Friedrich Nietzsche, not only for a pure philological reason.

Indeed, if we look both to the biographical facts and the texts, we can easily recognize that Camus has been engaged with Nietzsche in a constant, deep dialogue: from the high school, when he quoted Nietzsche 'at every opportunity, even inopportunely'[1], to the fatal car accident where he died, when in his bag has been found a copy of *The Gay Science*, Nietzsche's presence has traced a long red line in Camus' life[2]. But that does not mean that Camus has always looked in the same way at his old philosophical

---

[1] The French expression 'à tout propos et meme hors de propos' is taken from the witness of Camus' professor Paul Mathieu. Cf. *Dictionnaire Albert Camus*, Jeanyves Guérin (editor), Editions Robert Laffont, Paris 2009, p. 604.

[2] Cf. Roger Grenier, 'Le fil rouge nietzschéen', in *Le Magazine Littéraire*, n° 298, April 1992.

master: being a good pupil, he has surpassed his teacher, following to the letter Zarathustra's advice: 'One repays a teacher badly if one always remains a pupil only'[3].

In the following pages we are going to retrace the history of this relationship, dividing it in three different stages: first, the early passionate agreement to Nietzsche's aesthetic philosophy; second, the critique of his fatalism in *The Rebel*; third, the late presumed re-evaluation.

Nothing but Nietzsche I: the first essay 'On Music'

The young nineteen years old student of Algeri is looking both for a literal style and a philosophical inspiration. Under the advice of his philosophy professor Jean Grenier he reads plenty of authors: among all Gide, de Richaud, Bergson, Proust, Schopenhauer and, of course, Nietzsche. In the journal *Sud*, directed by Grenier himself, Camus writes six articles in two years (1931-1932), through which he exercises his literal and philosophical attitude. In one of them, named *Sur la musique*, he exposes his personal conception of Music and Art, starting from Schopenhauer and Nietzsche's positions. Because it is the first real appearance of Nietzsche's name in Camus' works, it is worth to stop a little on it.

In spite of his young age, or maybe just because of it, Camus seems to have a clear head, even too clear, on what Art really is – or, at least, on what it should be: he refuses at the same time the realist conception of Art, for which the artist should merely give a neutral portrait of reality, and the idealist one, for which instead the artist should correct reality imperfection through his art work[4].

What is, then, Camus' conception of Art? According to his words, Art is 'creation of a world of Dream, seductive enough to hide the world where we

---

[3] Friedrich Nietzsche, *Thus Spoke Zarathustra*, edited by Adrian Del Caro and Robert Pippin, Cambridge University Press, 2006, p. 59.

[4] In Camus' words, the first point of view 'not only dishonours Art, but it destroys it', while the second one 'too often becomes moral theory, that produces dull, false and annoying works'. Cf. Albert Camus, *Sur la musique*, in *Œuvres complètes*, 4 tomes, Éditions Gallimard, 2008, pp. 522-540 of the first tome. My translation.

live with all its atrocities'[5]. In few words, for the young Camus Art has a consolatory function. Music is, in this perspective, the most consolatory of all the different disciplines, because it creates a world with no relations to the real one where Beauty can be contemplated without any support of Reason.

Here Camus is totally in line with Nietzsche's first conception of Art and Music, defined by a critic as 'aesthetic cosmodicy'[6]. This conception is exposed for the most in Nietzsche's first published text *The Birth of Tragedy*. Indeed, arguing in favour of his perspective Camus will relate just to this text, considered by himself as 'the most important and characteristic work' of Nietzsche.

Here is the main problem: not only the Nietzschian critics will later belittle *The Birth of Tragedy* as a minor and overpassed work, but already Nietzsche himself in *Ecce homo* will say that 'in order to be fair to [this book] it is necessary to forget a few things', because 'it created a sensation and even fascination as a consequence of its flaws'. One thing more: Camus in his essay on music affirms that 'the thought of Nietzsche is directly derived from Schopenhauer', although with some divergences; but we all know what has been the last judgement of Nietzsche on Schopenhauer; still in *Ecce Homo*, he brutally affirms that 'Schopenhauer blundered in everything'.

The situation is then clear: for what we have seen the nineteen years old Albert Camus has for the most an anachronistic and reductive position on Nietzsche, being attracted more from 'the strange personality of this poet-philosopher' than from his thoughts. Here we agree with Michel Onfray, who affirms in his last work that 'Camus has approached the metaphysics of Art as a Romantic seduced by the Dionysian'[7].

---

[5] We underline that in the original French text the following terms are all written with the capital letter, in a rhetorical way: Dream, Art, Reason, Music, Life, Will, Genius, Nature and others.

[6] Alexander Nehamas, *Life as Literature*, Harvard University Press, Cambridge, 1985.

[7] Michel Onfray, *L'ordre libertaire. La vie philosophique d'Albert Camus*, Paris, Flammarion, 2012, p. 71.

Nothing but Nietzsche II: the first novel 'A Happy Death'

Approximatively between 1936 and 1938 Camus writes his first novel *La mort heureuse*, which will be published just later in 1971. This novel is full of explicit references to Nietzsche's philosophy and, above all, it has clearly a Nietzschian structure: the two Nietzschian concepts of 'natural death' and 'conscious death', exposed by Nietzsche in an aphorism that Camus reported in his *Notebooks*[8], give the title to the two parts of the novel; the protagonist Patrice Mersault follows with lucidity his 'will to happiness', that is nothing but a variation of the well-known Nietzschian 'will to power'; in the second part of the novel, the protagonist finally 'becomes what he is', namely he becomes one thing with his destiny, declaring "if I had my life to live over again' -- well I would live it over again just the way it has been'; lastly, the same conception of the body as a prerequisite for happiness is clearly taken from Nietzsche.

We do not have to stop too much on the analysis of this work because, in my opinion, such an interpretation is not a particular problematic point. In any case, if someone wants to investigate it thoroughly I will suggest in note some useful articles[9].

However, in short, the novel *La mort heureuse* is proof of a new awareness regarding Nietzsche's philosophy. Camus seems to understand the real importance of its contents in a deeper way, becoming gradually more interested in Nietzsche's thought than to his personality.

Nothing but Nietzsche III: 'The Myth of Sisyphus'

Nietzsche's presence in *The Myth of Sisyphus* is something different from the former ones: while in the essay *On Music* he was with Schopenhauer the main point of reference and still in the novel *A Happy Death* he was the main

---

[8] In the first *Notebook*, exactly in August 1938, Camus records: 'Sur la mort consciente, cf. Nietzsche. Crépuscule des Idoles, p. 203'.

[9] Mainly cf. Maurice Weyembergh, *Une lecture nietschéenne de* La mort heureuse, in *Albert Camus ou la mémoire des origines*, De Boeck, Paris-Bruxelles, 1998, pp. 75-84. Also cf. Michel Onfray, *L'ordre libertaire*, cit., the chapter *Mourir heureux*, pp. 89-91. At last cf. Roger Grenier, 'Le fil rouge nietzschéen', cit.

hidden inspirer, in *The Myth* instead his philosophical predominance seems to vanish, giving way to a Camus' more autonomous meditation.

Indeed, the twelve mentions of Nietzsche, whereof just five are textual quotations, are for the most methodological indications rather than substantial references to his philosophy: for example, in order to justify the philosophical relevance of the suicide problem, Camus refers to what he calls the 'Nietzschian criterion'[10], that is the necessity for the philosopher to 'preach by example'; farther, talking about the Actor, Camus paraphrases Nietzsche, who would have said that 'what matters is not eternal life but eternal vivacity'[11]; finally, in the appendix on Kafka he defines Nietzsche as 'the only artist to have derived extreme consequences of an aesthetic of the absurd, inasmuch as his final message lies in a sterile and conquering lucidity and an obstinate negation of any supernatural consolation'[12].

As we can see, the references to Nietzsche in the *Myth* are not essential nor indispensable to Camus' reasoning, like it was before in the essay *On Music* for example. It is not exaggerate to say that if we delete Nietzsche's name from the book everything will remain at his own place: to use a metaphor, the absurd building of Camus can stand upright without Nietzsche's support, which is here a decoration rather than a bearing wall.

Nevertheless, it does not mean that Nietzsche's influence on Camus is over. On the contrary, if we broach the text with a hermeneutic approach we can clarify – of course with a certain prudence – the character of Sisyphus at the light of the Nietzschian conception of the Eternal Return of the Same.

In order to understand this interpretation, one must firstly know what the Eternal Return is in the eyes of Nietzsche. Far from being an ontological affirmation on what things really are and far from being also a new original physical theory on the universal time cyclicity, it is instead an ethical-philosophical stratagem meant to permit the realization of the *Übermensch*, term which is better to translate with 'beyond-man' or 'over-man', excluding

---

[10] Albert Camus, *The myth of Sisyphus,* Penguin, London, 2000, p. 14.

[11] *Ivi.*, p. 78.

[12] *Ivi.*, p. 123.

'superman' for reason on which we will linger just in note[13]. How does this stratagem work? It is a kind of existential experiment in which to a person is asked the following questions: what will you do if you will have to live your life eternally in the same way you now live it and have lived it, without anything new nor different from the way you did? What if you are bound to live over and over again your pain, your suffering, your sacrifices, without any promise of redemption? Will you accept with joy to live this eternal return or will this thought crush and choke you?

Let us pose the same questions to Sisyphus: will him undertake and keep on his effort knowing not only that his rock will always fall, but also that at the end of his days there will be no one to reward him for his eternal sacrifice? Yes, he will. And he will with joy and pride.

On the contrary, if Sisyphus were not Sisyphus, we could imagine an alternative ending, in which we see him kneeling at the feet of the mountain near his rock, asking the gods to stop his torture. In this case, he would not have passed the trial of the Eternal Return: tiredness, dejection and cowardice would have prevailed on his pride and lucidity; the rock would have won, crushing and chocking him.

But fortunately Sisyphus is Sisyphus: 'negating the gods' and accepting his 'fatal and despicable' destiny, he is always 'the master of his days'. We do not have to imagine Sisyphus happy, because he is already so. That is, in conclusion, what I personally mean with the expression 'the Eternal Return of Sisyphus'.

---

[13] The German preposition '*Über*', which derives from the Latin *super* and the Greek *hyper*, can express both a sense of 'overstepping' (beyond) and 'superiority' (above, at the top of). For example, Heidegger and Jünger's dialogue '*Über die Linie*' can be translated both with 'Crossing the line'/'Over the line' and 'On the line'/'Regarding the line'. Anyway, it is just analysing Nietzsche's philosophy that we can resolve the ambiguity. Indeed, far from being a kind of superior and aristocratic man among the others, the *Übermensch* is a human future condition beyond the present one, as Zarathustra's image suggests: 'Mankind is a rope fastened between animal and overman – a rope over an abyss. A dangerous crossing, a dangerous on-the-way, a dangerous looking back, a dangerous shuddering and standing still'. Cf. *Thus Spoke Zarathustra*, cit., p. 7.

'Amor fati' Vs. 'Odium fati': Camus' critique of Nietzsche's fatalism

After the *Myth*, Camus will have to reconsider his position because of the dramatic events that took place in the '40s. Indeed, the Absurd cannot do anything in front of the twenty century's atrocities: as Camus himself remembers, 'nothing remains in the absurdist attitude which can help us answer the questions of our time. [...] It leaves us in a blind alley'[14]. Camus will formulate his concept of Revolt just to come out from this blind alley.

However, the passage from Absurd to Revolt coincides also with a new reconsideration of Nietzsche's philosophy. Indeed, as all the European intellectuals of the after-war also Camus is forced to face the problem of the so-called 'Nazification of Nietzsche'. He will give his personal resolution of this problem in 1951, in *The Rebel*, in the about fifteen pages of the chapter 'Nietzsche and Nihilism'.

Let us analyse these pages. First of all, a bitter remark: in the first note of this chapter, which incredibly does not appear in the Penguin Book edition translated by Anthony Bower[15], Camus underlines that he will broach just the last part of Nietzsche's philosophy, from 1880 to madness. He adds also that this chapter can be considered as a commentary of the *Will to Power*[16]. Now, this is a big controversial philological matter, because this presumed Nietzschian book never existed[17]. Camus, who uses a French translation of 1935 by Geneviève Bianquis, find himself in front of a false systematic work, in which Nietzsche seems to expose with precision both his final

---

[14] *The Rebel*, Penguin, London, 2000, p. 16

[15] *The Rebel*, Penguin Books Edition, 2000. Personally I've never seen such a bad edition of a philosophical book: wrong index, missing epigraph and dedication, missing pages (more than 30!), missing titles and even entire chapters, bad translations, etc., all of that makes Anthony Bower's translation a useless tool for those who want to read *L'Homme révolté* in English. For these reasons, I strongly advise a new English edition of *The Rebel*.

[16] The original note was: 'C'est évidemment la dernière philosophie de Nietzsche, de 1880 à l'effondrement, qui nous occupera ici. Ce chapitre peut être considéré comme un commentaire à *la Volonté de Puissance*'.

[17] Cf. Mazzino Montinari, '*La volonté de puissance' n'existe pas*, edited by P. D'Iorio, L'eclat, Paris, 1997.

system of the *Will to Power* and his European political project. Nietzsche clearly denied such a possibility in his last notebooks[18].

In any case, leaving aside this question, in these pages Camus defends and criticizes Nietzsche at the same time: on the one hand, he affirms that 'we can never confuse Nietzsche with Rosenberg', 'we must be the advocates for the defence of Nietzsche'; on the other hand, he affirms that Nietzsche has an 'involuntary responsibility' to not have posed a limit to his rebellion logic.

In particular, Camus criticizes the Nietzschian conception of 'amor fati', which is, in his words, 'the individual's absolute submission to Becoming'[19]. According to Camus, Nietzsche has tragically concluded his philosophy in a 'deification of fate', in which the individual has to accept everything that happens, including evil. Even though I personally do not agree on this interpretation of Nietzsche's fatalism for reasons that I will explain in note, I instead agree with Camus on his correction of Nietzsche's excess: using his notion of measure, he affirms that one must always counterbalance his Yes to the positive aspects of reality with a No to the negative ones; every 'amor fati' must always be balanced with an opposite 'odium fati'.[20]

After all, in conclusion, Sisyphus' lesson was clear: the destiny that we are forced to accept remains nonetheless despicable; far from renouncing to live, we still have to refuse every oppressive aspect of this world 'where children are tortured with no reason'.

---

[18] In 1888 Nietzsche substituted in his notes the 1885's title 'Der Wille zur Macht' with 'Versuch einer Umwerthung aller Werthe', changing – that is even more important – also the order in which he wanted to pose the different aphorisms. Elisabeth Förster-Nietzsche and Peter Gast ignored this and other notes just because they wanted to create a 'Nietzschian best-seller'.

[19] Antony Bower translates here the French term 'devenir' as 'self-realization', completely missing the point. Indeed, talking about Nietzsche's 'amor fati' the French term cannot but be the philosophical concept of 'Becoming' or, with a slightly different translation, 'fate', 'destiny' – anyway, the German original term is the noun 'das Werden', not the verb 'werden'.

[20] Michel Onfray defines this Camus' critique of Nietzsche's fatalism 'the great No to the great Yes'.

'Retour à Nietzsche': a presumed re-evaluation

Here we are at the last part of the paper, which is mainly a working hypothesis. Indeed, as Maurice Weyembergh has suggested, we can reasonably affirms that after *The Rebel* Camus has started a slow and silent re-evaluation of Nietzsche's position. If we read carefully all the texts of the 50s we will find plenty of Nietzsche's name quotations: in a letter to Breton and Patri, talking about Nietzsche, he affirms that 'such a soul infinitely overpasses us all'; elsewhere, he confesses 'I owe to Nietzsche a part of what I am'; as epigraph to *Actuelles II* he utilizes an aphorism of Nietzsche; finally, in the speech for the Nobel prize, he quotes the German philosopher more than one time. In particular, he quotes two of his main teachings. First, an advice for the 20th century's artist: 'to create today, is to create dangerously'. Second, an advice for the 20th century's philosopher: 'thoughts that come with doves' footsteps guide the world'.

Essential bibliography on the subject

W. E. Duvall, *Camus's Fall? From Nietzsche*, Historical Reflections, Spring 1995, pp. 537-552

W. E. Duvall, , *The Nietzsche Temptation in the Thought of Albert Camus*, Willamette Journal of Liberal Arts, Estate 1989, pp. 33-43

J.-F. Mattei, *Le premier ou le dernier homme?*, in *La pensée de midi*, 2010/1 N° 30, p. 99-106

B. Rosenthal, *Die Idee des Absurden. F. Nietzsche und A. Camus*, Bonn, Bouvier, 1977

R. Siena, *Nietzsche, Camus e il problema del superamento del nichilismo*, in "Sapienza", Vol. XXVIII, 1975

M. Weyembergh, *Camus und Nietzsche*, in *Sinn und Form*, 1993, pp. 654-664

M. Weyembergh, *Albert Camus, ou la mémoire des origines*, De Boeck universite, Paris-Bruxelles, 1998

M. Onfray, *L'ordre libertaire. La vie philosophique d'Albert* Camus, Paris, Flammarion, 2012

Dictionnaire Albert Camus, Jeanyves Guérin (editor), Editions Robert Laffont, Paris 2009

Roger Grenier, 'Le fil rouge nietzschéen', in *Le Magazine Littéraire*, n° 298, April 1992

"Rien, rien n'avait d'importance et je savais bien pourquoi" ("Nothing, nothing mattered, and I well knew why"): The World According to Meursault—or A Critical Attempt to Understand the Absurdist Philosophy of the Protagonist of Albert Camus' *The Stranger*

By George Heffernan

Introduction: The philosophical dilemma of Camus' *The Stranger*

The atheist-nihilist dilemma of Camus' *The Stranger* is this:[1] Either one believes in God and one's life has meaning, or one does not believe in God

---

[1] The French text of *L'Étranger* is found in the Pléiade edition of *Albert Camus*, vol. I: *Théâtre, Récits, Nouvelles*, ed. Roger Quilliot (Paris: Bibliothèque de la Pléiade, 1962), pp. 1127–1212. I refer to the text in parts (1 or 2), chapters (6 in 1 and 5 in 2), and paragraphs (from 1 to 27), which is a much more precise way of citing and quoting it than by mere pages. The English translations may contain a few paragraph changes with respect to the French original. A good English translation of *L'Étranger* is: *The Stranger*, tr. Matthew Ward (New York: Vintage, 1989). Finally, thanks to the efforts of Jean-Marie Tremblay (University of Quebec at Chicoutimi), an electronic edition of the French text of *L'Étranger* is now available on-line at: http://classiques.uqac.ca/classiques/camus_albert/etranger/etranger. In this paper, I reprise and revise some statements from my study "'Mais personne ne paraissait comprendre' ('But no one seemed to understand'): Atheism, Nihilism, and Hermeneutics in Albert Camus' *L'Étranger/The Stranger*", *Analecta Husserliana*, vol. 109 (2011), pp. 133–152. I urge the readers to consult my first treatment of the philosophy in Camus' *L'Étranger/The Stranger*.

and one's life has no meaning.[2] The Jewish-Christian variation on the theme is this: Either one accepts the vicarious atonement of Jesus Christ as the solution to the problem of one's guilt and one's salvation is assured, or one does not accept his self-sacrifice and one's damnation is certain. In the novel, the magistrate,[3] the prosecutor,[4] and the chaplain[5] seem to believe that, because Meursault is an atheist,[6] he must also be a nihilist.[7] They also tempt the readers to accept their inference. Yet it is not inconceivable that Camus is suggesting, by intent or in effect, that there is a third alternative here, and that Meursault too fails to find a "way out" of this "absurd" binary "logic".[8]

Now Meursault says that he does not accept Christ[9] and that he does not believe in God.[10] These statements are foundational to his sentiment that life cannot be understood as "rational"[11] but must be undergone as "absurd".[12]

---

[2] The God that is at issue here is the subject of the faiths of the revealed religions of the Abrahamic tradition, who is omnibenevolent, omnibeneficent, omnipotent, and omniscient (et cetera), as well as who has a providential plan in mind for the completeness or happiness of all his creatures. History and the history of philosophy are, of course, full of examples of people who believed in deities but not in a personal God to whom one can pray and with whom one can have a personal relationship.

[3] Cf. 2.1.7–13.

[4] Cf. 2.3.19, 2.4.5.

[5] Cf. 2.5.11–25.

[6] Cf. 2.1.13: "… monsieur l'Antéchrist …".

[7] This emerges most clearly in Meursault's examination by the magistrate. Cf. 2.1.11: "Mais il m'a coupé et m'a exhorté une dernière fois, dressé de toute sa hauteur, en me demandant si je croyais en Dieu. J'ai répondu que non. Il s'est assis avec indignation. Il m'a dit que c'était impossible, que tous les hommes croyaient en Dieu, même ceux qui se détournaient de son visage. C'était là sa conviction et, s'il devait jamais en douter, sa vie n'aurait plus de sens. 'Voulez-vous, s'est-il exclamé, que ma vie n'ait pas de sens?' À mon avis, cela ne me regardait pas et je le lui ai dit." Cf. also 2.5.13.

[8] Cf. 2.1.10–13, 2.5.13–25. Cf. also 1.1.27: "Il n'y avait pas d'issue." Cf. finally 2.2.17: "Non, il n'y avait pas d'issue …."

[9] Cf. 2.1.9–13.

[10] Cf. 2.5.13: "J'ai répondu que je ne croyais pas en Dieu." Cf. also 2.1.11.

[11] Cf. 2.5.3–4, 2.5.6, 2.5.8–9, 2.5.25.

[12] Cf. 2.5.25: "Rien, rien n'avait d'importance et je savais bien pourquoi. Lui aussi savait pourquoi. Du fond de mon avenir, pendant toute cette vie absurde que j'avais menée, un souffle obscur remontait vers moi à travers des années qui n'étaient pas encore venues et ce souffle égalisait sur son passage tout ce qu'on me proposait alors dans les années pas plus

Accordingly, Meursault disagrees with the authorities about whether to believe in God or to accept Christ, but he agrees with them that the only alternative is the absurdist option. For he uncritically acquiesces in their dominant narrative, according to which one who does not receive Christ or believe in God cannot live a meaningful life, that is, what they dogmatically believe to be the one and only truly meaningful life. Thus Meursault plays into the hands of those who confuse the problem of finding the meaning of life with the task of living a meaningful life. As a result, he ends up trying to accept the alleged indifference of the world, attempting to perceive it as "gentle",[13] and telling himself that he feels happy—and this in a way in which hardly anyone else would.[14]

The philosophical question in all this is whether and why the readers should follow the characters in assuming that human life is absurd because God does not exist or Jesus died in vain. In fact, it is not hard to see that there is a third way here, a way out of the atheist-nihilist dilemma, and it would be a fatal misunderstanding of the novel to assume that, because the characters did not see it, neither did the author nor should the readers. Therefore the only hermeneutically charitable interpretation of the novel, that is, the only one that does not gratuitously and precipitously posit inconsistency or incoherence where there may be none, is to suppose that, in not letting Meursault or the authorities recognize the possibility of a meaningful human life without Christ or God, Camus is challenging the readers to grasp what neither the protagonist nor the prosecutors were able to understand. Thus Camus, as distinguished from Meursault, may be understood as suggesting, by intent or in effect, that atheism does not entail nihilism.

Indeed, one can argue, with Nietzsche, for example, that the view that only the divine essence makes a human existence meaningful is an insidious kind

---

réelles que je vivais. Que m'importaient la mort des autres, l'amour d'une mère, que m'importaient son Dieu, les vies qu'on choisit, les destins qu'on élit, puisqu'un seul destin devait m'élire moi-même et avec moi des milliards de privilégiés qui, comme lui, se disaient mes frères. Comprenait-il, comprenait-il donc?"

[13] Cf. 2.1.11, 2.5.13, 2.5.26: "... je m'ouvrais pour la première fois à la tendre indifférence du monde."

[14] Cf. 2.5.26: "... j'ai senti que j'avais été heureux, et que je l'étais encore."

of nihilism.[15] For it is because "God is dead" that human beings must assume responsibility for finding or formulating an answer to the question about the meaning of human existence.[16] Thus "existentialism" may be understood, in a phenomenological sense, as the position that human life does not make sense due to a pre-established universal content,[17] but rather that individual human beings must make sense of their own lives by performing particular meaning-bestowing acts.[18] That is, one may contend that it is a religious form of nihilism to insist that, if God does not exist, then human existence is meaningless.[19] Nor does the elimination of God entail the destruction of morality.[20] To the contrary, according to Sartre, for example, if God is dead, then human beings alone become responsible for their words,

---

[15] The historical paradox of *The Stranger* is that it was written long after Nietzsche's *Thus Spoke Zarathustra* (1883–85), a prophetic work in many ways, especially with respect to atheistic existentialism.

[16] For Nietzsche, the assertion that "Gott ist tot" does not entail that God once existed and then died or was killed. It is not a historical-biographical claim about God but a meta-statement about the loss of belief or faith in God on the part of human beings. Cf. *Die fröhliche Wissenschaft*, bk. 3, aph. 1 ff.

[17] It is supposed to do so according to theistic essentialism. Jewish-Christian existentialism, for example, that of Kierkegaard, is another matter for another essay. Cf. especially Søren Kierkegaard, *Fear and Trembling* (1843), tr. Howard and Edna Hong (Princeton: Princeton University Press, 1983); *The Concept of Anxiety* (1844), tr. Reidar Thomte (Princeton: Princeton University Press, 1980); *The Sickness Unto Death* (1849), tr. Howard and Edna Hong (Princeton: Princeton University Press, 1983).

[18] From the perspective of phenomenological existentialism, human existents *constitute* the meanings of human existences, since existence is, in each and every case, the existence of an existent, so that being, conscience, and death, for example, are always and everywhere the being, the conscience, and the death of a concrete particular instance of *Dasein*. Cf. Martin Heidegger, *Sein und Zeit* (Tübingen: Max Niemeyer, 1977 [Fourteenth Edition]), pp. 41, 240, 278. Heidegger emphasizes the influence of Edmund Husserl's phenomenology, especially of his *Logische Untersuchungen* (Tübingen: Max Niemeyer, 1900/1901), on his work. Cf. *Sein und Zeit*, p. 38.

[19] Nietzsche's Zarathustra does not think, like Ivan Karamazov, that, "if God is dead, then all is permitted", but rather that, because God is dead, human beings must take responsibility, including moral responsibility, for human existence. Cf. *Also sprach Zarathustra: Ein Buch für Alle und Keinen*, ed. Giorgio Colli and Mazzino Montinari (Berlin: Walter de Gruyter, 1980), pp. 253, 340.

[20] As soon as one moves beyond the divine command theories of such thinkers as Augustine and Aquinas ('what is right, is right because God wills it, and what is wrong, is wrong because God wills it not': this view is ubiquitous in *Civitas Dei* and *Summa theologica*), it becomes seriously questionable whether the core of the human condition, namely, morality, rests on religion.

deeds, and lives.[21] Finally, as Heidegger, for example, argues, from the fact that human existence (*Dasein*) is temporally finite, it does not follow that life is rendered meaningless, but rather only that time (*Zeit*) emerges thematically as the hermeneutical horizon within which the resolute shaping of the "thrown project" (*geworfener Entwurf*) that is existence—authentic and truthful existence beyond God and "them" (*das Man*)—takes place, so that, properly understood, the awareness of finitude does not eliminate the need for meaning but rather enhances it.[22]

The question of Camus' connection to existentialism is genuinely vexed. Although he is commonly thought of as an existentialist *sui generis*, Camus is critical of Kierkegaard and other existentialists, arguing, for example, that the notion of a "leap of faith" underestimates the gravity, profundity, and ineluctability of the absurd.[23] Yet the virtue of *The Stranger*, properly understood, is not that it exhorts the readers to embrace Meursault's assertion of the absurdity of life, but rather that it challenges them to dig to a deeper level of reflection than that of which Meursault is capable. The readers also have good reason to be skeptical of the absurdist approach adopted by Meursault. For how can one make a difference in an indifferent world by

---

[21] Cf. Jean-Paul Sartre, *L'existentialisme est un humanisme* (presented in 1945 and published in 1946), ed. Arlette Elkaïm Sartre (Paris: Éditions Gallimard, 1996), pp. 26, 29, 31, 39: "... l'existence précède l'essence ...". Cf. also ibid., p. 30: "... l'homme n'est rien d'autre que ce qu'il se fait. Tel est le premier principe de l'existentialisme." Correctly or not, Sartre understands himself and Heidegger as atheistic existentialists, but Jaspers and Marcel as theistic (Catholic) existentialists. Cf. ibid., p. 26.

[22] This statement is an attempt, however awkward, to formulate the philosophical argument of *Sein und Zeit* in one sentence. On the *Sein* of *Dasein* as "geworfener Entwurf" ("thrown project") cf. *Sein und Zeit*, p. 285. The argument of Heidegger's *Letter on Humanism* (*Über den Humanismus*) (1945/1947) is another matter. Cf. my study "Phenomenology Is A Humanism: Husserl's Hermeneutical-Historical Struggle to Determine the Genuine Meaning of Human Existence in *The Crisis of the European Sciences and Transcendental Phenomenology*", *Analecta Husserliana*, vol. 115 (2013), forthcoming.

[23] Cf. the section on "Philosophical Suicide" in *Le Mythe de Sisyphe: Essai sur l'absurde*. The French text is found in the Pléiade edition of Camus' works, vol. 2: *Essais*, ed. Roger Quilliot and Louis Faucon (Paris: Bibliothèque de la Pléiade, 1965), pp. 119–135. A good English translation of the *Mythe* is: *The Myth of Sisyphus and Other Essays*, tr. Justin O'Brien (New York: Alfred Knopf, 1955).

responding with indifference?[24] And why should one assume that one must not make a difference?

The methodological approach that I take in this paper is *phenomenological* in that it provides an original description of the course and content of *The Stranger*, *hermeneutical* in that it focuses on the significant topic of the levels and moments of reflection of the protagonist, and *existentialist* in that it yields a tenable account of the philosophical relationship between the author Camus, who, I submit, appears to have eschewed existentialism as he understood it, and his protagonist Meursault, who, I suggest, seems to have embraced existentialism without having understood it.

Hermeneutics I: Is Meursault as unreflective as he seems?

The plot of the novel appears fairly evident:[25] Meursault's mother has died at an old people's home and he indifferently attends her wake and funeral in a somnambulant state of insensibility. Back home the next day, Meursault goes to the beach and bumps into Marie, a former coworker, with whom he begins what is, for his part, a non-committal relationship. The next week, Meursault helps Raymond, a neighbor who claims to be a warehouse guard but is said to be a pimp, by writing a letter to entice his allegedly unfaithful mistress, an Arab, into a situation in which Raymond will abuse her emotionally, physically, and sexually. A few days later, Raymond beats the woman, the police detain him, and Meursault testifies for him. A few days after that, Meursault's boss offers him a life-changing career opportunity, to which he reacts negatively, and Marie makes him a marriage proposal, to which he reacts ambivalently. The next weekend, when Meursault, Marie, and Raymond go to the beach to visit a couple of Raymond's friends, the abused woman's brother, the Arab, and another Arab follow them, and Meursault, after a series of three tense encounters between friends and foreigners, ends up killing the Arab by shooting him once and his inert body four more times. Arrested and interrogated, Meursault encounters an examining magistrate who urges him to acknowledge Christ's sacrifice and to beg God's forgiveness for his crime, as well as a legal system that is more

---

[24] Cf. again 2.5.26: "… je m'ouvrais pour la première fois à la tendre indifférence du monde."

[25] In this paragraph I provide neither references nor quotations since they are supplied elsewhere.

focused on his perceived insensitivity at his mother's funeral than on his alleged actions at his crime. During the investigation, which lasts eleven months, the deprivations of prison occasion Meursault to recollect the simple pleasures of his former life and to reflect on the loss of his freedom. At the trial, the prosecutor, seeking to establish a connection between his insensitive behavior at his mother's funeral and his callous actions on the fatal beach, argues that Meursault is guilty of premeditated murder because he buried his mother with a criminal heart, that is, that he is in effect guilty of matricide. His court-appointed lawyer mounts a hapless defense, Meursault makes an apparently ridiculous statement, namely, that he killed his victim "because of the sun", the jury swiftly returns a guilty verdict, and the judge imposes the sentence of death by public guillotining. Waiting in his cell for execution or pardon, with the fatal outcome looming much more likely, Meursault refuses to see the prison chaplain, concludes that life is not worth the trouble of having lived it, and, when the chaplain visits him against his will, shouts at him that nothing matters in his whole absurd life—after which he calms down and opens up to what he feels to be the gentle indifference of the world.

What does not appear comparably evident is the character of the protagonist, for Meursault's way of life is at once both simple and complex. He leads a life of immediate and impulsive "insensitivity"[26] in a world that he perceives to be one of "indifference",[27] and his mantra is "it does not matter", "it is not important", or "it does not mean anything".[28] By his own admission, he has "a taciturn and withdrawn character",[29] as well as "a nature such that [his] physical needs often get in the way of [his] feelings".[30] His tendency to let the natural elements get the better of the human emotions—though this is not entirely unambiguous[31]—becomes especially evident at the funeral of his

---

[26] Cf. 2.1.4, 2.4.2, 2.4.5 ("insensibilité").

[27] Cf. 1.6.4, 2.3.7, 2.3.17, 2.5.10, 2.5.26 ("indifférence").

[28] Meursault often says "cela ne signifiait rien" or something similar. Cf. 1.1.1–2, 1.1.13, 1.1.17, 1.2.2, 1.2.11, 1.4.3, 1.4.5, 1.5.3–4, 1.6.20, 2.3.3, 2.5.10, 2.5.23, 2.5.25–26.

[29] Meursault is "un caractère taciturne et renfermé". Cf. 1.1.4, 1.4.3, 1.5.4, 2.1.4, 2.1.8, 2.3.14, 2.3.16–17.

[30] Cf. 2.1.4: "Cependant, je lui ai expliqué que j'avais une nature telle que mes besoins physiques dérangeaient souvent mes sentiments."

[31] Cf. 2.1.5: "Il m'a demandé s'il pouvait dire que ce jour-là j'avais dominé mes sentiments naturels. Je lui ai dit: 'Non, parce que c'est faux.'"

mother and at his killing of the Arab.[32] The connection, rational or absurd, between these two expressions of his insensitivity has dire consequences for him.[33] With respect to traditional moral virtue, Meursault's insensitivity toward others and his hypersensitivity toward himself evoke the personal qualities of Dostoyevsky's unnamed existentialist par excellence, "the underground man".[34] With respect to traditional intellectual virtue, it is as if Camus designed Meursault as a negation of Socrates, for whom "the unexamined life is not worth living for a human being":[35] "... my purpose ... was to describe a man with no apparent awareness of his existence".[36] In any case, Meursault has, by his own admission, long given up both "[his] studies" and "the habit of examining [himself]".[37] In the words of Nietzsche, Meursault is not a human being (*Mensch*) striving to become a "superhuman being" (*Übermensch*) but a "last human being" (*der letzte Mensch*): one who eschews effort and examination of life and embraces the quotidian contentment and trivial satisfaction of work, love, and "happiness" understood as a feeling of complacency with whom or what one is.[38]

---

[32] Cf. 1.1.26: "Autour de moi, c'était toujours la même campagne lumineuse gorgée de soleil. L'éclat du ciel était insoutenable." Cf. also 1.6.25: "La brûlure du soleil gagnait mes joues et j'ai senti des gouttes de sueur s'amasser dans mes sourcils. C'était le même soleil que le jour où j'avais enterré maman et, comme alors, le front surtout me faisait mal et toutes ses veines battaient ensemble sous la peau."

[33] Cf. 2.1.4–5, 2.3.11, 2.3.14–17, 2.3.20, 2.4.2, 2.4.5, 2.4.7, 2.5.25.

[34] Cf. Fyodor Dostoyevsky, *Notes from Underground* (1864), tr. Richard Pevear and Larissa Volokhonsky (New York: Alfred Knopf, 1993), passim. Meursault also shares the "underground man's" skepticism of consciousness as a means to solve or even to address the problems of human existence. Cf. *Notes from Underground*, Part I, Section 2, where the notion that consciousness is a "sickness" emerges.

[35] Cf. Plato, *Apology of Socrates* 38a.

[36] Cf. Camus, *Essais*, p. 1426 ("Interview", *Les Nouvelles littéraires*, Nov. 15, 1945): "... mon propos ... était de décrire un homme sans conscience apparente." For an English translation of the remark cf. Camus, *Lyrical and Critical Essays*, ed. Philip Thody and tr. Ellen Kennedy (New York: Alfred Knopf, 1969), p. 348.

[37] Cf. 1.5.3: "Quand j'étais étudiant, j'avais beaucoup d'ambitions de ce genre. Mais quand j'ai dû abandonner mes études, j'ai très vite compris que tout cela était sans importance réelle." Cf. also 2.1.4: "J'ai répondu cependant que j'avais un peu perdu l'habitude de m'interroger et qu'il m'était difficile de le renseigner."

[38] Cf. 1.5.3, 1.6.25, 2.5.7, 2.5.26. Cf. also *Also sprach Zarathustra*, Prologue, ch. 5.

On the other hand, it is not as if Meursault exhibits no character development at all in the course of the novel. For after his crime he does not so much discover a new worldview as uncover the same one that he entertained before his crime, in that he displays a low degree of introspection[39] but not a high level of reflection.[40] It is in prison, for example, that he learns how to remember things.[41] Also, in the course of his incarceration, he attempts to be "reasonable",[42] but concludes that 'life is absurd',[43] and tries to make the best of it.[44] Thus Meursault is no Roquentin, who ultimately seeks to overcome the anxiety, despair, and forlornness of the nothingness of his own existence by freely choosing to determine being through writing about something other than himself.[45] The irony is that, although Meursault eschews the Delphic Oracle's moral and intellectual imperative ("Know thyself!"),[46] it is unlikely that any other spokesman for the unexamined life has inspired more people to examine their own lives.[47] Yet it is hard to say whether this was Camus' intent or Meursault's effect, or both, and to what extent, since the author seems to have created the character as someone who "does not take the

---

[39] Cf. 2.1.1–13, 2.3.2, 2.3.4, 2.4.1, 2.5.1, 2.5.3, 2.5.6, 2.5.10, 2.5.13–14.

[40] Cf. 2.2.17. Cf. also 1.2.5.

[41] Cf. 2.2.13: "J'ai fini par ne plus m'ennuyer du tout à partir de l'instant où j'ai appris à me souvenir."

[42] Cf. 2.5.3: "Mais ce n'était pas raisonnable." Cf. also 2.5.4: "Mais, naturellement, on ne peut pas être toujours raisonnable." Cf. finally 2.5.9: "Il fallait que je m'applique à réduire ce cri, à le raisonner."

[43] Cf. 2.5.25: "... pendant toute cette vie absurde que j'avais menée ...".

[44] Cf. 2.5.7: "Maman disait souvent qu'on n'est jamais tout à fait malheureux." Cf. also 2.5.26: "... j'ai senti que j'avais été heureux, et que je l'étais encore."

[45] Cf. Jean-Paul Sartre, *La Nausée* (Paris: Éditions Gallimard, 1938). A good English translation of the work is: *Nausea*, tr. Lloyd Alexander (New York: New Directions, 1959). For Camus' review of the novel cf. *Essais*, pp. 1419–1422. The review originally appeared in *Alger républicain* (October 20, 1938). An English translation of it is available in: Camus, *Lyrical and Critical Essays*, pp. 199–202.

[46] Cf. 1.2.5, 1.5.3, 2.1.4, 2.2.17.

[47] *The Stranger* may be the most widely read philosophical novel of the twentieth century. The original has sold more than six million copies, and it has been translated into more than forty languages.

initiative", who "does not respond to questions", and who "does not affirm anything", let alone articulate a philosophy, except perhaps at the very end.[48]

All this poses the question about the development of Meursault's character between the two parts of the novel. Without naming names,[49] one can say that it is generally accepted that there is a remarkable development in Meursault's character between Part One and Part Two of the narrative, and that this development consists in the fact that the Meursault of Part One is unreflective whereas the Meursault of Part Two is reflective. The evidence for this reading—to refrain from merely rounding up and crudely juxtaposing the usual suspects, namely, the "naturalistic" scenes surrounding the death of his mother in the country and his killing of the Arab on the beach versus the "societal" scenes at his interrogation, trial, and testament[50]—is supposed to consist in the fact Meursault in prison undergoes a metamorphosis (but not a "conversion", for that word would have inapplicable religious connotations) that enables him to see and feel people and things in Part Two that he had not been able to see and feel in Part One, that is, to see and feel them "the first time" or "for the first time".[51] In my analysis of the novel, I suggest that this understanding of Meursault's character is inaccurate because the evidence shows that he is an intelligent, perceptive, and reflective protagonist throughout, that is, from the beginning to the end of his narrative. I approach *The Stranger* within a hermeneutical horizon, rendering the description phenomenological by consistently focusing on the protagonist's levels and moments of conscious reflection.[52] I propose that, despite his noticeable

---

[48] Cf. Camus, *Théâtre, Récits, Nouvelles*, p. 1933 (a passage from an unsent letter to the literary critic "A. R."): "Le personnage principal du livre n'a jamais d'initiatives. Vous n'avez pas remarqué qu'il se borne toujours à *répondre aux questions*, celles de la vie ou celles des hommes. Ainsi il n'affirme jamais rien. Et je n'en ai donné qu'un cliché négatif. Rien ne pouvait vous faire préjuger de son attitude profonde, sinon justement le dernier chapitre."

[49] An exception to this rule would be the otherwise excellent translation and commentary: Brigitte Sahner, ed., *Albert Camus: L'Etranger* (Stuttgart: Philipp Reclam jun., 1984/2003), pp. 149–154.

[50] By "testament" I mean Meursault's "spiritual" legacy as bequeathed to the readers in his "last will and testament". Cf. 2.5.11–26.

[51] Cf. 1.5.9, 1.6.6, 2.1.1, 2.1.8, 2.2.17, 2.3.14–15, 2.3.17, 2.5.10, 2.5.26. Note, however, that not all occurrences of "la première fois" or "pour la première fois" are pregnant and not all occur in Part Two.

[52] In brief, I attempt to perform a phenomenological reduction on Meursault's perceptions and reflections in order to clarify the contents of his thoughts as such. This is a novel approach.

moral and intellectual evolution from Part One to Part Two of the novel, Meursault's defining character feature remains a deep philosophical flaw, namely, profound superficiality or an utter absence of genuine depth, in so far as he has an idiosyncratic world-view but not a rigorous philosophy.[53] The crucial point is that, contrary to Camus' suggestion, Meursault is in no case "a man with no apparent awareness of his existence", and that this holds for both parts of the novel, but that it is not tenable to assert without further ado that a coherent world-view, if not a rigorous philosophy, can be attributed to him.

An explication of the text: Meursault's reports on his levels and moments of reflection

As one who appears to have "pretty much lost the habit of analyzing [himself]",[54] as one who asserts that "life is not worth the trouble of having

---

Cf. Jean-Paul Sartre, "Explication de *L'Étranger*" (1943), in: *Situations I* (Paris: Éditions Gallimard, 1947), pp. 92–112; Roland Barthes, "*L'Étranger*, roman solaire", *Bulletin du Club du Meilleur Livre*, vol. 12 (1954), pp. 6–7; Germaine Brée, *Camus* (New Brunswick, N.J.: Rutgers University Press, 1961); René Girard, "Camus' Stranger Retried", *Proceedings of the Modern Language Association*, vol. 79 (1964), pp. 519–533; Conor Cruise O'Brien, *Albert Camus: Of Europe and Africa* (New York: Viking Press, 1970); Brian Fitch, "*L'Étranger*" *d'Albert Camus: un texte, ses lecteurs, leurs lecteurs* (Paris: Librairie Larousse, 1972); G. V. Banks, *Camus' "L'Étranger"* (London: Edward Arnold, 1976); Kenneth Dutton, *Camus' "L'Étranger": From Text to Criticism* (Sydney: Macquarie University Press, 1976); Adele King, *Notes on "L'Étranger"* (London: Longman/York Press, 1980); Brian Fitch, *The Narcissistic Text: A Reading of Camus' Fiction* (Toronto: University of Toronto Press, 1982); Patrick McCarthy, *Albert Camus: "The Stranger"* (Cambridge: Cambridge University Press, 1988/2004); English Showalter, *"The Stranger": Humanity and the Absurd* (Boston: Twayne Publishing, 1989); Harold Bloom, *Albert Camus' "The Stranger"* (Philadelphia: Chelsea House, 2001); Robert Solomon, *Dark Feelings, Grim Thoughts: Experience and Reflection in Camus and Sartre* (Oxford: Oxford University Press, 2006); David Carroll, *Albert Camus the Algerian: Colonialism, Terrorism, Justice* (New York: Columbia University Press, 2007); Edward Hughes, ed., *The Cambridge Companion to Camus* (Cambridge: Cambridge University Press, 2007), especially pp. 147–164 (Peter Dunwoodie, "From *Noces* to *L'Étranger*"); David Sherman, *Camus* (Oxford: Wiley-Blackwell, 2009).

[53] My interpretation was inspired by Roger Shattuck, *Forbidden Knowledge: From Prometheus to Pornography* (New York: Houghton, Mifflin, Harcourt, 1997), pp. 137–164 (on Camus' The Stranger).

[54] Cf. 2.1.4: "J'ai répondu cependant que j'avais un peu perdu l'habitude de m'interroger et qu'il m'était difficile de le renseigner."

lived it",[55] and as a remorseless, unregretful, condemned murderer expecting execution who seems to find the inner peace to accept "the gentle indifference of the world",[56] Meursault emerges for some readers as a kind of Camusian Sisyphus—a rebel with a cause, a courageous man who lives a meaningless life and dies a happy death. By means of the existentialist hero Meursault, according to this reading, Camus has bestowed philosophical respectability on the view that 'this whole life is absurd'.[57] Therefore, to understand the protagonist's take on life and death, I explicate Meursault's narrative in such a way as to elucidate his defining levels and moments of reflection, and I do so as he reports on them in the first-person. After all, the best way to accomplish the task of establishing what Meursault knows about himself and others is to take the narrator himself, who is neither an idiot nor a sage, as the prima facie (*caveat lector*) most reliable guide to his own feelings, thoughts, and actions. In any case, one should certainly not dismiss Meursault's story as categorically as the prosecutor does:[58]

What Meursault reports on his levels and moments of reflection before his crime:[59]

Meursault reports that, not knowing the day she died (1.1.1) or how old she was (1.1.25; cf. 1.3.1, 2.3.14), he experienced the death of his mother like a sleepwalker, not wanting to talk to anyone during the events surrounding her wake and funeral (1.1.4). He mentions that he turned down the caretaker's and the director's offers to let him see his mother one last time (1.1.9,

---

[55] Cf. 2.5.8: "Mais tout le monde sait que la vie ne vaut pas la peine d'être vécue."

[56] Cf. 2.5.26: "Comme si cette grande colère m'avait purgé du mal, vidé d'espoir, devant cette nuit chargée de signes et d'étoiles, je m'ouvrais pour la première fois à la tendre indifférence du monde."

[57] Cf. 2.5.25: "Du fond de mon avenir, pendant toute cette vie absurde que j'avais menée, un souffle obscur remontait vers moi à travers des années qui n'étaient pas encore venues et ce souffle égalisait sur son passage tout ce qu'on me proposait alors dans les années pas plus réelles que je vivais."

[58] Studies of the way in which Meursault tells his story include the excellent: Maurice-Georges Barrier, *L'Art du récit dans "L'Étranger"* (Paris: A. G. Nizet, 1962), and Brian Fitch, *Narrateur et narration dans "L'Étranger" d'Albert Camus: analyse d'un fait littéraire* (Paris: Minard, 1968). Cf. also Brian Fitch, ed., *Autour de "L'Étranger": Albert Camus I* (Paris: Revue des Lettres modernes, 1968).

[59] In this section the parts and paragraphs of the synopsis correspond to the parts and chapters of the novel. The first part contains six chapters and the second part contains five chapters.

1.1.20). He also remembers that he slept on and off through a good part of the wake (1.1.10, 1.1.14–15, 1.1.18, 1.1.19). Observant, he felt that his mother's friends were at the wake to judge him, and he wonders whether the dead woman lying there meant anything to them (1.1.15, 1.1.17). He noticed many of the smallest details of the funeral procession and its natural environment (1.1.24–27). Meursault describes how, although the whole experience enabled him to understand his mother (1.1.24), he could hardly wait to get back home, get some sleep, and return to his routine (1.1.27). At one point, a point that would later become fateful, Meursault thought about whether or not to smoke at his mother's wake, but then he thought that it did not matter, so he decided to do it (1.1.13).

Meursault reports that, having risen on the day after he returned home, he wondered, while he was shaving, what to do and decided to go swimming at the beach, where in the water he bumped into Marie, a former typist in his office whom he had once found attractive, a feeling that, he believed, was mutual (1.2.2). Meursault recalls that he and Marie engaged in physical contact, went to see a Fernandel film at which they exchanged physical displays of affection, and spent the night together (1.2.2–3). According to his account, Marie was already gone when he woke up in the morning, and Meursault spent most of that day on his balcony observing at length and analyzing in detail the comings and goings of the people of his quarter, even understanding why people said that a certain man was "distinguished" (1.2.6–11, especially 1.2.6). He explains that at his apartment he now lived in one room with only a few pieces of furniture, including a wardrobe whose mirror had gone yellow but still permitted a minimum of reflection given adequate light (1.2.5, 1.2.11). Meursault reflected that nothing had really changed now that his mother was buried and he would be going back to work (1.2.11).

Meursault reports that, returning from his first day back at work, he encountered his neighbor Salamano and his dog, who looked like but hated each other, which occasioned him to reflect on their troubled relationship at length and in detail (1.3.4; cf. 1.3.13, 1.4.3, 1.4.7–8, 1.5.7–1.5.9, 2.3.18, 2.5.25). He recalls that, running into his other neighbor, Raymond Sintès, who claimed to be a warehouse guard but was said to be a pimp (1.3.5), Meursault accepted his apparently spontaneous invitation (1.3.6), quickly and easily became his pal (1.3.7, 1.3.12), and eventually agreed to help him punish his allegedly unfaithful mistress by writing a letter that would entice her into a situation in which he could abuse her emotionally, physically, and sexually: Raymond wanted to go to bed with her and "juste au moment de finir"[60] spit in her face and throw her out (1.3.11). Meursault suggests that he wrote the letter for Raymond because he could not see any reason not to, but he also reports that he refused to write the letter until Raymond revealed, by divulging her name, that the woman was an Arab (1.3.12). Meursault remembers that, leaving Raymond's room, he had a strong physical reaction to the act that he had just performed (1.3.13). Yet Meursault also reports that he and Raymond seemed to have understood each other (1.3.7, 1.3.9, 1.3.11, 1.3.13).

Meursault reports that a few days later, when Meursault and Marie were at his apartment making love again and again, they heard the terrifying screams of the woman whom Raymond was beating, Marie asked Meursault to call the police but he refused because he did not like cops, and a neighbor summoned a policeman who intervened and summoned Raymond to the police station (1.4.4). Meursault recalls that he and Raymond later discussed the incident, that Raymond asked him to testify on his behalf, and that he, who told Raymond that it did not matter to him and that he did not know what to say, agreed to help him again by doing as he was asked (1.4.5). Meursault also suggests that he approved of how Raymond had treated the woman (1.4.6) and that he understood Salamano's loss of his dog in terms of the death of his own mother (1.4.7–8; cf. 2.5.25).

Meursault reports that, when his boss offered him the chance to change his life by going to Paris to help open a new branch office of his freight company, Meursault told him that it was all the same to him, that people never changed their lives, that one life was as good as another, and that he was not dissatisfied with his own, or, in other words, that he could not see any reason to change his life (1.5.3). Meursault recalls that, when that evening Marie asked him whether he wanted to marry her, he answered that he did not think that he loved her, but that he would marry her if she wanted—as he would marry any other woman who asked him under the same circumstances—yet that they would not be going to Paris, and this despite her expressed strong desire, upon hearing of his boss's proposition, to see the city (1.5.4). He also notes that, when they went for a walk through town, he noticed the beautiful women and he noticed that Marie noticed that he noticed them (1.5.5). He remembers that, eating alone at Céleste's

---

[60] I leave it to the readers to decide whether Ward's translation captures the full force of the original: "… 'right at the last minute' …".

restaurant, he was joined by a strange little woman whom he describes at length and in detail as acting like a robot (1.5.6). Finally, Meursault mentions that back home Salamano told him that, given that his dog had gone missing, his life had changed (1.5.7–9).

Meursault reports that at the beach on the fatal day, on the first of his three walks after lunch, with Raymond and Masson, he was not thinking about anything (1.6.11). He recalls that on the second of his three walks on the beach, with Raymond, he thought to tell him not to shoot unless the Arab drew his knife, and that he defused the situation by taking Raymond's gun away from him (1.6.18). Meursault recollects that it was then that he realized that Raymond had a choice in that one could either shoot or not shoot (1.6.19). Meursault also remembers that he realized that he did not have to take a third walk on the beach, this time alone, but he did, although in the event he was wrong to think that, whether he did or did not, it would amount to the same thing (1.6.20). Meursault further reports that after a long walk under the hot sun he was thinking about the cool spring behind the rock (1.6.17, 1.6.22, 1.6.25). He claims that he was surprised that the Arab was still there, this time alone, lying on his back with his hands behind his head, since, as far as he was concerned, the whole thing was over and he had gone back without even thinking about it (1.6.23). Yet he says that he watched the Arab carefully and gripped Raymond's revolver inside his jacket (1.6.24). Finally, Meursault reports that, aware that all he had to do was to turn around and that would be the end of it, he first waited, but then, knowing that he was making a stupid move, he moved forward, and, when the Arab drew his knife and held it up to him but was not close enough to cut him, he shot him once, and then, after he recognized that he had shattered the harmony of the day and his own happiness, he fired four more times at the motionless body lying on the beach (1.6.25; cf. 2.1.8–10, 2.4.2).

What Meursault reports on his levels and moments of reflection after his crime:

Meursault reports that, arrested and interrogated, at first he thought that his case was pretty simple, and that in his initial encounter with the examining magistrate the meeting seemed like a game to him (2.1.1–2). He recalls that, when his court-appointed defense attorney informed him that the prosecution had learned that he had shown "insensitivity" on the day of mother's funeral, and the attorney inquired into his feelings that day, he responded that it was hard for him to answer because "[he] had pretty much lost the habit of analyzing [himself]", that "[he] probably did love [his] mother" but that "did not mean anything" and "at one time or another all normal people have wished that their loved ones were dead", and that "[his] nature was such that [his] physical needs often got in the way of [his] feelings" (2.1.4). He says that he also could not state that he "had held back [his] natural feelings" the day of the funeral "because it's not true" (2.1.5). Yet Meursault reports that he also felt the urge to reassure his lawyer that he was "like everybody else, just like everybody else" (2.1.6). Meursault further explains that, in his second encounter with the examining magistrate, who sought to understand why he had fired four more times at a body lying on the ground, he, who opted to speak without his defense attorney present (2.1.7), could not say anything (2.1.8–9). Uncomprehending, the magistrate told Meursault that he believed in God and that he was convinced that no one is so guilty that God would not forgive them, but that for this to happen one would have to repent (2.1.10). On Meursault's account, the magistrate became passionate over the fact that he, Meursault, did not believe in God, for he, the magistrate, believed that all human beings believe in God, and that, if he doubted it, his life would become meaningless; he also shouted irrationally over the fact that Meursault did not believe that Christ had suffered for him (2.1.11). Finally, Meursault reports, the magistrate asked him whether he was "sorry" for what he had done, and he answered that he was more "annoyed" than "sorry" (2.1.12). In the course of the eleven months that the investigation of his case lasted, Meursault recollects, he came to feel like "one of the family" in his meetings with the judge and his lawyer, since the former gradually lost interest in his case, treated him more cordially, and usually addressed him as "Monsieur Antichrist" (2.1.13).

Meursault reports that, a few days after entering prison, he realized that this part of his life was going to be one of the things that he would never like talking about, but that, after a while, he no longer saw any point to his reluctance (2.2.1–2). He recalls that, from the day he received Marie's letter telling him that her first visit would be her last (since she was not his wife), he felt that he was at home in his cell and that his life was coming to a standstill (2.2.2). Meursault recollects that, when he was first imprisoned, the hardest thing was that his thoughts were still those of a free man, whereas afterwards his only thoughts were those of a prisoner, so that he remembered his mother's idea that after a while one could get used to anything (2.2.10). He admits that in the first months (of the eleven-month investigation: 2.1.13) he was tormented by his desire for a woman, and that he thought so much about the women whom he had known that his cell was filled with their faces and crowded by his desires, but that with time he understood that this loss of freedom was his punishment (2.2.11). Meursault reports that another punishment was the loss of cigarettes, which he also got used to (2.2.12; cf. 2.3.2). He recounts that, although the main problem in prison was killing time, he was not bored once he learned how to remember things (2.2.13). Meursault recollects that, after reading a newspaper story "a thousand times" about a family tragedy in Czechoslovakia in which a rich man who plays a joke on his mother was killed by her unwittingly (she then committed suicide), he thought that "one should never play games" (2.2.15). Finally, Meursault reports that he lost track of time (2.2.16), slept "sixteen to eighteen hours a day" (2.2.14), and, in the remaining time, which he spent reflecting on and talking to himself, he remembered what the nurse had said at his mother's funeral, namely, "there is no way out" (2.2.17; cf. 1.1.27).

Meursault reports that, having noticed a row of faces in court all looking at him, he realized that they were the jury (2.3.3). He recalls that at first he did not realize that all the people who were crowding into the courtroom had come to see him, that it required an effort on his part to understand that he was the focus of attention, that he noticed that everyone was acting as if they were all "a club where people are glad to find themselves among others from the same world"—and that is how he explained to himself "the strange impression" that he had of being "an odd man out, a kind of intruder" (2.3.4). Meursault recalls that he noticed that one reporter, who was much younger than the others and who had very bright eyes, was "examining [him] closely without betraying any definable emotion", so that he had "the odd impression of being watched by [himself]" (2.3.7; cf. 2.3.10, 2.3.13, 2.4.9, 2.4.11), and he thought that this was part of the reason why he did not understand everything that happened next (2.3.7). Meursault was also conscious of being watched by "the little robot woman" from Céleste's restaurant (2.3.10). He reports that he understood when the judge mentioned "some questions that might seem irrelevant to but might in fact be significant for [his] case", and that he was "irritated" by inquiries into why he had put his mother into a home (2.3.11). He recollects that the prosecutor asked Meursault whether he had gone back to the spring by himself armed and intending to kill the Arab, and that he said that he had not but it had just happened that way (2.3.12). Meursault says that after that things got confused and the court was adjourned, but that he did not have time to think before the court was reconvened (2.3.13). Meursault reports that he then realized "for the first time" that he was "guilty" when the director and the caretaker from the home testified that his mother had complained that he had put her in the home, that he had not wanted to see her, that he had been calm and not cried at her funeral, that he had not paid his last respects at her grave, that he had not known how old she was, and that he had smoked and slept and drunk coffee at her wake (2.3.14–15). Meursault adds that Céleste testified that his crime was a matter of "bad luck" and that his testimony was "the first time in [his] life that [he had] ever wanted to kiss another man" (2.3.16); that Salamano pleaded with the court "to understand" but that no one seemed to understand (2.3.18); and that Raymond testified that Meursault's presence at the beach was just "chance", but that the prosecutor, connecting Meursault's letter to Raymond's girlfriend and his killing of Raymond's enemy, described him as "a monster, a man without morals" (2.3.19). Finally, Meursault reports that, when the prosecutor accused him of "burying his mother with crime in his heart", he understood "that things were not going well for [him]" (2.3.20), and he realized that his life had changed (2.3.21).

Meursault reports that, in the continuation of his trial, he felt that "everything was happening without [his] participation", and that he should break in and say something, until he realized, on second thought, that "[he] did not have anything to say" (2.4.1). He recalls that he was bored with the prosecutor's speech, but also admits that, if he understood him correctly, he was saying that his crime was "premeditated", and that his way of viewing events had a certain consistency and plausibility (2.4.2). Meursault recollects that the prosecutor asserted that he was "intelligent", that he had killed "with full knowledge of his actions", that no one could say that "he acted without realizing what he was doing", and that his crime was "no thoughtless act … with mitigating circumstances" (2.4.3). Meursault concedes that, when he heard the prosecutor say that he had never expressed remorse for or shown emotion over his offense, he could not help but admit that he was right, indeed, that he "had never been able to truly feel remorse for anything"—yet that he could not say this "given the position [he] had been put in" (2.4.4). Meursault records no reaction of his own to the prosecutor's argument that he had "no soul" in him and "nothing human within his reach", that "the emptiness of his heart" was "an abyss threatening to swallow up society", that he was morally guilty of killing his mother, and that he must be executed (2.4.5). Meursault reports that in his own statement he said that he had never intended to kill the Arab, and that, when asked by the judge to state the motives for his act, he blurted out, realizing how ridiculous he sounded, that "it was because of the sun" (2.4.6). Meursault remembers that, in his summation, his defense attorney talked about him in the first person, as if "to reduce [him] to nothing" and "to substitute himself for [him]", only to emphasize what an honest man, tireless worker, and model son he was, but, "in a glaring omission", without saying anything about the funeral (2.4.7). In the end, Meursault remembers being assailed by the memories of a life that was not his anymore (2.4.8). Finally, Meursault reports that the jury quickly found him guilty of premeditated murder without extenuating circumstances and that the judge swiftly sentenced him to death by public guillotining (2.4.11).

Meursault reports that after the verdict and sentence all he cared about was escaping the machinery of justice and avoiding the inevitable (2.5.1–2). He recounts that he remembered a story that his mother used to tell him about how his father had gone to watch a murderer be executed and come back throwing up, that he understood that it was "natural", and that he resolved that, if he ever got out of prison, then he would go and watch every execution he could—only to realize that he was not "being reasonable" in imagining himself in the role of a spectator at an execution (2.5.3). But Meursault also recalls that he recognized that "one cannot always be reasonable", and that he made up new laws to reform the penal code so as the give the condemned man a chance (2.5.4)—only to realize that the whole point of the guillotine is to kill with great precision (2.5.5). Meursault recollects that his mother used to say that "one can always find something to be happy about", even if it is only one more day to live (2.5.7). Meursault remarks that he thought that "everybody knows that life is not worth the trouble of having lived it", that "it does not much matter whether one dies at thirty or at seventy, since in either case other men and women will naturally go on living—and for thousands of years", and that "nothing could be clearer", in other words, that "it is obvious that, since we are all going to die, when and how do not matter" (2.5.8). Meursault reports that, when the chaplain, whom he had refused to see for the fourth time (2.5.1, 2.5.10), came to see him, he told him that he did not believe in God, that he was not interested in discussing whether he was sure about it, that he was not talking this way out of despair, and that he lived with the thought that nothing remains after death (2.5.13–16). He also reports that, when he told the chaplain that he was guilty (though he added that he did not know what sin was), that he was paying for it, and that nothing more could be asked of him (2.5.18), the chaplain countered that he could be asked to see "a divine face" emerge from the darkness of the stones of the walls of his cell (2.5.20), which, Meursault says, he found impossible (2.5.21). Meursault explains that, when the chaplain refused to believe that Meursault "loved this earth as much as all that" and did not wish for another life in the way in which he himself did, he told him that he had had enough, that he had only a little time left, and that he did not want to waste it on God (2.5.22–23). He recalls that the chaplain put his hand on his shoulder and told him that, although he could not know it because his heart was blind, he was on his side and would pray for him

(2.5.24). Meursault reports that at this point he started yelling at the top of his lungs, grabbed the chaplain by the collar of his cassock, and poured out to him everything that was in his heart, namely, that none of the chaplain's certainties was worth anything, that he, Meursault, was sure about himself and about everything about himself, or that he "had been right", that he "was still right", and that he "was always right", that he had lived his life one way and could just as well have lived it another, that "nothing, nothing mattered" and that he "knew why" and so did the chaplain, and that in "the whole absurd life" everyone was "elected by the same fate" to be "privileged" by life and "condemned" to death (2.5.25). Finally, Meursault reports that, calmed down, washed clean, and ridden of hope, and thus prepared for his "departure from a world that now and forever meant nothing" to him, he felt as if he understood why his mother at the end of her life must have felt, as he did, "ready to live it all again", and opened himself to "the gentle indifference of the universe", so that he felt "happy"—wishing only for a large crowd of spectators at his execution to greet him with cries of hate (2.5.26).

This explication of the text suggests that the key to understanding Meursault's defining levels and moments of reflection, as reported in his own first-person narrative, is a matter of two basic aspects. On the one hand, a close reading of his narrative shows that it is necessary to posit a certain moral and intellectual development on the part of the protagonist in the transition from Part One to Part Two. On the other hand, it also shows that it is not tenable to suppose that the difference between Part One and Part Two of the novel is that in the former Meursault is unreflective whereas in the latter he is reflective. Nor does Meursault emerge, on a judicious weighing of the evidence, as "a man with no apparent awareness of his existence", and this holds for both Part One and Part Two.[61] For instance, even if one accepts the premise that it was indeed in prison that Meursault "learned how to remember",[62] he would first have to have collected all the things that he

---

[61] Symmetry seems to suggest that Part One and Part Two consist of five chapters each and that the sixth chapter of the former serve as a link between the parts and their respective plots. Cf. Meursault's "awakening" in 1.6.25: "J'ai compris que j'avais détruit l'équilibre du jour, le silence exceptionnel d'une plage où j'avais été heureux."

[62] Cf. again 2.2.13: "J'ai fini par ne plus m'ennuyer du tout à partir de l'instant où j'ai appris à me souvenir." It is not necessary, and it is impossible, to interpret this observation as a statement by Meursault that prior to his imprisonment he did not know how to remember, or that he remembered nothing before his incarceration—which would make nonsense of his

then recollected after he went to prison, and he would have to have done this before he went to prison. In fact, in his narrative Meursault clearly indicates both that he reflects and that he notices that others reflect in both Part One and Part Two. As he says, and not just once but rather often: "J'ai réfléchi ...."[63] The verb in question does, of course, occur more frequently in Part Two than in Part One.[64]

For examples, a close reading of his own narrative shows that in Part One Meursault deliberates, however briefly, about whether to smoke at his mother's wake, decides to do so, and does so (1.1.13). He decides, however impulsively, to go for a swim, and he and Marie come closer together, and not without thought (1.2.1–4). He hesitates to write the letter for Raymond to his mistress, yet on second thought he does it, not only because he is trying his best to please Raymond and he did not have any reason not to please him, but also because he learns that the woman is an Arab (1.3.11–12). He refuses to call the police when Marie asks him to as Raymond is beating his mistress, because he does not like cops (1.4.4); he also agrees to testify for Raymond even though he has no reason to do it and does not know what to say (1.4.5); but he refuses to accompany Raymond to a house of prostitution because he does not like that sort of thing (1.4.6). He refuses to consider his boss's life-changing career choice because he thinks that people never change their lives and he is not dissatisfied with his own (1.5.3), and he reacts ambivalently to Marie's marriage proposal (1.5.4), but later he really thinks that he is going to get married (1.6.6). Finally, he voluntarily goes to the beach on three different occasions and on the third he deliberately shoots the Arab five times without adequate provocation, all the while thinking about what he is doing, including his crucial, stupid one step forward under the blazing gaze of the sun (1.6.11–25, especially 1.6.25). In fact, Meursault tells the reader that he deliberates, decides, and acts all the time, and that he does what he does because of this or that cause, circumstance, or condition.

---

narrative. It makes much more sense to understand him to say that it was in prison that he began to reconstruct his past in memory. Cf. ibid.: "Ainsi, plus je réfléchissais et plus de choses méconnues et oubliées je sortais de ma mémoire."

[63] Cf., for example, what Meursault reports about his wish to smoke at his mother's wake (1.1.13): "J'ai eu alors envie de fumer. Mais j'ai hésité parce que je ne savais pas si je pouvais le faire devant maman. J'ai réfléchi, cela n'avait aucune importance."

[64] Cf. 1.1.20, 1.3.11, 1.5.3, 2.1.5, 2.1.9, 2.1.12, 2.2.10, 2.2.13, 2.3.8, 2.3.13, 2.4.2–3, 2.4.11, 2.5.4, 2.5.6, and 2.5.10, for occurrences of the verb "réfléchir".

For examples, a close reading of his own narrative also shows that in Part Two Meursault lets himself be defined in his encounters with the examining magistrate and his defense attorney as "a taciturn and withdrawn person" (2.1.8) who keeps quiet because he does not have much to say (2.1.8), and who, out of laziness (2.1.6), weariness (2.1.8), and annoyance (2.1.12), also has little or nothing to say about his own case (2.1.9), which he has a hard time taking seriously (2.1.1–2). In prison, he reflects (2.2.17) on his own desires, needs, and wants (2.2.1, 2.2.10–14), but not on his act, its motives, and its consequences, for, other than to tell the other prisoners, most of whom are Arabs, what he is in prison for, namely, having killed an Arab (2.2.2), he does not consider his victim. At his trial, advised by his lawyer not to speak unless spoken to and not to volunteer anything (2.3.5), he is again "taciturn and withdrawn" (2.3.17), to the point of not contradicting the prosecutor (2.3.12), even when he realizes that he is guilty (2.3.15) and that things are not going well for him (2.3.20). During the continuation of his trial, when he feels that everything is happening without his participation (2.4.1, 2.4.7), and that he should say something, he realizes, on second thought, that he does not have anything to say (2.4.1), except that he never intended to kill the Arab and that he did it "because of the sun" (2.4.6)—without articulating any of the particular circumstances of his actions (cf. 1.6.17–18, 1.6.22, 1.6.25, 2.1.8, 2.3.12), his statement sounds ridiculous to the court. Condemned in his cell, he thinks, too late, that, "if something is going to happen to [him], then [he] wants to be there" (2.5.7), and for the first time he acts like it, so that he finds within himself the feelings to contradict the chaplain's religious world-view and to accept 'the absurdity of life' and "the gentle indifference of the world" (2.5.25–26).

Therefore the significant difference between Part One and Part Two of *The Stranger* is not the presence of reflection on the part of Meursault in the former and its absence in the latter. It is rather, formally speaking, the higher level and the greater number of moments of reflection on the part of Meursault in Part Two as compared to and contrasted with Part One. But it is also, materially speaking, the presence in Part One of a recognition of guilt on his part for his treatment of his mother and the presence in Part Two of an admission of guilt on his part for his treatment of the Arab. The evidence that he both senses and reports these respective kinds of guilt is convincing beyond a reasonable doubt.[65] At the same time, Meursault may not be a

---

[65] Cf. 1.1.2, 1.1.5, 1.1.15, 1.2.1–2, 1.3.11, 1.4.5–6, 2.1.10–11, 2.3.3, 2.3.15, 2.4.1, 2.4.4–5, 2.4.10–11, 2.5.8, 2.5.15, 2.5.18, 2.5.25.

complete idiot, but he is also not a wise philosopher. His belated attempts at reflection do not make him a keen observer of his own condition, and his self-reflection does not translate into self-criticism. The world-view that he articulates is barely consistent and hardly coherent. Above all, it is untenable in the face of cogent evidence to the contrary to portray Meursault as a man deprived of choice and driven by necessity, or as a man bereft of reflection and without any self-awareness. This holds for both Part One and Part Two of the novel. From a Sartrean standpoint, Meursault is a case study in "bad faith", since he repeatedly asserts facticity and denies transcendence.[66] According to Meursault's account, for example, the thoughts that he records himself as having thought during his crime are not afterthoughts that occur to him in prison or at trial, but the very thoughts that he was thinking "in real time" as he was acting on the beach.[67] Thus the prosecutor also argues that the defendant is "an intelligent man"[68] who, in committing his crime, acted "in a reflective manner"[69] and did not perform "an unreflective act",[70] and even Meursault finds this argumentation "plausible".[71]

Among the things that Meursault registers and reports is the "strangeness" of himself and of others. In fact, the strangeness of the stranger is a leitmotif of *The Stranger*. For example, at his mother's wake Meursault realizes that some of the old people are making "weird" sounds.[72] When Salamano loses his dog, Meursault understands from "the peculiar little noise"[73] coming from next door that the old man is crying. Dining at Céleste's restaurant, Meursault thinks that "the little robotic woman" who seats herself at his table

---

[66] Cf. Jean-Paul Sartre, *L'Être et le Néant: Essai d'ontologie phénoménologique* (Paris: Éditions Gallimard, 1943), Part One, Chapter 2: "Bad Faith" (*mauvaise foi*).

[67] Cf. again 1.6.10–25.

[68] Cf. 2.4.3: "'Cet homme, Messieurs, cet homme est intelligent. Vous l'avez entendu, n'est-ce pas? Il sait répondre. Il connaît la valeur des mots. Et l'on ne peut pas dire qu'il a agi sans se rendre compte de ce qu'il faisait.'"

[69] Cf. 2.4.2: "Et 'pour être sûr que la besogne était bien faite', j'avais tiré encore quatre balles, posément, à coup sûr, d'une façon réfléchie en quelque sorte."

[70] Cf. 2.4.3: "Car il ne s'agit pas d'un assassinat ordinaire, d'un acte irréfléchi que vous pourriez estimer atténué par les circonstances."

[71] Cf. 2.4.2: "Ce qu'il disait était plausible."

[72] Cf. 1.1.17: "... un bruit singulier ... ces clappements bizarres ...".

[73] Cf. 1.4.8: "... au bizarre petit bruit qui a traversé la cloison ...".

is "strange".[74] Before his crime, Marie tells Meursault that he is "peculiar".[75] After his crime, Meursault thinks that his lawyer is wearing "an odd-looking tie"[76] and looking at him "in a peculiar fashion".[77] At his trial, Meursault has "the strange impression" of being "a little like an intruder"[78] and "the odd impression of being watched by [himself]".[79] Adducing his peculiar behavior at his mother's funeral, the prosecutor portrays Meursault as "a stranger"[80] to society. This behavior seems to Meursault to be "foreign to [his] case".[81] But Meursault is a stranger to the law.[82] Thus the judge tells Meursault "in bizarre language"[83] that he will be guillotined. Now Meursault does not like questions, especially those which begin with "why".[84] Yet Camus' challenge to readers is to understand what Meursault cannot, namely, why he, "the stranger", killed the Arab.[85] For Meursault's intense perceptions and lengthy reflections do not reveal an accurate or adequate answer to this question.

Hermeneutics II: How do Meursault's reflections reflect on him?

A critical reading of *The Stranger* must test Meursault's acts and attitudes against the evidence of his own narrative. Meursault wants to tell his lawyer and the examining magistrate, of course, that he is "like everybody else, just like everybody else".[86] If this basic self-perception involves self-deception,

---

[74] Cf. 1.5.6: "… une bizarre petite femme …. J'ai pensé qu'elle était bizarre …."

[75] Cf. 1.5.4: "… bizarre …".

[76] Cf. 2.1.3: "… une cravate bizarre à grosses raies noires et blanches …".

[77] Cf. 2.1.5: "… d'une façon bizarre …".

[78] Cf. 2.3.4: "… la bizarre impression que j'avais d'être … un peu comme un intrus …".

[79] Cf. 2.3.7: "… l'impression bizarre d'être regardé par moi-même …".

[80] Cf. 2.3.15: "… un étranger …".

[81] Cf. 2.3.11: "… questions étrangères à mon affaire …".

[82] Cf. 2.1.1.

[83] Cf. 2.4.11: "… dans une forme bizarre …".

[84] Cf. 1.1.9, 1.2.4, 2.1.9–10, 2.3.11–12, 2.3.18.

[85] Cf. 1.6.22, 2.1.8, 2.4.6.

[86] Cf. 2.1.6: "J'avais le désir de lui affirmer que j'étais comme tout le monde, absolument comme tout le monde." Cf. Meursault's subsequent response to the examining magistrate (2.1.9): "… il m'a demandé si j'aimais maman. J'ai dit: 'Oui, comme tout le monde' …."

however, then so does virtually everything else that Meursault thinks and says about himself in regard to others. In their reflections on his reflections, therefore, the readers cannot unreflectively adopt Meursault's level of reflection as their own. Nor is it begging the question to hold Meursault logically responsible for his peculiar manner of reasoning, since he indicates that he regards himself as torn between what he describes as rationality and absurdity.[87]

A case in point is the one in which Meursault insists that, although "one cannot always be reasonable",[88] he himself "had been right, was still right, and was always right".[89] Yet before his crime he also insists on living a relatively unreflective life,[90] and he confirms this conviction in the conversation with his boss over a possible change of location, position, and life.[91] In addition, after his arrest he tells his lawyer "that [he] had pretty much lost the habit of questioning [himself]", and that therefore it was hard for him to tell him what he wanted to know.[92] As a result, too, he does not understand why the examining magistrate is interested in understanding him or his deed, he is less interested in understanding himself or his own deed than the magistrate is, and he is not very interested in understanding himself or his deed at all.[93] Once Meursault, in prison, engages in what is, at least by

---

[87] Cf. 2.1.9, 2.5.3–4, 2.5.6, 2.5.8–9, 2.5.25. Cf. especially 2.5.3: "Mais ce n'était pas raisonnable." Cf. also 2.5.4: "Mais, naturellement, on ne peut pas être toujours raisonnable." Cf. also 2.5.6: "Il y avait aussi deux choses à quoi je réfléchissais tout le temps: l'aube et mon pourvoi. Je me raisonnais cependant et j'essayais de n'y plus penser. ... Je finissais par me dire que le plus raisonnable était de ne pas me contraindre." Cf. also 2.5.8: "Donc (et le difficile c'était de ne pas perdre de vue tout ce que ce 'donc' représentait de raisonnements), donc ...." Cf. finally 2.5.9: "Il fallait que je m'applique à réduire ce cri, à le raisonner."

[88] Cf. again 2.5.3–4, 2.5.6, 2.5.8–9.

[89] Cf. 2.5.25: "J'avais eu raison, j'avais encore raison, j'avais toujours raison."

[90] Cf. 1.2.5 (especially the metaphor of the mirror that became opaque long ago).

[91] Cf. 1.5.3: "Il m'a demandé alors si je n'étais pas intéressé par un changement de vie. J'ai répondu qu'on ne changeait jamais de vie, qu'en tout cas toutes se valaient et que la mienne ici ne me déplaisait pas du tout. ... je ne voyais pas de raison pour changer ma vie. En y réfléchissant bien, je n'étais pas malheureux. Quand j'étais étudiant, j'avais beaucoup d'ambitions de ce genre. Mais quand j'ai dû abandonner mes études, j'ai très vite compris que tout cela était sans importance réelle."

[92] Cf. 2.1.4: "J'ai répondu cependant que j'avais un peu perdu l'habitude de m'interroger et qu'il m'était difficile de le renseigner."

[93] Cf. 2.1.1–2, 2.1.7–13, especially 2.1.9, where the examining magistrate asks Meursault repeatedly (the first time and four subsequent times) why (*pourquoi*) he first fired one shot,

his own personal standard, reflection in depth, it is too little and too late to make a decisive difference in his critical situation.[94] Hence the prosecutor is wrong in characterizing the defendant as 'a moral monster lacking a soul and an abyss empty of anything human',[95] but he is right in describing his crime as a reflective act,[96] arguably even a premeditated act.[97] After all, Meursault is reflective enough to know the difference between right and wrong, but not resolute enough to conform his actions to right, and so he does wrong.

The evidence of Meursault's narrative confirms this reading beyond a reasonable doubt. For example, Meursault admits that he shot the Arab repeatedly without sufficient provocation, and he does this by failing repeatedly to provide an adequate explanation for why he did what he did.[98] On his third trip to the beach, Meursault did something similar to what he had warned Raymond not to do on their second trip to the beach.[99] In any event, in the world according to Meursault, a European may shoot an Arab who draws a knife, even if the Arab has not cut the European.[100] Meursault

---

then paused, and finally fired four more shots at the Arab, only to encounter Meursault's bored silence in response.

[94] Cf. 2.2.17. The metaphor of the tin plate in prison that enables a little bit of reflection reiterates the symbol of the wardrobe mirror at home that disenabled reflection by turning yellow. Cf. 1.2.5.

[95] Cf. 2.3.19: "Il s'agissait d'un drame crapuleux de la plus basse espèce, aggravé du fait qu'on avait affaire à un monstre moral." Cf. also 2.4.2–5.

[96] Cf. 2.4.2: "Et 'pour être sûr que la besogne était bien faite', j'avais tiré encore quatre balles, posément, à coup sûr, d'une façon réfléchie en quelque sorte." Cf. also 2.4.3: "Car il ne s'agit pas d'un assassinat ordinaire, d'un acte irréfléchi que vous pourriez estimer atténué par les circonstances."

[97] Cf. 2.4.2: "Le fond de sa pensée, si j'ai bien compris, c'est que j'avais prémédité mon crime." Cf. also 2.4.10.

[98] Cf. 1.6.25 (Meursault gives his original, inadequate account), 2.1.8–10 (Meursault cannot explain the motive or rationale for his deed to the examining magistrate), 2.3.12 (Meursault cannot explain to the prosecutor at trial why he went back to the beach alone and armed), 2.4.2–5 (Meursault cannot argue with the prosecutor's summation), 2.4.6 (Meursault cannot explain to the court in his own words why he did what he did).

[99] Cf. 1.6.18: "Puis Raymond a dit: 'Alors, je vais l'insulter et quand il répondra, je le descendrai.' J'ai répondu: 'C'est ça. Mais s'il ne sort pas son couteau, tu ne peux pas tirer.'" Meursault suggests that Raymond *may* shoot the Arab if he draws his knife, but not that Raymond *must* shoot the Arab if he draws his knife.

[100] Cf. 1.6.18: "'Non, ai-je dit à Raymond. Prends-le d'homme à homme et donne-moi ton revolver. Si l'autre intervient, ou s'il tire son couteau, je le descendrai.'" Implying that the

also recognized, again on their second trip to the beach, that Raymond had a choice to shoot or not to shoot.[101] And Meursault realized that he did not have to return to the beach a third time, alone, for his final and fatal trip.[102] In fact, Meursault says that, even after having sighted and been sighted by the Arab on the third trip, it occurred to him that all he had to do was to turn and go and that would have been the end of it.[103] Thus he acted knowingly and willingly. For Meursault says that he knew, "in real time", so to speak, that it was "stupid" to advance on the Arab, who, lying on his back, drew his knife, evidently in self-defense, but was not close enough to stab him, only to be shot by him.[104] Finally, the numerous temporal markers in Meursault's account indicate that the thoughts that he recounts throughout are not the mere afterthoughts that he had in prison but the thoughts that he was thinking *while* he was acting on the beach.[105]

Meursault finds himself compelled to admit that the case against him makes sense.[106] Thus his lack of comprehension for the prosecutor's argument that his act was "premeditated"[107] is not evidence of lack of consciousness of guilt on his part.[108] Rather, it shows that, even after he has realized that he is

---

other Arab has a knife too (for which he has no visible evidence—cf. 1.6.13–14—though he may hold the prejudice that "they all carry knives"), Meursault anticipates shooting the Arab—an Arab, any Arab—merely for drawing his knife on him or Raymond. Cf. 1.6.25.

[101] Cf. 1.6.19: "J'ai pensé à ce moment qu'on pouvait tirer ou ne pas tirer."

[102] Cf. 1.6.20: "Rester ici ou partir, cela revenait au même. Au bout d'un moment, je suis retourné vers la plage et je me suis mis à marcher."

[103] Cf. 1.6.25: "J'ai pensé que je n'avais qu'un demi-tour à faire et ce serait fini." Cf. 1.6.23–24.

[104] Cf. 1.6.25: "À cause de cette brûlure que je ne pouvais plus supporter, j'ai fait un mouvement en avant. Je savais que c'était stupide, que je ne me débarrasserais pas du soleil en me déplaçant d'un pas. Mais j'ai fait un pas, un seul pas en avant."

[105] This observation is neutral with respect to an answer to the question as to whether there is an omniscient narrator in the novel.

[106] Cf. 2.4.2: "J'ai trouvé que sa façon de voir les événements ne manquait pas de clarté. Ce qu'il disait était plausible."

[107] Cf. again 2.4.2, 2.4.10.

[108] Given that the defendant is a *pied-noir* (an ethnically French "blackfoot" or settler) and the victim an Arab, as well as that Meursault is the only eyewitness against himself, one is tempted to regard the charge of premeditated murder as implausible. On the other hand, Meursault would have been tried under the *Code napoléonien*, that is, he would not have been presumed innocent until proven guilty—to the contrary. According to the principles of

guilty,[109] he remains remorseless.[110]   With his shaky grasp of moral motivation,[111] Meursault testifies that he killed the Arab "because of the sun",[112] leaving the *explanans* as much in need of an explanation as the *explanandum*.   Yet this "explanation" is not totally absurd but partially rational, at least in the world according to Meursault. On his third trip to the beach, namely, Meursault sought refuge from the fierce heat of the sun in the cool spring behind the rock,[113] and the Arab was blocking the way to it.[114] The source symbol even becomes a narrative leitmotif.[115]   Thus, given that Meursault admits to his defense attorney that "[his] nature was such that [his] physical needs often got in the way of [his] feelings",[116] one can at least begin to make some sense of his "senseless" act of killing the Arab. Yet the physical "explanation" could not constitute a moral or legal *justification*. In

---

contemporary American jurisprudence, Meursault would most likely have been charged with and probably found guilty of a form of second degree murder, that is, a murder involving a display of depraved indifference toward the preservation of the life of his victim.

[109] Cf. 2.3.15: "J'ai senti alors quelque chose qui soulevait toute la salle et, pour la première fois, j'ai compris que j'étais coupable."

[110] Cf. 2.1.12. Cf. also 2.4.4: "Sans doute, je ne pouvais pas m'empêcher de reconnaître qu'il avait raison. Je ne regrettais pas beaucoup mon acte." Cf. finally 2.4.8.

[111] The testimony about "chance" (cf. 1.3.12, 2.3.12, 2.3.19, 2.4.6: "un hasard") and "bad luck" (cf. 2.3.17: "un malheur") proves unhelpful both legally and ethically. One also cannot but notice how Meursault's narrative repeatedly posits chance instead of projecting choice. Cf. especially 1.3.12: "J'ai fait la lettre. Je l'ai écrite un peu au hasard, mais je me suis appliqué à contenter Raymond parce que je n'avais pas de raison de ne pas le contenter." Here Meursault already suggests that his motivation is overdetermined, that is, that there is more moving him to perform his action than mere chance alone.

[112] Cf. 2.4.6: "J'ai dit rapidement, en mêlant un peu les mots et en me rendant compte de mon ridicule, que c'était à cause du soleil."

[113] Cf. 1.6.22: "Je voyais de loin la petite masse sombre du rocher entourée d'un halo aveuglant par la lumière et la poussière de mer. Je pensais à la source fraîche derrière le rocher. J'avais envie de retrouver le murmure de son eau, envie de fuir le soleil, l'effort et les pleurs de femme, envie enfin de retrouver l'ombre et son repos. Mais quand j'ai été plus près, j'ai vu que le type de Raymond était revenu."

[114] Cf. 1.6.23: "Il était seul. Il reposait sur le dos, les mains sous la nuque, le front dans les ombres du rocher, tout le corps au soleil. Son bleu de chauffe fumait dans la chaleur. J'ai été un peu surpris. Pour moi, c'était une histoire finie et j'étais venu là sans y penser."

[115] Cf. 1.6.17–18, 1.6.25, 2.1.8, 2.3.12. The full meaning of the symbol would be the proper topic of another study: "The Source in *The Stranger*".

[116] Cf. again 2.1.4: "Cependant, je lui ai expliqué que j'avais une nature telle que mes besoins physiques dérangeaient souvent mes sentiments."

fact, the sun plays an oppressive role against Meursault in the two crucial death scenes of the novel, that is, at the funeral of his mother in the country and in the encounter with the Arab on the beach.[117] In the second scene, the sun does not enlighten but rather blinds him, leading him not to do good but driving him to do evil. Having failed to propose an alternative narrative even remotely acceptable to that of the prosecution, Meursault insists that he has been condemned, by "men who change their underwear",[118] for "not having wept at his mother's funeral".[119]

No one, of course, especially not his over-challenged, under-involved defense attorney, can read Meursault "like an open book".[120] The readers must, however, avoid the reflective fallacy,[121] namely, the error of adopting Meursault's underdeveloped level of reflection as their own instead of adapting a thoughtful approach of their own to his acts and attitudes. It is not a valid objection to this procedure to say that Meursault might feel oppressed by it, for against his own best self-interest he reacts apathetically and even allergically to any and all attempts by others to understand him.[122] Yet, if Meursault himself, and he alone, is allowed to determine the only level of reflection that the readers may apply in examining his life and legacy, then it is incomprehensible why anyone would undertake to understand him or his narrative in the first place. The hermeneutical point is that Camus' "stranger" is "like everybody else, just like everybody else", not in the sense in which he thinks, but in the sense that he is the *author* of his narrative yet not the *authority* on its meaning. It is not only possible but also necessary to

---

[117] Cf. 1.1.24–27, 1.6.11–25.

[118] Cf. 2.5.2: "Le fait que la sentence avait été lue à vingt heures plutôt qu'à dix-sept, le fait qu'elle aurait pu être tout autre, qu'elle avait été prise par des hommes qui changent de linge, qu'elle avait été portée au crédit d'une notion aussi imprécise que le peuple français (ou allemand, ou chinois), il me semblait bien que tout cela enlevait beaucoup de sérieux à une telle décision."

[119] Cf. 2.5.25: "Qu'importait si, accusé de meurtre, il était exécuté pour n'avoir pas pleuré à l'enterrement de sa mère?" Cf. also 2.1.4, 2.3.11, 2.3.15, 2.3.20, 2.4.5.

[120] Cf. 2.4.7: "'Moi aussi, a-t-il dit, je me suis penché sur cette âme, mais, contrairement à l'éminent représentant du ministère public, j'ai trouvé quelque chose et je puis dire que j'y ai lu a livre ouvert.'"

[121] The reflective fallacy may be regarded as a variation on the mimetic fallacy.

[122] Cf. my study "'Mais personne ne paraissait comprendre' ('But no one seemed to understand'): Atheism, Nihilism, and Hermeneutics in Albert Camus' L'Étranger/The Stranger", especially pp. 135–144.

understand Meursault better than he understood himself.[123] The same holds for understanding the world according to Meursault. He may be the maker of his world, but he is not, and certainly not alone, the decider of the meaning of that world and its contents. In the end, the thematic problem is not that Meursault is utterly lacking in empathy, but rather that he, who displays very little of it, and does so in odd ways that are hidden or hard for others to perceive,[124] allows himself to become crucially dependent on the sympathy of others, who then control his fate and decide his destiny. This is what is not rational but absurd about the plot of *The Stranger*, and it is a direct function of the character of Meursault, who, feeling excluded from participation in his trial,[125] and reduced to nothingness in his lawyer's summation,[126] is left to muse: "If something is going to happen to me, I want to be there."[127] Yet, because Meursault could not control his actions in Part One, he cannot control "his" narrative in Part Two.

Conclusion: Meursault, Camus, existentialism—and beyond

The aim of this investigation, which seeks to adhere rigorously to the evidence of the case, is neither to commend nor to condemn Meursault, but rather to comprehend him. Its modest but sober proposal is that it makes sense to understand Camus' novel as a *reductio ad absurdum* argument against Meursault's narrative, according to which 'life is absurd'.[128] In

---

[123] Cf. Hans-Georg Gadamer, *Wahrheit und Methode: Grundzüge einer philosophischen Hermeneutik* (Tübingen: Mohr {Siebeck], 1960), pp. 180–181, 280–281. The only way to understand Meursault is by means of "a fusion of horizons" (*Horizontverschmelzung*). Cf. ibid., pp. 284–290.

[124] Cf. 1.3.4, 1.3.13, 1.4.3, 1.4.7–8, 1.5.7–9, 2.3.18, 2.5.25.

[125] Cf. 2.4.1: "En quelque sorte, on avait l'air de traiter cette affaire en dehors de moi. Tout se déroulait sans mon intervention. Mon sort se réglait sans qu'on prenne mon avis."

[126] Cf. 2.4.7: "Moi, j'ai pensé que c'était m'écarter encore de l'affaire, me réduire à zéro et, en un certain sens, se substituer à moi."

[127] Cf. 2.5.7: "Quand il m'arrive quelque chose, je préfère être là."

[128] One can also read the work as if Camus were neutrally regarding Meursault from the perspective of a non-participant observer. The character who understands Meursault best may be the young journalist at his trial from whom he gets "the odd impression of being watched by [himself]" (2.3.7, 2.3.10, 2.3.13–14, 2.4.11). The press needed a sensational story to relieve the summer boredom of the reading public in Paris (2.3.4, 2.3.7, 2.3.10, 2.3.13, 2.4.11), but this particular journalist distinguishes himself as somehow on Meursault's side. Cf. Olivier Todd, *Albert Camus: une vie* (Paris: Éditions Gallimard, 1996), pp. 187–188. The

general, it is clear that, because Camus argues from the absurd, whereas Meursault argues to the absurd,[129] the author does not use the character as a spokesman for his own philosophy.[130] In particular, Meursault resolves to attend "all the executions" if his appeal is granted,[131] whereas Camus opposes the death penalty, at least as a firm rule with some initial hesitation.[132] This alone is a major difference between two men who, by their mothers' accounts, have in common fathers who attended executions that made them sick.[133] Hence the author suggests, and not at all subtly, that the readers recognize the protagonist's plan not as reasonable but as absurd.

Thus the author exhorts the readers to overcome Meursault's initially confined and ever narrowing horizon.[134] For Meursault shouts that 'he is always right'.[135] Yet he is wrong that "people never change their lives" and

---

character of the young journalist is one of those by means of which the author writes himself into the novel. Cf. Camus, *Théâtre, Récits, Nouvelles*, p. 1934: "Trois personnages sont entrés dans la composition de *l'Étranger*: deux hommes (dont moi) et une femme."

[129] Cf. Camus, Interviews, *Les Nouvelles littéraires*, Nov. 15, 1945, and May 10, 1951.

[130] Cf. Camus, *Essais*, p. 448: "Un personnage n'est jamais le romancier qui l'a créé. Il y a des chances, cependant, pour que le romancier soit tous ses personnages à la fois."

[131] Cf. 2.5.3: "Si jamais je sortais de cette prison, j'irais voir toutes les exécutions capitales."

[132] Cf. Camus, *Réflexions sur la guillotine/Reflections on the Guillotine* (1957), in: *Essais*, pp. 1019–1064. In his *Notebooks*, Camus writes "that it is impossible to say [*dire*] whether a person is absolutely guilty [*absolument coupable*] and consequently impossible to pronounce [*prononcer*] total punishment [*châtiment total*]". Cf. Camus, *Carnets II: janvier 1942–mars 1951* (Paris: Éditions Gallimard, 1965), p. 200 (entry dated June 1947). Camus' initial doubts about the legitimacy of capital punishment hardened into resolute opposition in the wake of the inadequate purge trials in France after the Second World War. Cf. *Camus at "Combat": Writing 1944–1947*, ed. Jacqueline Lévi-Valensi with a Foreword by David Carroll (Princeton: Princeton University Press: 2006), pp. xi–xix. The original French edition appeared without the English foreword (Paris: Éditions Gallimard, 2002). Cf. also Camus, *Essais*, pp. 253–327.

[133] Cf. 2.5.3: "Je me suis souvenu dans ces moments d'une histoire que maman me racontait à propos de mon père. Je ne l'avais pas connu. Tout ce que je connaissais de précis sur cet homme, c'était peut-être ce que m'en disait alors maman: il était allé voir exécuter un assassin. Il était malade à l'idée d'y aller. Il l'avait fait cependant et au retour il avait vomi une partie de la matinée." This part of Meursault's narrative reflects a part of Camus' own story. Cf. *Essais*, p. 1021.

[134] Cf. 1.3.2, 1.6.24, 2.2.2, 2.5.1.

[135] Cf. again 2.5.25: "J'avais eu raison, j'avais encore raison, j'avais toujours raison."

that "one life [is] as good as another".[136] For example, Meursault indicates that his mother's life did change as a result of his having put her into an old people's home.[137] He also points out that Salamano's life changed after the loss of his wife and the disappearance of his dog.[138] In addition, Meursault certainly changed the Arab's life for him. Moreover, one cannot argue that people do not change their lives, but rather that their lives are changed for them, for Meursault changed his own life, for the worse, going not to Paris but to prison.[139] In fact, Meursault was happy before his crime,[140] but became unhappy after it,[141] and in the end he wants to be happy again.[142] Accordingly, if it is true that "after a while you could get used to anything",[143] and that "you can always find something to be happy about",[144] then it is also true that some things are more worth getting used to and being happy about than others.[145] Resentment aside, one can both appreciate the absurdity of life and reasonably prefer the freedom of the sun, the beach, and the sea to the punishment of incarceration, prosecution, and decapitation. Thus Meursault helps readers realize that people do change their lives and that one life is not as good as another, though he may understandably find all this difficult to admit in retrospect.

---

[136] Cf. 1.5.3: "J'ai répondu qu'on ne changeait jamais de vie, qu'en tout cas toutes se valaient …."

[137] Cf. 1.1.7, 1.1.21, 2.5.26.

[138] Cf. 1.5.9: "Sa vie avait changé maintenant et il ne savait pas trop ce qu'il allait faire."

[139] Cf. 1.5.3–4, 1.6.25, 2.2.1–17, especially 2.3.21: "Et pourtant quelque chose était changé …."

[140] Cf. 1.6.25: "J'ai compris que j'avais détruit l'équilibre du jour, le silence exceptionnel d'une plage où j'avais été heureux. Alors, j'ai tiré encore quatre fois sur un corps inerte où les balles s'enfonçaient sans qu'il y parût. Et c'était comme quatre coups brefs que je frappais sur la porte du malheur."

[141] Cf. 2.3.21: "Dans l'obscurité de ma prison roulante, j'ai retrouvé un à un, comme du fond de ma fatigue, tous les bruits familiers d'une ville que j'aimais et d'une certaine heure où il m'arrivait de me sentir content."

[142] Cf. 2.5.26: "… j'ai senti que j'avais été heureux, et que je l'étais encore."

[143] Cf. 2.2.10: "C'était d'ailleurs une idée de maman et elle le répétait souvent, qu'on finissait par s'habituer à tout."

[144] Cf. 2.5.7: "Maman disait souvent qu'on n'est jamais tout à fait malheureux."

[145] Cf. 2.2.10: "J'ai souvent pensé alors que si l'on m'avait fait vivre dans un tronc d'arbre sec, sans autre occupation que de regarder la fleur du ciel au-dessus de ma tête, je m'y serais peu à peu habitué."

Other prominent examples of the incoherence of his proclamations on the meaninglessness of life include Meursault's bizarre argument that, "since we're all going to die ... when and how don't matter".[146] This claim too is not cogent, because decades of life and the manner of death do matter, and a great deal, if not for him then for others.[147] It is not dispositive in this regard that Meursault in prison seems to have established a different relation between himself and time,[148] or that he appears to have embraced a version of the "lived present",[149] or even accepted a kind of "eternal return of the same".[150] The same untenability holds for his generalizing thesis that "life is not worth the trouble of having lived it",[151] which surely depends on whose life is at issue and how it is lived. Hence Meursault is clearly mistaken in feeling that he is "like everybody else, absolutely like everybody else".[152] Certainly not all readers of his narrative think that they are "just like Meursault, absolutely like Meursault". In any case, he cannot speak for anyone but himself, and to think otherwise is arrogance on his part. In the end, then, Meursault is also dead wrong that "nothing mattered".[153]

---

[146] Cf. 2.5.8: "Du moment qu'on meurt, comment et quand, cela n'importe pas, c'était évident."

[147] Meursault's argument echoes Kierkegaard's equally problematic statement that, if a human life is not eternal, then it is empty. Cf. the opening lines of "A Tribute to Abraham" in *Fear and Trembling* and *The Myth of Sisyphus*, p. 41 (*Le Mythe de Sisyphe*, p. 128), where Camus refers to this passage in Kierkegaard: "Ce cri n'a pas de quoi arrêter l'homme absurde ...." The question is whether Meursault exemplifies "the absurd human being", and the answer is not at all clearly in his favor.

[148] Cf. 2.2.13–17, starting in 2.2.13: "Toute la question, encore une fois, était de tuer le temps. ..."

[149] Cf. 2.2.16: "Ainsi ... le temps a passé. J'avais bien lu qu'on finissait par perdre la notion du temps en prison. Mais cela n'avait pas beaucoup de sens pour moi. Je n'avais pas compris à quell point les jours pouvaient être à la fois longs et courts. Longs à vivre sans doute, mais tellement distendus qu'ils finissaient par déborder les uns sur les autres. Ils y perdaient leur nom. Les mots hier ou demain étaient les seuls qui gardaient un sens pour moi." One is reminded of Augustine's treatment of time in Book 11 of his *Confessions*.

[150] Cf. 2.5.26: "Et moi aussi, je me suis senti prêt à tout revivre."

[151] Cf. 2.5.8: "Mais tout le monde sait que la vie ne vaut pas la peine d'être vécue." In *The Stranger* (p. 114), Ward translates this sentence thus: "But everybody knows life isn't worth living." In doing so, he turns a hypothetical original into a categorical translation.

[152] Cf. 2.1.6: "J'avais le désir de lui affirmer que j'étais comme tout le monde, absolument comme tout le monde."

[153] Cf. 2.5.25: "Rien, rien n'avait d'importance et je savais bien pourquoi."

The case for Meursault's world-view is as weak as the case against his crime is strong. As mutable beings, human beings age, weaken, and die. Why? According to the Jewish-Christian narrative, it is because they are guilty. Therefore they must be punished, not only because they sin, but also because the first human beings sinned.[154] Now Meursault tells the prison chaplain that he does not know what "sin" is.[155] Yet he also repeatedly indicates that he does accept the notion that all human beings are "guilty" and "condemned" without having done anything evident or determinate to merit being so.[156] Hence he has internalized the grim Jewish-Christian theological anthropology that places human beings between a punishment that they do not deserve, allegedly stemming from original sin (*peccatum originale*), and a reward that they cannot earn, ostensibly linked to eternal life (*vita aeterna*).[157] Yet from the brute fact that human beings must die it does not follow with any cogent evidence that death is a punishment for guilt from sin.[158] The philosophical question is: Why must death be interpreted penally, that is, as an extraneous punishment? Why can it not be understood naturally, that is, as an organic occurrence? Meursault does not reflect on this aspect of his condition, the human condition, but Camus does.[159]

In retrospect, Camus summarized *The Stranger* with a paradoxical formulation: "In our society any man who does not weep at his mother's funeral runs the risk of being sentenced to death."[160] Accordingly, Meursault

---

[154] Cf. Gen. 2–3.

[155] Cf. 2.5.18: "Je lui ai dit que je ne savais pas ce qu'était un péché."

[156] Cf. again 1.1.2, 1.1.5, 1.1.15, 1.2.1–2, 1.3.11, 1.4.5–6, 2.1.10–11, 2.3.3, 2.3.15, 2.4.1, 2.4.4–5, 2.4.10–11, 2.5.8, 2.5.15, 2.5.18, 2.5.25, but this time especially 2.5.25, whose context does not mitigate its text: "Tout le monde était privilégié. Il n'y avait que des privilégiés. Les autres aussi, on les condamnerait un jour. Lui aussi, on le condamnerait."

[157] Cf. Augustine, *City of God*, bks. 13–14, 20–22, passim.

[158] Cf. Nietzsche, *Thus Spoke Zarathustra* 2.20: "On Redemption".

[159] Cf. Camus, *Entre Plotin et Saint Augustin or Métaphysique chrétienne et Néoplatonisme*, in: Camus, *Essais*, pp. 1224–1313, especially pp. 1293–1307 (on Augustine). This seminal text of Camus was written as his thesis for his *diplôme d'études supérieures* under the direction of René Poirier at the University of Algiers in 1936. It is available in an excellent English edition: *Christian Metaphysics and Neoplatonism*, tr. Ronald Srigley (Columbia, Missouri: University of Missouri Press, 2007).

[160] Cf. Camus, "Preface to *The Stranger*" (1955/56), in: *Lyrical and Critical Essays*, p. 335. This Preface was written in 1955 (signed by Camus on January 8 of that year) and published in the American University Edition of *The Stranger* in 1956. The original French version is

is convicted, arguably absurdly, more because of his lack of emotion at his mother's funeral than because of his state of mind at his victim's death.[161] What Camus wants to say with this plot summary is that "the hero of the book is condemned because he does not play the game".[162] Thus Camus does not view Meursault so, as some readers have, namely, as "a piece of social wreckage", but rather as "a foreigner to the society in which he lives, wandering, on the fringe, in the suburbs of private, solitary, sensual life".[163] Camus explains that, to understand more accurately his author's intention in creating his character, one must ask how it is that Meursault does not play the game:[164] "The response is simple: He refuses to lie. To lie is not only to say what is not true. It is also, and above all, to say more than is true, and, as far as the human heart is concerned, to express more than one feels."[165] It is striking that Camus' characterization contradicts Meursault's claim that he is "like everybody else, absolutely like everybody else": "This [to lie] is what we all do, every day, to simplify life. Contrary to appearances, Meursault does not want to simplify life. He says what he is, he refuses to hide his

---

found in Camus, *Théâtre, Récits, Nouvelles*, pp. 1928–1929. Cf. p. 1928: "J'ai résumé *l'Étranger*, il y a longtemps, par une phrase dont je reconnais qu'elle est très paradoxale: 'Dans notre société tout homme qui ne pleure pas à l'enterrement de sa mère risque d'être condamné à mort.'"

[161] Cf. again 2.1.4, 2.3.11, 2.3.15, 2.3.20, 2.4.5, especially 2.5.25: "Qu'importait si, accusé de meurtre, il était exécuté pour n'avoir pas pleuré à l'enterrement de sa mere?" Cf. also Camus, *Notebooks* (*Carnets II, janvier 42 à mars 51* [Paris: Éditions Gallimard, 1964]), pp. 29–30. Cf. finally Camus, *Théâtre, Récits, Nouvelles*, p. 1932: "Dans tout cela naturellement, il s'agit des moyens artistiques et pas de la fin. Le sens du livre tient exactement dans le parallélisme des deux parties. Conclusion: La société a besoin de gens qui pleurent à l'enterrement de leur mère; ou bien on n'est jamais condamné pour le crime qu'on croit. D'ailleurs je vois encore dix autres conclusions possibles."

[162] Cf. "Preface to *The Stranger*", pp. 335–336. Cf. also *Théâtre, Récits, Nouvelles*, p. 1928: "Je voulais dire seulement que le héros du livre est condamné parce qu'il ne joue pas le jeu."

[163] Cf. "Preface to *The Stranger*", p. 336. Cf. also *Théâtre, Récits, Nouvelles*, p. 1928: "En ce sens, il est étranger à la société où il vit, il erre, en marge, dans les faubourgs de la vie privée, solitaire, sensuelle. Et c'est pourquoi des lecteurs ont été tentés de le considérer comme une épave."

[164] Cf. "Preface to *The Stranger*", p. 336. Cf. also *Théâtre, Récits, Nouvelles*, p. 1928: "On aura cependant une idée plus exacte du personnage, plus conforme en tout cas aux intentions de son auteur, si l'on se demande en quoi Meursault ne joue pas le jeu."

[165] Cf. "Preface to *The Stranger*", p. 336. Cf. also *Théâtre, Récits, Nouvelles*, p. 1928: "Le réponse est simple: il refuse de mentir. Mentir ce n'est pas seulement dire ce qui n'est pas. C'est aussi, c'est surtout dire plus que ce qui est et, en ce qui concerne le coeur humain, dire plus qu'on ne sent. "

feelings, and society immediately feels threatened. For example, one asks him to say that he regrets his crime in the approved manner. He replies that what he feels in this regard is annoyance rather than genuine regret. And this nuance condemns him."[166] For Camus, then, Meursault is not "a piece of social wreckage" but "a poor and naked man enamored of a sun that leaves no shadows".[167] Especially his alleged lack of feeling is supposed to be a gross misperception on the part of others and readers: "Far from being bereft of all feeling, he is animated by a passion that is profound because it is stubborn, the passion for the absolute and for the truth."[168] That "this truth is still a negative one" does not diminish its importance for life.[169] According to Camus, *The Stranger* is even "the story of a man who, without any heroic attitude, agrees to die for the truth".[170] Finally, Camus says, in another paradoxical statement, that Meursault is "the only Christ that we deserve", adding that he says this "without any blasphemous intent" but only "with the slightly ironic affection" of an artist for a character of his creation.[171]

---

[166] Cf. "Preface to *The Stranger*", p. 336. Cf. also *Théâtre, Récits, Nouvelles*, p. 1928: "C'est ce que nous faisons tous, tous les jours, pour simplifier la vie. Meursault, contrairement aux apparences, ne veut pas simplifier la vie. Il dit ce qu'il est, il refuse de masquer ses sentiments et aussitôt la société se sent menacée. On lui demande par exemple de dire qu'il regrette son crime, selon la formule consacrée. Il répond qu'il éprouve à cet égard plus d'ennui que de regret véritable. Et cette nuance le condamne."

[167] Cf. "Preface to *The Stranger*", p. 336. Cf. also *Théâtre, Récits, Nouvelles*, p. 1928: "Meursault pour moi n'est donc pas une épave, mais un homme pauvre et nu, amoureux du soleil qui ne laisse pas d'ombres."

[168] Cf. "Preface to *The Stranger*", p. 336. Cf. also *Théâtre, Récits, Nouvelles*, p. 1928: "Loin qu'il soit privé de toute sensibilité, une passion profonde, parce que tenace, l'anime, la passion de l'absolu et de la vérité."

[169] Cf. "Preface to *The Stranger*", p. 336. Cf. also *Théâtre, Récits, Nouvelles*, p. 1928: "Il s'agit d'une vérité encore négative, la vérité d'être et de sentir, mais sans laquelle nulle conquête sur soi et sur le monde ne sera jamais possible."

[170] Cf. "Preface to *The Stranger*", pp. 336–337. Cf. also *Théâtre, Récits, Nouvelles*, p. 1928: "On ne se tromperait donc pas beaucoup en lisant dans *l'Étranger* l'histoire d'un homme qui, sans aucune attitude héroïque, accepte de mourir pour la vérité."

[171] Cf. "Preface to *The Stranger*", p. 337. Cf. also *Théâtre, Récits, Nouvelles*, pp. 1928–1929: "Il m'est arrivé de dire aussi, et toujours paradoxalement, que j'avais essayé de figurer dans mon personnage le seul christ que nous méritions. On comprendra, après mes explications, que je l'aie dit sans aucune intention de blasphème et seulement avec l'affection un peu ironique qu'un artiste a le droit d'éprouver à l'égard des personnages de sa création."

Yet must the readers so understand Meursault as Camus does? Meursault may die for *his* truth, but he does not die for *the* truth. He certainly does not die for the truth of his victims, the abused Arab woman and her murdered brother. Thus his narrative may not be a lie as a whole, but it is false in crucial respects. For example, when Meursault writes the letter for Raymond to his mistress, he then says more than is true, or at least more than he knows to be true, since he naïvely relies on a one-sided, self-serving version of events.[172] In writing the letter, which sets off a chain of events that leads to the murder,[173] Meursault, flaunting the principle of sufficient reason, does what Raymond wants him to do because he wants to please his new pal and because he has no reason not to do it.[174] Also, when Meursault testifies for Raymond to the police, he then says more than is true, or at least more than he knows to be true, and he even admits that he does not know what he is supposed to say.[175] All this is to say *more* than is true, to express *more* than one feels, to do *more* than is justified. For his part, Meursault insists that he cannot admit to feelings that he does not have.[176] Yet what about his colonialist, racist, and sexist attitudes toward his victims?[177] Did Meursault not harbor feelings of resentment against Arabs that he did not admit to but acted on?[178]

---

[172] Cf. 1.3.7–11.

[173] Cf. 1.3.11–12, 1.4.1, 2.3.19, 2.4.2.

[174] Cf. 1.3.12: "J'ai fait la lettre. Je l'ai écrite un peu au hasard, mais je me suis appliqué à contenter Raymond parce que je n'avais pas de raison de ne pas le contenter."

[175] Cf. 1.4.5, 1.6.3, 2.3.19.

[176] Cf. 2.1.5: "Non, parce que c'est faux."

[177] Cf. 1.6.25: "La gâchette a cédé, j'ai touché le ventre poli de la crosse et c'est là, dans le bruit à la fois sec et assourdissant, que tout a commence." Yet Meursault's involvement in the case does not begin with the encounter with the Arab on the beach, but rather with the letter that he wrote for Raymond to entice the Arab's sister to Raymond's apartment so that he could brutally punish her for her alleged infidelity. It is uncertain whether Meursault would have written the letter if he had not realized that the woman was an Arab. For, after having demurred, Meursault only then wrote the letter when he realized, as Raymond told him her name, that the woman was an Arab (1.3.12). Also, a reasonable person must doubt whether Meursault would have so killed a European as he did the Arab (1.6.25).

[178] One cannot overlook how Meursault looks at the Arabs looking at him and his fellow Europeans as they depart for the beach (1.6.3): "Ils nous regardaient en silence, mais à leur manière, ni plus ni moins que si nous étions des pierres ou des arbres morts." Cf. my study "'J'ai compris que j'étais coupable' ('I understood that I was guilty'): A Hermeneutical

As a result, it is safe to say that it is not the case that "everything is true and nothing is true" at Meursault's trial.[179] The hermeneutical focus on levels and moments of reflection, combined with a phenomenological description of the evidence, enables readers of *The Stranger* to recognize that, despite Meursault's rejection of God and Jesus Christ, atheism need not yield nihilism.[180] Nor is the character's atheistic existence, absurd or rational, evidence of nihilism on the author's part.[181] In fact, it is an ironic twist of *The Stranger* that the protagonist Meursault seems to have embraced "existentialism" without having understood it, whereas the author Camus appears to have eschewed *existentialism* as he understood it.[182] It is worth noting that a thorough investigation of Camus' skeptical response to essentialism in general, and to Husserl's essentialist phenomenology in particular, remains a desideratum.[183] This is not to mention Husserl's critical attitude toward what was in his time called "Existenzphilosophie" (Jaspers) but would later be known as "existentialisme" (Marcel),[184] or his own inquiry

---

Approach to Sexism, Racism, and Colonialism in Albert Camus' *L'Étranger/The Stranger*", *Journal of Camus Studies*, vol. 1 (2011), pp. 64–87.

[179] Cf. 2.3.16: "'Tout est vrai et rien n'est vrai!'"

[180] Camus was hardly an atheist without further ado. He once stated, for example, his nuanced view 'that he did not believe in God but that he was not an atheist for all that' (*Le Monde*, August 31, 1956): "Je ne crois pas en Dieu, mais je ne suis pas athée pour autant—et … je trouve à l'irréligion quelque chose de vulgaire et d'usé."

[181] Cf. Camus, "Preface" (to the American Edition of *The Myth of Sisyphus and Other Essays*, tr. Justin O'Brien [New York: Alfred Knopf, 1955]), p. v: "… this book declares that even within the limits of nihilism it is possible to find the means to proceed beyond nihilism. In all the books I have written since, I have attempted to pursue this direction." It is evident that, although Camus wrote *The Stranger* (finished in May 1940) before *The Myth of Sisyphus* (finished in February 1941), the remark about transcending nihilism from within applies not only to the later but also to the earlier work.

[182] Cf. Robert Spector, "Albert Camus 1913–1960: A Final Interview [December 20, 1959]", *Venture*, vols. 3/4 (Spring/Summer 1960), pp. 26–40. Cf. also Camus, "Interview [with Jeanine Delpech]", *Les Nouvelles littéraires*, November 15, 1945: "Non, je ne suis pas existentialiste …. Sartre est existentialiste, et le seul livre d'idées que j'ai publié: *le Mythe de Sisyphe*, était dirigé contre les philosophes dits existentialistes …." Condensed versions of the interviews are reprinted in Camus' *Essais*, pp. 1424–1427 and 1925–1928, respectively.

[183] Camus' response to, and critique of, Husserl is concentrated in *The Myth of Sisyphus*, Chapter One: "An Absurd Reasoning", specifically in the section on "Philosophical Suicide".

[184] Cf. again my "Phenomenology Is A Humanism: Husserl's Hermeneutical-Historical Struggle to Determine the Genuine Meaning of Human Existence in *The Crisis of the European Sciences and Transcendental Phenomenology*", *Analecta Husserliana*, vol. 115 (2013), forthcoming.

into the conditions of the possibility of an essential analysis (*Wesensanalyse*) of the personal character of a particular individual.[185]

Finally, it should go without saying, but it probably goes better with saying, that the ordinary Meursault is not comparable to the heroic Sisyphus. It is, to be sure, generally understood that, since Camus published *The Myth of Sisyphus* in 1943, after having published *The Stranger* in 1942, there must be a close but unclear connection between these two seminal texts of the thinker. It is, none the less, hard to understand how it can matter to Meursault whether the stone is up or down the hill. In fact, it makes much more sense to understand Meursault as someone who, in violation of the letter and spirit of *The Myth of Sisyphus*, commits "philosophical suicide" by leaping all too precipitously and superficially, not *over* the absurd, but *to* the absurd. Thus he emerges as precisely the kind of "existentialist" with whom Camus should have had little sympathy and for whom he should have had a lot of criticism—"the slightly ironic affection" of the author for the character of his creation notwithstanding. In the end, both Meursault and Sisyphus are supposed to be happy.[186] Wherein their respective happinesses are supposed to consist, however, is another question, an open one.

---

[185] Cf. Edmund Husserl, *Zur Lehre vom Wesen und zur Methode der eidetischen Variation: Texte aus dem Nachlass (1891–1935)*, ed. Dirk Fonfara (Dordrecht: Springer Publishing, 2012), Husserliana XLI, pp. 366–372.

[186] Cf. 2.5.26: "… j'ai senti que j'avais été heureux, et que je l'étais encore." Cf. also *Le Mythe de Sisyphe*, the last sentence of the part entitled "The Myth of Sisyphus": "Il faut imaginer Sisyphe heureux."

Selfishness in Albert Camus' *La Chute*

By Emily Holman

> Selfishness is not wishing as one wishes to live, it is asking others to live as one wishes to live.[1]

What selfishness is and how (im)moral are two questions that have long plagued both moral philosophers and writers of literature. Even lexicographers offer scant clarification. The OED provides two definitions for 'selfish'.[2] The first is split into three aspects, only two of which concern us here (the third refers to genetics): 'Devoted to or concerned with one's own advantage or welfare to the exclusion of regard for others' and 'Used (by adversaries) as a designation of those ethical theories which regard self-love as the real motive of all human action'. Each is telling. The lack of punctuation between 'welfare' and 'to' in the first denotes that in order for self-concern to be classified as selfish it must within itself involve exclusion of the concerns of others: exclusion of others is an inherent aspect of self-concern if that self-concern is to be 'selfish'. The second indicates the likelihood of derogatory usage. It also points at the complex nature of selfishness' connection with self-love, suggesting the ease with which the latter can be denigrated by dint of that connection. Both aspects of the first definition are pejorative. The second introduces an alternative: 'By etymological re-analysis used for "pertaining to or connected with oneself".' The definition is not obsolete. Yet that the qualification 'by etymological reanalysis' is deemed necessary suggests that the possibility for selfishness to refer to the self in a neutral fashion, as here stated, is in fact remote.

What the OED definitions demonstrate, in terms both of the meanings given and the meticulous way in which they are choreographed, is that calling something 'selfish' usually suffices to condemn it. Selfishness' spectrum of

---

[1] Wilde 2001: 156

[2] http://www.oed.com/view/Entry/175306

meaning is both deeply related to the context of its usage (which depends also on the motive of its user) and, regardless of how it is used, extremely difficult to separate from a halo of negativity. Impossible, though, to separate from the self: whilst many moral notions (such as the 'moral emotions': guilt, shame, pride etc) relate to the self, the concept of selfishness regards the concern of the self, with the self. The very meaning depends on self-involving thought and action, which makes potentially disconcerting its propensity toward the negative. *Mansfield Park*'s Miss Crawford expresses this well: '[s]elfishness must always be forgiven, you know, because there is no hope of a cure.'[3] The word generates a sense of paradox. Is it possible not to be selfish? Many literary representations of selfishness have sought to clarify the meaning of a moral notion that denotes self-involvement and also entails censure; others, however, revel in its ambiguity. Such is the position of Albert Camus' *La Chute* (1956), which thrives on the haziness of 'selfishness' as a moral concept. In probing the paradox at the word's root, it comments on the implication of a moral notion that condemns self-interested action, ultimately suggesting that the double-bind of selfishness' definition can be detrimental to human desire, and ability, to live.

The tripartite nature of the OED's entry provides a useful formula for thinking about three dominant aspects of selfishness: thinking of or acting for oneself over others (1a); an insult that performs a degrading of self-love by calling it 'selfish' (1b); anything to do with the self (2). The selfishness conceived by narrator Jean-Baptiste Clamence derives its meaning from OED(1a) and especially (1b): it can only mean pejoratively. Indeed the possibility for it to be a word that refers to the self in a neutral fashion does not occur to Clamence at all. His selfishness occupies a substantial realm— any thought or action motivated by the self is included—and for him, all thoughts and actions are contaminated by that connection. As per OED(1b), self-love is selfish and therefore immoral. Clamence goes still further: selfishness is a fundamental and inevitable aspect of mankind, meaning that part of one's essential condition is immorality. A sense of this is generated throughout the text; in fact, it is Clamence's self-appointed task to prove it so. The text, which in offering us only one voice immerses us in Clamence's perspective, proffers Miss Crawford's light-hearted observation: that, as everything that stems from the self is selfish, selfishness is inescapable. For her this is a humorous instance of paradox, and she treats it ironically. But

---

[3] Austen 2004: 89

Clamence allows it to rest neither as light-hearted nor as paradox: he turns it into a strait-jacket. With selfishness *applicable* to anything 'to do with the self', but *meaning* only pejoratively, anything 'to do with the self' can be polluted with the tarnishing brush of the word. Selfishness and immorality become, straightforwardly, the truths of the human condition.

As this suggests, Clamence is no gentle, occasionally misbehaving Miss Crawford; this self-identified 'juge-pénitent' (judge-penitent)[4] revels in duality and duplicity.[5] His voice governs the text. Many critics have been rightly reluctant to call the book a novel or novella; some prefer philosophical essay.[6] First and foremost, though, the text is a *récit*: a narrative or account.[7] This is essential to understanding *La Chute*. Those who interpret Clamence as a mouthpiece for Camus inevitably misread the text, even 'systematically distort' it.[8] We are steeped in Clamence's perspective from first word to last, following him and a silent companion through five days of talks—or rather, speeches, for though we are not privy to the companion's interjections, they are but sparse:[9] it is Clamence who guides and directs the conversation. Clamence's speeches are geared towards a very specific objective; his every word is shaped, targeted and focused. His aim is to persuade his listener that all of humanity, including each of them, is guilty. Selfishness lies at man's core and characterises him; it is inescapable, and man's pretensions to selflessness are hypocrisy. Because the world is inhabited by man, it, too, is sullied. From the beginning, Clamence impresses these as facts on his listener, with every adjective or ostensibly casual aside specific to his intention: 'méfiance' is 'fondée' (distrust is justified); the deportation and death of 75,000 Jews is 'lessivage!'(a clean-up); people 'grouillant' (swarm); even the sea, in a deliberate echo of his casual collation of genocide and cleaning, 'fumante comme une lessive' (steams like a wet

---

[4] All translations are my own.

[5] Camus 1983: 6

[6] See Ford 2004; Hanna 1958; Hartsock 1961; Madden 1966; Roberts 2008.

[7] See Rey 1970.

[8] Viggiani 1960: 69

[9] See Otten 1982 for claims Clamence talks to himself.

wash). Yet the case Clamence 'plaide' (pleads) is not impartial, however much he tries to present it so.[10]

This is because *La Chute*'s exploratory focus differs from Clamence's 'démonstration'.[11] Rather, it is the character of Clamence which comes under the spotlight. This is a man whose adopted name draws evident parallels with John-the-Baptist. Viggiani describes 'Camus' punning as too obvious to be missed', but it is important to remember that Clamence has selected the name himself.[12] It is he who has chosen to create a connection between himself and a prophet both beheaded for telling an uncomfortable truth and endowed with the responsibility of proclaiming the world's future. This 'most enigmatic of Camus' works' speaks beyond its protagonist:[13] although the sum of monologues proffered aim individually and with gathering force at nothing less than corrupting the listener, Clamence's view is sufficiently unrelenting in its scathing attitude towards himself, as well as towards humanity, to shift attention from his 'démonstration' and onto him. For Clamence's unhappiness and disillusion are evident from the moment of introduction, prompting questions about how he was brought to this drastic, destructive perspective. In this way the narrative with which we are presented is double. If narrative 'recounts a story that happened in the past [and] drama enacts a story and makes it present',[14] *La Chute* combines narrative and drama, and goes further still: it does not represent or re-enact, but re-construct, a past event: it alters it with its retelling. Rosemarie Jones' argument for extending the *récit* is persuasive: 'the story of Clamence's fall is...a *récit* inside *La Chute* which is itself a *récit*.'[15] The mode of narrative is crucial to understanding what the book says about selfishness: Clamence's words betray more than he realises, assert though he does that his speech is 'dirigé' (directed).[16] As he delights in revealing at the end, the story of his selfishness has been all along shadowed by the desire to persuade his companion of his own guilt. But the desire itself merits investigation. It is useful to turn now to

---

[10] Camus 1983: 3-9

[11] *Ibid* 47

[12] Viggiani 1960: 66

[13] Locke 1967: 306

[14] Perez 2000: 56

[15] Jones 1994: 76

[16] Camus 1983: 80

---

examining Clamence's trickery so as to distinguish it from what the *récit* tells us.

Let us begin by considering the manipulative techniques Clamence uses, consciously, to intensify a sense of man's guilt, selfishness, hypocrisy, and the essential falsity of his existence. Before even the pair's gin has arrived, Clamence has referred to the impossibility of 'une vie propre' (a clean life) and 'l'eczéma' beneath 'style'; he has summarised 'l'homme moderne' (modern man) with 'une phrase': 'il forniquait et lisait les journaux' (he fornicated and read the newspapers). It is not only life and man that he has presented in a particular way. He has referred to himself as educated and of a 'nature communicative', one who has 'beaucoup médité sur l'homme' (much-meditated on man), which again emphasises the John-the-Baptist connection. He positions himself as prophet laden with the duty of dispensing unwelcome truth. (At the beginning of the second meeting he points out that he lied about his name, a remark that itself contributes to generating the sense of duplicity and hypocrisy with which he wishes to taint mankind.) Comments dropped into his story apparently offhandedly have the aura of considered conclusions and are similarly slanted to his end: 'mon métier est double, violà tout, comme la créature' (my profession is double, that's all, like man himself). '[V]oilà tout' presents the observation as simple, harmless fact; yet these small facts are what will convince his listener of man's guilt. Man's selfishness is described but also dramatised, as Clamence forces his companion to experience selfish treatment himself. 'Décidément,' he says, 'vous m'interéssez' (Decidedly, you interest me). This three-word sentence is followed by a paragraph break, implying a pause, then 'Quant à moi... ' (As for me ...).[17] Such seemingly careless speech-habits establish from the first meeting that Clamence cannot avoid returning to his favoured subject: himself. This persists throughout the *récit*, as Clamence highlights the self-involved patterning of his speech so as to construct and then enliven the portrait of his selfishness. He even tells his interlocutor, 'vous me répondrez plus tard' (you'll tell me later).[18] Clamence is indeed a caricature, as Elizabeth Trahan put it; but he caricatures himself.[19]

---

[17] *Ibid* 3-7

[18] *Ibid* 26

[19] Trahan 1966

He is careful to provide a strong impression of his *past* selfishness, as it is on this that generating a sense of his guilt depends. In speaking of his old life Clamence depicts himself as naive: he was happy but unreflective. He presents his past as that of an everyman, precisely so that anyone might recognise himself in his actions. The detailed listing of charitable acts in which he indulges disconcerts, for his companion will almost certainly have performed at least one of these acts, and Clamence's insistence on his immoral motive, hidden even to himself, obliges consideration of whether one, too, may have been alternately motivated. He demonstrates the impossibility of selflessness by showing how even the most virtuous acts have at their root what Iris Murdoch called 'the fat relentless ego'.[20] The care with which he focuses on and narrates the hypocrisy of his ostensibly selfless Parisian life allows him to make a deliberate comment on Christian morality. In accordance with his mission, Clamence takes care to demonstrate the selfishness beneath the selflessness in as disquietingly vivid a manner as possible: he 'adorais' (adores) helping others, 'exultais' (exults) if beggars come to his door, 'rejouissais' (rejoices) at giving lifts.[21] He brings together Aristotelian and Kantian ethics, and undermines each, showing how Aristotle's assertion that it is good to enjoy virtuous action can be perverted, and also demonstrating that the dear self Kant warned against is dearly, inescapably pervasive. Yet readings of this such as Azzedine Haddour's are incomplete: '*La Chute* parodies dogmatic Christology: selfless concern for the widow and orphan dominates Clamence's life. The doubleness of *La Chute* changes this selflessness into selfishness.'[22] The 'doubleness' is Clamence's. *La Chute* has multiple layers—David Ellison surmises the text as invoking 'the rhetoric of dizziness'[23]—enabling Clamence's parodying, his dogged and single-minded cynicism, his insistence on selfishness and guilt, as well as the conversion from 'genuinely virtuous' Parisian to one characterised precisely by the above, to reflect on selfishness itself.[24]

Clamence's coming-to-awareness of his selfishness is a relatively recent development. The seeds are first sown when he hears a woman fall into water

---

[20] Murdoch 2003: 51

[21] Camus 1983: 12-3

[22] Haddour 2000: 88

[23] Ellison 1983

[24] Solomon 2004: 57

and does not move to help, and from this point they develop steadily, as Clamence hears laughter at his back and begins to analyse human action during the loop of life and death, including his own. 'Par degrés, j'ai vu plus clair' (Bit by bit, I saw more clearly):[25] astutely, Clamence presents his realisation as a movement towards truth. He assures his listener of his unthinking past, appearing to walk a well-trodden path in philosophy, one in which he 'self-interprets',[26] viewing his old self differently now that his perspective has changed. But it is not simply this that is happening. Were Clamence, in his view, coming to a 'clair' point as to his selfishness, he might make his case for the selfishness 'at the core of human action' in a correspondingly clear manner.[27] Instead his narrative relies on generating, not presenting, a sense of past and ongoing selfishness. He traps the listener into agreement with the 'démonstration' by means of subtle asides, contrived observations and, as he reveals at the end, the movement from 'je' to 'vous', which covertly extends to all mankind his condemnation, without the awareness or agreement of his listener. He removes from his listener the possibility to assent to logic: for his argument does not rely on logic but on semblance: on the creation of an impression. 'Avouez...que vous vous sentez, aujourd'hui, moins content de vous-même que vous ne l'étiez il y a.cinq jours?' (Confess...that you feel, today, less content with yourself than you did five days ago?), Clamence asks, delighting in the accomplishment of his mission. Yet that he has had to do it through subtlety and trickery offers response to those critics who see in Clamence the maturing of one who is becoming 'increasingly aware':[28] it implies lack of trust in his position. The 'clair' standpoint he claims is rather one to which he hopes, through his polluting words, to inveigle others. Ellison writes of the 'presence of evil...within language itself':[29] Clamence's method is words that lull and sway all the way to coercion, when one finds oneself enmeshed in Clamence's own obscured perspective. (Solomon describes him as 'a black widow spider'.[30]) For his perspective is obscured and he knows it; but he cannot get past it. Far better 'd'étendre le jugement à tout le monde pour le

[25] Camus 1983: 27

[26] Taylor 1985

[27] Ellison 1990: 145

[28] Jones 1994: 52

[29] Ellison 1990: 163

[30] Solomon 2004: 41

rendre plus léger à mes propres épaules' (to extend judgement to everybody in order to make it weigh less heavily on my own shoulders).[31] In spite of what he thinks, it is not 'jugement' Clamence extends, but a polluting mode of perception, one that insistently searches for evidence of man's inherent and inescapable selfishness. Clamence is right to think of himself as spreading a burden to others so as to lighten his load; but the burden is his own 'poisonous' perspective.[32]

That the argument depends on a successful rendition of past selfishness reveals a tension exerted on Clamence's narrative. Clamence must add in the selfishness of his past actions in the present. Given that he has been practising 'mon utile profession' 'aussi souvent que possible' (my useful profession as often as possible), it is evident that this is not done without reflection.[33] (Elsewhere the interweaving between past and present serves his argument: comments like '[j]'y viens, ne craignez rien, j'y suis encore, du reste' (I'm getting there, don't worry, in fact, I've never left the subject) boost the interrelatedness of all of his tale:[34] the subjects of selfishness and guilt can never really be left behind.) Clamence's depiction of selfishness as an inherent part of the past is as 'dirigé' as all of his speech. Consider one of his earliest instances of the self-steeped reality of his selfless behaviour. '[J]'adorais aider les aveugles à traverser les rues' (I loved to help blind people cross the street):

> Du plus loin que j'apercevais une canne hésiter sur l'angle d'un trottoir, je me précipitais, devançais d'une seconde, parfois, la main charitable qui se tendait déjà, enlevais l'aveugle à toute autre sollicitude que la mienne et le menais d'une main douce et ferme sur le passage clouté, parmi les obstacles de la circulation, vers le havre tranquille du trottoir où nous nous séparions avec une émotion mutuelle.[35]

---

[31] Camus 1983: 75-8

[32] Solomon 2004: 54

[33] Camus 1983: 76-7

[34] *Ibid* 21

[35] *Ibid* 12

(From as far away as I could see a cane hesitating on the side of a pavement, I would rush forth, sometimes just a second ahead of another charitable hand which was already stretching out, whisk the blind person away from all other solicitude other than my own and lead him, with a gentle, firm hand, across the crosswalk, through the traffic, towards the safe haven of the pavement, where we would separate with mutual emotion.)

Clamence is careful to show that he does not see a person but 'une canne' faltering at the pavement's edge, managing to suggest that all that mattered to him was this wiggling piece of wood, which he knew meant opportunity, and 'je me précipitais' accordingly. The imperfect tense bolsters his case by indicating that this is all that matters to him still: his sense of enjoyment in this bygone moment continues. (Indeed he shortly afterwards refers to these 'années dont à vrai dire, j'ai encore le regret au cœur' (years which, true to say, I still yearn for in my heart), the period of a 'lumière édénique' (prelapserian glow))[36]. The pointed reference to the stick allows him to highlight his opposition to the traditional notion of selflessness: thinking of other people. He takes a moment to attend to his 'main douce et ferme', strengthening the impression of his revelling in the retelling of his putative altruism. Clamence immerses himself in these old actions in a way that fully establishes the nostalgia he feels for them: the description of his movement 'sur le passage clouté', through the 'obstacles' of traffic, towards the safe haven of the pavement all illustrate a similar delight in his own action and his own body.

That this is one sentence is vital for a similar reason: the sentence gathers momentum as it continues, immersing the listener and reimmersing Clamence in a sensual, prolonged gratification of times past. One solo sentence suggests that Clamence has become lost in the retelling—something that works to his advantage in showing the extent of his selfishness. But it shows its extent *now*: the description tells of his present motive rather than of the past moment. The depiction of the past itself is false. That even the narrative perspective of the present does not register that there is a person attached to the 'canne' indicates how deliberate, how purposeful, a retelling this is. Likewise the pair of adjectives that describe his hand show Clamence's present, not previous, involvement. (After all, this event took

---

[36] *Ibid* 16-7

place an undisclosed number of years ago, and Clamence later refers to his 'etonnant pouvoir d'oubli' (astonishing ability to forget)).[37] The decision to remark on the hand, on the movements of his body, on the wobbling cane is made now, as calculated as the decision to depict each of these as felt at the time. The constructed nature of the depiction betrays Clamence's determination to find and prove selfishness, and spawn as strong a sense of it as possible.

Despite the attempt to portray this as enlightenment ('[a]vec quelques autres vérites, j'ai découvert ces évidences peu à peu' (with some other truths, I discovered these facts bit by bit)),[38] this is not straightforwardly a development in perspective. Clamence's 'évidences' for his (and by extension mankind's) selfishness are discerning, duping—and he knows it. 'Ce sont là de petits traits,' Clamence tells his interlocutor of these past stories, 'mais qui vous feront comprendre les continuelles délectations que je trouvais dans ma vie, et surtout dans mon métier' (these are small touches, but they will make you understand the continual delights that I was finding in my life, and above all in my profession).[39] These 'petits traits' have the canny present purpose of generating a sense of his selfishness that overwhelms: they take up a third of the book. But they also function in a way that Clamence does not realise at all: inadvertently, they demonstrate how carefully created his presentation of selfishness is. His 'trouvais' is of the wrong tense: the 'délectation' is contrived now so as to trick his listener. Clamence's purpose—corruption—overpowers the possibility not only for his narrative to be sincere, but also to flow easily from his current perspective. When Richard Kamber describes the book as 'show[ing]' that mankind is 'fundamentally flawed by selfishness', then, he is falling for Clamence's resourceful rhetoric. The showing is itself flawed. Yet Clamence is not 'demonic'.[40] However much he tries to prove it, neither Clamence nor mankind are inherently evil—according, at least, to *La Chute*).

It is helpful here to consider a novel by Ayn Rand, *The Fountainhead* (1947), which stresses that it is 'how' words 'come to mean' that is most

---

[37] *Ibid* 27

[38] *Ibid* 27

[39] *Ibid* 13

[40] Viggiani 1960: 66

significant.[41] Through the self-belief that it engenders, selfishness can liberate; selflessness, though, can cripple, as one fears to act in favour of oneself for fear of societal condemnation. It is this that lies behind the novel's vendetta against the conventional notion of selfishness: it contests the definition because of what that definition comes to signify in practice. The indistinct way in which selfishness is used for indictment—as, for instance, 'what you're saying is very ugly and selfish'[42]—means that one can be denounced for selfishness without speaker or listener knowing precisely what it is that is being named selfish. Any act associated with the self is liable to be assessed 'selfish' and so denigrated, thus engendering a fear of committing any action that might be called selfish. Similarly, when altruism is described as 'the doctrine which demands that man live for others and place others above self',[43] this refers not to a dictionary definition of altruism but to what 'preach[ing]' altruism effects psychologically. Once celebrated, once preached as virtuous, altruism becomes a hallmark of morality, associated so strongly with virtue that its insistence on thinking of others before oneself can lead to a loss of the conception of self and its 'functions' (to 'think, feel, judge, or act').[44] Such a loss is equal to what the novel terms 'selflessness': the state of an absence of self altogether. The promotion of altruism leads ultimately to 'self-immolation', as those seeking virtue struggle to become selfless. This connection is hinted throughout the novel and given explicit, exclamatory statement in a climactic end-speech:

> Preach selflessness. Tell man that he must live for others. Tell men that altruism is the ideal. Not a single one of them has ever achieved it and not a single one ever will. His every living instinct screams against it. But don't you see what you accomplish? Man realizes that he's incapable of what he's accepted as the noblest virtue—and it gives him a sense of guilt, of sin, of his own basic unworthiness. Since the supreme ideal is beyond his grasp, he gives up eventually all ideals, all aspiration, all sense of his personal value.[45]

---

[41] Rand 1961: 664-70. See Hare 1952; Stevenson 1937.

[42] Rand 1961: 585

[43] *Ibid* 666

[44] *Ibid* 667

[45] *Ibid* 621

With the impossible posited as virtue, man will condemn himself. It is an attitude that resounds with a comment made by Clamence: 'Dieu n'est pas nécessaire pour créer la culpabilité, ni punir. Nos semblables y suffisent, aidés par nous-mêmes.'[46] For Clamence, man's readiness to find himself guilty is simply part of the wretched condition of mankind. But *The Fountainhead* presents the possibility that the fault lies with the power of moral categories themselves, and the urge to conform to or avert them. In the case of selfishness this is particularly dangerous: if '[e]gotism [is] held to mean the sacrifice of others to self' and altruism 'the sacrifice of self to others', no way out is left for man, who is 'forced to accept masochism as his ideal—under the threat that sadism [is] his only alternative'. For *The Fountainhead* this double-bind is, like the standard definition of selfishness, simply wrong, underhandedly so: the choice between 'self-sacrifice [and] domination' is 'the greatest fraud ever perpetrated on mankind'. For man to be guiltless he must ignore those who try to burden him with guilt.

Clamence burdens himself. *La Chute*, too, explores the psychological ramifications of the act of moral categorisation. Although it is to his own judgement that Clamence submits himself, the judgement follows inevitably from the moral appraisal he performs of his actions. Toohey, who uses man's sense of guilt to his advantage, would be well-pleased with Clamence, who, in deciding his guilt, pursues it to the fullest extent: bringing together all aspects of the OED's definitions, and condemning any 'self'—all mankind— accordingly. Thus the view he presents of happiness and success finds each immoral by their very definition:

> On ne vous pardonne votre bonheur et vos succès que si vous consentez généreusement à les partager. Mais pour être heureux, il ne faut pas trop s'occuper des autres. Dès lors, les issus sont fermées. Heureux et jugé, ou absous et misérable.[47]

> (You are not forgiven your happiness and success unless you generously consent to share them. But to be happy, one must not occupy oneself too much with others. So there is no escape. Happy and judged, or absolved and miserable.)

---

[46] Camus 1983: 61

[47] Camus 1983: 44

According to this, happiness and success are, of themselves, anti-social. They need to be 'pardonn[és]', as though there is in them something intrinsically dangerous to others. Interestingly (given the lack of foundation for the comment) happiness cannot exist in a shared realm: but misery can.[48] Clamence does not provide a reason for his contestable claims: in accordance with the rhetoric of all his narrative, he presents possibility as fact so as to strengthen the 'démonstration'. Something else is also happening here. Clamence invokes the language of religion ('absous') to depict happiness as sinful, but also to emphasise that, in the godless world he has portrayed throughout his talks, it is society (the ominous 'On') which offers absolution and judges, which bestows guilt or forgives. That Clamence puts society in this position of power indicates the way in which he thinks of moral judgement: in terms of guilt and forgiveness, of judges and the judged. (Indeed he has referred to this earlier, using, intriguingly—whether Camus and Rand knew one another's work is unknown—the same terms for the moral choice Roark called a 'trap': '[j]e sais bien qu'on ne peut se passer de dominer ou d'être servi' (I know well that one cannot do without domineering or being served)).[49]

What of the turning-point itself, which kindles Clamence's realisation of selfishness and so leads him to 'créer la culpabilité' (creat guilt)?[50] Clamence still remembers minute details of its occurrence, and references them with lyricism: '[i]l était une heure après minuit, une petite pluie tombait, une bruine plutôt, qui dispersait les rares passants' (it was an hour after midnight, a light rain was falling, a drizzle rather, which dispersed the few passers-by). The blood running through his body is as 'doux' (gentle) as the falling rain; 'heureux' (happy) with the walk, he is enjoying the sensation of being alive. He sees 'une mince jeune femme' (a slight young woman) on the bridge. Between her dark hair and the collar of her coat 'on voyait seulement une nuque, fraîche et mouillée, à laquelle je fus sensible' (one could see only a small part of her neck, cool and damp, which impacted me). He hesitates—implying that he considered approaching her—then walks on. Moments later he hears the body fall. There is a silence, which 'me parut interminable' (seemed to me interminable):

---

[48] Compare Arendt 1970: 15. '[S]haring joy is absolutely superior...to sharing suffering.'

[49] Camus 1983: 25

[50] Various critics argue the story is false; see Brombert 1999.

> Je voulus courir et je ne bougeai pas. Je tremblais, je crois, de froid et de saisissement. Je me disais qu'il fallait faire vite et je sentais une faiblesse irrésistible envahir mon corps. J'ai oublié ce que j'ai pensé alors. « Trop tard, trop loin... » ou quelque chose de ce genre. J'écoutais toujours, immobile. Puis, à petits pas, sous la pluie, je m'éloignai.[51]

> (I wanted to run and I didn't move. I was trembling, I thought, from cold and from shock. I told myself that it was necessary to move quickly and I felt an irresistible weakness invade my body. I have forgotten what I thought then. 'Too late, too far', or something like that. I was still listening, still. Then, with small steps, under the rain, I moved away.')

The description of the moment before the event is as significant as that of the event itself. The attention to the back of the woman's neck evokes a strange intimacy, particularly as it struck Clamence sufficiently for him to recall it now, the fresh, wet skin peeking between the dark hair and clothing. That Clamence is 'sensible' to the sight of this neck, affected enough to hesitate, and moved enough to walk on, is indicative: there is no sign of the exploitation of women that Clamence has spent precisely that day's conversation explaining he was never able to avoid; and the contrast strengthens the impression that this encounter was something unusual. His careful, delicate words suggest that for him the moment was one of extraordinary insight into what it is to be another human being. The gentleness with which he looks at her, sees her vulnerability, and walks on, indicates a capacity for empathy that Clamence later bolsters with his account of his time as a prisoner of war.

His reaction after the fall is telling: Clamence's description does not suggest the selfishness for which he will condemn himself. His distress is evident: his brief happiness flees, he is cold and shocked, he trembles, he cannot move. As a turning-point that leads him to the extreme position in which we meet him, the prophet imposing 'l'esclavage' (slavery) on mankind,[52] it is surprisingly lacking in selfishness. Though he does not run for help, it is not for lack of interest in the woman's fate: he waits, listens, 'immobile'. Were it

---

[51] Camus 1983: 39

[52] *Ibid* 75

the selfishness of OED(1) or even lack of interest he would walk on, unconcerned and unmoved. Clamence is neither. He is sufficiently affected to avoid reading the papers, a reaction Kamber has used to demonstrate his selfishness, though it speaks rather of distress: lack of care would see not the slightest change in Clamence's habits. What prevents Clamence from helping is something more disturbing than selfishness, and more insidious: an apparent sense of the meaninglessness of action. The 'faiblesse irrésistible' that invades Clamence's body and solidifies his stasis is a sign of his fundamental apathy towards life. '[J]e n'ai jamais pu croire profondément,' he says later, 'que les affaires humaines fussent choses sérieuses' (I have never been able to seriously believe that human affairs are serious things).[53] Nothing seems meaningful because he believes in no meaning.

What become evident to Clamence in this moment are two things he has long suspected: the harshness of life and the impossibility of one human ever caring fully for another. During the second meeting, while talking of friendship, he makes a sardonic, but revealing, comment: 'la mort seule réveille nos sentiments' (death alone awakens our feelings). He is providing evidence for his subject, the falsity of relations and the 'deux faces' (two faces) that characterise all interaction, but his outrage at the hypocrisy of general behaviour after a death is striking.[54] He returns to the subject of death again and again; and indeed, insofar as the woman's fall is the axis of both his life and the text, he never leaves it. This itself indicates a non-selfishness: Clamence has recreated every aspect of his life since the death of somebody else. The selfish hypocrisy that revolts him in others (such as the father who 'oublia' (forgets) his daughter's death)[55] he does not himself exhibit. The comment about death echoes, again now, as Clamence finds himself 'réveill[é]' after the death of the unknown woman. Even in the forceful, urgent immediacy of the moment in which the life of a woman who occasions such subtlety of feeling in Clamence is endangered, Clamence cannot muster the impulse of energy required to respond. His response is one of lethargy, betraying a lack of instinct for life-preservation.

---

[53] *Ibid* 48

[54] *Ibid* 19

[55] *Ibid* 41

That the death is apparently suicide is also significant. At no other point in his narrative has Clamence indicated such closeness with another living being, aside perhaps from the Frenchman he nicknames Duguesclin. The woman's suicide posits her at odds with life, not only a victim of life's cruelty, as she might be had her death been definitively accidental, but also one who does not desire the opportunity of life at all. Whether her death was or was not suicide, that it might have been casts the woman, importantly, as in opposition to life. Her death, like Duguesclin's, is surely part of what prompts in Clamence the revulsion in life he now exhibits and tries to compel in his listener. Clamence's references to suicide throughout his narrative cement the impression that this is a moment that will never leave him. Camus' earlier work *Mythe de Sisyphe* begins: '[i]l n'y a qu'un problème philosophique vraiment sérieux: c'est le suicide. Juger que la vie vaut ou ne vaut pas la peine d'être vécue, c'est répondre à la question fondamentale de la philosophie' (There is only one truly serius philosophical problem: suicide. To judge whether or not life is worth being lived, that is to respond to the fundamental question of philosophy).[56] Clamence has made that judgement carefully. He has decided not to think that life is worth living. What he is doing as we meet him is not 'v[ivant]' at all, nor is it 'vaut...la peine': his existence is based on spreading guilt. We find him revelling in self-hate, determined to spread it to others. He claims to want death; as with the lethargy of attitude exemplified in his lack of instinctive response to the sound of the fall, he has no drive to act. 'Tout serait consommé, j'aurais achevé' (everything would be over, I would be saved), he says, envisioning his decapitation.[57] Clamence's health declines throughout his narrative, his non-life, non-death instinct—his apathy—exhibiting itself in a physical stasis. It is significant that he ends the *récit* lying down; it suggests a relinquishing of will altogether. Just as he foretells on the second day, without self-esteem man cannot stay 'debout' (upright) or 'avancer' (advance). The *récit* ends, of course, with reference to the woman. This 'central, all-determining' moment is responsible for Clamence as we now meet him.[58]

Perhaps the clearest, most unambiguous, aspect of *La Chute* is that the man we meet now is unpleasant. As Solomon writes, 'even if [the] accusation of

---

[56] Camus 1973: 1

[57] Camus 1983: 81

[58] Ellison 1990: 146

duplicity and selfishness against the earlier Clamence is false and unfair, it accurately characterizes him now'.[59] Clamence has become the man he had judged himself for being. Solomon attributes this to 'resentment', seeing Amsterdam-Clamence as bitter and envious of his earlier self. Clamence certainly exhibits cynicism, yet it is not resentment that now characterises him. It is sadness. Clamence has taken the disconcerting possible truth of the 'fat relentless ego' and applied it drastically. He has turned confession to corruption.[60] That Clamence's action after deciding on his selfishness, and so on his guilt, is so much more vicious than before, towards others as well as himself, emphasises the powerful psychological effect that moral categories can have. It also shows Clamence's vulnerability: for him to accept guilt so readily—and apply it so drastically—implies a vulnerability that predates the discovery of selfishness, a readiness to find 'la tristesse de la condition commune' and the 'malconfort' torture-box of life.[61]

Most critics agree that Clamence's early life was happy. Ellison describes Clamence as a 'materially successful Parisian lawyer who enjoyed the admiration of his colleagues and the adulation of his clients';[62] Solomon compares him to Aristotle's *megalopsychos*, calling him as 'close as any of us can imagine coming to the Western urbane ideals he so clearly embodies'.[63] Clamence was indeed a fully-functioning, impressive member of society. For the episode with the woman to have struck him so significantly, however, points to a less happy Clamence than the one he has portrayed, 'profondément content de lui-même' (profoundly contented with himself), 'surhomme' of a 'vie réussie' (superman of a successful life). He makes brief reference to its emptiness: '[j]'étais à l'aise en tout...mais en même temps satisfait de rien' (I was at ease with everything, but at the same time satisfied with nothing). The comment's concision, combined with the fact that it does not serve Clamence's abject objective, indicates the likelihood of its truth. He goes on to mention rare, blissful moments of being 'fou des êtres et de la vie' (enraptured with people and with life), something that evokes both the lack of this feeling most of the time, and a yearning to

---

[59] Solomon 2004: 56

[60] See Shklovsky 1993 on 'confession as device'.

[61] Camus 1983: 79; 53

[62] Ellison 1990: 143

[63] Solomon 2004: 51

feel it more. Indeed he continues '[p]arfois…il me semblait…que je comprenais enfin le secret des êtres et du monde' (sometimes it seemed to me that I finally understood the secret of humans and of the world). The need to find this 'secret' conveys desire for more from life.[64]

The Fountainhead had suggested that, in neglecting one's profoundest desires, which is to neglect one's self, life can be only meaningless. *La Chute* makes a similar argument using different terminology, demonstrating with both Clamence's words and the character of Clamence himself the necessity of self-esteem. To live without it is akin, not to living without a self, but to living as 'chiens écumants':

> Le sentiment du droit, la satisfaction d'avoir raison, la joie de s'estimer soi-même, cher monsieur, sont des ressorts puissants pour nous tenir debout ou nous faire avancer. Au contraire, si vous en privez les hommes, vous les transformez en chiens écumants.[65]

> (A sense of legality, the satisfaction of being right, and the joy of self-esteem, dear sir, are powerful incentives in keeping us upright or making us advance. On the other hand, if you deprive men of these, you transform them into rabid dogs).

The 'joie de s'estimer soi-même' is part of what makes man man. (This, coming at the beginning of the second meeting, is before Clamence has turned the word 'homme' into one that suggests the 'petits sournois, comédiens, hypocrites' (little sneaks, play actors, hypocrites) of the *récit*'s end.[66]) In accordance with his aim, Clamence shows both how precarious a being man is (without these three, he is a rabid dog) and also how false are the things on which he relies. For Clamence self-esteem is illusion. The law is unreliable, for it depends on men, who above all else are selfish; knowledge of being right, too is dependent on others. Self-esteem is as vulnerable, if not more: it depends on one's self-conception, which depends on other, fallible creatures, and, as Clamence's character itself confirms, it is unstable.

---

[64] Camus 1983: 16-7

[65] Camus 1983: 11

[66] *Ibid* 74

All of this Clamence will seek to explain and prove with his narrative, for this (again, apparently offhand) comment comes at the start of the second meeting. Unbeknown to his listener, the Clamence speaking now has lost the 'sentiment', 'satisfaction' and 'joie' of believing in his rightness and self-esteem. His words are as 'dirigé[s]' as ever: the simplicity of each word suggests the naiveté with which these three qualities are regarded, so that the listener's trust in them is, slyly, undermined: he too will begin to distrust the notion of self-esteem, and believe it merely an illusion that will someday be dissipated. The repetitive structure Clamence uses to introduce these qualities (rhetoric's 'power-of-three') conjures a sense of importance that is immediately punctured by the following sentence, which establishes man's susceptibility. Not only are we meeting Clamence as a chien écumant; he is planning to turn his listener into one.

It is crucial to remember that Clamence speaks from outside: self-esteem is already mere memory. 'The world of innocence', says Solomon, 'is always vulnerable when it is viewed from within the world of bitter reflection. Unless, that is, the world of bitter reflection is itself exposed to its own "truths," and its own motives...are displayed for all to see.'[67] Clamence's words are meant in irony, but they reflect on him and substantiate their claim. His loss of self-esteem has had wider implications: he has become convinced of the pointlessness of all human endeavours and their essential crudity and malevolence. Clamence's sadness, his inability to believe in the possibility of his goodness, has led him to espouse selfishness—as both concept and act. His 'cowardly failure of nerve' during the bridge-episode leads him to a sufficiently drastic loss of self-worth to condemn all aspects of the self.[68]

At issue is not only the delicacy of his self-esteem ('je ne me reconnaissais que des supériorités, ce qui expliquait ma bienveillance et ma sérénité' (I recognised in myself only superiority, which explained my good will and serenity))[69]. His reaction also reveals his dependence on conventional morality. Clamence deems his non-action selfish, when it rather betrays something more disturbing, and judges himself immoral accordingly. His utter adherence to the moral definition of selfishness illustrates how

---

[67] Solomon 2004: 48

[68] Viggiani 1960: 66

[69] Camus 1983: 27

dangerous this can be, for he allies himself so thoroughly with the notion of selfishness that he can detect no other characteristic in himself or in mankind: he limits man to selfishness and thus guilt, and this for him defines man. The extension of selfishness that he performs—including anything of the self—is logical but perverse and masochistic: he removes from man the possibility of being anything other than selfish.

This radical application of a moral notion queries its definition in the way Roark does more explicitly in *The Fountainhead*. The moral state Roark dreads, in which 'life, as such, is [thought to be] evil' because of the way that the word 'selfishness' has been permitted to function,[70] is taking place in Clamence's mind. In aligning himself with selfishness as extensively and as thoroughly—any concern with, any enjoyment of, the self—Clamence places himself, along with every other individual, in an impossible moral position: how can a person live morally, if living involves selfish activity, and selfishness is immoral? The answer he gives is that one cannot: the life he chooses as 'solution' is void of moral goodness.[71] His idea of selfishness is as destructive for and ruthless towards the self, towards mankind, as that which Roark aimed to clarify for his fellows.

The corrosive reaches of 'selfishness' extend even to loving oneself, which becomes *per se* something to be condemned. Clamence's view of the anti-social nature of self-love is revealing: '[j]e jouissais de ma propre nature, et nous savons tous que c'est là le bonheur bien que, pour nous apaiser mutuellement, nous fassions mine parfois de condamner ces plaisirs sous le nom d'égoïsme' (I rejoiced in my own nature, and we all know that there lies happiness, even though, to appease one another, we pretend to condemn such pleasures under the name of egoism).[72] Clamence is not only here condemning the happiness of loving the state of being alive—as oneself—as an extension of the selfish instinct of mankind. (Note that to slot loving oneself 'sous le nom d'égoïsme' *is* to condemn it.) He also aligns life in society—life outside of 'ma propre nature'—with unhappiness, and necessarily so. '[C]'est là le bonheur'; happiness can belong nowhere else. Yet it is condemned so as to contribute to social harmony, which itself

---

[70] Rand 1970: ix

[71] Camus 1983: 80

[72] *Ibid* 12

asserts that society is not conducive to, or compatible with, 'bonheur'. Clamence does not query *why* self-love should be something that troubles others to the extent that it requires 'apais[ant]'; he takes it as given that the individual's love for himself is anti-social. His characterisation of happiness in life as anti-social is a perspective that evokes the necessary misery of life in the people-filled world. Clamence attributes to ennui 'la plupart des engagements humains' (most human endeavours): '[i]l faut que quelque chose arrive, même la servitude...la guerre, ou la mort' (something must happen, even servitude, war, death).[73] Every event, however appalling, is merely man's method of deflecting the sheer inanity of being alive. Prisoners of war, rape, murder, genocide: life is just a place for man to play out his selfishness. 'Ah! 'chère planète! Tout y est clair maintenant. Nous nous connaissons, nous savons ce dont nous sommes capables' (Ah! Dear planet! All is clear now. We know ourselves, we know what we are capable of.)[74] Life is malevolent, for man is selfish and he inhabits the world.

Yet *La Chute* makes it clear that Clamence's judgement is selective. Walking with his interlocutor in the fourth chapter, Clamence asserts that he is the only guide who can 'vous montrer ce qu'il y a d'important ici' (show you that which is important here): what he points out is 'le plus beau des paysages négatifs!' (the handsomest of negative landscapes): the (again) 'lessive' water, 'la digue grise' (grey dike), the 'tas de cendres' (pile of ashes) of a dune. 'Un enfer mou, vraiment!' (A soggy hell, indeed!) His companion points out the sky, which 'vit' (lives). This reference to the beauty of their surroundings, which Clamence has neglected, stresses the discriminating nature of Clamence's narrative, and perspective. Clamence's response: '[i]l s'epaissit, puis se creuse, oeuvre des escaliers d'air, ferme des portes de nuées' (it thickens, becomes concave, opens up air shafts and closes doors of cloud). His language is pointedly flat and bathetic, particularly given the juxtaposition with his vivid description of all that is 'négatif' in the landscape.[75] Clamence's choice is the dirty, the paltry, the squalid. What Ellison calls Clamence's expression of the 'moral nullity of our time' is rather his perception of the nullity of existence.[76] It follows

---

[73] Camus 1983: 21

[74] *Ibid* 25

[75] *Ibid* 40

[76] Ellison 1990: 163

partly from his application to himself of 'selfishness'. Solomon says Clamence 'think[s] too much', and insofar as he applies 'selfishness' to its fullest extent, condemning anything of the self, he does; yet his inability to think beyond the conventional, and Christian, moral definition, suggests one who might think too little. He never goes to the moral notions themselves.

Camus has been described by Peter Roberts as 'one of the most...hopeful moral philosophers' of his time.[77] The *récit*, in generating and then challenging its own duplicity, offers a plausible account for the complexity of moral conceptualisation. It suggests the impossibility of ever knowing the self. Clamence is a character who refuses 'to live in a tension' between 'good and evil',[78] and destroys his life and tries to destroy everyone else's because of his belief that the defeat of the ego is morally desirable but impossible. 'Ma solution, bien sur, ce n'est pas l'ideal' (of course my solution is not ideal), he says, '[m]ais quand on n'aime pas sa vie, quand on sait qu'il faut en changer, on n'a pas le choix, n'est-ce pas?' (but when one does not love one's life, when one knows it has to change, one does not have any choice, right?)[79] That there is not an explicit answer does not prevent a suggestion from emerging; Clamence's 'solution' is sufficiently unattractive as to render undesirable what brought him to it. Whatever else created this 'derniers des derniers' (lowest of the low),[80] the fault lies partly with Clamence's definition of selfishness: with the collation he performs of the OED's definitions. He is 'lock[ed] in an inferno of his own making'.[81] It is a position that becomes clearer when read alongside *The Fountainhead*. Absurdity has developed into apathy: a loss of desire for meaning altogether.[82] This has taken place before the text begins; but it also occurs as the narrative progresses. 'Happy men are free men', says one of Rand's characters, 'so kill their joy in living'.[83] Clamence is trying.

---

[77] Roberts 2008: viii. See Denton 1964

[78] Hartsock 1961: 362

[79] Camus 1983: 80

[80] *Ibid* 77

[81] Otten 1982: 114

[82] See Camus 1973; Barnes 1959; Henry 1975; Sartre 1955; Sefler 1974.

[83] Rand 1961: 622

Works Cited

<u>Primary Texts</u>

Austen, Jane. 2004. *Mansfield Park* [1814] (London: CRW Publishing Limited, Collector's Library)

Camus, Albert. 1973. *Mythe de Sisyphe* [1942] (Paris: Gallimard)

---. 1983. *La Chute* [1956] (London: Methuen Education Ltd)

---. 2006. *The Fall*, transl. Robin Buss (London: Penguin Books)

Kant, Immanuel. 2002. *Groundwork for the Metaphysics of Morals* [1785], trans. Allen W. Wood (New Haven: Yale University Press)

Rand, Ayn. 1961. *The Fountainhead* [1947] (New York: HarperCollins)

---. 1970. *The Virtue of Selfishness* [1964] (New York: Signet)

---. 1993. *The Fountainhead* (New York: Signet)

Wilde, Oscar. 2001. *The Soul of Man under Socialism and Selected Critical Prose* [1891], ed. Linda Dowling (London: Penguin Books)

Secondary Sources

Arendt, Hannah. 1970. *Men in Dark Times* (New York: Harcourt Brace & Company)

Barnes, Hazel. 1959. *Humanistic Existentialism: The Literature of Possibility* (Lincoln: University of Nebraska Press)

Brombert, Victor. 1999. *In Praise of Antiheroes: Figures and Themes in Modern European Literature 1830-1980* (London: U of Chicago P)

Denton, David. 1964. "Albert Camus: Philosopher of Moral Concern", *Educational Theory*, Vol. 14, No. 2, pp. 99-127

Ellison, David. 1983. "Camus and the Rhetoric of Dizziness: *La Chute*", *Contemporary Literature*, Vol. 24, No. 3, pp. 322-348

---. 1990. *Understanding Albert Camus* (Columbia: U of South Carolina P)

Ford, Russell. 2004. "Critiquing Desire: Philosophy, Writing and Terror", *Journal of Human Rights*, Vol. 3, No.1, pp. 85–98.

Frankfurt, Harry. 2001. "The Dear Self", *Philosophers' Imprint, Vol. 1, pp. 1-14*

Haddour, Azzedine. 2000. *Colonial Myths: History and Narrative* (Manchester: Manchester UP)

Hanna, Thomas. 1958. *The Thought and Art of Albert Camus* (Chicago: Henry Regnery)

Hare, Richard. 1952. *The Language of Morals* (New York: Oxford U P)

Hartsock, Mildred. 1961. "Camus' The Fall: Dialogue of One", *Modern Fiction Studies*, Vol. 7, pp. 357-364

Henry, Patrick. 1975. *Voltaire and Camus: the Limits of Reason and the Awareness of Absurdity* (Oxfordshire: Voltaire Foundation)

Jones, Rosemarie. 1994. *Camus: L'Etranger and La Chute* (London: Grant & Cutler Ltd)

Kamber, Richard. 2002. *On Camus* (Belmont: Wadsworth)

Locke, Frederick. 1967. "The Metamorphoses of Jean-Baptiste Clamence", *Symposium*, Vol. 21, No. 4, pp. 306–315

Murdoch, Iris. 2003. *The Sovereignty of Good* [1970] (London: Routledge)

Otten, Terry. 1982. *After Innocence: Visions of the Fall in Modern Literature* (Pittsburgh: U of Pittsburgh P)

Perez, Gilberto. 2000. *The Material Ghost: Films and their Medium* (Baltimore: John Hopkins UP)

Rey, Pierre. 1970. *La Chute: Camus* (Paris: Hatier)

Roberts, Peter. 2008. "Bridging Literary and Philosophical Genres: Judgement, Reflection and Education in Camus' *The Fall*", *Educational Philosophy and Theory,* Vol. 40, No. 7, pp. 873-887

Sartre, Jean-Paul. 1955. *Literary and Philosophical Essays*, trans. Annette Michelson (London: Rider and Company)

Sefler, George. 1974. "The Existential vs. the Absurd: The Aesthetics of Nietzsche and Camus", *The Journal of Aesthetics and Art Criticism*, Vol. 32, No. 3, pp. 415-421

Shklovsky, Victor. 1993. *Theory of Prose*, trans. Benjamin Sher (Illinois: Dalkey Archive Press)

Solomon, Robert. 2004. "Pathologies of Pride in Camus' The Fall", *Philosophy and Literature,* Vol. 28, No.1, pp. 41-59

Trahan, Elizabeth. 1966. "Clamence vs. Dostoevsky: An Approach to La Chute", *Comparative Literature*, Vol. 18, No. 4, pp. 337-350

Viggiani, Carl. 1960. "Camus and the Fall from Innocence", *Yale French Studies*, No. 25, pp. 65- 71

Absurdism and Lyricism: Stylistic Extremes in Camus' Novels

By Peadar Kearney

"Eh ! là, je dérive, moi aussi, je deviens lyrique ! Arrêtez-moi, cher, je vous en prie."

— Jean Baptiste Clamence, *La Chute*

Introduction

Albert Camus was born in 1913 in Mondovi in French Algeria and tragically killed in a car accident in Villeblevin, France in 1960. During this time that was his short life he deeply marked both francophone and world literature. Within the francophone sphere, his work symbolizes a transition point between the attempts at an underlining of a universal truth of Marcel Proust and André Gide and the dry objectivism of writers of the nouveau roman. His global status is seen in 1957 when he wins the Nobel Prize for "making sense of the absurd and supporting the deep need for hope from the bottom of the abyss". He is the youngest Frenchman to have won this award. Historically, he existed in interwar, war and post-war years. He was a novelist, playwright, essayist, philosopher, and journalist; in each genre what binds is his philosophical culture.

In discussing Camus, one speaks often at the same time of Jean-Paul Sartre. Both were trying to build a new 'humanism' in denouncing the absurd aspects of the human condition. Both use their fiction to put their own philosophies to work. But Sartre is the great "existentialist" writer while Camus denied being an existentialist, saying that man finds his end in himself and not in God (Christian existentialism) or history (atheist existentialism). He believes that we must pose the question directly to man, not to "existence" as an abstract being. At first they knew and appreciated each other through their works. In 1944 they met for the first time, they shared an initially friendly relationship but from the period when Camus wrote *The Rebel* they quarrelled, when Sartre criticised Camus for his 'bourgeois humanism'.

After a literary debut that shows an almost feverish ardour to live with *Nuptials*, "the distress of a troubled era ends to convince him that the world is plunged into absurdity"[1] and Camus engages more and more. By engaging however, he deals with abstract questions on the human condition. Although the references are not direct, the era shapes him; the trajectory of his treatment of the absurd shows that between *The Outsider* (1940; written before the war, during the time he left his native country, finding himself alone in a foreign country) and *The Plague* (written in large during the war when he participated in collective resistance) the opposition facing the same absurd changes from 'I' to 'we'. On this same line there is a parallel evolution between the lyricism of *Nuptials*, (1939, written when he was still in Algeria), *The Plague* and *The Outsider,* the emphasis shifts from nature to fraternity. Then he comes back on himself in *The Fall* when he feels alone between the extremists; in Algeria for example he is seen as radical by the right and conservative by the left. Politically, he rejects violent revolt, to which he prefers the passive resistance.

It must be remembered that all these works serve to express his philosophy; his theoretical work explicitly state it, then the novels, short stories and plays put it to work. A deceptively simple style of writing is an artistic choice that serves one of his principal desires as a writer; widespread comprehension. He produced a body of work that may seem pessimistic but we must not ignore traits that show a desire for happiness. He said of himself: "Pessimistic with regards to the human condition, I am optimistic when it comes to man."[2]

I want to show that throughout his major novels there are two stylistic discourses that function together to create one stylistic dichotomy: a detached lucidity that describes the absurdity of the human condition and a living lyricism that often evokes what refuses the absurd.

I understand the absurd according to Camus as the confrontation between what is expected of existence ("the human call") and what there really is. Our

---

[1] P.-G Castex and P. Surer, 154.

[2] P.-G Castex and P. Surer, 156

expectations and our lives are not absurd; the absurd is born from the confrontation of the two[3]. For me, Camus' lyricism is the stylistic expression of we often refer to as 'the revolt' in his work. The revolt is the refusal to accept absurdity as reality in favour of an alternative. Be it poetically evoking that which seems to answer this same 'human call' or the sense brotherhood that is found by bathing with a friend, or the beauty of Algerian countryside. What refuses the absurd demonstrates the means for progress. By demonstrating this bipolar stylistic discourse, I identify one of many implicit dichotomies present in Camus' writing that contributes to the totality of the writer's artistic expression. Camus' nihilism recognizes a way to no longer be nihilist.

Absurdism

Camus describes his comprehension of the absurd as a divorce; for him the absurd is born from the divorce of "a state of being and a certain reality". We can interpret this divorce as the dissonance that exists between man's hopes and what he achieves in reality. The absurd is neither man's hope or bleak reality but a confrontation of the two; human condition.

"Mother died today. Or maybe yesterday, I don't know[4]"; the sentence with which we are introduced to Meursault at the beginning of *The Outsider*. He talks about his mother's death without plunging himself into it. He doesn't ask how this came to happen. He regrets nothing. He states the fact that his mother is dead as he would observe the weather. Here and throughout this novel, this sombre, lucid manner with which Meursault perceives his surroundings permits the narrative to be understood as "absurdist". A similarly cold and detached narrative perspective is just as immediately evident in *The Plague*. Although it is a third person perspective, in revealing himself to be Rieux, the narrator is just as subjective in theory and objective in practice as Meursault. This narrative distance is consciously taken by the fictional character/narrator as a commitment to the truth. Rieux "accepts only truth with no reserves". With this transparent narrative position in *The Outsider* and *The Plague* the narrator stands between the reader and the narrative, but we see through him and objects and events speak for

---

[3] Pierre Lapaire, 610.

[4] Camus, *The Outsider*, 9

themselves. Although Meursault may not be struck by his mother's death the reader certainly is, and even more so by his apparent detachment. Yet this transparent narrative position seems to be a commitment to objectivity that produces different results; Rieux does so to remove himself from the horror that surrounds him and give an impartial account of the plague. Without Rieux's logic, Meursault's insensitivity produces a more brutal effect.

The reader is not the only witness to Meursault's apparent detachment. Meursault's first person perspective objectively recounts the inevitable clash with a society unwilling to understand his detachment. This clash is a treatment of social rules that is present in all three novels. 'Social codes' are obviously expected to be followed at the risk of being punished by the majority; you have to cry at your mother's funeral, you have to want to get married, you have to hope to obtain a high social class. These rules are depicted and interacted with in two different ways throughout *The Outsider* and *The Fall*.

Meursault's interaction with these social rules brings about many paradoxes; he often describes much of his conduct by saying 'naturally' or 'like everyone else' but in reality he is in a very isolated social position. He appears to want to blend-in socially but there remain certain accepted social practices that to him are unnatural and therefore impossible. For example, during the questioning with the magistrate (chapter I, part II) Meursault refuses the opportunity to help himself because he knows that doing so could prevent him from getting the punishment he deserves. He cannot express a false regret and Meursault is the principal victim of the brutality of his truth.

On the other hand, Jean-Baptiste Clamence knows that one must know when to appear sad, in love, loyal or religious or risk being rejected like Meursault[5]. The world is a stage where men play their role and all are designated a "sign":

---

[5] Sophie Doudet, 164

"I know mine in any case; a double face, a charming Janus and above it the motto of the house; 'Don't rely on it'. On my cards: 'Jean-Baptiste Clamence, play-actor.'"[6]

By mastering and manipulating the game Clamence ridicules it. Let's take for example the 'role' he invents to seduce women:

"Hence I played the game. I knew they didn't like one to reveal one's purpose too quickly. First, there had to be conversation, fond attentions as they say. I wasn't worried about speeches, being a lawyer, nor about glances, having been an amateur actor during my military service. I often changed parts, but it was always the same play."[7]

For Clamence these social codes are no more that than the stage directions in an absurd spectacle. Camus often depicts social space in a very theatrical light and the court scene in *The Outsider* reminds us of this, yet where Clamence manipulates, Meursault is the victim:

"[...] my lawyer lost his temper. He asked Perez in what seemed to me an exaggerated tone of voice whether he'd noticed me 'not crying'. Perez said, 'No.' The Public laughed"[8].

The jury are the audience, Meursault is the villain, the prosecutor the hero and defence lawyer the laughing stock.

Camus said "the novel is no more than a philosophical concept put into images"[9]. This concept is played out via the dynamic between the camusian protagonist and the circumstances in which they find themselves. The protagonist may represent a certain value but the raison d'être of the circumstance is to test what they represent. The court room scene in *The Outsider* is a means of representing the absurd. In this case the absurd is expressed as social farce. In the most straightforward sense this process

---

[6] Camus, *The Fall*, 36.

[7] *Ibid*, 45

[8] Camus, *The Outsider*, 73

[9] Joël Malrieu, 155

achieves what it must; ensuring Meursault will be punished for the crime he has committed. But, in theory, Meursault's insistence on his own guilt renders the whole process redundant. In place of the simple court case of a guilty murderer prepared to openly admit to his guilt, the trial seems to develop into the social unveiling of he who lurks amongst them trying to blend in, but refuses to sacrifice his conception of normal in favour of the majority's:

> "And I felt something stirring up the whole room; for the first time I realised that I was guilty. The caretaker was asked to repeat the story of the white coffee and the cigarette."[10]

The insistence on this story's relevance to an unrelated murder becomes ridiculous. The jury seem more affected by Meursault having smoked and drank a coffee beside his mother's corpse than the fashion in which he murdered. Meursault's lawyer questions this event's relevance to the murder the prosecutor successfully responds "'I accuse this man of burying his mother like a heartless criminal."[11]

A similar sense of farce is obvious in *The Plague*. There is a stark contrast between Rieux's capacity to objectively describe a situation the way it is and the Oran authorities unwillingness to acknowledge the elephant in the room (i.e., the plague in Oran):

> "The question,' old Castel cut in almost rudely, 'is to know whether it's plague or not'.
> Two or three of the doctors present protested. The others seemed to hesitate. The prefect gave a start and hurriedly glanced towards the door to make sure it had prevented this outrageous remark from being heard."[12]

While social circumstance seems to be a means of expressing the absurd in the novels in question, the perception of self oscillates between rationality

---

[10] Camus, *The Outsider*, 71-72

[11] Camus, *The Outsider*, 76

[12] Camus, *The Plague*, 46

and absurdity. Rieux's rational sense of self and purpose provides stark contrast with those of Meursault and Jean-Baptiste Clamence.

Although Clamence purports a very assured image of himself can we really believe what he says? Oppositions such as the image Clamence wishes to give of himself and his actual image are central. For example, Clamence compares himself to Janus, the two faced Greek god with one face turned towards the future and the other towards the past. This idea can allow us to understand the portrait he gives of himself to have a double significance; one face is what he wants to be seen as, the other is reflected by this need itself to purport a certain image of himself. Tracing a trajectory of his state of self, with the present of the narrative being the end point, he begins as the 20th century man par excellence:

> "[…]a man at the height of his powers, in perfect health, generously gifted, skilled in bodily exercises as in those of the mind, neither rich nor poor, sleeping well and fundamentally pleased with himself without showing this otherwise than by a happy sociability. You will readily see how I can speak, without modesty, of a successful life."[13]

Yet moving forward, this apparently impenetrable confidence is very easily deconstructed. Stopping at during an evening stroll at the Pont des Arts in Paris, he hears someone laugh behind his back. All of a sudden this "happy sociability" that he uses as a means to show his self contentment is brought into question. The very thought, even in passing, that someone could laugh at someone so happy with themselves turns the totalitarian universe constructed on vain foundations in which Clamence had seen himself at the centre upside down[14].

At home later that same evening Clamence looks in the mirror and considers what he sees not as a reflection but as a representation. Once again there is this idea of a duplicate self, where the exterior and interior selves are flip sides of the same coin: "My reflection was smiling in the mirror, but it seemed to me my smile was double [. . .]"[15] The choice of 'mon image' (as in

---

[13] Camus, *The Fall,* 22

[14] Sophie Doudet, 169

[15] Camus, *The Fall,* 31

Camus' original text) is quite vague. Although O'Brien has translated it as 'my reflection', this could possibly take away from the author's intention. Camus' choice separates appearance and the actual state of self; Clamence seems to observe his own reflection from an objective perspective. Yet this idea itself of a dissonance between reality and the reflection that one must accept as identical to this reality is a surrealistic impression which is even more present in *The Outsider:*

> ". . . I looked at myself in my tin plate. My reflection seemed to stay serious even when I tried to smile at it . . . and for the first time in several months, I clearly heard the sound of my own voice. I recognised it as the one that had been ringing in my ears for days on end and I realised that all that time I'd been talking to myself"[16]

The opposite of Clamence until the Pont des Arts, Meursault hardly has a perception of self. Instead, he seems willing to accept how others see him as his true state of self. Although he does not recognise himself in either lawyer's speeches he never objects out of commitment to objectivity:

> "At that point though I listened because he said, 'it's true that I killed a man.' Then he went like that, saying 'I' every time he meant me (. . .)It seemed to me that it was just another way of excluding me from the proceedings, reducing me to insignificance and, in a sense, substituting himself for me."

At this point his perception of self is entirely generated not by himself and his actions but everything that is attributed to him by others, so much so that his lawyer hijacks Meursault's person by switching from "he" to "I". Once again this transparency contributes to Meursault being opaque character; he is there but he is merely a reflection of what other says he is, this in turn makes all the more mysterious what his actual image may be. The dissonance between the imagined self (i.e. the image one has of one's self) and the reflection of the self brings us back to Camus' definition of the absurd as "a state of being and a certain reality".

---

[16] Camus, *The Outsider,* 65

Camus' absurd is the difference to what is thought to be real and what actually is real. This understanding of Camus' absurd and the style in which it is expressed is essentially a series of perception. It can be understood in the order in which it has been laid out here; the detached manner in which the narrative is presented by the narrator, the manner in which the protagonist and the circumstance to which they must submit confront perceive each other and the way in which the self is perceived and the discourse used to express this are the stylistic elements from which Camus' absurd is constructed. Man's call is met by the world's unreasonable silence.

Lyricism

Radically opposed to the sombre style that Camus uses to evoke the Absurd, Lyricism in Camus' work is a vivid and rich means of recognising what refuses the absurd.

If we can look through the state of detachment that seems to define Meursault the first time that we come across him, there are moments of sensitivity that ought to be impossible for a character who's *raison d'être* we initially conceive to be having nothing to do with humanity. A sunny day hits him like "a slap". He never takes account of the time; he only notices an absence or presence of sunlight. This sensitivity brings about a much more vivid lexical field through which Meursault abruptly evokes his surroundings: "For two hours now the day had stood still, for two hours it had been anchored in an ocean of molten metal"[17]. Following this idea of closeness to the most basic natural elements, it has been said that even his name is made from natural elements: Meursault = Mer (Sea) +Soleil (Sun) +Eau (Water)[18]. This perception that is at the same time detached and trenched in it's surroundings is a natural perception, which is to say that he feels so obliged to surrender to natural conditions that what would be at the top of another character's agenda does not cross his mind:

---

[17] Camus, *The Outsider,* 49

[18] Joel Malrieu, 131.

> "I realised now that I only had to turn round and it would all be over. But the whole beach was reverberating in the sun and pressing against me from behind. I took a few steps towards the spring."[19]

This way of perceiving the world that depends so strongly on natural conditions is almost animalistic; he follows where it leads him.

Proximity to nature is a theme often present in Camus' work and perhaps nowhere more so than in *Nuptials*. Camus, himself the first person narrator, shares his reactions to the Algerian countryside, where he shows a deep desire to experience the totality of his surroundings to a very profound level. He wants to "tie onto his skin the embrace for which the earth and sea sigh together, lips to lips". He "needs to plunge into the sea, nude." He loves the sensation of being immersed in water as much as Meursault or Tarrou. Written during the same period of his career as *Nuptials, The Outsider* shows a similar desire for closeness to all that is natural but in a style that is consciously more sombre. In both cases, the narrator shows a desire to "harmonise his breath with the turbulent sighs of the world"[20].

In *The Plague* this theme is not as central yet there are certain similarities that can be found between *Nuptials*'s narrator, Meursault and Rambert. He wants to escape the quarantine in Oran because what he understands to be freedom (his lover, the country) is unreachable within the limits of this town. These passions are much the same as Meursault's: the smell of summer, the neighbourhood he loves, the evening sky, Marie's dresses and her laugh. Both only understand their freedom and how much it is worth to them when they are locked away from it (be it Oran in quarantine or an Algiers prison). To establish a link from *Nuptials* to *The Plague*, it is interesting that Camus himself, who we understand to be the narrator of *Nuptials*, said that Rambert was the character to which he felt the closest[21]. One can easily imagine that the narrator of *Nuptials* would feel just as grief-stricken if he could no longer freely access what he understands to be liberty: the right to experience the sea, the earth and the woman he loves.

---

[19] Camus, *The Outsider*, 49

[20] Camus, *Noces,suivi de L'Été,* 13 (translation from French my own)

[21] Roger Quilliot, 176

Throughout certain works, the protagonist displays a burning desire to seize the moment in time where he finds himself. Roger Quilliot used an interesting term to put this theme into context: Romanticism of the present. All these images of states of self projected on nature lead to a temptation to use the word 'romanticism' but what separates Camus from any romantic writer is rejection of nostalgia; the present is the catalyst for this fervent desire. This idea is illustrated most clearly in *The Outsider*. Al though there isn't the constant yearning that we see in *Nuptials*, there is a rejection of monotony, to which the total experience of the present , be it positive or negative, is preferred. This culminates during the final moments of the narrative:

> As if this great outburst of anger had purged all my ills, killed all my hopes , I looked up at the mass of signs and stars in the night sky and laid myself open for the first time to the benign indifference of the world. And finding it so much like myself, in fact so fraternal, I realised that I'd been happy, and that I was still happy. For the final consummation and for me to feel less lonely, my last wish was that there should be a crowd of spectators at my execution and they should greet me with cries of hatred. [22]

This "benign indifference" is the unreasonable silence of the world that Camus refers to in his definition of the absurd. Acceptance is impossible and society refuses to ignore him, so if he is obliged to be judged he wants it to be a judgement executed in the most sincere fashion. Meursault's function as a character is to act as a means through which all that is natural and honest is expressed; if he was innocent he would wish that someone would see this but as he is guilty he wants to be seen as the criminal he is. Rather than regretting the past act of rendering himself a criminal, he finally finds solace by realising that for the first time he is being perceived for what he actually is.

Among the stylistic bipolarities of the narratives in question, perhaps the most extreme is found when analysing the way in which Camus fictionalises human relations. Meursault's trial, Oran's authorities self-imposed paralysis, Jean-Baptiste Clamence's formula for seducing women; social interaction can be depicted in a cynically satirical light.

---

[22] Camus, *The Outsider*, 95

Yet this is not to say human relationships are constantly debased; satire serves to ridicule cynical social practices. It is the practice which inspires the situation that's cynical, not necessarily the writer's own opinion. Amid the spectacle of Meursault's trial faith in man is subtly expressed. Céleste, the owner of a restaurant where Meursault eats but "also a friend" is questioned to give a character statement for Meursault. He describes the murder as "unfortunate". It's clear that he doesn't want to say anything that would potentially constitute evidence against Meursault but at the same time this isn't possible when there is so much evidence against him. Meursault sees that "tears come to his eyes and his lips tremble". The fact that a mere acquaintance would not only avoid joining in with his accusers but be so moved and still resist the temptation to lie makes Meursault "experience the desire to kiss a man" for the first time. It is not because Céleste wants to help him but the fact that he acknowledges that he could not possibly help Meursault without lying and still refuses to. To further illustrate this, Meursault isn't moved when Raymond and Masson falsely give the impression to know him very well in order to help him.

The relationship between Rieux and Tarrou in *The Plague* demonstrates furthermore this faith in man's capacity to overlook immediate circumstances in order to remain loyal to a greater moral truth. Coming from two very different backgrounds, circumstance places them together. Although opposing the same adversary, their positional logic differs; Rieux does so to practice his profession, while Tarrou revolts against all that kills men. On ideological and personal levels they don't share much, yet their relationship illustrates man's implicit selflessness. Beyond the most obvious selflessness (fighting the plague), they are willing to look at something and admit to themselves that they may not see the same thing, but feel the same way:

> [...] the sea spread out before them, a gently heaving expanse of deep-piled velvet, supple and sleek as a creature of the wild. They sat down on a boulder facing the open. Slowly the waters rose and sank, and with their tranquil breathing sudden oily glints formed and flickered over the surface in a haze of broken lights. Before them the darkness stretched out into infinity. Rieux could feel under his hand the gnarled, weather-worn visage of the rocks, and a strange happiness possessed him. Turning to Tarrou, he caught a

glimpse on his friend's face of the same happiness, a happiness that forgot nothing, not even murder.[23]

Tarrou may not have this sameway of seeing things as Rieux, but he can allow himself to look beyond his own personal struggle, while never forgetting that everywhere men are dying, in order to accept that to a certain extent, everyone feels the same way as him.

There is a variety of intersexual relationships in the works in question: Raymond's brutality is undoubtedly condemned, Rieux affectionately misses his wife, Jean-Baptiste Clamence seduces out of vanity and Rambert longs to see his lover. From a purely stylistic standing point, women are objects that inspire aesthetically animated passages, and although such a representation could possibly lead to a broader question on gender roles, it remains necessary to identify the method in which female characters are described in these works to understand Camus' style. Meursault's relationship with Marie seems to contain elements from many of these scenarios. For example, marrying her 'would be all the same to him' yet when he sees her in court he displays a deep familiarity with her physical appearance; "From where I was sitting I could just make out the slight swell of her breasts and the familiar little pout of her lower lip" [24]. Their emotional link may not be profound but there is certainly an appreciation of an 'object' that appeals to physical desire. In *Nuptials*, the appreciation borders on admiration:

> "I remember at least one big, magnificent girl who had danced the whole afternoon. She wore a necklace made of jasmine with her tight blue dress was dampened with sweat from the small of her back to her thighs. She laughed while dancing and threw her head back. When she passed by tables, she left an odour mixed of flowers and skin."[25]

This is not to say that this is the only way in which women are treated (see Rieux's relationship with his wife), yet for the purpose of this

---

[23] Camus, *The Plague*, 246

[24] Camus, *The Outsider*, 74

[25] Camus, *Noces suivi de L'Été*, 40 (translation from French my own)

discussion of Camus' style, the evocation of women's physical appearance produces an aesthetic effect similar to the one produced in the other cases highlighted.

This section serves to highlight the vivid, aesthetically pleasing lyricism in the works in question; be it closeness to nature, a burning desire to experience the temporal present, faith in man's tendency towards selflessness and honesty or an appreciation of woman's physical appearance. Camus reserves this style for what refuses the absurd and responds to 'the human call'.

Stylistic Dichotomy

After identifying the grouping of these two extremes the logical progression is to find out how these two discourses interact. What is the purpose of putting these two styles together? How do they work together and complement each other? What does the meeting of the two produce? The paradoxes at the heart of the works in question expose a balance of the absurd and the lyrical that is central to what we understand to be the camusian aesthetic.

To begin this question of a link between these two stylistic discourses, it is beneficial to bear in mind a Camus quote which introduces *The Myth of Sisyphus:* "…this book declares that even within the limits of nihilism it is possible to find the means to proceed beyond nihilism"[26]. In recognising the causes and sources of nihilism, its limits are identified and it's possible to go beyond this nihilism. Taking the novels as the illustration of the theoretical works, this idea of balancing the sources of nihilism with the means for not being nihilist is widespread. The absurd sentiment does not prevent the search for happiness. By applying this quote to the works in question, we begin to receive the message produced by this stylistic bipolarity. *The Outsider* establishes solitude of confronting the absurd. *The Plague* shows the collective facing the same absurd. *The Fall,* not following the same thematic trajectory, concentrates on man's implicit tendency towards duplicity. Yet once the source of nihilism is identified, so too are it's limits. After the living lyricism of *Nuptials, The Outsider* retains this passion for

---

[26] Camus, *The Myth of Sisyphus,* V

pureness by refusing the absurd. Faith in man is further explored by calling for a revolt against the absurd in *The Plague*. *The Fall*, still not on the same path, weakens nihilism via the negation of negativity. Progress beyond the absurd takes place only after recognising the absurd.

In *The Outsider* the protagonist's perception of his surroundings and of himself is so detached that he cannot socially interact in a place where one's self awareness and acceptance of responsibility are the means by which participation can be accepted. He is as a result seen as a monster by others. Yet from the reader's privileged position, as witness to his lucid honestly, he is exposed as a sensitive being in a very profound relationship with nature.

To briefly synopsize this narrative, one could say that the this novel serves the dual purpose as an illustration of the absurd set out in *The Myth of Sisyphus,* and of man's capacity to come to terms with this absurd to progress beyond it. Meursault's passive refusal to justify his actions seems absurd yet this is what makes him consistent. To attempt to give logic to Meursault's actions would be to contextualise them in terms of human condition (i.e. the absurd), when the very refusal to do so is why he exists: Meursault is man who will have nothing to do with the human condition. He therefore cannot lie, he cannot follow social rules, and he cannot differentiate between what he thinks and what he says. The only forces he submits to are the most natural ones. This is what makes him the 'outsider' of the title.

For all his passivity, Meursault's nihilism is active; the action itself of refusal, passive as it may be, remains an active choice. From this point, the rebellion against the absurd is born. Yet Meursault's 'rebellion' is not consciously committed, his self perception is so warped that he sees himself "like all the others" and qualifies much of what he does by saying "naturally". Being an untraditional protagonist and, one can be tempted to call Meursault an "anti-hero" but is this applicable to the character who is unaware of differences between himself and the society he ought to stand-out from to justify the (anti-)'hero' title? Or is this the definition of the anti-hero par excellence? By dying he wins a sort of moral victory by never giving in. By letting himself go, events flow over him like water.

Although *The Outsider* and *The Plague* demonstrate a similarly active nihilism, the rebellion committed is passive in the former and active in the later. These works show the same absurd but the faces opposing them are not the same:

> "*The Outsider* describes man's nudity in front of the absurd; *The Plague,* the profound equivalence of all points of view in face of the same absurd. It's a progression that will go further in subsequent works. But what's more is that *The Plague* demonstrates that the absurd teaches nothing. This is the ultimate progress."[27]

Faith in the collective's ability to come to terms with the plague opposes the surrounding horror. Rieux is so committed to objectively paying tribute to this that he does not invest himself in his narrative. His reason for creating this account is to serve as a reminder of man's ability to form a collective but also his tendency to forget this. The plague is an opposition large enough for the collective Camus wishes to pay tribute to. Such terms make us think of heroism but the cold sobriety of Rieux's narrative never allows his homage to go so far. The resistance described is not heroic but human. The tribute is to the average. The circumstances are extraordinary but the characters are not. Average morality wins a victory against badness; not by ending the plague but by allowing themselves to develop even within the temporal and physical space of the plague. The oppositions are widespread; good will instead of heroism, health instead of salvation, and humanity in place of saintliness[28]. The limits of nihilism are very clearly marked here; they are (meta)physically present in Oran's walls. Yet these closed walls do not prevent the characters progressing mentally and emotionally beyond them. Camus justifies that even within the limits of nihilism the means for progressing beyond this nihilism are obtainable. Faith is declared and the call to revolt is made.

This comprehension of Camus' style as a balance of extremes is a standing-point from which one can access meaning to various aspects of his work. Victory through death, flourishing in a confide space; such contradictions are omnipresent and are often a means of presenting a paradox which permits theme to take on a binary function. This sense of implicit dichotomy is omniscient in *The Fall.* We can use Roger Quilliot's identification of Apollonian and Dionysian tendencies in Camus' work as a means of contextualising Jean-Baptiste Clamence. Whereas at one end we have Rieux's cold Apollonian reason and at the other, *Nuptials'* narrator has a Dionysian appreciation for any aesthetic appeal, Jean Baptiste Clamence

---

[27] Roger Quilliot, 182

[28] Ibid, 184

acknowledges both extremes by having traits that respond to both sets of values. His elastic morals allow him to engage with vice in hedonist measure but his profound self-awareness allows him to systematically rationalise this.

This simultaneous engagement of polar discourses reflects *The Fall*'s position in the evolution of the stylistic dichotomy; the progression between *Nuptials*, *The Outsider* and *The Plague* is linear and conveniently comprehensible in the same order as their chronological appearance. Trying to impose *The Fall* on this same scale becomes problematic. Whereas in the previous works the two discourses in question are independent from each other and can be separated to be sequentially discussed, the distinction between the two in *The Fall* becomes blurred. The sea for example, the point of departure for a lyrical passage in *The Plague,* is transformed into an image of the infinity of the absurd (chapter 5). In this passage and elsewhere we have the impression that even lyrical discourse is not immune to Clamence's cynical satire. To add to the sea as a symbol for the infinite abyss, scenic islands are reduced to a point to reign above others, acting out of kindness serves the only purpose of having others think you are generous, accusing oneself is a way of implicating others. Clamence acknowledges that "separating the truth and lies is difficult" in his narrative that exposes the weakness of reader's position that depends on the narrator's honesty. The interest of the narrative is not its subject but the manner in which the subject is presented.

The way in which Clamence reveals his supposed 'profession' says more about the nature of the narrative of which it is part than about Clamence himself:

> I accuse myself up hill and down dale. It's not hard, for I have now acquired a memory. But let me point out that I don't accuse myself crudely, beating my breast. No, I navigate skilfully, multiplying distinctions and digressions too – in short I adapt my words to my listener and lead him to go me one better. I mingle what concerns me and what concerns others , I choose the features we have in common, the experiences we have endured together, the failings we share – good form, the man of the moment, in fact, such as reigns in me and in others. With all that I construct a portrait which is the image of all and of no one. A mask, in short, rather like those carnival masks which are both lifelike and stylized so that they make people say: 'Why surely I've met him!' When the portrait is finished, as it is this evening, I show it with great sorrow: 'This, alas, is what I am!' The prosecutor's

charge is finished. But at the same time the portrait I hold out to my contemporaries becomes a mirror.[29]

He recites his lines to win the confidence of his audience. The listener, taken by a false sense of fraternity, empties his heart. In doing so he reduces himself to zero. As a result, Clamence can take back his superior position, he 'reigns' again. Penance allows the 'judge-penitent' to deliver judgement.

Yet this is not to say that *The Fall*'s binary discourse serves the purpose of deride lyricism. It does not lose its stature from previous works because the narrative voice in *The Fall* is intentionally turned on itself. Rather than belittling the subject of his own discourse, Clamence decreases his own credibility as a legitimate narrator. As a result, his own negativity, rather than the subject of his discourse, is what is negated. The call to revolt is no longer so fervent as in *The Outsider* or *The Plague* but the critique of misconduct is ever-present.

The progressive trajectory of the relationship between these stylistic poles reflects the evolution of Camus' treatment of the absurd and the different manners it is opposed. As *The Fall* prevents a linear depiction of this progression, the most logical approach is chronological: *Nuptials* captures an ardent joie de vivre. *The Outsider* defines and engages with the absurd and opposes it in a manner that meanders between active and passive. *The Plague* shows an absurd which sets itself up as totalitarian and underlines "the profound equivalence of all points of view" yet man's capacity to surpass the most imposed limits, both physical and metaphysical, appears to raise a question to which the opposing side cannot respond. *The Fall* mixes discourses to the effect that it is constructed upon a series of binary poles and one discourse only serves to embellish another, yet Clamence's own recognition of his dishonesty opposes the infallibility of his narrative externally to the text itself; all of the 'values' presented in the text are subject to scathing satire. The two discourses function in a stylistic dichotomy that conveys the bipolar nature of Camus' style as a novelist.

---

[29] Camus, *The Fall*, 102

Conclusion

Albert Camus is most widely recognised in connection with the absurdist literary movement yet to not look beyond the absurd in his work is to miscomprehend him as a writer. Yes, the absurd is confronted and defined from the very outset of his work, but the importance is not what this definition consists of, but the act of confrontation itself. Because the absurd is not subject to a simple summary or composition, but rather it is derived from the product of other elements. The dissonance between what is expected of existence and what existence actually amounts to is Camus' absurd. All of this is presented for the purpose of being opposed. But, this is only part of the fabric with which Camus constructs a fictional representation of the human condition as an existential experience. The absurd and its opposition are the totality of the representation in question. The agent mostly commonly described opposing the absurd is the revolt; this refers to humanity's implicit capacity to use the recognition of the absurd as a lesson to progress beyond the absurd. The interaction between the two is the tension responsible for the interest of much of Camus' work. The revolt is described as the evidence of progress, as Camus declares in *The Rebel*; "I revolt, therefore we are".

These values that balance Camus' writing are stylistically accessible via the discourses identified here. We can justify the absurd and revolt being negative and positive values that counteract and balance each other by comparing these discourses and examining the manner in which they function together to construct one stylistic dichotomy. Neither outweighs the other and this is one of many ways in which Camus' writing is a fine work of balance.

Works Cited

Works studied:

Camus, Albert. *The Outsider*. Trans. Joseph Laredo, London, Hamilton, 1982.

---. *The Plague.* Trans. Robin Buss, London, Penguin, 2010.

---. *The Fall.* Trans. Joseph O'Brien, Middlesex, Penguin, 1963.

---. *Noces suivi de L'Été* , les éditions Gallimard, Paris, Gallimard, 1959.

Works by the same author:

Camus, Albert, *The Myth of Sisyphus.* Trans. Joseph O'Brien, New York, Vintage, 1955.

---. *L'homme révolté*, Paris, Gallimard, 1951.

Criticism:

Doudet, Sophie, *"Dossier", La Chute,* Folio plus classiques edition, Barcelona, Gallimard, 2008.

Pierre Lapaire, "Un Style polarisé ; éléments de la binarité stylistique chez Camus", *The French Review*, (4) 1993, p.610. Web. Nov. 2011.

Lazare, Donald, *The Unique Creation of Albert Camus*, London, Yale University Press, 1973.

Mailhot, Laurent, *Albert Camus ou l'imagination du désert,* Montreal, Montreal University Press, 1973.

Malrieu, Joël, "Dossier", *L'étranger*, folio plus edition, France, Gallimard, 1996.

Quilliot, Roger, *La mer et les Prisons ; Essai sur Albert Camus*, France, Gallimard, 1970

Rey, Pierre-Louis, L'étranger : profil d'une œuvre, Paris, Hatier, 1991.

Broader context:

Castex, P.-G. et Surer, P., Manuel *des études littéraires françaises : XXe siècle*, Paris, Hachette, 1967.

Kayser, Wolfgang, "Qui raconte le roman ?" in Gérard Genette and Tzevtan Todorov, *Poétique du récit*, Paris, Seuil, 1977, p.59-p83.

Camus' Literary Criminal and the Law: Loathing the Outsider

By Stefan Lancy

Introduction

Albert Camus' infamous literary criminal, Meursault, is a remarkable and disconcerting creation[1]. Colin Wilson identifies him as a man with 'no genius, no unusual feelings to bestow' yet his character has captivated generations of readers[2]. He is difficult to empathise with, his freezing honesty and inability to lie simultaneously draws the reader to him and then repels. Perhaps the now famous opening lines of *The Outsider* most succinctly illustrate his character:

> Mother died today. Or maybe yesterday. I can't be sure.[3]

Who is this startlingly frank man? Why is his tone so indifferent? In an Afterword to *The Outsider*, Camus summed up his work by saying that 'any man who doesn't cry at his mother's funeral is liable to be condemned to death'[4]. This is indeed the case in the text where Meursault is ostensibly condemned to death for the murder of an Algerian man. However his lack of repentance and unwillingness to seek forgiveness, in the words of the prosecutor, mark him as a man without a soul with 'no access to humanity nor to any of the moral principles which protect the human heart'[5]. Camus goes on to say that the hero of his book is an outsider to the society in which

---

[1] Albert, Camus, *The Outsider*, (Joseph Laredo trans, 2000).

[2] Colin Wilson, *The Outsider*, (2001), 27.

[3] Camus, as above n 1, 9.

[4] Ibid, 118.

[5] Ibid, 98.

he finds himself tried – on 'the outskirts of life, solitary and sensual'[6]. He says what he believes to be true and will not lie or hide his feelings. It is for this reason that society feels threatened by him. This is evidenced when he is asked if he regrets his crime, to which he replies that he is more annoyed than truly regretful. Camus argues that it is this nuance that condemns Meursault – his conviction for 'an absolute truth'[7].

Society will almost always look for repentance in criminals, to find a human side to their persons - something we can sympathise or pity them for. Meursault will not bow to this demand. A man who has committed a murder generally shows some interest in what he has done and what will be done to him. He may weep, protest or seek a strong defence to increase his chances of acquittal or appeal to our mercy. Meursault's indifference marks him as something other than the common man. It disconcerts his questioners who put it down to 'callousness'[8]. The prosecutor colours Meursault's heart as 'so empty that it forms a chasm which threatens to engulf society'[9].

Subsequently, Meursault is struck by the 'unreality' of his trial, often compared to Franz Kafka's *The Trial* in this sense. For Wilson the trial 'had the least importance' for Meursault and the people admonishing him but simple figures foisted onto him 'in the equally unreal years I was then living through'[10]. It is not until the final pages of the text when Camus reveals this secret of Meursault's indifference, his lack of interest in the unreality of his existence as it does not torment him. It is only the imminent prospect of death that awakens our non-hero who, to 'feel less lonely', wishes only for the crowds to greet his execution with 'cries of hatred'[11].

*

---

[6] Ibid, 118.

[7] Ibid, 119.

[8] Wilson, as above n 2, 29.

[9] As above n 1, 98.

[10] As above n 2, 29.

[11] As above n 1, 117.

With this in mind, what questions do *The Outsider* and Camus' other works present to a lawyer or scholar? I argue that the text presents a fertile field in which to delve further into questions of law in literature through the text's ability to question legal norms. It poses fundamental questions concerning how judges, lawyers and other members of the legal profession, as well as the arms of law enforcement, assert social norms and how they deal with an individual who is substantially at odds with a traditional understanding of the law's role in society – the Outsider. Indeed, such questions are explicitly raised in Richard A. Posner's analysis of *The Outsider*[12]. Conversely, Weisberg focuses his analysis on how a legal system struggles to fit a figure into easily defined categories in order to make decisions (guilty, innocent, manslaughter, murder)[13].

When a text such as *The Outsider* addresses the social and ethical facets of society's existence and structural norms, the language of literature and the language of law come together and address the same aspects of life, with at times varying degrees of similarity[14]. Literature can probe emotions, narrative and character whereas law mostly concerns itself with facts, codes and punishment. Literature is the mirror to the face of the law. The text's appropriation of the law can be interpreted and discussed, 'read as (a) constitutive text, as forms of ethical and political action'[15].

This essay will assert that *The Outsider* questions the conventional wisdom of legal discourse and reflects an at times ugly image of the law and how it treats its unwilling subjects. An image that is fearful and vengeful, unwilling to tolerate outsiders, unable to conceive of appropriate methods of punishment or understanding when faced with unwilling subjects. In particular, I will analyze why the law sees Meursault as guilty not just of criminal offences, but as a person, why the trial is farcical in its creation of the accused and its desire to subject Meursault to its authority.

---

[12] Richard A. Posner, *Law and Literature*, (revised ed, 1998), 44-45.

[13] Richard H. Weisberg, *The Failure of the Word: The Protagonist as Lawyer in Modern Fiction* (1984).

[14] James, B, White, 'What Can a Lawyer Learn from Literature?', Book review of *Law and Literature: A Misunderstood Relation* by R. A. Posner (1989), 102 *Harvard Law Review* 2014.

[15] Ibid, 2032.

Part 1: The Witness, The Guilt and Law

Meursault's Guilt or the Law's - Which Is It?

Meursault's 'guilt' lies at the heart of *The Outsider* and the most disturbing aspect of Meursault's guilt lies in its ambiguity. It is Camus' reluctance or intention not to disclose just how much it is Meursault's absence of remorse rather than the crime itself that condemns him. As Camus outlined in the Afterword, Meursault's apparent callousness is used to colour the injustice of what befalls him before the law. An inoffensive act, not crying at his mother's funeral, is constructed as a sign of a truly sinister man. As he himself notes, 'a great deal was said about me, possibly even more about me than about my crime'[16]. Posner even asserts that 'a case can be made that Meursault is a psychopath'[17]. Others have asserted that he is in fact 'the sanest character in Twentieth Century literature'[18]. Meursault's murder of the Algerian is but a pretext. In order for Camus to create his existentialist hero, he had to commit a reprehensible crime but remain innocent in essence, to be later wronged by the justice system. Without it, his monotonous life would have never drawn the eyes of the law. Immediately thereafter, the text is infused with the somber certainty that Meursault will be found guilty.

Meursault 'does not play the game' and wholly submits to the scrutiny of the law without protest. What marks the text as a seminal work is the depiction of the law's inability to resolve human ambiguity. Meursault is effectively a spectator at his own trial, distanced by his 'estrangement from the society the court represents' who, like Voltaire's *Candide*, sees an at times astonishing and amusing process being played out[19]. The court is seen to be 'conducting the case independently' of Meursault and his 'fate was being decided without anyone asking (his) opinion'[20]. Meursault is thus condemned by his alienation. He dies for a crime many have argued could have been defeated

---

[16] Camus, as above n 1, 95.

[17] Camus, as above n 12, 89.

[18] See generally, Weisberg, as above n 11, at 116, 120. .

[19] Ernest Simon, 'Palais de Justice and Poetic Justice in Albert Camus' "The Stranger"' (1991) 3 *Cardozo Studies in Law and Literature* 1, 122.

[20] Ibid.

with a self-defence claim at the time the text is set[21]. Instead, every detail of the trial is used to demonstrate that the judges resent the murderer not for his crime, but for himself[22].

It has been argued that the judges want to 'destroy the truth he embodies' and the challenge he presents to society as an Outsider[23]. This truth is presented in Meursault's knowledge that individuals will forever be isolated from one another by their very human condition and his actions thus reflect an instinct that human relationships do not exist and the idea of homogenous community is mistaken[24]. Furthermore, Meursault presents the grim conclusion that 'everybody knows that life isn't worth living', reflecting a bleak and sobering outlook on human existence, indeed even purpose[25]. But the law has its own stories to tell and views to assert and it will silence the stories it does not want to hear or conform to its protocols and proceedings. Meursault's is such a story. His is one of neither guilt nor innocence when it comes 'before the law' (in Kafka's terms) where he is really deemed guilty until proven innocent[26]. As Camus himself wrote in his essay, "Reflections on the Guillotine", every society contains criminals but no one is ever absolutely guilty or innocent – a major argument he puts forward against capital punishment. *The Outsider* is an indication of his later conviction that no system of justice can be considered legitimate or just where it murders its own citizens[27].

---

[21] See Louis Hudon, "*The Stranger* and the Critics", *Yale French Studies*, No. 25, Albert Camus (1960), 59-64.

[22] René Girard, 'Camus' Stranger Retried' (1963) 79 *PMLA* 5, 521.

[23] Ibid.

[24] Hudon, as above n 21, 62.

[25] Camus, as above n 1, 109.

[26] David Caroll, 'Symposium: Failure of the Word: Guilt by "Race": Injustice in Camus' The Stranger' (2005) 26 *Cardozo Law Review* 2331, 2338.

[27] On June 17, 1947, Camus wrote about 'how impossible it is to say that anyone is absolutely guilty, and hence impossible to decree total punishment'. *Notebooks, 1942-1951*, at 157 (Justin O'Brien trans, 1966). In 1957, in '*Reflections on the Guillotine, in Resistance, Rebellion, and Death*', he challenges the right of society to impose the death penalty on anyone: 'Capital punishment is not simply death…It is a murder." (Justin O'Brien trans, 1960), 199.

Meursault is judged guilty not for what he did, but for what he is – an Outsider – for what society and the judicial system construct him as being (or subsequently transform him into) through the stories of his life recounted by the prosecution. His soul is judged as 'dark' as is his strange 'nature' and inner being. Despite seeing himself as 'an ordinary man of good qualities', his intelligence and philosophical detachment from the vagaries of human existence are reworked into 'crushing accusations', a barrage of which he cannot withstand[28]. He dies for 'refusing to play the game' when in fact he often does. This is seen when he lies to the police to protect his dubious friend, Raymond. Some critics, notably Caroll, see Meursault's guilt as extending beyond this sense of alienation, into a characterization of Meursault being 'an alien enemy of the collective', the French state[29]. This is seen in Meursault's refusal to repent before the judge when he beseeches him to do so – seen here by Caroll as a rejection of French identity. His refusal also marks a broader refusal to assimilate into a homogenous group in colonial Algeria. This leads the magistrate to condemn him as an enemy of 'Christian France' and refer to him as 'Mr. Antichrist'.

Hudon takes Meursault's character to be 'nothing less than an intellectual, free from all hierarchies of values' and who subscribes to none[30]. He has freed himself from what others consider to be normal 'values', materialistic ambition and thus is free to be totally honest. This can be seen in his luckless lover, Marie, who feels the full brunt of his honesty when he tells her that love 'didn't mean anything' and who must later propose to him herself[31]. His consciousness is highly attuned to the pitfalls of illusion and human frailty, intensely attached to the few things in life which are without question – the sun, the beach, death and so on. Yet he does not despair for his 'life was a good as another and that I wasn't at all dissatisfied with mine', indeed he says he wasn't even unhappy[32]. His analytical consciousness does not turn him into the soulless monster the prosecution sees him as representing. Rather, as Camus points out, his character is one of searing honesty who sees 'no constructed image of the world, but an explosion of the real in incoherent

---

[28] See Matthew Ward, Translator's Note To Albert Camus, (Matthew Ward trans, 1988), 100.

[29] Carroll, as above n 26, 2336.

[30] Hudon, as above n 21, 63.

[31] Camus, as above n 1, 38.

[32] Camus, as above n 1, 44.

psychological fragments'[33]. Again this character is seen to confront both the norms proposed both by a religious, colonial culture and Western judicial demands.

Meursault's guilt can thus be seen as the embodiment of 'intersubjective warfare' fought between himself and the judges, representatives of the dichotomy between the Self and the Other[34]. Camus sets out to prove that society will punish the hero who acts according to his heart (or more accurately, his conscience and intellect). The truth of this statement is contentious but what is clear is that The Outsider reveals a tragedy keenly felt by those beyond the ready conception of a legal system. The court chooses to eschew the 'wholly negative ethic of tolerance' of 'others' to the 'stricter but loftier ethic of justice' and condemns him[35]. Meursault must die because it is impossible for society to allow him to live his own life according to his own philosophy. This is reflected in The Outsider's mood of despair and is captured in Meursault's tension between desiring solitude and seeking out 'the others' – his dying wish to be acknowledged, to be greeted 'with cries of hatred'[36]. A final acknowledgement of a desire to return to the company of others which cannot be satisfied.

Meursault's Fellow 'Others' – Camus Other Protagonists

This theme is later taken up in Camus' novel *The Fall* with its protagonist, a former defence barrister, Clamence[37]. In a five-day monologue in which he presents himself to a silent court, he urges the reader as witness to listen to his own self-judgment and findings of guilt. As in *The Outsider*, the final determination of guilt is generally reserved for the last moment (Oedipus in exile, Othello takes his own life, Josef K submits to execution) but Clamence sees his role as a 'judge-penitent', asserting that self-inflicted penance

---

[33] Hudon, as above n 21, 63.

[34] Girard, as above n 22, 525.

[35] Camus, as above n 1, 98.

[36] Camus, as above n 1, 117.

[37] Albert Camus, *The Fall*, (Robin Buss trans, 2006).

provides a solution to the neither absolute innocence nor guilt of humanity. Meursault's guilt attempts to reach this solution[38].

As mentioned above, Camus' trial scene operates to provide an external arena where the individual is pitted against society, to the misfortune of the former[39]. The guilty conscience of Meursault is determined by a hostile court. To find the self-determination of guilt by an individual, we must look to *The Fall* and the protagonist Clamence who is plagued by 'existential guilt' for failing to risk his life for another (a suicidal woman throwing herself off a bridge); placing him under a moral obligation to make reparations through admissions of guilt and desiring penance[40]. Clamence's self-trial culminates in his recognition of guilt but he chooses to repent through proclaiming his guilt in a 'public *mea culpa*'[41]. Thus Camus throws the question of guilt back onto the reader, the silent witness in this literary court-room – forcing one to formulate our own verdict, much like in *The Outsider*.

Like Meursault, Clamence exhibits no desire to remove himself from judgment nor escape the judgment of society – instead he is weighed down by the burden of self-judgment. A fate shared by Meursault who eventually comes to realize his own guilt but does not persecute himself for it. Although both are forced to face the judgment of others, Clamence's ultimate tribunal is that of his own conscience[42]. This is a significant development from *The Outsider*; reaffirming that one's conscience as the sole valid tribunal is highly significant. To make each man 'his own judge' breaks down the

---

[38] For an example of how Meursault's questionable guilt (raising questions of self-defence, manslaughter and mental capacity) is explored in university level criminal law courses and comparisons between the text and current American legislation see Robert Batey, 'Symposium: Law and Popular Culture: Literature in a Criminal Law Course Aeschylus, Burgess, Oates, Camus, Poe and Melville' (1998) 22 *Legal Studies Forum* 45, 8-14.

[39] It is worth noting that Camus himself had hands on experience in witnessing court room scenes as a journalist for the *Alger –Republican* and is seen as the source of his literary descriptions in the text. See Albert Camus, *Carnets, mai 1935 – février 1942* (Paris, 1962).

[40] 'Existential guilt' is defined in Martin Buber, 'Guilt and Guilt Feelings' (1957) *Psychiatry*, 114-29.

[41] Marilyn K. Yalom, 'Albert Camus and the Myth of The Trial' (1964) 25 *Modern Language Quarterly* 434, 448.

[42] Ibid, 449.

tension that exists in *The Outsider* between judgment and sympathy; the law's firm hand and the reader's emotional reaction to Meursault's end. Camus' later hero has taken the law's sword of justice and wielded it against himself, rejecting all other forms of higher authority.

Man is thus seen as being able to become the sole arbiter of his own existence. Camus may well pass judgment on society in *The Outsider* but he opts to focus on the more personal question of the self-trial in *The Fall*. Again, a link can be made here to Franz Kafka's *The Trial* where the image of a man on trial, accused by the incomprehensible law, defending and finally condemning himself, creates a desperate and frightening experience. Kafka's vision of the trial, like Meursault's own experience, culminates in a sense of guilt that extends guilt beyond the victim to all mankind[43]. Such a sense of shared guilt is also present in Camus' *The Plague* which contains another emotive trial scene where we see a crisis between witnessing injustice and balancing our own conscience[44]. Rieux, the narrator, is called to give evidence and feels a sense of responsibility to balance the restraint he feels as a law abiding citizen, and the urgency he feels to protect his fellow man from injustice:

> All the same, following the dictates of his heart, he had deliberately taken the victim's side and tried to share with his fellow citizens the only certitudes they had in common – love, exile and suffering.[45]

In Existentialist thought, human subjects are 'condemned to be free', asserting that each individual must face an immense anguish in trying to determine the meaning of things; often concluding that there is no human nature but only choice[46]. Such a philosophy can be used to fill the void left by those who fail to see, or do not recognize the regulations and power of the law. In *The Plague*, the law is shown to fail its citizens and legal problem

---

[43] Ibid, 450.

[44] See S. Felman, 'Crisis of Witnessing: Albert Camus' Postwar Writings' (1991), 3 *Cardozo Studies Law and Literature* 197. Albert Camus, *The Plague* (Gilbert S trans, 1957).

[45] Ibid, Camus, 278

[46] This is the view proposed by Jean Paul Sartre, 'Existentialism is a Humanism', (P. Mairet, trans) in Langiulli, (ed) *The Existentialist Tradition: Selected Writings* (1971), 393. There are of course divergent views.

solving does little to stem the outbreak of plague in the town. For example, as the plague rapidly spreads through the town, the law is seen as being unable to recognize human suffering and it introduces measures without 'any real discussion'[47]. The law is seen to resort to force to combat the 'spirit of lawlessness' that engulfs the town[48]. It is only when the main character, Rieux, is leaving the offices of the Prefect's in town that the law's operation is seen as flawed. Once removed from the law's stronghold (the Prefect's office) Rieux can see that people are suffering. It is only when we physically and psychologically distance ourselves from the sites of the law that one sees the reality of the human subjects' condition under the law. Rieux sees 'a woman screaming in agony...her arms towards him' but the legal mind cannot see what the healing hands of the town's doctors confront[49]. This is also seen in the depiction of legal discourse that is seen as heavily formalized and abstracted like in *The Outsider*. The law must act inflexibly for public welfare but in the trial scene, the very words of the law are abstracted and difficult to grasp. Seen where the 'defendant' is but 'the little man in the dock' and the law's 'priests', the lawyers, must don their red gowns to become 'another man, no longer genial or good natured'[50] – dehumanized and dehumanizing[51].

This existentialist critique of institutions that ignore individual pain is clearly evident in Camus' work, especially *The Outsider* and *The Plague*. The law is seen as so abstracted that it becomes entirely removed from the very persons and interests it claims to be concerned with and dedicated to preserve[52]. It is for this reason that Camus champions a form of self-trial and examination that fits comfortably into the sentiments expressed in Existentialist thought.

---

[47] In the text, the law rolls outs harsh measures to stem the outbreak of the plague, rationing sneaks in discreetly, at 76, martial law is imposed at 159.

[48] Camus, as above n 44, 108,

[49] Camus, as above n 44, 51.

[50] Camus, as above n 44, 230.

[51] Yalom, as above n 41, 4.

[52] Paul McHugh writes of another abstraction process in modern common law: "The law of negligence...is a tale of how a snail in a bottle finds itself imaginatively relocated in law twentieth-century high finance and deal-making. In the mind of the common lawyer, the common law's past is there to be put into the present" in 'The Common-Law Status of Colonies and Aboriginal "Rights": How Lawyers and Historians Treat the Past' (1998) 61 *Saskatchewan Law Review* 393, 401.

Having now discussed the at times farcical nature of the legal trial against Meursault and his fellow outsiders in both *The Fall* and *The Plague*, I will now analyze the question of judgment itself. We have seen that, for Camus, the law cannot provide the outsider with a sustaining truth – it can only punish, persecute or fear them for their position and philosophy.

Presenting Meursault to the Law

The Outsider is constructed in two clean parts: Meursault's life leading up to the murder followed by part two which is devoted to his trial. As mentioned above, the murder is often seen as but a pretext to bring Meursault 'before the law'. It is only after Meursault has killed the unidentified Arab, and fired another four shots, that he realizes the law has him. For him it 'was like giving four sharp knocks at the door of unhappiness', four sharp knocks at the doors of the law[53]. The immediately ensuing trial is the occasion for reviewing Meursault's actions in Part One and subjecting his character to detailed public scrutiny[54].

The trial, Part Two, is really a chance for the reader to evaluate his former life which until then had allowed Meursault to avoid public and self-scrutiny. Fitch has argued that Part 1 thus functions as a 'trap' in which to ensnare the reader, or at least make them find Meursault uncomfortable, and make them more likely to adopt the view of the prosecutor. Part Two then operates to assist the reader in rejecting the prosecutor's points of view and sympathize with the accused[55]. Of note is that Posner adopts the former, and Weisberg the latter, sympathies. The murder he commits, however random it may appear to the reader or is portrayed in the text, is also a 'flight from senselessness' which removes Meursault from his meaningless, monotonous life and subjects him to the 'meaningful world' of the penal system[56]. The murder, once committed, carries Meursault into the cold bosom of the legal system. Ironically he seems to welcome this development and is ready to submit himself to the higher authority of the law.

---

[53] Camus, as above n 1, 60.

[54] Brian T. Fitch, *The Narcissistic Text* (1982), ch. 4.

[55] Ibid.

[56] Colin Davis, 'The Cost of Being Ethical: Fiction, Violence and Altericide' (2003) 9 *Common Knowledge* 2, 246.

At the very beginning of Part Two, Meursault is quite pleased with the seamless, fluid like functioning of the law where the examining magistrate helps him to explicitly approve of the law. This is seen in him being provided with a lawyer, leading him to conclude that it is 'most convenient that the legal system should take care of such details' and, effectively, himself[57]. Furthermore the Magistrate affirming just 'how well the law worked' compounds this positive statement[58]. It is perhaps an example of Camus' cruel humor towards the law. By committing this murder, Meursault can embrace the structure that his life would otherwise lack and agrees to become but an actor is his own life in which the law will have the final say[59]. One early conclusion that can be made from such a situation, artfully constructed by Camus, is that Meursault, seeking truth, must murder to make it possible for him to maintain the belief that some other body or person may know the truth[60]. Or, to simply submit to a higher order even if that order is seen as absurd or arbitrary. Again, this is partly the underlying cause of Meursault's inner guilt.

Camus has insisted elsewhere, notably in *The Fall*, that we are all 'accomplices' in the claim of innocence. Clamence, the protagonist, asserts that he has no friends, 'I have only accomplices'[61]. He goes on to claim that 'we all claim to be innocent, at any price, even if, to this end, we have to accuse both heaven and humankind'[62]. Yet Meursault does not do this, even his friendly witnesses try to introduce the excuse Clamence also uses to defend himself, that of 'unfortunate circumstances' which are, in Raymond's words, 'a matter of chance', for Celeste, a 'misfortune'. Weisberg especially comes down on the side of Meursault when he stresses that the 'natural environment of the day of the murder – coupled with the slight drunkenness' in effect robs Meursault of his free will[63]. Yet these points are unconvincing and ineffectual to Meursault's trial and cannot explain the subsequent four shots. Conversely, Posner opines that Meursault is guilty for being 'utterly

---

[57] Camus, as above n 1, 63.

[58] Ibid.

[59] Davis, as above n 56, 247.

[60] Ibid.

[61] Camus, as above n 37, 1517.

[62] Ibid.

[63] Weisberg, as above n 13, 121.

self-absorbed and incapable of any feelings for his fellow human-beings'[64]. This is but another distortion of Meursault's life and reflects the untenable position of the shopkeeper in Camus work, *The Plague*, whose reaction to news of a suspiciously similar crime, a young office worker killing an Arab on the beach, suggests that 'if they put all that rabble in jail, decent folks could breathe more freely'[65]. Yet as Simon deftly points out, Camus maintains the ambiguity of guilt and innocence in the text and one cannot resolve it easily[66].

However, by ignoring Camus' ironic signposts, misleading and confusing as they are, Weisberg takes the part of an accomplice, Posner the part of the executioner, and many a reader but a confused witness to a legal process that both baffles and fails to convince either way. Camus later wrote that if one cannot prove one's own virtue, the prisons must be opened[67]. That statement is a clear indicator of his views on the ambiguity and inherent difficulties in attributing guilt or maintaining innocence – the question of punishment, trial and retribution engulfed in confusion and emotion. Meursault is the embodiment of this confusion. As Girard points out, the text is truly 'divided against itself' – each page reflecting the contradictions and divisions inherent in the murder; every denial of communication and emotion an effort to communicate; every gesture of indifference but an appeal in disguise[68]. One must now consider the trial in the text and consider how the law is depicted as struggling with this very issue.

The Outsider and Legal Language on Trial

In *The Outsider*, a relatively simply court trial is transformed by Camus into an analysis about how human irregularity and personal traits, normally immune to the law, are prosecuted in a court so that the law itself can be exposed and satirized[69]. The law's mechanical application of judgment,

---

[64] Posner, as above n 12, 89.

[65] Camus, as above n 44, 1262.

[66] Simon, as above n 19, 122.

[67] Albert Camus, *Oeuvres Completes*, Vol. 2 (1970), 144.

[68] Girard, as above n 22, 530.

[69] Camus, as above n 1, 123.

coupled with its simplistic distinctions between guilt and innocence 'does violence' to human diversity, splitting individuals in exclusive misleading categories[70]. Camus goes to some lengths to establish a believable courtroom scene; replete with accurate conventions and procedures, focusing in on the participants and the mechanical regularity of the trial itself. Indeed Meursault finds the most 'annoying thing was that the condemned man had to hope the machine worked properly'[71].

The language of the courtroom is not 'literary' nor is it stylized, it is the real language of legal discourse articulated by the prosecutor and judge, defense attorney and witnesses. Meursault's own knowledge of the 'value of words' is seen by the prosecutor as a sign of intelligence and used against him to show that Meursault has 'no place in a society whose fundamental rules (he) ignored'[72]. Meursault's lawyer appeals to the jury for leniency, citing 'extenuating circumstances' and arguing that his 'surest punishment…was eternal remorse' – an appeal that doesn't get him very far[73]. Camus even throws in a wry comment on the linguistic flexibility of lawyers with the misleading truthfulness of witness testimonies in the character of Marie who breaks down when the prosecutor 'forced her to say the opposite of what she was thinking'[74].

Camus' reason for bringing the law so accurately into the text is not simply for accuracy, it is to allow the law, in all its practical and formal manifestations, accompanied by its social assumptions and political clout, to be subjected to unexpected scrutiny. Camus seeks to analyze and critique the law's underlying pretenses and deficiencies. The *modus operandi* of the author appears to be that – if the law itself is incapable of resolving ambiguities relating to innocence and guilt and being wholly unable to recognize and accommodate 'the other' in the law - its role as a forum of judgment and punishment is forfeit. The law must be seen in a critical light, and thus the character of Meursault becomes but a spectator at his own trial and can look upon it with an irony similar to that of his creator.

---

[70] Ibid, 124.

[71] Ibid, 107.

[72] Ibid, 97, 99.

[73] Ibid, 101.

[74] Ibid, 90.

> ...What with all these long sentences and the endless days and hours that people had been talking about my soul, I just had the impression that I was drowning...[75]

Others however have accused Camus of deliberately making the trail implausible to appeal to his readership. Posner has contended that the sentence is 'unrealistic' in its harshness within a French colonial setting when self-defence remains a plausible argument[76]. Perhaps what is intended is not a full out assault on the law, but a tactile method by which Camus can critique judgment in particular. In this vein, Weisberg points out that Continental jurisprudence 'as depicted by European novelists' often involves the author substituting himself for the investigative magistrate and thus both the inquisitor and the novelist merge to aid in the perception of a structure of meaning and fullness otherwise difficult to grasp in legal proceedings[77]. In other words, the author tries to appropriate the voice of justice to help build the story. What invalidates the prosecutor's rather forceful interpretation of Meursault's reality, despite the early protection of the Magistrate, is his blindness to ambiguities and his inability to exclude his own feelings for the accused in the case. Weisberg goes on to say that the trial would never have produced a guilty verdict in an American court and that Camus is here critiquing the failure of the French criminal procedure to allow character evidence in murder trials[78]. As always, Posner is contrary to Weisberg on this point, arguing that Camus faithfully portrays French procedure and such claims are irrelevant in literary considerations of poetic justice[79]. A view favored by this author.

Arguably, Camus is trying to tackle the behemoth of absolute legal reasoning and its supreme reluctance to acknowledge other philosophical views. The figure of the Magistrate as a figure of the law is a useful example here. When the Magistrate asks Meursault to repent, and he again refuses, his unwillingness as a defendant to conform to the Magistrate's views by

---

[75] Ibid, 101.

[76] Posner, as above n 12, 88, 'A colonial French court would not have been so eager to convict and sentence to death a Frenchman accused of murdering a "native"'.

[77] Weisberg, as above n 13, 121.

[78] Ibid.

[79] Posner, as above n 12, 88-89.

repenting of his crime and sin (note he hasn't even been found guilty yet!) enrages the Magistrate who starts to wave the Crucifix at his face (after Meursault refuses to repent before God – that a Magistrate would exhibit such a personal outburst is highly improbable and must be assigned to Camus' poetic license). He goes on to say that it was his belief that all men believed in God and that 'if he should ever doubt it, his life would become meaningless'[80]. He then shouts at Meursault – 'do you want my life to be meaningless?'[81]. This is exactly the threat that Meursault embodies. His figure as an outsider threatens the very assumptions upon which the law is founded – regularity, homogeny and a shared morality.

To reiterate my contention, Meursault's crime is not simply murder, it is refusing to accept or acquiesce to the law's worldview. The trial thus descends into a caustic farce. The succeeding days in which the trial takes place is marked by the Magistrate who treats Meursault 'cordially' occasionally betraying his true thoughts by referring to him as 'Mr. Antichrist'[82]. Yet one must view this with caution, keeping in mind the agenda of the author here. As Robert Batey has stated regarding his use of *The Outsider* in teaching criminal law, discussion of these characters allows him to 'conclude with a plea that is direct and personal – 'I ask the students to try *not to practice law* the way the legal professionals in *The Outsider* do'[83].

How The Outsider allows for an Examination of the Law

The trial in *The Outsider* shows the law to be at times highly prejudicial and without mercy, hateful of outsiders and vengeful. The examining magistrate sees that Meursault cannot be saved and uses his role to insulate himself from the reality of the murder he will permit upon Meursault by treating him as unrepentant before God and not worthy of his mercy (note the positioning of the examining magistrate in a god like role here). The bloodthirsty prosecutor is seen as 'relentless' in his assault on Meursault, turning 'an ordinary man's good qualities' into those of 'crushing accusations' and demands his head for

---

[80] Camus, as above n 1, 68.

[81] Ibid.

[82] Ibid, 70.

[83] Batey, as above n 38, 12 (emphasis added).

his crime 'with an easy mind'[84]. The Magistrate who presides over the trial, a figure who is meant to feel a sense of great responsibility before sentencing a man to death, does little but ask numerous questions behind a mask of formality after deciding Meursault is unredeemable[85]. The judge here exhibits such an absence of thoughtful consideration, knowing the pain he will inflict at the trial's close, has led critics to conclude that Camus' law and trial 'takes place in a field of death and pain'[86].

Part 2: Judgment, Crime and the Absurd

Meursault is judged not for his crime, but for his being. Despite having killed a man, he is not the real villain in the story. The villains are those that punish him and the 'institution through which this punishment is administered' – the law and its actors[87]. Whilst initially taken aback by this man's alien nature and lack of shared human feeling towards events, we are slowly stripped of our 'normal conceptual lenses' and see the world as he sees it, increasingly hypocritical and arbitrary[88]. By the end of our novel, many readers are prepared to find fault with the prosecutor and judge rather than Meursault himself.

Faulting Meursault's Case

There is clearly an injustice evident here – the overwhelming sense that the law did not treat Meursault as it should have. We have seen how Camus depicts a court that is unwilling to accept any narrative outside the sphere of its' own assumptions and, when met with explanations for conduct indifferent to its ideas of causation (or Meursault's lack there of), it is seen to assume facts are being withheld and deliberates accordingly[89]. When the

---

[84] Camus, as above n 1, 99.

[85] See generally Eric L. Muller, 'The Virtue of Mercy in Criminal Sentencing' (1993) 24 *Secton Hall Law Review* 288.

[86] Robert M. Cover, 'Violence and the Word' (1986) 95 *Yale Law Journal* 1601, 1601.

[87] Emlyn W. Cruikshank, *Dialogues of Indifference: Albert Camus' 'The Outsider' and Criminal Punishment Theory* (2010) ANU College of Law Research Paper No. 10-29.

[88] David Sprintzen, *Camus: A Critical Examination* (1988), 23-24.

[89] Cruikshank, as above n 87, 3.

court is met with the demeanor of an outsider such as Meursault, whom it deems inappropriate and lacking in adequate remorse, it makes inferences as to his subjective character and intent. It is for this reason that Meursault's judgment strikes the reader as unjust. It is the literary paradigm for how agents indifferent to legal assumptions are treated and how varied philosophical understandings of when and how to punish can justify such treatment[90]. As Judge Orthon puts it in *The Plague* – 'It's not the law that counts, it's the sentence'[91]. *The Outsider* thus affords us with an opportunity to reexamine how to regulate the state practice of criminal punishment and the advocacy of criminal trials.

The existing, predominant approach to Camus' work in relation to jurisprudence and criminal punishment theory has focused upon Camus' 'theory of the Absurd'[92]. Camus' philosophy of the Absurd developed throughout his texts and its evolution is beyond the scope of this paper[93]. Yet, as is clearly evident in the texts already discussed, the philosophy of the Absurd, at its core, is concerned with the tension between the insistence one places on reason, order and meaning and the observation that there is often a sense of disinterest and indifference in the world, even chaos. This 'absurdity' is epitomized in the court's treatment of Meursault. Its construction of the case and imbuing his character with sinister traits better suited to proffer an explanation of his crime is at odds with Meursault's true conduct - done in the absence of real emotion. They take up the two threads of Camus' philosophy, the insistence of meaning and reason being applied to human behavior where there is really none[94]. It is this tension that snaps in

---

[90] Ibid.

[91] As above n 44, 118. As an aside, the New South Wales Law Reform Commission has previously stated that it was 'impossible to identify among the varying philosophical approaches a dominate rationale' in sentencing. See *Sentencing,* Discussion Paper 33 (1996), 56. Available at: http://portsea.austlii.edu.au/au/other/nswlrc/dp/33/DP33CHP1.html, (last accessed 24/05/2011).

[92] For example, see Dwight Newman, 'Existentialism and Law – Toward a Reinvigorated Law and Literature Analysis' (2000) 63 *Saskatchewan Law Review* 87. In addition, Lenora Ledwon cites *The Outsider* as one of the dominant works in law and literature: *Law and Literature: Text and Theory* (1996), 122.

[93] See Lev Braun, *Witness of Decline: Albert Camus, Moralist of the Absurd* (1974) for a studied analysis of his philosophy. Please note I use the word 'Absurd' within this paper as it relates to Camus' theory, not its everyday meaning.

[94] Cruikshank, as above n 87, 11.

Meursault's face when the need for reason and attributing blame fails where none can be found, to the great frustration and fear of the court. *The Outsider* is thus seen as a very critical meditation on legal practice and can be placed under the 'literary texts as legal text' arm of Posner's distinction, as a way to 'subversively question advocacy in criminal trials' and accord us with a chance to appraise contemporary punishment theory[95].

Legal Narratives and Dialogue: Disabling Assumptions

One of Meursault's failures, in the eyes of the court, is to adequately frame the why and how of his crime within an acceptable narrative. Some commentators hold that legal narratives such as this are entrenched in 'epistemological assumptions' which make the choice between narratives the key point in determining who has 'control' over any given legal dispute[96]. The strength of one's legal narrative or story gives a greater or lesser weight in the legal arena. This is of course seen in *The Outsider* where Meursault's truthful but utterly unconvincing story seriously jeopardizes his case. Others contend that assumptions of chronological narrative are themselves unjust and possibly violate presumptions of innocence[97]. In this vein, critics such as Dershowitz have called for statutory reform such that rules of evidence should be allowed to consider or permit the vagaries of real human experience to enter the courtroom, rather than be subjected to the filter of legal jargon and restrictions[98]. Newman also contends that allowing such existentialist literature such as *The Outsider* back into legal academia is warranted as it allows one to experience how possible injustices are individually experienced[99]. This would require a revision of how the law applies its 'template ethics' to all to accommodate the subjectivity of human experience:

---

[95] Ibid, 13.

[96] Kim Scheppele, 'Just the Facts, Ma'am: Sexualized Violence, Evidentiary Habits, and the Revision of Truth' (1992) 37 *New York Law Review* 145, 145-172.

[97] Alan Dershowitz, 'Life is Not a Dramatic Narrative' in P. Brooks and P. Gewirtz (eds), *Law's Stories: Narrative and Rhetoric in the Law* (1996), 4.

[98] Ibid, 105.

[99] Newman, as above n 92.

...Underneath legal doctrine is a true story suppressed by the official narrative assumptions of the doctrine...there is a contestable set of stories suppressed by the doctrine's claim of timeless Cartesian truth.[100]

The thrust of Camus' work deals directly with this subjective experience of the law. Jurisprudence should be concerned with the crucially absurd depictions of the law's operations and processes which (in Camus' texts) ultimately fail its followers and outsiders alike. Its' assumptions concerning causative and emotional meaning blind the court, prohibiting it from considering subjective actualities of individual experience such as Meursault or Clamence. Punishment should instead be dialogical and absent such assumptions[101]. Furthermore, the courts' refusal to consider the plausibility of this subjective view, as distinct from its own absurd objective assumptions heavily influence the way in which it treats Meursault. His character cannot be explained by rationally deterministic conclusions. His is one that, as we have seen, is sensual in nature and driven by the immediate, being able to explain his actions accordingly and not to any higher motive or reasoning[102]. We have already seen this behavior. Meursault agrees to marry Marie only 'to give her pleasure' despite not loving her and hesitates at a promotion to Paris as it would involve him moving from Algiers where 'life is as good as another' and his present one suits his needs 'well enough'[103]. His indifference to evocative situations demonstrates Camus' concern with logic and emotion inherent in the human condition and the multiplicity of possible responses '...that which a human being can experience with body and soul'[104]. The law responds with great frustration to this indifference and it can indeed be unsettling, even for the reader, such as Meursault's lack of premeditation or remorse.

---

[100] Robert Weisberg, 'Proclaiming Trials as Narratives: Premises and Pretenses', in P. Brooks and P. Gewirtz (eds), as above 97, 67.

[101] Cruikshank, as above 87, 15.

[102] See Maria Aristodemou, *Law and Literature: Journeys from Here to Eternity* (2000), 132-138.

[103] Camus, as above n 1, 48.

[104] Cruikshank, as above 87, 16.

Equally troublesome is the way Meursault treats the legal process, matched only by the indifference with which the court treats Meursault. It is concerned with its absurd narrative rather than engaging in a dialogue with this cold outsider who it cannot understand. This is why the Court creates its own normative narrative and constructs a chronological sequence of events. Meursault cannot explain himself at all and we see that when he does try to explain himself, he becomes only too conscious 'that I sounded ridiculous'[105]. Meursault eventually becomes aware of how the court is constructing the chain of events and ultimately the lack of interest the court shows in his own narrative, compounding his own indifference to the point where he sees the case as being conducted 'independently of me'. The construction of his story by his own lawyer, who uses the word 'I' every time he means Meursault, is but another way of 'excluding me from the proceedings, reducing me to insignificance'[106].

What is demonstrated here is the pervasive judicial belief in the universality of sequence and motive. This belief renders the court incapable of considering Meursault's 'truth' and he is found guilty. Not only is he found guilty of the murder of the Algerian, but also guilty for not crying at his mother's funeral and incredibly, the prosecutor goes on to say that 'the man sitting here in the dock is also guilty of the murder which this court is to judge tomorrow' for Meursault has shown that 'he has no place in a society whose most fundamental rules' he ignores[107]. Even mercy is not granted to Meursault for his soul is colored as knowing 'nothing of the most basic human reactions' and thus must be denied to him[108].

This absurdity has been picked up by several leading law and literature critics' explanations of *The Outsider*. Maria Aristodemou notes the inherent falsity of the law's 'will to explain' all situations and events, being 'unwilling to acknowledge the idea of a life made up of discontinuous isolated events without a logical sequence'[109]. Meursault is thus transformed from an idle, somewhat cold, sun lover to a soulless, murderous monster

---

[105] Camus, as above n 1, 99.

[106] Camus, as above n 1, 100.

[107] Camus, as above n 1, 99.

[108] Camus, as above n 1, 99.

[109] Aristodemou, as above 102, 139.

once the law finishes with its' tale. Similarly Weisberg criticizes the focus of the law upon incidents wholly unrelated to the crime and without any legal weight in their original form[110]. Even Posner who upholds Meursault's conviction notes that the reader is invited by Camus to reject the 'state ideology that men are primarily spiritual beings endowed with souls and that man's actions possess a coherence'[111]. Meursault's indifference is thus characterized as remorselessness and the court superimposes criminal characteristics upon him and unrelated actions based on the assumption that all people express emotion in objectively identifiable ways that transcend subjective characteristics. Cruickshank notes that this indifference is particularly noteworthy because it draws attention to the variety of subjective influences on the conduct of an indicted in court which can range from trauma repression to reasons of anxiety[112].

Where is Camus taking us?

Camus highlights the Existentialist view that human behavior and thought is not always rational or anticipated, nor can it be. Is he calling for a rejection of a judicial system informed by Judeo-Christian models of behavior and morality or is he simply advocating a new means by which one must consider individual action as opposed to template understandings of individual character? It is argued that Camus is not advocating such a radical approach. The very construction of Meursault, and to a lesser extent Clamence, is to provide the reader, the scholar, lawyer or judge an opportunity to see the law through the eyes of an individual uncolored by sentiment or faith. Meursault's unwillingness to 'participate in the social market' of our society gives him a functional value which demonstrates the value of punishment to society as a whole[113]. His punishment is justifiable because of its market efficiency – a constructive response to those whom, by commissioning crimes, have upset this 'market'. What does this mean? In essence one can support the trial of Meursault on basic deterrence grounds. Posner defends

---

[110] Weisberg, as above n 13, 115.

[111] Posner, as above n 12, quoting Patrick McCarthy, 44.

[112] Cruikshank, as above n 87, 20. See also Bryan H. Ward, 'Sentencing Without Remorse' (2006) 28 *Loyola University Chicago Law Journal* 131.

[113] See Richard A. Posner, 'An Economic Theory of the Criminal Law' (1985) 85 *Columbia Law Review* 1193, 1196.

the conviction because Meursault was emotionless and 'odious to a civilized person'[114]. This idea is seen to support the basic framework of deterrence in Utilitarian punishment theory.

Simon prefers to contend that Camus' court and its judgment is invalidated because of its 'blindness to ambiguities and its exclusion of any feeling for the absurd'[115]. This has been called a passionately 'self-interested and value-attuned' mode of judgment, predicated on a combination of 'pseudo-moralism and imposed behaviorism'[116]. The law should be seen to be able to justify itself above the behavioral indifference of the indicted, as argued by Cruikshank. Camus' court is one where the neutral adjudication of a criminal trial goes horribly wrong, and deliberately so, for it allows Camus to critique the lack of dialogue in legal proceedings between the subject and the law. *The Outsider* depicts an indifferent administration of punishment, true. The themes of the text are Existentialist in essence and depicts how absurd legal belief in causative narrative and template expression of emotions are liable to abuse and injustice. It is an 'illustration of how legal analysis can fundamentally misunderstand human beings and their interaction'[117]. What Camus seeks to outline is that a court must be more communicative and more inclined to engage with its subjects as individual subjects as opposed to beings defined by general collective feelings and attributes. This is the ultimate challenge of the text, Meursault must be punished, but given his unique nature, how can we punish him?

Punishing the Other without Punishing Ourselves?

Punishment theory focuses upon how States can justify their actions in inflicting suffering upon their citizens for the common good – generally falling under the banner of utilitarian or retributive[118]. Camus' courtroom can

---

[114] Richard A. Posner, *Law and Literature* (revised ed, 2009), 96.

[115] Simon, as above n 19, 123.

[116] Weisberg, as above n 13, 115.

[117] Batey, as above n 38, 70.

[118] Frederick Schaeur and Walter Sinnott-Armstrong, *The Philosophy of Law: Classic and Contemporary Readings with Commentary* (1996). See also H J. McClocksey, 'Utilitarian and Retributive Punishment' (1967) 64 *The Journal of Philosophy* 91, 91-110; Michael Lessnoff, 'Two Justifications of Punishment' (1971) 21 *The Philosophical Quarterly* 83, 141-148.

be seen as retributive and authoritarian but there is a further detail. When its methods of punishment and legal structure fail to accommodate the outsider, it is seen as failing to uphold basic tenets of justice and equality before the law.

A multiplicity of punishment theories exist ranging from the aforementioned Utilitarian approach favored by Posner to more recent theories such as Duff's 'communicative theory'[119]. Duff's theory can be particularly attuned to the issues outlined in *The Outsider*. Duff proposes a theory that impresses upon the court a need to communicatively engage with the accused so that they are understood and can thus understand their own punishment. This is a development from traditional retributivism, which sees 'intrinsic good by inflicting suffering on wrongdoers'[120]. That form of retributivism shares much with Posner's view that the court was correct in punishing Meursault as he was an agent who refused to engage with it. Duff defends his new communicative approach to punishment by arguing it is a 'two-way rational activity' whereby we:

> ...communicate with another, who figures not simply as a passive recipient, but as a participant with us in this activity[121].

This 'communication' stands in stark contrast to theories which assert that the purpose of punishment requires condemnation and reprimand[122]. Metz has pointed out here that it is 'possible to censure someone without communicating with her or even without communicating at all'[123]. It is argued that these traditional understandings of the law's role in punishment is what concerns Camus in these many trials scenes across his oeuvre. Not only

---

[119] R A. Duff, 'Penance, Punishment and the Limits of Community' (2003) 5 *Punishment and Society* 295. See also R A. Duff and David Garland, 'Thinking About Punishment' (1996) 20 *Crime and Justice* 1, 27.

[120] See Immanuel Kant, 'On the Right to Punish' (M. der Sitten, trans) in *The Metaphysics of Morals* (1991), 140.

[121] Duff, as above n 119, 79.

[122] See Joel Feinberg, *Doing and Deserving* (1970); Jean Hampton, 'An Expressive Theory of Retribution' in Wesley Cragg (ed) *Retributivism and Its Critics* (1992), 1-25.

[123] Thaddeus Metz, 'Censure Theory and Intuitions About Punishment' (2000) 19 *Law and Philosophy* 491, 492.

is the reader at times forced to bear witness to patently unjust trial procedures (*The Outsider*), the reader is also at times called be a judge (*The Fall*) and see the failings of legal institutions before indifferent subjects who are demonized for being so (*The Plague*).

Duff's communicative theory offers some redemption within the realm of Camus' texts. It would give voice to the outsider and enable courts to tear off their blindfold and see the individual before them as not just as a subject, but an individual constructed both by society and their own subjectivity. It could thus avoid the indifference of Camus' court. How relevant is this to Meursault? One could argue that such a communicative approach could well have saved him from death. The implications of *The Outsider* are met with a great deal of sympathy in communicative punishment theory as it brings actual communicative engagement to the fore; preventing the abstraction of the accused and his subsequent alienation from proceedings. In other words, it imbues the outsider with a voice where otherwise he would be rendered mute by the law and its practitioners.

This is a theory of punishment actually concerned with the welfare of those it punishes. It is more likely to allow a court to accord concern to the agents before it and inhibit the assumption of narrative nor read emotional character and motive into the absence of palpable remorse[124]. In other words, Meursault would not become 'Mr. AntiChrist'. Duff goes on to say that trials serve 'not just the much acclaimed appearance of justice but...the very essence of justice' and defines the trial process as an attempt to engage with the defendant, to try and seek their assent to their own verdict – to reach a mutual understanding of their wrongdoing[125]. Thus the court is moved from a focus upon punishment and vengeance to a position of dialogical engagement with the accused. For Meursault, one can perhaps foresee his acquittal based on self defence (if he had been properly allowed to speak) or a lesser charge of manslaughter for he has no motive nor malicious intent.

---

[124] Duff (1996), as above n 119, 38.

[125] Ibid, 33.

Conclusion

Meursault's trial is multifaceted in its meaning and speaks on several levels – ranging from critiques of the justice system, to the exploration of the absurd in legal proceedings and the treatment of indifferent subjects by the law. It is also at its heart a human tale – one of a misunderstood man who harbors few illusions and is punished for his honesty and 'refusing to play the game'. *The Outsider* subtly implies that Meursault's trial does in fact lead him to acknowledge the wrongfulness of his actions and leads almost to repentance – 'it was then that I felt a sort of wave of indignation spreading through the courtroom, and for the first time I understood that I was guilty'[126]. As discussed above, the notion of guilt is complex in *The Outsider* and can be either moral or legal guilt – Camus refuses to say which. Perhaps Meursault's later 'awakening' where he becomes 'sure of my life' is a telling hint[127]. It is still questionable whether or not Meursault is now prepared to renegotiate his former self or assimilate into his society and it is perhaps relates to his impending death that he is much more attune to his situation and status[128]. For out of the injustice perpetrated against him, he becomes aware that 'the essential thing was to give a condemned man a chance' and when all a condemned man can do is to hope the legal 'machine worked properly', he states that 'I'd reform the punishment system'[129].

There can be no definite way of determining whether or not Meursault could have progressed to the point where the law and his person could co-exist. It has no direct bearing on the purpose of the novel – that being to allow Camus to critique the elements of legal process and punishment and how the law can or cannot deal with its unwilling subjects or simply those who do not subscribe to its moral reasoning. Meursault's trial is nevertheless a travesty for its failure to engage with the Outsider as a subject. It is hoped however that an investigation of this text has allowed others, both insiders and outsiders, to reassess the methodology of the justice system in regards to

---

[126] Camus, as above n 1, 87.

[127] Camus, as above n 1, 115.

[128] Duff has pointed out that the moral development of Meursault at the end of the text makes little sense given Camus' neglect in demonstrating Meursault's shift from a life of immediate sensuality to one of rational realization. See R A. Duff and S E. Marshall, 'Camus and Rebellion: From Solipsism to Morality' (1982) 5 *Philosophical Investigations* 116, 123-126.

[129] Camus, as above n 1, 106, 107.

punishment and subjective understanding of individuals to avoid similar miscarriages of justice, both literary and real.

Works Cited

Aristodemou, Maria. Law and Literature: Journeys from Here to Eternity (2000).

Batey, Robert. 'Symposium: Law and Popular Culture: Literature in a Criminal Law Course Aeschylus, Burgess, Oates, Camus, Poe and Melville' (1998) 22 *Legal Studies Forum* 45.

Braun, Lev. *Witness of Decline: Albert Camus, Moralist of the Absurd* (1974).

Buber, Martin. 'Guilt and Guilt Feelings' (1957) *Psychiatry.*

Camus, Albert. *Carnets, mai 1935 – février 1942* (1962).

---. *The Fall* (Robin Buss trans, 2006).

---. *Notebooks*, 1942-1951, at 157 (Justin O'Brien trans, 1966).

---. *Oeuvres Completes*, Vol. 2 (1970).

---. *The Outsider* (Joseph Laredo trans, 2000).

---. *The Plague* (Gilbert S trans, 1957).

---. *'Reflections on the Guillotine, in Resistance, Rebellion, and Death'* (Justin O'Brien trans, 1960)

Caroll, David. 'Symposium: Failure of the Word: Guilt by "Race": Injustice in Camus' The Stranger' (2005) 26 *Cardozo Law Review* 2331.

Cover, M Robert. 'Violence and the Word' (1986) 95 *Yale Law Journal* 1601.

Cruikshank, W Emelyn. *Dialogues of Indifference: Albert Camus' 'The Outsider' and Criminal Punishment Theory*, ANU College of Law Research Paper No. 10-29   (2010).

Davis, Colin. 'The Cost of Being Ethical: Fiction, Violence and Altericide' (2003) 9 *Common Knowledge* 2.

Dershowitz, Alan. 'Life is Not a Dramatic Narrative' in P. Brooks and P. Gewirtz (eds), *Law's Stories: Narrative and Rhetoric in the Law* (1996).

Duff, A R, and David Garland. 'Thinking About Punishment' (1996) 20 *Crime and Justice* 1.

Duff, A R, and Marshall, S. E. 'Camus and Rebellion: From Solipsism to Morality' (1982) 5 *Philosophical Investigations* 116.

Duff, R A. 'Penance, Punishment and the Limits of Community' (2003) 5 *Punishment and* Society 295.

Dwight, Newman. 'Existentialism and Law – Toward a Reinvigorated Law and Literature Analysis' (2000) 63 *Saskatchewan Law Review* 87.

Feinberg, Joel. *Doing and Deserving* (1970).

Felman, S. 'Crisis of Witnessing: Albert Camus' Postwar Writings' (1991), 3 *Cardozo Studies Law and Literature* 197.

Fitch, T Brian. *The Narcissistic Text* (1982).

Girard, René. 'Camus' Stranger Retried' (1963) 79 *PMLA* 5

Hampton, Jean. 'An Expressive Theory of Retribution' in Wesley Cragg (ed) *Retributivism and Its Critics* (1992).

Hudon, Louis. 'The Stranger and the Critics', *Yale French Studies*, No. 25, Albert Camus (1960).

Kant, Immanuel. 'On the Right to Punish' (M. der Sitten, trans) in *The Metaphysics of Morals* (1991).

Ledwon, Lenora. *Law and Literature: Text and Theory* (1996).

Lessnoff, Michael. 'Two Justifications of Punishment' (1971) 21 *The Philosophical Quarterly* 83.

McClocksey, H, J. 'Utilitarian and Retributive Punishment' (1967) 64 *The Journal of Philosophy* 91.

McHugh, Paul. 'The Common-Law Status of Colonies and Aboriginal "Rights": How Lawyers and Historians Treat the Past' (1998) 61 *Saskatchewan Law Review* 393.

Metz, Thaddeus. 'Censure Theory and Intuitions About Punishment' (2000) 19 *Law and Philosophy* 491.

Muller, L Eric. 'The Virtue of Mercy in Criminal Sentencing' (1993) 24 *Secton Hall Law Review* 288.

New South Wales Law Reform Commission. *Sentencing,* Discussion Paper 33 (1996).

Posner, A Richard. 'An Economic Theory of the Criminal Law' (1985) 85 *Columbia Law Review* 1193.

---. *Law and Literature* (revised ed, 2009).

---. *Law and Literature,* (revised ed, 1998).

Sartre, Jean-Paul. 'Existentialism is a Humanism', (P. Mairet, trans) in Langiulli, (ed) *The Existentialist Tradition: Selected Writings* (1971).

Schaeur, Frederick and Walter Sinnott-Armstrong. *The Philosophy of Law: Classic and Contemporary Readings with Commentary* (1996).

Scheppele, Kim. 'Just the Facts, Ma'am: Sexualized Violence, Evidentiary Habits, and the Revision of Truth' (1992) 37 *New York Law Review* 145.

Simon, Ernest. 'Palais de Justice and Poetic Justice in Albert Camus' "The Stranger"' (1991) 3 *Cardozo Studies in Law and Literature* 1.

Sprintzen, David. *Camus: A Critical Examination* (1988).

Ward, H Bryan. 'Sentencing Without Remorse' (2006) 28 *Loyola University Chicago Law Journal* 131.

Ward, Matthew. 'Translator's Note To Albert Camus, (Matthew Ward trans., Alfred A. Knopf, 1988).

Weisberg, Robert. 'Proclaiming Trials as Narratives: Premises and Pretenses', in P. Brooks and P. Gewirtz (eds) (1996).

---. *The Failure of the Word: The Protagonist as Lawyer in Modern Fiction*, (1984).

White, B James. "What Can a Lawyer Learn from Literature?", Book review of *Law and Literature*: *A Misunderstood Relation* by R. A. Posner (1989), 102 *Harvard Law Review* 2014.

Wilson, Colin. *The Outsider* (2001).

Yalom, K Marilyn. 'Albert Camus and the Myth of The Trial' (1964) 25 *Modern Language Quarterly* 434.

Albert Camus: The Politics of Poverty and the Misery of Kabylie[1]

By Jerry Larson

The subject of poverty was a central concern of Albert Camus, as it was of Tolstoy and Orwell, and this had a major influence on his political philosophy. Camus' early relationship with Communism and his later ideas on socialism, clearly expressed in his articles in *Combat*, were primarily the result of the poverty that he witnessed in Algeria. Nowhere is this seen more clearly than in the articles he wrote for the *Alger Républicain* in 1938-1939, on the economic conditions in Kabylie. This paper presents these articles for the first time in English translation, and I will argue that they played a crucial role in forming Camus socialist thought, his philosophy of revolt, and the basic premises of his moral philosophy.

In *Lyrical and Critical Essays*, Albert Camus wrote "Poverty kept me from thinking all was well under the sun and in history; the sun taught me that history was not everything,"[1] and the awakening of Camus' political consciousness began in his early years in Algeria as a result of the poverty and the economic inequalities that he witnessed between the French colonialist and the Arab population. In ways very similar to Tolstoy's *What Then Must We Do?* (1886), and Orwell's *Down and Out in Paris and London* (1933), and *The Road to Wigan Pier* (1937) this issue of poverty lies at the center of Camus' entire literary canon,[2] and it substantially determined his

---

[1] Albert Camus, *Lyrical and Critical Essays* (New York: Vintage, 1963) p. 7-8.

[2] Tolstoy, Orwell and Camus not only shared an interest in the poor and the problems of poverty in their work, but they also focuses on the ideas of socialism and social justice. See V.C. Letemendia's "Poverty in the writings of Albert Camus" *Polity* 24:3 (1997): 441-460, and Gordon B. Beadle's "George Orwell's Literary Studies of Poverty in England," *Twentieth Century Literature* 24:2 (1978) p. 188-201. Tolstoy was a major influence on Camus and Olivier Todd relates in *Albert Camus: A Life* (New York: Carroll & Graf, 1997) that Camus kept a picture of Tolstoy in his office near his writing lectern along with those of Nietzsche and Camus' mother (see page 359). For a concise article on Tolstoy and Orwell, see Robert

commitment to social justice, human freedom, and the philosophy of socialism.[3] In his view,

> ...the most revolting justice is consummated when poverty is wed to the life without hope or the sky that I found on reaching manhood in the appalling slums of our cities: everything must be done so that men can escape from the double humiliation of poverty and ugliness.[4]

Camus experienced first-hand the despair and hopelessness of poverty both in his own life growing up in the Belcourt neighborhood of Algiers and in the conditions of the Arab population. The effects of this are most clearly depicted in the autobiographical novel *The First Man*, where he describes the main character as having "grown up in the midst of a poverty naked as death."[5] In his early journalistic writings, Camus captures the stark images of Arab poverty when he writes: "In the early hours, I have seen in Tizi-Ouzou children fighting with dogs in Kabylie over the contents of a garbage can."[5] However, despite these conditions in Algeria, he still maintained that: Although I have known and shared every form of poverty in which this

---

Pearce's "Orwell, Tolstoy, and *Animal Farm*," *The Review of English Studies* 49:193 (1998) p. 64-69.

[3] Malcolm Crowley in "Camus and Social Justice" (*The Cambridge Companion to Camus*, Cambridge: Cambridge University Press, 2007) divides Camus' social justice into two categories: "First, there is the kind of concern...in which what is at stake is the equitable organization of social structures, especially as they relate to the distribution of wealth. Secondly, Camus' commitment to the idea of justice is also articulated through his engagement with world historical events" 94. Roger Quillot in *Critical Essays on Albert Camus* (Boston: G. K. Hall & Co., 1988) relates that Camus once remarked "I have not learned about freedom in Marx, I have learned about it in poverty" p. 37. And in *Resistance, Rebellion, and Death*, he makes the statement that "Poverty increases insofar as freedom retreats throughout the world, and vice versa" p. 94.

[4] Camus, *Lyrical and Critical Essays*, p. 8.

[5] Albert Camus, *The First Man* (London: Penguin Books, 1996). In this novel, probably no image is as stark as that of his grandmother groping "around in the excrement" searching for a two-franc that the young Jacques lied about dropping into the toilet. Camus writes, of the "terrible need that made two francs a significant amount in this house" p. 70.

[5] Albert Camus, *Essais* (Paris: Gallimard et Calmann-Lévy, 1965), p. 907-8: "Par un petit matin, j'ai vu à Tizi-Ouzou des enfants en loques disputer à des chiens kabyles le contenu d'une poubelle."

---

country abounds, it is for me the land of happiness, of energy, and of creation. And I cannot bear to see it become a land of suffering and hatred.[7]

Camus' criticism of colonialism and his support for the Moslem Arabs in Algeria, which differed from the attitudes of the French *pied noirs*, stemmed from the inequalities and the poverty that he witnessed. This concern formed the basis for his early political activism against social injustices; it led him to join the Communist Party and support independence for the Algerians; and it is reflected in his journalistic articles for the *Alger Républicain* and later for *Combat*. For Camus, "The injustice from which the Arab population has suffered is linked to colonialism itself, to its history, and its administration."[8]

The effects that poverty had on Camus in these early years resulted in a life-long interest in socialist ideas and economic reform that would form the basis of his later political, social, and humanistic philosophy. While many of these ideas would find their expression in his novels, it is specifically in the articles he wrote for newspapers and magazines in Algeria and in France that we find his relationship to the philosophy and the politics of socialism most clearly articulated. They also provide an important background from which to gain a better understanding of his reasons for writing *The Rebel*, and the troubled relationship he had with left-wing politics over his lifetime. As he once remarked "I was born into the leftist family, and I'll stay there until I die."[9] This strong commitment to leftist politics and the belief in the need for social change would eventually lead to his interest in and early association with socialist ideologies and his later hopes for a "moderate Utopia."[10]

---

[7] Camus, *Resistance, Rebellion and Death* (New York: Vintage, 1974), p. 141.

[8] Camus, p. 144.

[9] Olivier Todd, *Albert Camus* (New York: Carroll & Graf, 2000), p. 408.

[10] For references to Camus' idea of a moderate or relative Utopia, see Lévi-Valensi, Jacqueline, ed. *Camus at Combat: Writing 1944-1947* (Princeton: Princeton University Press, 2006), p. 260-261.

Camus' first involvement with journalism: The communist years under the "Front Populaire"

Camus' ideas of socialism are most clearly articulated in the eight articles "Neither Victims Nor Executioners" that appeared in *Combat* between November 19-30 in 1946,[11] but the importance of his early association with Communism and the Communist Party is far less acknowledged. In his early years, his desire for political action to improve society outweighed his reservations. In a letter to Jean Grenier in August of 1935, he wrote:

> I confess to you that everything attracts me to it [Communism] and I have decided to undergo this experience....Any doctrine can and must evolve. It is sufficient that I firmly subscribe to ideas that bring me back to my origins, to the friends of my childhood, to everything that formed my perceptions and feelings. You understand what my doubts and my hopes are. I have such a strong desire to see a decrease in the amount of misfortune and bitterness that poisons men.[12]

In the same letter, Camus also writes:

> You are right to advise me to join the Communist Party...What has stopped me for a long time and what stops so many minds, I believe, is the religious sense that is missing in communism. It is also the claim that Marxists make about constructing a morality where man is self-sufficient.[13]

---

[11] These eight articles appear in *Camus at Combat* on pages 255-276.

[12] See *Correspondance: Albert Camus—Jean Grenier 1932-1960* (Paris: Gallimard, 1981): (Je vous avoue que tout m'attire vers eux et que j'étais décidé à cette expérience...Toute doctrine peut et doit évoluer. Cela est suffisant pour que je souscrive sincèrement à des idées qui me ramènent à mes origines, à mes camarades d'enfance, à tout ce qui fait ma sensibilité....Vous comprenez quels peuvent être mes doutes et mes espoirs. J'ai un si fort désir de voir diminuer la somme de Malheur et d'amertume qui empoisonne les hommes), p. 22-23. (All translations from the French are mine).

[13] *Correspondance*, p. 22-23. (Vous avez raison quand vous me conseillez de m'inscrire au parti communiste....Ce qui m'a longtemps arrêté, ce qui arrête tant d'esprits je crois, c'est le sens religieux qui manqué au communisme. C'est la prétention qu'on trouve chez les marxistes d'édifier une morale dont l'homme se suffise...).

The beginning of the mutual disillusionment and split between Camus and the Communists, however, started when a former Governor General of Algeria, Maurice Viollette, introduced a bill in the Chamber of Deputies in France that would have given the vote to a select group of Moslems in Algeria.[14] Camus wholeheartedly supported the Blum-Viollette bill and when the Radical Socialists in Algeria opposed the plan, Camus published an article in the Culture Center magazine in 1937, entitled "A Manifesto of Algerian Intellectuals," in which he attacked the colonial attitude towards the Algerian population.[15] Following the publication of the "Manifesto," the French Communist Robert Deloche sent a report to the Comintern in Moscow calling Camus a "Trotskyite agitator" and asking that he be purged from the party for not following the Party Line, which eventually led to his expulsion.[16]

---

[14] Alistair Horne in his book *A Savage War of Peace: Algeria 1954-1962* (New York: New York Review of Books, 2006) says of Viollette: "His declared ideal was that 'Muslim students, while remaining Muslim, should become so French in their education, that no Frenchman, however deeply racist and religiously prejudiced he might be…will any longer dare to deny them French fraternity'. It spelt, in one word "assimilation" p. 37.

[15] Todd, p. 59-61. Herbert R. Lottman in *Albert Camus: A Biography* (London: Axis, 1997) remarks that the Blum-Viollette Plan called for the vote to be given to 21,000 Moslems (p. 165), and Todd writes that as a result of opposition from the Radical Socialists (the rich colonists) and other French political classes, the bill was defeated (see p. 60-62). According to Camus in *Combat* (May 18, 1945): "In 1936, the Blum-Viollette plan marked a first step toward a policy of assimilation after seventeen years of stagnation. It was by no means revolutionary. It would have granted civil rights and voting status to roughly 60,000 Muslims. This relatively modest plan aroused immense hopes among the Arabs. Virtually the entire Arab population, represented by the Algerian Congress, indicated its approval. But leading colonists, banded together in the Financial Delegations and the Association of Mayors of Algeria, mounted a counteroffensive powerful enough to ensure that the plan was never even presented to the Chambers" (see *Camus At Combat: Writing 1944-1947* (Princeton: Princeton University Press, 2006), p. 208-9.

[16] Todd, p. 61-62. According to Lottman, at the time of the creation of the Algerian Communist Party on July 4, 1936, the anti-colonialism stance of the Communist Party was relegated to a secondary role by Stalin, who was more concerned with the Fascist threat. The result of this policy both in France and Algeria would be a greater division between the Moslem population, its leaders like Messali Hadj and Amar Ouzegane, as well as its supporters like Camus. It would also create an unbreachable divide between those who favored the idea of Moslem integration into French-Algeria and those who advocated Moslem nationalism and independence. In this debate, Camus came down clearly on the side of the Moslems (see Lottman, p. 161-168).

Camus' membership in the Communist Party lasted from 1935 to 1937, and had a profound impact on his philosophical vision of political problems and his subsequent activism.[17] His interest in politics continued, but it was now sustained through literature, the theatre, and a more personal form of journalism. Although he was no longer a political activist, he would soon find a new outlet in journalism in a left-wing newspaper, the *Alger Républicain*, which supported both the socialist policies of the Popular Front headed by Léon Blum and the Moslem population in Algeria. Founded in October, 1938 by Jean-Pierre Faure, who hired Pascal Pia as editor, the *Alger-Républicain* was modeled on the *Oran Républicain*, and promoted itself as "the daily newspaper of the Popular Front, that is, of Democracy."[18]

The Misery of Kabylie

Camus' first articles in 1938 were book reviews. However, with the right-wing government of Edouard Daladier now in power in France and the subsequent shift to the right in the French-Algerian government, Camus began to defend the policies of Blum's government and to criticize the right-wing administration in Algiers through letters to the Governor General.[19] As Lottman relates, at the beginning of his time at the *Alger Républicain*, Camus was responsible for covering criminal trials and investigating the social and political problems of the local population, which brought him face to face with the problems of colonial justice and the rights of the Moslem

---

[17] Lottman states that Camus' membership lasted between "autumn 1935 until 1937," (160), while Olivier Todd states that it ran "sometime between July 1937 and early 1938" (p. 62).

[18] For a discussion of the founding of the *Alger Républicain*, see Lottman 198-200. For the source of the quote and a complete list of the dates and the articles that Camus wrote for this paper, see the article by Charles A. Viggiani (C.A.V.) entitled "Camus and *Alger Republicain* 1938-1939," *Yale French Studies 25* (1960), p. 138-143. Olivier Todd remarks that "The politics of *Alger Républicain* were that of the failed political movement of the Popular Front, led by the socialist Léon Blum. The paper declared that its enemies were 'the traveling salesmen of fascism, and industrial, agrarian, and banking feudalism'" p. 74.

[19] Viaginni, p. 139-140. Camus' first articles appeared under the heading of "Le Salon de Lecture" beginning on October 9, 1938 (138), and on January 10, 1939, Camus published an open letter to the Governor General, p. 140.

population, especially in the cases of Michel Hodent, Sheikh El Okbi, Abbas Turqui, and the arsonists of Auribeau.[20]

The great majority of Camus' novels, short prose, and plays, as well as his essays, revolve around crime and the justice system as core issues. Camus' interest in the issues of crime and justice was not just sociological and political--it also coincided with his deepest philosophical intuitions. We might venture to say that Camus' propensity to juxtapose the ephemeral (and in some cases sordid) aspects of everyday existence with the metaphysical, reflects his particular genius. Camus also used crime as a mirror that he held up to society to question its fundamental values about freedom and justice.

More important than these judicial accounts, however, was the series of eleven articles that Camus wrote on the poverty in the region of Kabylie between June and July, 1939, entitled "Misère de la Kabylie," in which he describes the economic and social conditions of this area.[21] The articles focus on the destitution and the agricultural realities of the Kabyle, which Camus supports with facts, statistics, and vivid descriptions of the struggles

---

[20] Lottman, *Albert Camus,* p. 207-210. Michel Hodent had been charged with the theft of wheat by a rich farmer, along with six other Moslems and one French Algerian and through the paper Camus "exposed methods used to obtain false testimony, the bias of the judge, making it clear that he and his newspaper felt Hodent was completely innocent" p. 208. The El Okbi affair concerned the assassination of the Grand Mufti of Algiers on August 2, 1936, who supported the colonial administration (p. 208), and the last case concerned ten farm workers who were arrested for setting fire to straw huts and were sentenced to hard labor. Camus insisted they were innocent and he showed that torture was used to get them to confess to the crime. He also demanded that the torturers be brought to justice and that the wage system should be looked into (p. 210). It is striking to note how this involvement with the inequities of the colonial judicial system later translated into a major thematic thread in Camus' literary work, as it did in Orwell's *Burmese Days*. Gordon Bower in *George Orwell* London (Little, Brown, 2003) relates that the philosopher A.J. Ayer met both Camus and Orwell in Paris, and that he was "struck by the similarity of their outlook" p. 324. Camus quotes Orwell's *Burmese Days* in *Notebooks: 1945-1951* (New York: Harcourt Brace, 1965): "Most people can be at ease in a foreign country only when they are disparaging the inhabitants" 150. For an article on Camus and Orwell, see Miho Takahashi's "George Orwell and Albert Camus: A Comparative Study—Their Views and Dilemmas in the Politics of the 1930s and 40s," *International Journal of the Humanities* 2:3 (2004), p. 2517-2526.

[21] These articles began on June 5, 1939 in the *Alger Républicain* and appeared daily until June 15. The first article was entitled "La Grèce en haillons," but does not appear in the *Oeuvres complètes* edition (Paris: Gallimard et Club de l'Honnête Homme, 1983). For a list of the dates and the titles, see the article by Viaginni. The translations of these articles are my own.

of poor families forced to depend on government supplies of wheat for survival,[22] as in the following passage: "I believe I can affirm that at least 50% of the population feed on grasses and on roots and the rest wait for administrative charity in the form of distributions of grains."[23] Camus points out that these handouts, which were often inadequate, were used for political purposes.[24] They were also alarmingly unfair. For instance, in the area of Bordj-Meanaïl, the poor got 10 kilos of wheat every month, but in other localities it was every three months, and a family of eight needed 120 kilos a month just for bread.[25] As a result of this: They maintained that the paupers whom I saw prolonged their 10 kilogrammes of grains during the month and for the rest fed on roots and on stems of thistles that Kablyles, with an irony which it is impossible not to consider bitter, call donkey's artichokes.[26]

---

[22] Camus, *Oeuvres complètes* (Paris: Gallimard et Club de l'Honnête Homme, 1983), p. 311. Camus relates that "According to an official report, 40% of Kabyle families currently live on less than 1,000 francs a year, that is to say, …less than 100 francs a month…when one realizes that a Kabyle family always consists of at least five or six members, one gets an idea of the inexpressible destitution in which the Kabyle peasants live." (Un rapport officiel évalue à 40% les familles kabyles qui vivent actuellement avec moins de 1000 francs par an, c'est-à-dire…moins de 100 francs par mois….Quand on saura que la famille kabyle compte toujours au moins cinq ou six membres, on aura une idée du dénuement indicible où vivent les paysans kabyles).

[23] Camus, p. 311. (Je crois pouvoir affirmer que 50% au moins de la population se nourrissent d'herbes et de racines et attendent pour le reste la charité administrative sous forme de distribution de grains).

[24] Camus remarks that "They maintain in Tizi-Ouzou that the last elections of the General Council were determined on the basis of the distribution of grain….and I know… that in Issers they refused grain to those poor people who had voted for the Algerian Popular Party" p. 317. (On affirme à Tizi-Ouzou que les dernières élections au conseil général ont été faites avec le grain des distributions…Et je sais…qu'aux Issers on a refusé du grain à ceux des indigents qui avaient voté pour le parti populaire algérien).

[25] Camus, p. 311. (À Bordj-Menaïel, cette charité se renouvelait tous le mois, dans d'autres localités tous les trois mois. Or il faut à une famille de huit membres environ 120 kilos de blé pour assurer le pain seulement pendant un mois).

[26] Camus, p. 311. (On m'a affirmé que les indigents que j'ai vus faisaient durer leurs 10 kilos de grains pendant un mois et pour le reste se nourrissaient de racine et de tiges de chardon que les Kabyles, avec une ironie qu'on peut juger amère, appellent artichauts d'âne). He also writes that "I did know that the stem of the thistle constituted one of the basic Kabyle food sources. I later verified that this was true pretty much everywhere. But what I did not know is that last year, five small Kabyle children of the region of Abbo died following the consumption of poisonous roots." (Je savais en effet que la tige de chardon constituait une des bases de l'alimentation kabyle. Je l'ai ensuite vérifié un peu partout. Mais ce que je ne savais

In addition to the problems of hunger and food supplies, Camus focused on the unemployment and the problems of emigration, as well as the consequences of colonial exploitation in the form of low wages paid to the workers in the area and long working hours.[27] Camus later remarks that: "As for the idea that has been spread about the inferiority of the indigenous work force, it is on this that I would like to end. Because it finds its source in the general contempt in which the colonist holds the unhappy people of this country."[28]

It is in the article on education, however, that Camus expresses some of his harshest criticism of the colonial administration and its educational policies in Kabylie, beginning with the number of children who were deprived of education due to the lack of schools.[29] He points out that "today only a tenth

---

pas c'est que l'an passé, cinq petits Kaybles de la région d'Abbo sont morts à la suite d'absorption de racines vénéneuses), p. 315.

[27] For his discussion of wages and working hours, see Camus' *Oeuvres complètes* p. 319-323. He also discusses the importance of the Kabyle peasant's freedom to emigrate to France and the benefit that this had on relieving their poverty. Camus advocated steps to make it easier for the Kabyles to emigrate and suggested that they replace the Italians who were leaving southern France. While some countered that the Kabyles were too tied to the mountains, Camus replied by writing that "...I would respond by first reminding them that in France there are 50,000 Kabyle who left them. And I will let a Kabyle peasant answer to whom I posed the question and who answered: "You forgot that we do not have enough to eat. We have no choice." (D'autre part, tout le sud de la France se dépeuple et il a fallu que des dizaines de milliers d'Italiens viennent coloniser notre propre sol. Aujourd'hui, ces Italiens s'en vont. Rien n'empêche les Kabyles de coloniser cette région. On nous a dit: "Mais le Kabyle est trop attaché à ses montagnes pour les quitter." Je répondrai d'abord en rappelant qu'il y a en France 50 000 Kabyles qui les ont quittées. Et je laisserai répondre ensuite un paysan kabyle à qui je posais la question et qui me répondit: "Vous oubliez que nous n'avons pas de quoi manger. Nous n'avons pas le choix"), p. 336.

[28] Camus, p. 322. (Quant à l'idée si répandue de l'infériorité de la main-d'oeurvre indigene, c'est sur elle que je voudrais terminer. Car elle trouve sa raison dans le mépris général où le colon tient le malheureux people de ce pays).

[29] Camus, p. 323. In Camus' view: "The Kabyle's thirst for learning and his taste for study are legendary. But it is because the Kabyle, besides their natural disposition and practical intelligence, quickly understood what an instrument of emancipation the school could be...this is the whole problem of education in Kabylie: this country lacks schools, but nevertheless it does not lack the desire for education. (La soif d'apprendre du Kabyle et son goût pour l'étude sont devenus légendaires. Mais c'est que le Kabyle, outre ses dispositions naturelles et son intelligence pratique, a vite compris quel instrument d'émancipation l'école pouvait être...c'est tout le problème de l'enseignement en Kabylie: ce pays manque d'écoles, mais il ne manque pourtant pas de crédits pour l'enseignement). In the pages that follow, Camus

of Kabyle children who are old enough to attend school can benefit from this education."[30] He also faults the colonial government for failing to live up to the promises made in regards to the construction of schools and the flawed policy of building "palace schools" in economic and tourist areas--when many more schools could have been built elsewhere for the same cost. Camus writes that: "I have the impression that these schools are made for the tourists and investigating committees and that they sacrifice to the prejudice of prestige the elementary needs of the indigenous people....Nothingseems to me more reprehensible than this same policy."[31]

In his concluding remarks on education, Camus expresses his desire to see full equality between the two populations, and a complete assimilation of the indigenous subjects:

> Kabyles desire schools as they desire bread. But I also have the conviction that the problem of education must undergo a more general reform....Kabyles will have more schools when they will have abolished the artificial barrier which separates the European education from indigenous education, on the day where on the benches in the same school, two people will begin to understand each other by getting to know each other.....if they really want assimilation, and that these worthy people are French, you should not begin by separating them from Frenchmen.[32]

---

gives specific figures on the number of students who were turned away from classes or schools because there was no place for them.

[30] Camus, p. 324. (...aujourd'hui, un dixième seulement des enfants kabyles en âge de fréquenter l'école peuvent bénéficier de cet enseignement).

[31] Camus, p. 326-327. (Mai j'ai l'impression que ces écoles sont faites pour les touristes et les commissions d'enquête et qu'elles sacrifient au préjugé du prestige les besoins élémentaires du people indigène...Rien ne me paraît plus condemnable qu'une pareille politique).

[32] Camus, p. 327. (Les Kabyles réclament donc des écoles, comme ils réclament du pain. Mais j'ai aussi la conviction que le problème de l'enseignement doit subir une réforme plus générale....Les Kabyles auront plus d'écoles le jour où on aura supprimé la barrière artificielle qui sépare l'enseignement européen de l'enseignement indigène, le jour où, sur les bancs d'une même école, deux peuples faits pour se comprendre commenceront à se connaître...En tout cas, si l'on veut vraiment d'une assimilation, et que ce people si digne soit français, il ne faut pas commencer par le séparer des Français).

In the remaining articles, Camus considers the economic and social future of the Kabyle and what policies the government should enact. In these pages, the connection between the concrete realities he witnessed and reported and his vision of the absolute centrality of the notion of social justice comes out very strongly. In the final article, for example, he concludes with these words:

> It seems that it is, today, bad for a Frenchman to take action that reveals the misery of a French country. I must say that it is difficult today to know how to be a good Frenchman...But, at least, it is possible to know what it is like to be a just man. And my prejudice is that France will never be better represented and defended than by acts of justice....It is not for a political party that this is written, but for men. And if I wanted to give to this inquiry the sense that it would make them admit it, I would like to say that it is not trying to say: 'Look what you have done in Kabylie,' but 'Look what you have not done.'[33]

From his perspective, it may have been unclear what a national culture or the specific program of a political party should be, but it was perfectly clear what justice and a true humanism demanded. As he wrote in *Combat*, "The face that a nation wears is that of its system of justice."[34] This, more than anything, encapsulates the basic premise at the heart of Camus' political thinking. It is precisely this intuition which will drive his famous polemics with Sartre, Merleau-Ponty, as well as the Communist-leaning philosophers, and that will fuel his reflections in *The Rebel*.

These articles on Kabylie resulted in Camus being criticized by the rightists and the colonial government. He was also accused of idealizing the poor, a

---

[33] Camus, p. 341-342. (Il paraît que c'est, aujourd'hui, faire acte de mauvais Français que de révéler la misère d'un pays français. Je dois dire qu'il est difficile aujourd'hui de savoir comment être un bon Français...Mais, du moins, on peut savoir ce que c'est qu'un homme juste. Et mon préjugé, c'est que la France ne saurait être mieux représentée et défendue que par des actes de justice...Ce n'est pas pour un parti que ceci est écrit, mais pour des hommes. Et si je voulais donner à cette enquête le sens qu'il faudrait qu'on lui reconnaisse, je dirais qu'elle n'essaie pas de dire: "Voyez ce que vous avez fait de la Kabylie", mais: "Voyez ce que vous n'avez pas fait de la Kabylie").

[34] Lévi-Valensi, *Camus at Combat,* p. 165. This quote was taken from an article in *Combat* entitled "Justice and Freedom" dated September 8, 1944.

criticism later brought against Sartre and Fanon in similar fashion for their portrayal of the Algerian peasantry.[35] More importantly, Camus' attempts at exposing the poverty and the injustice of colonial policies sustained his fervent desire for social reform in Algeria, an interest that would continue unabated in his writing, especially in his next journalistic activities as editor and writer of *Combat*.[36]

Camus wrote his last article for the *Alger Républicain* in August of 1939 (the paper eventually closed on October 28), and in September of that year, Camus became the editor-in-chief of a small paper called *Le Soir Républicain*.[37] Pia and Camus reportedly turned it into an anarchist paper that did everything it could to resist the military censorship that started in July of 1939.[38] Camus signed his own name to the editorials, in particular an article called "Explanation of the War," which attracted the attentions of the authorities. After several criticisms by the censors, he was told to stop writing it.[39] *Le Soir Républicain* was eventually closed by the police and the

---

[35] Todd, p. 83. This following note is particularly interesting: "After his articles appeared, Algerian Governor General Le Beau went to Kabylia, perhaps in part impelled by the reporter's descriptions. Some ethnologists who read Camus' articles found they idealized the poor too much, and spoke from too haughty a position, yet no journalist in memory had written such a powerful series of articles." Tolstoy was also criticized for idealizing the peasantry.

[36] It is also worth noting that Frantz Fanon would later be stationed in the Kabylie area in the French army. His books *The Wretched of the Earth* and *A Dying Colonialism,* however, would show a different approach to colonialism and the Algerian problem. This difference in viewpoint also helps to explain the conflicts that would later develop between Camus and the group of Fanon, Jeanson, and Sartre.

[37] See Vigianni, p. 138. Lottman states 'that "…the war was making printing and distribution more costly, and *Alger Républicain* lost readership beyond the city limits. Pia decided to publish a two-page afternoon paper which could be sold by street hawkers. Thus was founded *Le Soir Républicain*, on September 15, which would coexist with *Alger Républicain* until October 28, when the latter was shut down because of the scarcity of newsprint" p. 223.

[38] According to Lottman: "Indeed, their anarchistic tendencies were similar, which is certainly why they worked so well together at the time….Their skepticism, their outspoken dissent, had to cause difficulties with the censors….it [*Le Soir Républicain*] would be a pure journal of opinion, and Pia and Camus, twin mischief-makers, had soon turned it into an anarchist organ" p. 222-224.

[39] Todd relates that in a letter to Francine Faure, Camus said "…Things will get nastier when we publish a new column of 'Explanation of the War' in the paper. A captain in the censorship office told one of the writers about me that I'd better watch out, adding, 'What a shame that boy with such talent should be a bad Frenchman—sic and double sic! This

copies seized on January 10, 1940, and the board of directors blamed Camus for the closure.[40] After this, he found it very difficult to find any job in journalism in Algeria, which forced him to leave for Paris on March 14, 1940,[41] and because of the political situation in Algeria and his journalistic writings, I believe that this, in effect, forced Camus to leave for France. Through the help of Pascal Pia, Camus found work at *Paris-Soir* before ending up as the editor of the resistance paper *Combat*. It is in the articles that he wrote for that paper that we find the clearest development of his political philosophy in regards to socialism and democracy, most notably on the issues of freedom, justice, and morality in politics.

Camus' articles in *Combat* appeared over a period of more than three years from 1944 to 1947.[41] The social analyses and the political positions he expressed there form the basis of many of the ideas that he would later develop in *The Rebel*. Indeed as Lottman has indicated, in October 1945, Camus wrote an article for an anthology published by Jean Grenier entitled "Remarque sur la révolte," which was already the draft of the first chapter of *The Rebel*, six years before the book was actually published in 1951. This

---

morning, as I was again asked to stop running the 'Explanations of the War,' I replied that to fight Hitler, we had to fight Frenchmen who wanted to introduce Hitler's methods in France. That's where things stand now" p. 88-89.

[40] See Lottman, p. 227. He also says that "The board discovered (so said the unpublished statement), by examining articles that had not appeared in the paper because of censorship, that Camus had tried to give the afternoon daily an orientation absolutely contrary to the opinions of the paper's backers....While the board would not go so far as to say that Camus had willfully scuttled the newspaper, it felt that he was responsible for the present situation" p. 227-228.

[41] See Todd, p. 101. Regarding this period, Lottman says that "All sorts of stories have been told about Camus' own situation at this time. That he had to hide out in Oran, that he was expelled to France—as if a man considered subversive would be expelled toward the battlefront....What seems to have happened is that Camus found it difficult to obtain a job (although with so many eligible males away at war that should have been easy), and when he did find one, the government stepped in deftly and took it away from him" p. 230.

[41] Arthur Goldhammer in his online article "Camus At Combat" gives the dates as "from March 1944 until November of 1945" (p. 1). In the introduction to Jacqueline Lévi-Valensi's book *Camus at Combat*: Writing: *1944-1947*, David Carroll states that "Camus published a total of 165 entries in Combat between August 21, 1944, and June 3, 1947: 138 editorials and 27 articles..." p. vii. Goldhammer also makes the point that "Camus had become an important public figure in France more because of his journalism than because of his fictional and quasi-philosophical texts" (p. 1). Camus did, however, continue to contribute articles to *Combat* until 1949.

clearly indicates the crucial importance of his writing for *Combat* in the formation of his political ideas,[42] and I would argue that the source of the ideas contained in *The Rebel* is in fact to be found not just in the *Combat* articles, but indeed in Camus' sustained journalistic activity before his arrival in Paris, specifically in his articles on the poverty of the Kabyle.

Camus was referred to a "*moraliste*" by several writers, including Sartre,[43] and his moral philosophy was based on the belief that human dignity and happiness could only be achieved in a society where reducing poverty, hunger, and economic inequalities became a primary goal. These are the ideas that are clearly outlined in these very early articles on Kabylie, and when writing of the famine in Algeria in *Combat*, he asked, "Is it clear that in a country where sky and land are invitations to happiness, this means that millions of people are suffering from hunger?...When millions of people are suffering from hunger, it becomes everybody's business." [44]

The failure of Christianity, Utopian Socialism, Marxist Communism, and other ideologies to improve these conditions constituted a recurring theme and criticism in his works, notably in *The Rebel*. The subject remained a primary focus of Camus' mature political and social philosophy as he tried to understand the relationship between political institutions and the human struggle for freedom through revolt and revolution. His moral philosophy is based on the need to create human and social values in a world where poverty robs people of a basic sense of dignity and justice.[45] In *Combat*, he wrote that his definition of socialism "does not believe in absolute and infallible doctrines but in obstinate and tireless if inevitably halting

---

[42] See Herbert Lottman p. 386 and Olivier Todd: "The idea of revolt had obsessed Camus since at least 1943," and that the fifteen-page article on revolt was printed in the magazine *L'Existence* (300). Roger Quillot also comments in *The Sea and the Prisons* (University: University of Alabama Press, 1970) that "The first chapter of *L'Homme révolté* is, except for a few nuances, nothing more than the essay *La Remarque sur la révolte* written between 1943" p. 205.

[43] Stephen E. Bronner in *Camus: Portrait of a Moralist* (Minneapolis: University of Minnesota Press, 1999) called Camus "the great *moraliste* of twentieth-century letters," p. ix., and Sartre in his tribute at the time of Camus' death stated that he belonged to "that long line of moralists whose works represent perhaps what is most original in French Literature" (Jean-Paul Sartre, Modern Times: Selected Non-Fiction (London: Penguin Books, 2000), p. 302.

[44] Lévi-Valensi, *Camus at Combat* p. 203-204.

[45] This, in fact, was one of the main themes of his very first novel *A Happy Death*.

improvement of the human condition. It holds that justice is well worth a revolution."[46] True to this philosophy, Camus attempted through the articles on Kabylie to expose the poverty of this area and to improve the lives and the conditions of these poor native Algerians.

[46] This appeared in an article dated November 24, 1944. See *Camus as Combat*, p. 122.

Works Cited

Beadle, Gordon B. "George Orwell's Literary Studies of Poverty in England." *Twentieth Century Literature* 24:2 (1978): 188-201.

Bower, Gordon. *George Orwell*. London: Little, Brown, 2003.

Bronner, Stephen Eric. *Camus: Portrait of a Moralist*. Minneaopolis: University of Minnesota Press, 1999.

Camus, Albert. *Essais*. Paris: Gallimard et Calmann-Lévy, 1965.

---. *Lyrical and Critical Essays*. New York: Vintage, 1963.

---. *Notebooks: 1942-1951*. New York: Harcourt Brace, 1965.

---. *Oeuvres complètes*. Paris: Gallimard et Club de l'Honnête Homme, 1983.

---. *Resistance, Rebellion and Death*. New York: Vintage, 1974.

---. *The First Man*. London: Penguin Books, 1996.

--- and Jean Grenier. *Correspondance: 1932-1960*. Paris: Gallimard, 1981.

Crowley, Malcolm. "Camus and Social Justice." *The Companion to Camus*. Cambridge University Press, 2007.

Goldhammer, Arthur. "Camus at Combat." http:www.people.fas.harvard.edu/ agoldham/articles/Camus 6/11/07.

Horne, Alistair. *A Savage Peace: Algeria 1954-1962*. New York: New York Review of Books, 2006.

Letemendia, V.C. "Poverty in the Writings of Albert Camus." Polity 19:3 (1997): 441-449.

Lévi-Valensi, Jacqueline, ed. *Camus at Combat: Writing 1944-1947*. Princeton: Princeton University Press, 2006.

Lottman, Herbert. *Albert Camus: A Biography*. London: Axis, 1997.

Pearce, Robert. "Orwell, Tolstoy, and Animal Farm." *The Review of English Studies* 49:193 (1998): 64-69.

Quillot, Roger. *Critical Essays on Albert Camus*. Boston: G.K. Hall & Co., 1988.

---. *The Sea and the Prisons: A Commentary on the Life and Works of*

Albert Camus. University: University of Alabama Press, 1970.

Sartre, Jean-Paul. *Modern Times: Selected Non-Fiction*. London: Penguin, 2000.

Takahashi, Miho. "George Orwell and Albert Camus: A Comparative Study—Their Views and Dilemmas in the Politics of the 1930s and 40s." *International Journal of the Humanities* 2:3 (2004): 2517-2526.

Todd, Olivier. *Albert Camus*: A Life. New York: Carroll & Graf, 2000.

Viaginni, Charles A. "Camus and the Alger Repubicain1938-1939." *Yale French Studies* 25 (1060): 138-143.

Meursault: Mad, Bad, Messiah?

By Simon Lea

In *The Myth of Sisyphus* Camus criticizes what he sees as extreme reactions to the absurd; the Christian view that the absurd leads us to God and the existentialist position leading to nihilism. Popular views of Meursault tend often to lean towards the extreme. That is, he is mentally unbalanced or retarded, he is a nihilist lost in a meaningless universe, or a mythical being who kills men like plants lean towards the sun. I believe that Camus intended Meursault to be not that much different to you or I, that his thoughts, feelings and reflections on the world he finds himself in are not at all extreme, that he is, as he'd like to tell his lawyer, "just like everyone else."[1] In this paper I will be looking at three extreme, but popular, views of Meursault, that is that he is either mad, or bad or some kind of messiah. Readers familiar with C. S. Lewis will recognise an obvious similarity to his famous *Trilemma* regarding Jesus. That is, that Jesus of Nazareth can be considered either Mad, Bad or God.

One word of caution I would like to add, before we begin, is that we should remember that *The Stranger* is a first person narrative and that it may not be that reliable. Meursault, the narrator, admits that he is not very good at explaining himself and that he doesn't like discussing his ideas. He fails to make himself understood to various other people appearing in the novel and confesses to not understanding others, notably the examining magistrate. We should wonder why someone who doesn't like talking to others is bothering to talk to us. And why someone who is clearly intelligent would choose to express himself in ways that, at times, make him look rather simple. *The Stranger* can be seen as an attack on game-playing but, after taking a step back, one can't help but suspect that Meursault is playing a game with us. I want us to keep this at the back of our minds for now, until we reach the conclusion of this essay.

---

[1] A. Camus, *The Outsider*, Penguin (1982) p.65

In his 1955 preface to the American University edition of *The Stranger* Camus writes: "I summarized *The Stranger* a long time ago, with a remark that I admit was highly paradoxical: 'In our society any man who does not weep at his mother's funeral runs the risk of being sentenced to death.' I only meant that the hero of my book is condemned because he does not play the game [...] A much more accurate idea of the character, or, at least one much closer to the author's intentions will emerge if one asks just *how* Meursault doesn't play the game. The reply is a simple one: he refuses to lie. To lie is not only to say what isn't true. It is also and above all, to say *more* than is true, and, as far as the human heart is concerned, to express more than one feels. [...] One would therefore not be much mistaken to read *The Stranger* as the story of a man who, without any heroics, agrees to die for the truth. I also happened to say, again paradoxically, that I tried to draw in my character the only Christ we deserve."[2]

In any discussion of how to understand a literary character the simple objection is why not just go with whatever the author says. After all, isn't she or he the expert on their own creations? The short answer is no, authors are not necessarily the best judge of their own characters. Characters, quite early into the writing process, take on a life of their own. For sure, in the writer's mind, novels begin with a brief sketch of who each person is. Some are based on people known to the author, others are amalgams of various people, and some are complete inventions. We know that Meursault was initially based on Pierre Galindo, the brother of one of Camus' girlfriends and the incident on the beach was based in a large part on an incident that really happened to Galindo. We know that Raymond gives an account of an event that Camus overheard one day on a tram-ride. But Meursault is not Pierre Galindo, and Raymond is not some guy overheard on the tram. Once the novel is in print, the author's understanding of each character is as good (or bad) as anyone else's. Camus, annoyed that reviewers and critics had failed to understand Meursault also admitted that his conclusion was just one of many.

In order to understand Meursault we need to understand five events. Each event has many sub-events, some have more than others. First, we need to give them a name. I have chosen: (1) The Funeral, (2) Marie Cordona, (3) Raymond Sintès, (4) The Killing, and (5) Lack of Remorse. Each of these things are complex events made up of simpler parts. For example, *The*

---

[2] A. Camus, "Preface to The Stranger", *Lyrical and Critical Essays*, Vintage (1970) p.336-7

Funeral includes: Meursault's reaction to the telegram informing him of his mother's death, his decision not to see inside the coffin, drinking café au lait and smoking cigarettes during the vigil, and some other details. *Marie Cordona* includes meeting her on the beach the day after the funeral, going to the cinema and taking her home, odd comments regarding marriage, and some other details. These five events will be used in our discussion on whether Meursault is mad, bad or messiah. They are, if you like, the evidence against him.

If Meursault is mad, then his behaviour during the funeral, his treatment of Marie, assisting Raymond in the cruel punishment of his girlfriend, murdering the Arab and his lack of remorse can be explained by his mental illness. Other factors, such as his strange lack of emotion and ambition and his refusal to do anything to help himself in court can also be explained away. In the section dealing with madness and mental disability we look at the idea of Meursault being schizophrenic or mentally handicapped in some way. We also look into the possibility of his suffering a temporary 'psychotic break' brought on by depression, grief, and/or intoxication. However, it is never intended to prove that Meursault should be thought of as in some way mad, rather, the opposite, to rule out the idea.

We then turn to the idea that Meursault is not mad but bad. That is, that he is evil, some kind of monster. Using the events, described above, we look for evidence to suggest that Meursault is evil. The prosecutor, during the trial, does just this and he finds a monster in Meursault. However, what we will find is that Meursault, during these events, acts no differently than most of the people in his society, that far from being a monster he is, in his own words, "... just like everyone else, exactly like everyone else."[3] What we find is that all the evidence is explained away, leaving us with a Meursault neither mad nor bad.

We are left with the third option in our trilemma, messiah. This is the idea that Meursault is some kind of saviour hero, someone who will deliver us from evil, in Camus' words "the only Christ we deserve."[4] At this point in

---

[3] A. Camus, *The Outsider*, Penguin Books (1982) pp.65,66

[4] A. Camus, "Preface to The Stranger", *Lyrical and Critical Essays*, Vintage (1970) pp.336,337

our discussion we will no longer be interested in the evidence *against* Meursault but rather *for* Meursault. That is, what defense is there for the idea that he is some kind of hero? A trilemma is a choice of three options, none of which are satisfactory. In this paper I will discuss why Meursault can not be considered mad, or bad, but also why he doesn't work as a messiah. What this means for *The Stranger* I will deal with in my conclusion.

I. Is Meursault mad?

Camus reacted strongly against any idea that Meursault was schizophrenic. Philip Thody tells us that the 1955 preface was "directed first and foremost against critics like Father Troisfontaines, Wyndham Lewis, Pierre Lafue, and Aimé Patri, who have argued that Meursault was 'a schizophrenic,' or 'a moron'."[5] I agree with Camus. I don't think Meursault can be considered mad, nor is he a simpleton.

Meursault is sociable, takes an interest in others, and displays intelligence. For sure, he is not talkative and when forced to talk he is far from articulate but this failing is nothing very unusual. Camus himself was not a very good public speaker. In the care home, Meursault shows interest in the caretaker and they chat together. Meursault remembers things that the old man has said previously and engages in the conversation. He also shows an interest in his elderly neighbour, Salamano, whose scabby dog goes missing. Meursault is friendly and polite, saying good evening when they meet on the landing and enquiring after the dog. When the dog escapes (wriggling out of his collar whilst Salamano is watching a human escape artist) Meursault offers advice on finding the animal. And when it becomes apparent that the dog is never coming back, he tries to console the old man. It is noteworthy that Meursault says that he is upset by the dog's disappearance, showing empathy for his neighbour.

He successfully chats up Marie Cordona, asks her out to the cinema and takes her home with him. On the Sunday, the girls who see him watching them from his balcony recognise him and wave. Considering the ease with which he picked up Marie the day before, we can assume that Meursault has no problem attracting the opposite sex. Céleste, the café owner who

---

[5] Ibid.

sometimes goes to the races with Meursault, describes him as a man of the world. His neighbour Raymond Sintès also considers him a man of the world. He appears to charm Masson and his wife; Meursault is polite and friendly, complimenting the host on his chalet. Masson, who has only met him once and that was on the day Meursault came to his house and murdered a man, stands up for him in court, telling the jury that the man in the dock is a 'decent chap'.

On the day of the murder Meursault displays his intelligence in two ways. It is he who works out how the Arabs knew where to find them (they noticed Marie's oilskin bag and guessed correctly that the trio were going to the beach). And during the second run-in with the Arabs on the beach, Meursault skillfully disarms Raymond. Predicting that simply telling the hot-headed Raymond not to shoot would probably just make him more likely to pull the trigger, Meursault quickly finds the words that will persuade Raymond to hand over the gun without losing face.

At Meursault's trial, every one, but two, of his friends, associates and colleagues speak in his defense. The only two people we are introduced to, in the novel, that are not at the trial are Meursault's boss and his friend Emmanuel. Their absence can be explained for artistic reasons. The character of Emmanuel is interesting. He and Meursault would eat together, go to the cinema together and could accurately be described as friends. A possible explanation for his absence (and I admit this is pure conjecture) can be found in his name.[6] Emmanuel means 'God is with us' in Hebrew. Is his absence from court Camus' way of suggesting that God is absent from the proceedings? Whether or not Camus intended this character to be read in this way, we have to include Emmanuel in the list of people with whom Meursault has normal, friendly relations. He might not be at the trial but he is a witness to us, attesting to Meursault's good character.

---

[6] Camus chooses the names of his characters carefully. Raymond Sintès has Camus' mother's maiden name, and Marie Cordona has the maiden name of Camus' grandmother. Meursault's name itself is made up from two sounds blending the French for sea and sun (mer + sol). Camus will use versions of the Biblical names Mary and Martha in various works, Meursault's girlfriend is called Marie, Patrice Mersualt from *A Happy Death* has a girlfriend called Marthe. Jan's wife in the play *Cross Purpose* (*The Misunderstanding*) is called Marie, his sister is called Martha. In *The Fall*, Jean-Baptiste Clamence cries out, like his namesake Jean the Baptist, in the wilderness (Clamence sounds similar to *clamans*, 'crying' in Latin).

Taking into account all of the above, it is highly unlikely that we are supposed to read in the character of Meursault a schizophrenic or a 'moron'. That is, there is nothing organically wrong with his brain. He can maintain social relations and retain friendships. These friends are prepared to stand up for him in court. He is not bewildered by life, wandering around in a state of confusion. He's capable of reason and aware that others are too. All this would not be possible if he were handicapped in some way mentally.

However, it must be acknowledged that Meursault comes across as more than a little eccentric. Not for nothing have many commentators considered him mad. In the first half of *The Stranger* he senselessly kills a man, and then shows no remorse whatsoever in the second half of the novel. We have seen that Meursault is neither schizophrenic nor is he mentally challenged. However, another possibility remains. At the time of the killing he could have been suffering some kind of psychotic break from normal functioning possibly triggered by grief, excessive fatigue, excessive alcohol intake and the excessive heat of the Algerian sun.

Let's explore the idea that the death of Meursault's mother tipped him over the edge, bringing on some kind of psychotic depression. Psychotic depression is defined as "a mental disorder in which a person has depression along with a loss of touch with reality (psychosis)"[7]. Meursault's hallucinatory account of the killing, ending with the comment "And it was like giving four sharp knocks at the door of unhappiness"[8] seems to fit the diagnosis. The Arab appears to be laughing, when he almost certainly isn't. Everything shakes, then "The sea swept ashore a great breath of fire. The sky seemed to be splitting from end to end and raining down sheets of flame."[9] Something seems to be controlling Meursault. He is pushed forward by the sun. The gun mysteriously leaves his pocket and is pointed at the man before him (Meursault never tells us when the revolver he grips inside his jacket is brought out, does he know?). He does not fire the gun but the trigger gives way.

---

[7] A.D.A.M. Medical Encyclopedia
(http://www.ncbi.nlm.nih.gov/pubmedhealth/PMH0001929/)

[8] A. Camus, *The Outsider*, Penguin Books (1982) p.60

[9] Ibid. p.60

We have mentioned above that Meursault had relationships with other people; he is friends with Emmanuel, Céleste, Marie and Raymond, and gets on well with Masson and his wife. And that if he was suffering from schizophrenia he wouldn't have managed to create and maintain these relationships. So, if he was a depressed psychotic, wouldn't these people have noticed? Well, eventually they might have. If he is suffering from a temporary psychosis brought on by depression exacerbated by the death of his mother, it is possible that he could commit the murder before his illness has a chance to effect his relationships with others. That is, the killing of the Arab is the first clear indication to others that something is wrong with their friend. The events that take place in the first half of the novel take place over a very short period of time (compared to many months in the second half). The two major characters, Marie and Raymond, have only gotten to know Meursault after the death of his mother. They knew of him, he's not a complete stranger. Marie used be a typist at his place of work and Raymond lives in the same building, exchanging a few words every now and again. But neither of them get to know Meursault until the two weeks leading up to the murder. Salamano knew his mother but only really talks to Meursault after the death of his dog which occurs within this two week period. In fact, the only witness in Meursault's trial who really knew him before the death of his mother is Céleste. If Meursault's personality changed after the death of his mother, as a result of depression, the only person who might possibly notice the difference is Céleste, but given the short period of time and the fact that during this time he doesn't see him outside of the café (no trips to the races are mentioned) it is unlikely he would get the opportunity to register a change in Meursault if there was one.[10]

Meursault spends a lot of time feeling tired and sleeping in bed (so does Patrice Mersault in *A Happy Death*).[11] He dozes off during the vigil over his

---

[10] Even if we entertain the idea that the peculiar 'robotic' woman Meursault sees in the café, and later during his trial, is a hallucination – and I do not believe Camus intended her to be – then Celeste would have noticed nothing strange about Meursault's behaviour. He doesn't attempt to communicate with the woman in the café or when he follows her. If he had, and she is a hallucination, Celeste could have seen Meursault talking to himself. But since he doesn't attempt any communication all that Celeste would have seen was his friend eating dinner and then leaving the café.

[11] Meursault is a creature of habit. In notes taken for a novel, possibly *The Stranger* or *A Happy Death,* Camus writes: "He can be completely explained by his habits, of which the most deadly is to stay in bed."

mother's coffin; he is so tired that he can 'hardly think straight' during the funeral procession, and heads home to Algiers 'to go to bed and sleep for a whole twelve hours.'[12] The next day he has trouble getting up, the following day he sleeps until ten and then stays in bed until noon. Back at work, the first thing that his boss asks is 'if [he] wasn't too tired'[13] A strange thing to ask unless Meursault is coming across as unusually tired. At lunch with Emmanuel he has too much to drink and goes home to sleep it off. After the commotion of Raymond beating his girlfriend, Meursault is sleepy and takes a nap. The morning of the day of the murder Marie has to shout at him and shake him just to wake him up. He has a headache and, according to Marie, 'a face like a funeral'.[14] On his walk down the beach with Raymond and Masson, before the first run-in with the Arabs, Meursault says, '[I] wasn't thinking about anything because the sun beating down on my head was making me feel sleepy.'[15]

Alcohol plays an important part in the events that unfold in the first half of the novel. On the Monday back at work Meursault drinks too much wine at lunch and needs to sleep it off. Every time Meursault meets with Raymond, he drinks alcohol. On the first night he has over a litre of wine. After the 'punishment' of Raymond's girlfriend, they go out and have brandy. On the day of the murder, Meursault has too much wine at lunch. That morning, Marie had to shout and shake him to wake him up. Could this have anything to do with the fact that the day before he'd been out with Raymond to give his statement at the police station? It is likely that they drank together and Meursault's difficulty rising, his headache and the pain of the sunlight 'like a slap in the face' when he gets outside sounds a lot like a hangover. The murder itself takes place a couple of hours after heavy drinking at lunch-time. The wine was certainly flowing, Masson keeps refilling Meursault's glass and the drink gives him a 'thick head'. Walking down the beach, moments before meeting the Arab for the last time, Meursault describes the 'drunken haze' the sun was 'pouring' into him.[16]

---

[12] A. Camus, *The Outsider*, Penguin Books (1982) p. 22

[13] Ibid. p.23

[14] Ibid. p.49

[15] Ibid. p.54

[16] Ibid, p.58

Meursault was tired and he had been drinking a lot but this isn't proof that he was psychotic. If the murder was due to a brief psychotic break or due to a mixture of depression and grief, exacerbated by fatigue and excessive drinking then we could expect Meursault to have recovered before the end of the novel. He would no longer be drinking, since he is in prison, and if he had been suffering psychosis and was still suffering psychosis then there would have been further incidents of his losing touch with reality of which there are not.[17] His attempts to understand his fate, the surge of feeling he experiences at thoughts of being free and avoiding the guillotine, as well as the fear he expresses to the chaplain[18] demonstrate than he is a normal man in an extraordinary position. A quite lucid Meursault says at the end of the novel "I'd been right, I was still right, I was always right."[19] Add to this that it is Meursault who is narrating the tale and he doesn't come over as psychotic. I am reminded of Jean-Baptiste Clamence's narration in *The Fall*. That is, I suspect the man telling the story is not entirely sincere, that there is something more to it that he's letting on.

II. Is Meursault bad?

In Camus' essay 'Summer in Algiers' he provides a list of things that make up a code of morality for working class men in that region. The first of which is that you look after your mother[20]. One of the things held against Meursault, not only in court but, as Salamano confides in him, by some of the local people also, is a failure to look after his mother[21]. In what ways does Meursault fail in respect to her? He puts her in a care home, he is unsure when she died or exactly how old she was. He doesn't want to view the body and he drinks café au lait and smokes cigarettes during the vigil. The day after her funeral he goes swimming, picks up a girl and takes her to see a comedy before bringing her home and sleeping with her. Does this make Meursault a monster? Remember, we are not interested in whether or not he

---

[17] He is detached during the trial but this doesn't read as if the detachment is due to psychosis.

[18] Ibid. p.112 "I explained to him that I wasn't in despair. I was simply afraid, which is only natural."

[19] Ibid. p.115

[20] A. Camus, 'Summer in Algiers', *Lyrical and Critical Essays*, Vintage (1970) p.87

[21] A. Camus, *The Outsider*, Penguin Books (1982) p.48

is a nice guy but whether his actions are so outside the acceptable norm that he can be rightfully considered a monster.

The reason Meursault doesn't know the exact day his mother died is down to the ambiguous telegram he receives from the home: "Mother passed away. Funeral tomorrow. Yours sincerely."[22] Meursault's behaviour is no more or less callous than that of some of the others involved in the funeral. The telegram itself is a callous way to inform a son of his mother's death. The caretaker at the home is quite insensitive in his discussion of how bodies need to be buried quickly in Algeria because of the heat. And the treatment of Pérez, Madame Meursault's boyfriend, an elderly man who is forced to run behind the hearse and who faints with exhaustion when he arrives at the church, is outrageous by modern standards. People have their own way of dealing with grief and sometimes do not know how to feel or what to feel when a family member passes away. And we see, as time passes, that Meursault comes to understand his mother more and his feelings toward her death change. Nothing in Meursault's behaviour with regards to his mother shows him to be inhuman, a monster. But his behaviour is still odd. There are set and established ways to talk about the recently deceased. Telling his first lawyer, "I probably loved mother quite a lot, but that didn't mean anything' and to then acknowledge that, "To a certain extent all normal people sometimes wished their loved ones were dead"[23] is completely inappropriate for the situation. Does this failure to acknowledge what is appropriate display a callous disregard for his mother? What's happening in this situation is strange. Meursault doesn't have a callous disregard for his mother (if he did, why bother attending her funeral in the first place?) and he is intelligent. So why is he talking like this?

Meursault is also condemned for his lack of feeling towards Marie. However, his conversations with Marie are not as strange as they first appear. When she asks him if he loves her it has only been a week since they first met on the beach. Could she seriously have expected him to say yes? She appears hurt when he says he doesn't love her but is soon laughing again, so the conversation can not have been all that serious. Similarly, the following week when she asks if Meursault wanted to marry her it is not clear whether she is

---

[22] Ibid. p.9

[23] Ibid. p.65

actually proposing or just enquiring after his interest in her, on where their relationship is heading. Again, the scene ends with Marie smiling. Later on, after he points out some attractive women, she declines his dinner invitation, claiming that she has a prior engagement. We can assume she's referring to a date with another man because she doesn't say what the 'something' she has to do is and then immediately pulls Meursault up for not wanting to know where she's going (and presumably who she is meeting). The thing is that he *does* want to know but didn't think of asking. Read this way, he and she come over as young lovers unsure of where they stand in their new relationship and where things are headed. This is perfectly normal.

Then there is Meursault's reaction, or lack of reaction, to Raymond's story of beating his girlfriend and his agreement to write the letter that will entrap this girl in a cruel and humiliating punishment. Meursault does like Raymond, considers him a mate (just as much as Céleste, although Céleste "was worth more than him"[24]), and expresses no condemnation over his violence towards women. Why does Meursault contribute to the abuse of Raymond's girlfriend by writing the letter and by going to the police station to act as a witness on his behalf?

Meursault was quite drunk when he wrote the letter for Raymond. That might explain why he went along with the plan but it doesn't explain why he never regrets it. He does say, when he describes the trial, "I'd never really been able to regret anything. I was always preoccupied by what was about to happen, today or tomorrow"[25] but this hardly gets him off the hook. Most sociopaths would probably say much the same thing. It is quite possible that even if he were a man to regret things, he wouldn't have regretted writing the letter. However, there is every chance that he, and Camus, would not have seen much wrong in his actions. Beating a cheating woman may have been considered a natural response for a working class man in 1930s Algeria. After the beating Raymond asks Meursault to act as a witness for him that his girlfriend cheated; so presumably if Raymond can prove to the police that the girl had deceived him then the beating would be seen as justified. It is worth observing that in a 2005 survey on domestic violence carried out on behalf of

---

[24] A. Camus, *The Outsider*, Penguin Books (1982) p.116

[25] Ibid. p.97

the BBC, 30% of UK men and 31% of women agreed that domestic violence was acceptable if one of the partners had been unfaithful.[26]

Going back to Camus' essay on the working men of Algiers, we read:

> "I fully realize that such people cannot be accepted by everyone [...] People commonly reproach its "mentality" that is to say, its particular mode of life and set of values. And it is true that a certain intensity of living involves some injustice."[27]

Meursault's siding with Raymond over the domestic violence against his girlfriend could then be a reflection of his Algerian working class mentality, regrettable perhaps but a sign of institutionalized and deep-rooted sexism rather than one man's aberration. If this is so, then Meursault can not be singled out as a monster. Raymond's actions were worse: the plan was his idea and it was his fists striking the woman. However, even he does not come across as a monster but rather a pathetic character.[28] His plan doesn't even work. The woman fights back and he is slapped and humiliated by the policeman. He lives in fear of her brother's retribution and ends up slashed and bloody.

If we can find nothing evil in Meursault's reaction to his mother's death and funeral, or in his behaviour with Marie; if we find him reprehensible in his complicity with Raymond's abuse of his girlfriend but, not a monster, we are left with just *The Murder* and Meursault's subsequent *Lack of remorse*. Putting aside the actual killing for the moment, let's look at his lack of remorse over taking the life of another man.

One possible explanation is that Meursault fails to see the man he killed as a man. It has been noted by many critics and is immediately apparent to all but the most careless reader that while Meursault and all his European friends have names, none of the Arabs do. In any discussion of the novel, we are

---

[26] Hitting Home: Domestic violence survey part II (http://news.bbc.co.uk/1/hi/uk/2753917.stm)

[27] A. Camus, 'Summer in Algiers', *Lyrical and Critical Essays*, Vintage (1970) p.89

[28] "There is something tragic about him in his liking to humiliate her." A. Camus, Notebooks 1935-1942, Rowan & Littlefield edition (2010) p.100

forced to refer to the murdered man as 'the Arab' or the more clunky 'the brother of Raymond's girlfriend'. If Meursault (and Camus) lived in a climate of institutionalized sexism they most certainly lived in a country in which Arabs were treated and believed to be second class citizens. Camus, to his credit, recognized this earlier than most of his fellow Belcourt residents but, as Patrick McCarthy points out, "Few working class Europeans shared their concern or saw any link between their own struggles and the Arabs."[29] Camus believed in being generous and hoped for assimilation but he had no Arab friends. Meursault is so blind to Arabs that he fails to notice until it is pointed out to him that the Arab nurse in the care home, that he has just seen, has a bandage across her face. "Where her nose should have been, the bandage was flat. Her face seemed nothing but a white bandage."[30] Yet he notices the caretaker's white moustache, his beautiful blue eyes and reddish complexion. An animosity between Europeans and Arabs is shown by Camus. Meursault describes how the Arabs stare at him, not as if they were gazing at another human being but as if he were a block of stone or a dead tree. After the killing, Meursault himself will think no more of the man he leaves lying dead on the beach than he would of leaving a dead tree lying in the sand. None of this makes him a good man but no worse than the men he lives amongst, Camus himself included.

So we are left with the killing itself. The killing is inexplicable. Meursault cannot give a good account of himself at trial. As discussed above Camus describes the event in strange hallucinatory language. Camus scholar David Sprintzen in his analysis of the murder says: "Returning to the beach and Meursault's description of what took place, the *why* seems about as relevant as asking a plant why it grows towards the light."[31] In other words, the explanation is that this is just the way things are: plants are phototropic, Meursault's a killer and neither can be understood in moral terms. This answer seems, to me, unsatisfactory. Perhaps Meursault is a special case, someone who can not be judged like ordinary men. This brings us on to the third option in our trilemma, messiah.

---

[29] P. McCarthy, *Camus*, Hamish Hamilton (1982) p.25

[30] A. Camus, *The Outsider*, Penguin Books (1982) p. 12

[31] D. Sprintzen, *Camus: A Critical Examination*, Temple University Press (1988) p.30

III. Is Meursault a messiah?

When we talk of Meursault as a possible messiah it is with a lower-case 'm'. It is not to suggest that he is the expected deliverer of the Jewish people but a deliverer in a general sense. In other words, a hero. A man of extraordinary strength and courage, a saviour whose exploits will be revered. Meursault is often held up to be a hero. Conor Cruise O'Brien has commented that "I have found from reading a number of students' essays on Camus that a prevalent stock response is one as seeing Meursault as a hero and martyr for the truth."[32] This view is not restricted to students. Rachel Bespaloff, as O'Brien points out, reflects on Meursault's 'heroic firmness' that will cost him his life[33]. Adele King recognizes references to the life of Jesus Christ in Meursault's story. She argues that he "plays a Christ-like role, witnessing to a true relationship between man and the world."[34] She points out that Meursault's refusal to tell the examining magistrate why he fired four more shots into the dead body and his three refusals to see the chaplain are analogous to Christ's three refusals to be tempted by Satan. His silence during the trial representing Jesus' silence before Pontius Pilate. Jesus died before an angry crowd and Meursault hopes for a similar audience to his death. There may well be similarities between the lives of Meursault and Jesus of Nazareth but these similarities alone do not a messiah make. So what does Meursault do to make him a savior, a hero?

According to Camus, Meursault is condemned to death because he doesn't play the game. How does he not play the game? According to Camus: "he refuses to lie. To lie is not only to say what isn't true. It is also and above all, to say *more* than is true, and, as far as the human heart is concerned, to express more than one feels." There are numerous instances of game-playing in *The Stranger*. These games are of the sort described by psychiatrist Eric Berne in *The Games People Play* in which the 'players' adopt the roles expected of them in various social situations. Meursault is expected to play various roles throughout the novel. First, he is to be 'the grieving son', then 'the ambitious employee'. Marie wants him to play 'the courting lover' while Raymond wants him to be 'the man of the world'. His lawyer wants to get

---

[32] C. C. O'Brien, *Camus*, Fontana (1982) p.21

[33] Cited in O'Brien, p.21

[34] A. King, *Camus*, Oliver and Boyd (1968) p.54

down to business and discuss how they will play it in court. He is totally frustrated, disgusted even, by Meursault's refusal to play the game. "He thought for a moment. Then he asked me if he could say that I'd controlled my natural feelings that day. I said, 'No, because it's not true.' He looked at me in a peculiar way, as if he found me slightly disgusting."[35] In the examining magistrate's room Meursault is called upon to play a role he has read about in books and it seemed to him "like a game."[36] The magistrate wants him to weep before the crucifix like "The criminals who have to come to me before [who] have always wept at this symbol of suffering."[37] Meursault doesn't play that game, he keeps forgetting that his role is to be the criminal. When Marie visits him in prison she wants to play 'the everything is going to turn out alright' game. In the prison, the other prisoners are tormented by their need for a woman and play with themselves. Meursault, who accepts his punishment, abstains. Note Meursault's disapproval of the game-playing son in the found newspaper article: "I decided that the traveller had deserved it really and that you should never play around."[38] After this point Meursault is not called upon to play any games himself, rather he is a pawn in the games played by others. The journalists use him to create sensational news stories they've 'blown up a bit' (apart from the young journalist, played by Camus himself, who does not pick up his pen when the other reporters do). And the prosecutor uses Meursault's situation to help him play the role of top prosecutor (if the top defense lawyer can get a man off who should be condemned, the top prosecutor seeks the death penalty for a man who could get off.) Even Meursault's own lawyer gets in on the game, playing by the prosecutor's rules rather than coming up with a decent defense for his client. The man is completely outplayed by his rival. His own colleagues play a kind of congratulatory game, patting the lawyer on the back and telling him he was 'magnificent'. Meursault is actually drawn into this game himself and joins in, albeit half-heartedly. It is the only time he admits to playing a game. Although his pointing out the other beautiful women to Marie in chapter five smacks of game-playing to me. So, for the most part, Meursault doesn't play games but what about Camus' claim that he refuses to lie?

---

[35] A. Camus, *The Outsider*, Penguin Books (1982) p.65

[36] Ibid. p.64

[37] Ibid. p.69

[38] Ibid. p.78

Meursault does lie. He writes the letter for Raymond, knowing that the contents are untrue. And he gives a false testimony to the police on his friend's behalf. When he recounts his experience in the examining magistrate's office he says he did, "As *I always do* when I want to get rid of someone I'm not listening to, I gave the impression that I was agreeing with him." [my emphasis][39] Surely, deliberately giving somebody a false impression is a kind of lying? It is only because the magistrate insists on the point that Meursault puts him straight. Presumably before his arrest, with people who he wanted to get rid of, who didn't have the power to detain him and insist on answers, Meursault used this useful deceit freely. As just mentioned above, he joins in the back-patting game of congratulation during the trial when he lies to his lawyer agreeing with the man's colleagues that, after a poor performance, the lawyer was magnificent, "but it was hardly a sincere compliment, because I was tired."[40] If Meursault follows a strict ethic of sincerity, then surely his compliments ought to be sincere.

A possible answer to Meursault's lies has been suggested by various commentators, that when Camus says Meursault refuses to lie, he means only, telling lies about his feelings. That is, he lives honestly, according to the truth that life is absurd. David Sherman makes the point:

> "Meursault not only perceives the futility of hopes (not to mention forging ethical values) in the face of a meaningful universe in which 'all experiences are unimportant' [MS, p.62], but he actually lives his life accordingly. Therefore when Meursault coolly lies to the police on behalf of Raymond, he is being dishonest in a conventional sense, but from the viewpoint of our metaphysical condition he is being honest, for ultimately, just like the death of his mother it makes no difference."[41]

However, a problem remains. If it all makes no difference, why refuse to lie? As Sherman points out, in *The Myth of Sisyphus* Camus places importance on the quantity of life, rather than the quality. Meursault will have a greater quantity of life if he lies to the magistrate and plays the game expected of

---

[39] A. Camus, *The Outsider*, Penguin Books (1982) p.68-9

[40] Ibid. p.101

[41] D. Sherman, *Camus*, Blackwell (2009) p.63

him. In fact, it is almost certain that he will. As O'Brien rightly says, "In practice, French justice in Algeria would almost certainly not condemn a European to death for shooting an Arab who had drawn a knife on him and who had shortly before stabbed another European."[42] Some words of remorse and a few tears on the production of the crucifix and Meursault would have escaped his fate, adding to the quantity of his days.

If Meursault believes everything to be meaningless how do we explain his dislike of the police? If everything is meaningless then why does Meursault show a preference when Marie asks him to call the police on Raymond? He doesn't say something like *Marie asked me to call the police but I thought it was pointless*. No, he says, "I told her I didn't like policemen."[43] It could be an unanalyzed prejudice. Meursault is a working class man from Algiers and, as observed by Camus in his essay 'Summer in Algiers', these men don't like the police. Meursault might not question why he doesn't like police just as he doesn't question why he likes swimming, or sun-bathing, having sex with Marie or being friendly with Raymond. However, he does know that he enjoys these things and that in order to continue to enjoy them he needs to avoid being guillotined. So, the question again, why doesn't he say whatever he needs to in order to escape this fate? One solution suggested by Robert Solomon and favoured by Sherman, is "Meursault neither lies nor tells the truth, because he never reaches that (meta-) level of consciousness where truth and falsity can be articulated"[44] For Solomon Meursault is a 'philosophically fantastic character'. But Camus doesn't want his hero to be *incapable* of telling a lie, he wants Meursault to *refuse* to lie. We seem to have run into the same problem we did when trying to understand the murder by considering Meursault to be as morally unaccountable as a sun-seeking flower. Sartre, in his 'Explication of The Stranger', joins those commentators who claim Meursault's actions can not be understood, when he says that "[Meursault] is there before us, he exists, and we neither understand nor quite judge him."[45] This view of Meursault doesn't help us if we want to understand him as a hero or messiah. He can't agree to die for the truth if he

---

[42] C. C. O'Brien, *Camus*, Fontana (1982) p.22

[43] A. Camus, *The Outsider*, Penguin Books (1982) p.39

[44] Cited, D. Sherman, *Camus*, Blackwell (2009) p.63

[45] J. P. Sartre, 'Explication of The Stranger', *Camus: A Collection of Critical Essays*, Prentice-Hall (1962) p.114

is incapable of doing otherwise. And how can he save us if we can not understand him?

Let's look at Camus' claim that Meursault agrees to die for the truth. There is no sense that this is something he chooses to do when he finds himself in front of the examining magistrate or in court. At no point does he think along the lines of *I could fake remorse and escape the guillotine but I will not lie and will face death in order to stay true to my heart!* The death sentence imposed on Meursault comes as a complete surprise to him. Just before the sentence is read in court, his lawyer has assured him that things are going well. When told that he might get away with just a few years in prison Meursault even asks about the possibility of getting that sentence quashed. The only other place that Meursault can 'agree to die for the truth' is in prison.

In prison, he alternates between imagining that his appeal will be granted, with a surge of joy at the thought, and imagining that his appeal will be denied. Through a series of mental exercises he trains himself to accept that he will die. Not simply that if his appeal is denied he will die but that he *will* die either way. The imminence of his certain death (with the possibility of his appeal being rejected) allows him to realize the truth that he is going to die. We all know that it is a fact that one day we will cease to live, but most of us can not *feel* this fact as true. Unless death is imminent, the thought of death for us is simply an abstract idea. Meursault manages to accept that he will die regardless of what happens with his appeal and this acceptance allows him experience life without illusion or hope. This experience is a happy one. When Meursault thinks of winning his appeal, or escaping the guillotine, he feels a rush of joy in his body. In his mind he can understand that in the grand scheme of things it doesn't matter whether he dies at thirty or seventy. A series of meaningless events up until death is just as meaningless whenever the death occurs. Note also that the age mentioned is thirty. In 'Summer in Algiers' Camus tells us "A workingman of thirty has already played all his cards. He waits for the end with his wife and children around him. His delights have been swift and merciless. So has his life."[46] Until the prison meditations, Meursault could not harmonize his body's leap of joy at the thought of life with his understanding that life is meaningless. This failure in harmony meant he failed to grasp the truth. Once the harmony is

---

[46] A. Camus, 'Summer in Algiers', *Lyrical and Critical Essays*, Vintage (1970) p.86

achieved he can start to live. The lies, and the false hope, no longer get in the way, preventing him from living his life and being happy. His prison meditations help him to truly accept the fact that because his life must end in death, that it is limited. And this is why he is angry at the chaplain using up his time. His attack on the man is not an attack on society, inauthenticity, false hope, illusion or anything like that. He is simply angry because the time and happiness he has just won is being wasted by this man. Every time dawn passes without his being taken to the guillotine, Meursault has just "gained another twenty-four hours"[47] and he doesn't want to waste a minute of them. I suspect he would have thrown Marie out his cell if she wanted to waste time discussing impossible marriage plans or Raymond if he wanted to show off about some macho incident that occurred on the tram. It is also why he understands his mother, so close to death, choosing to take a boyfriend and start her life again.

However, for all this, acceptance of death is not *agreement* to die. So, it can neither be said that Meursault somehow agrees to die for the truth during the trial nor can it be said that once in prison, he makes some agreement to die for the truth. When he dies it won't be *for* anything. The only possible interpretation could be that Camus means 'agree' in the sense that everything is telling Meursault that he will die, whether by the guillotine or by old age, and he 'agrees' with this truth. In *The Myth of Sisyphus* Camus writes:

> "A man notices or says that he is thirty. Thus he asserts his youth. But simultaneously he situates himself in relation to time. He takes his place in it. He admits that he stands at a certain point on a curve that he acknowledges having to travel to its end. He belongs to time and, by horror that seizes him, he recognizes his worst enemy. Tomorrow, he was longing for tomorrow, whereas everything in him ought to reject it."[48]

This man has become aware that his time is limited and of the absurdity of longing for tomorrow. However, for most people this 'revolt of the flesh' is temporary and they return to thinking only of their future life – they no longer 'agree' that they will die. This interpretation is closer, I believe to what Camus must have meant, and it explains why he added that Meursault

---

[47] A. Camus, *The Outsider*, Penguin Books (1982) p.109

[48] A. Camus, *The Myth of Sisyphus*, Penguin Classics (2000) p.20

agrees to die without 'heroics'. He refuses to play games, he is sentenced to death and he agrees that he will die (one day). Meursault doesn't take any kind of heroic stand against game-playing. He is a victim of the games played by others and agreeing to die is not some kind of price he agrees to pay for refusing to play games.

What about Camus' claim that "In our society any man who does not weep at his mother's funeral runs the risk of being sentenced to death"? A similar way of putting this would be: anyone who refuses to *play the game* might end up dead. Most people would accept this as pretty uncontroversial. The risk may be slight for some and much greater for others but who hasn't been advised at some point in their lives to just 'play the game' and not cause waves? As the Japanese proverb says *The stake that sticks up gets hammered down* and people who refuse the go along with some games will 'stick up' and run the risk of getting 'hammered down'.

Meursault is different from the other characters in the novel in that he lives for the present rather than for tomorrow and future goals. We have seen that he lacks ambition. Ambition is always aiming at some future goal. This goal is always some kind of distinction, something that makes one distinct from others. In the original sense of the word, ambition referred to going around canvassing for votes. In today's use the word has a broadly similar meaning. Ambitious people go around doing things in the hope that these things will earn 'votes' of respect from others. People who have career ambitions seek to distinguish themselves in the workplace, so that others will recognize them as the person most deserving of promotion, more responsibility, or a pay rise. Ambitious actors seek to distinguish themselves in auditions, in productions and so on so that others hold them up as great actors and cast them in bigger roles. Ambitious academics need others to recognize them as leading experts (or even *the* expert) in their fields of study. The rewards, for the office-worker, the actor and the academic are all the same. The closer they get to reaching their ambitions, the more honour, respect and power[49] they are given by others. Raymond's ambition is to be seen as a man, he boasts of his macho exploits to Meursault, beats his girlfriend and gets into fights. But he's a failure. He is short and wears clothes that make him look ridiculous. His plan to humiliate his girlfriend fails and he is the one who ends up

---

[49] By *honour* I mean something that is paid to an individual by others. I do not mean anything like personal integrity or abiding by any moral principles.

humiliated, first by the policeman and then by the woman's brother. Most people don't like him and call him a pimp. Raymond's ambitions bring him unhappiness. Rather than enjoy the present, he schemes revenge on his cheating girlfriend and lives in fear of her brother and his friends. He carries a gun, for respect, protection or both? This ends up getting his friend arrested for murder and sentenced to death. The newspaper men (except the one played by Camus) want to write the most sensational stories, so they 'blow up' Meursault's case. The prosecutor wants to be distinguished as a top lawyer; he seeks the death penalty and gets it. Meursault's own lawyer gets drawn into the prosecutor's game and plays by his rules rather than act in the best interest of his client. And this all started with one man, the examining magistrate. He, I suspect Camus wants us to think, is preoccupied with thoughts of a different kind of future, the afterlife. Meursault's problems really start when he refuses to go along with the examining magistrate's expressions of faith.

O'Brien has criticized Camus saying: "What appears to the casual reader as a contemptuous attack on the court is not in fact an attack at all: on the contrary, by suggesting that the court is impartial between Arab and Frenchman, it implicitly denies the colonial reality and sustains the colonial fiction."[50] However, I don't think that Meursault's trial was supposed to be representative of trials currently held in Algiers. Camus goes out of his way to show that the trial is unusual, and therefore can be expected to have an unusual outcome. In fact, Meursault himself seems to agree with O'Brien. For shooting the Arab dead he expects to receive just a couple of years in prison, hard labour if he's unlucky. He even raises the possibly of having this very lenient sentence quashed. But Meursault is at no ordinary trial.

We don't know how the trial has been blown up because Meursault doesn't tell us. A clue comes from a journalist. He tells Meursault that they're blowing up the case. He also says that a reporter from Paris, down to cover the parricide case that follows Meursault's trial, has been told to cover his as well. Why? It may be the summer silly season but it's difficult to believe that Parisians would be that interested in a fight in Algiers between two thugs gone wrong. Meursault knows nothing about what his case has been blown up into, so neither do we, but it must be big to attract the Parisian press. Note that Meursault, who is completely unaware of the sensationalism of his trial,

---

[50] C. C. O'Brien, *Camus*, Fontana (1982) p.23

is taken completely by surprise at the vehemence of the prosecutor and can not understand why the man is so angry. How did things get like this? Things started so simply. The arresting police-officers were not much bothered and the examining magistrate seems to accept everything up until *after* the first shot. How did Meursault's inability to give a good account of why he fired the extra four shots lead to things getting so out of hand? My guess would be that Meursault's refusal to play the repentant sinner for the examining magistrate so shocked and appalled the man that the case became for him a battle between good and evil. Meursault the 'hardened soul' becomes 'Mr. Antichrist'. The magistrate then encourages the prosecutor to seek the harshest punishment. The prosecutor, in front of the assembled media (who are blowing up the case a bit because they've nothing else to write about) puts in the performance of a lifetime, making his trial every bit as newsworthy as the parricide trial taking place the next day. The press take advantage of this and lap up the prosecutor's attack on Meursault, blowing the story up even more.

Where do we stand in our pursuit of Meursault the messiah? He doesn't play the game, he won't say more than he feels but we are unsure why. If he truly believes that everything is meaningless, then why hold to an ethic of sincerity? He agrees that he will die and finds happiness but this agreement to die doesn't involve taking some kind of stand, he throws the chaplain out his cell but this wasn't a protest against anything more than having his time wasted. Meursault isn't a martyr. He doesn't foresee any risk in refusing to play the game, his death sentence is a total surprise. We don't even know that he will not be reprieved. We do know that his crime wouldn't normally earn someone the death penalty and the prosecutor's arguments are absurd. Meursault may well escape the guillotine. However, unlike Jesus, Meursault does not need to die after his trial.

Camus says that Meursault is the only Christ we deserve. Perhaps Meursault is a messiah, just not a very good one. The narrator of *The Stranger* is an inarticulate man who doesn't like talking. He can't explain himself properly to his lawyer and he can't adequately explain this failure of communication to us either. He understands little more about the world than the average working class man of Algiers. He doesn't have an enlightened attitude to Arabs or women. He likes swimming and making love and when the mother, from whom he'd drifted apart, dies, he doesn't pretend to feel a grief he doesn't feel. The little more about the world he does understand came to him first when he gave up his studies, then when he stopped analyzing himself and finally in his prison cell. But he is incapable of adequately passing on what he has learned to us. We get glimpses, we are intrigued and want to know more. Which is why Camus publishes *The Myth of Sisyphus* alongside *The Stranger*. That essay tells us more, in that Camus shares some of his thoughts. The plays *Caligula* and *Cross Purpose* explore more of the same ideas from different angles. Camus wants Meursault to entice the reader into finding out more. As Jacob Golomb in his study of Camus observes, "Fiction, with its fiction rhetoric and irony, shakes us, opens us to change and entices us to pursue change. But only the philosophical essay makes clear the purpose of this enticement and thereby removes any hesitation we may experience in following the traumatic adventures of the heroes of authenticity."[51]

The Stranger has its moments of ridiculousness: Meursault failing to notice the Arab nurse doesn't have a nose and huge bandage over her face, Salamano's dog escaping from his collar while his owner is watching a human escape artist, Raymond's silly hat. The narrator, a narrator who doesn't like talking and isn't good at explaining things, gets caught up in ridiculousness: first the killing, then the trial. Attempting to understand these things is like trying to understand Charles' ridiculous hat in Madame Bovary. Meursault gives us a glimpse of what an ordinary man who chooses not to play games looks like. Camus took those games away from him, leaving Meursault a person naked against the absurd. A stranger kind of messiah than we are used to.

---

[51] J. Golomb, *In Search of Authenticity: From Kierkegaard to Camus*, Routledge (1995) pp.170,171

Works Cited

Bree, Germaine (ed). *Camus: A Collection of Critical Essays*. Prentice-Hall (1962)

Camus, Albert. *Lyrical and Critical Essays*. Vintage (1970)

Camus, Albert. *The Myth of Sisyphus*. Penguin Books (2000)

Camus, Albert. *The Outsider*. Penguin Books (1982)

Camus, Albert. *Notebooks 1935-1942*. Rowan & Littlefield edition (2010)

King, Adele. *Camus*. Oliver and Boyd (1968)

McCarthy, Patrick. *Camus*. Hamish Hamilton (1982)

O'Brien, Connor Cruise. *Camus*. Fontana (1982)

Sherman, David. *Camus*. Blackwell (2009)

Sprintzen, David. *Camus: A Critical Examination*. Temple University Press (1988)

Camus' *Les Justes*: A Rebuff to Sartre's *Les Mains Sales?*[1]

By Benedict O'Donohoe

Preamble

These two strikingly similar plays fall into that period when Sartre and Camus enjoyed an uneasy friendship and rivalry in post-war Paris. It is also a period of tension between radically opposed ideologies, creating moral conflict for politically engaged French intellectuals, both within themselves and between each other. Sartre's evocation of a rigidly ideological and idealistic socialism, preached by his young protagonist Hugo Barine, set against the pragmatism of the mature realist, Hoederer, found an attentive audience in April 1948.[2] Sartre's ambiguous argument for *Realpolitik* at the expense of ethics, appeared to endorse collusion with ideological enemies: the means are justified by the ends, Hoederer insisted, and that invariably results in "getting one's hands dirty".

Twenty-one months later, in December 1949, Camus responded with *Les Justes*, whose characters propound an implicit rebuttal of the cynical Sartrean position. Ivan Kaliayev—like Hugo, an idealist and an intellectual—repudiates the criticism of his colleague, Fedorov, that he defied his orders by failing to throw his grenade at the Archduke's carriage because he was accompanied by children. Laying claim to the Camusian "quest for self",

---

[1] A longer version of this article has been published as "Revolution or Revolt? *Les Mains Sales* and *Les Justes*", in *Sartre Studies International*, Volume 18, Issue 2, 2012: 72–88. This abridged re-draft shifts the emphasis, as the new title suggests, towards the question whether Camus' play was a deliberate reply to Sartre's.

[2] Contat and Rybalka attribute this popular success to the public's "identification" with Hugo and consequent reading of the play as "anti-communist" (see Michel Contat and Michel Rybalka, *Les Écrits de Sartre*, Paris: Gallimard, 1970: 177). All translations from French sources are my own.

244

Kaliayev vindicates the moral conscience of the individual amidst collective action, and so doing delivers a counterblast to the arguably amoral position of Sartre's Hoederer. For Camus, the ends do not necessarily justify the means; there are ethical limits which ultimately guarantee the victory of human dignity over gradualist and morally compromised "progress".

What is each playwright's notion of authenticity, as embodied in their respective protagonists? What are we to make of their common futile deaths (for both Hugo and Ivan die remorseless and unenlightened)? How should we construe their attitudes by contrast with the more pragmatic characters such as Olga and Hoederer, or Fedorov and Annenkov? Is there a sense in which Camus used Kaliayev to critique Sartre's position, thereby provoking their subsequent and definitive dispute?

The Situation

Les Mains Sales

Hugo deliberately places himself in what Sartre calls *une situation-limite*, that is one in which he is obliged to make a decision upon which his own life depends: to assassinate or not to assassinate Hoederer. Nevertheless, even in the most extreme situations, Sartre insists, we remain free and capable of making choices. Should Hugo kill Hoederer in order to obey the orders which he has insisted be given to him, and risk being gunned down in turn by Hoederer's bodyguards? Or should he follow his inclination *not* to kill Hoederer and invite his own execution instead? In either case, Hugo's life is in jeopardy. However, he does not value his life, he says so explicitly, and as he falls under the influence of Hoederer, it becomes clear that life itself frightens him rather more than death.

Later on, when he has killed Hoederer and served three years in prison, Hugo finds himself in a subtly different dilemma. This situation is not of his choosing, but flows from a change in Party policy towards the position propounded by Hoederer. Now, if Hugo toes the new Party line, accepting the official "crime of passion" explanation of Hoederer's assassination, his life will be safe and he can re-join the Party ranks. If, on the other hand, he stubbornly insists that the murder was a political act, then the Party leaders will certainly have him shot. This ought to be an easy decision, and yet Hugo chooses to die, vindicating his action in a misguided tribute to Hoederer.[3]

Those on the political right saw this gesture as a moral self-sacrifice which safeguarded Hugo's integrity and by implication denounced the cynical duplicity of socialism in action. Those on the left construed it as implicitly anti-communist and decried it in the pages of *L'Humanité*, the official press organ of the French Communist Party (PCF). The play was produced in New York within a year, under the tendentious title *Red Gloves*, as a piece of pro-western propaganda.[4] Even Camus, having attended a dress rehearsal with Sartre, observed that it was surely Hugo who "loves men as they are", and not Hoederer, who was evidently "a dogmatic communist who considered men for what they might become, and deceived them in the name of an ideal".[5] Sartre was dismayed—"This was exactly the opposite of what I was trying to say"[6]—and in a bid to suppress such unintended interpretations of the play, he vetoed productions of it throughout the 1950s.

Les Justes

Camus' young hero, Ivan Kaliayev, also finds himself initially in a *situation-limite* of his own choosing. He has opted—out of intellectual conviction rather than class loyalty—to join the "Combat Organisation" of the Revolutionary Socialist Party, and similarly clamoured for the privilege to be entrusted with direct action, thereby risking his own life for the cause. Camus writes in the companion essay, "The Delicate Assassins", that this paradox of "respect for human life in general combined with contempt for one's own" was the defining feature of this anarchist group in *fin de siècle* Russia: "They are indeed living with the same paradox, which brings together within them a

---

[3] For a full plot summary, see Benedict O'Donohoe, "Jean-Paul Sartre, *Les Mains sales* [*Crime*

Passionnel / Dirty Hands]", in *The Literary Encyclopedia*, 2009, at:

http://www.litencyc.com/php/sworks.php?rec=true&UID=11115.

[4] See Benedict O'Donohoe, "Dramatically Different: The Reception of Sartre's Theatre in London and New York", *Sartre Studies International*, Volume 7, Issue 1, 2001: 1–18.

[5] See Contat and Rybalka, op. cit., 184.

[6] Ibid. This key text is cited in full below.

respect for human life in general and contempt for their own lives in particular, which extends to a kind of nostalgia for the supreme sacrifice."[7] Indeed, it appears that for the historical models of Ivan Kaliayev and Dora Doulebov, the idea of self-sacrifice was both a "passionate desire" and an "embellishment" of terrorist activity,[8] not some unfortunate but inevitable collateral risk. This, then, is a marked contrast with the ethos of the Proletarian Party as Sartre conceives it, in which the duty of the activist is rather to continue to make him / herself useful to the cause, so long as that is practically possible.

Like Hugo, Kaliayev discovers that situations are never stable, whether or not one chose them. As he awaits the Grand-Duke's carriage, he has not calculated that his target might not be alone, and he lets the carriage pass by when he sees the Grand-Duchess with her niece and nephew. Kaliayev's sensitivity is engaged, the "assassin's delicacy" is to the fore, and is endorsed by his comrades, whom he feared he had betrayed: "Disregard for one's own life combined with a profound respect for the life of others", writes Camus, "indicates that these delicate assassins lived out the destiny of the revolution in its most extreme contradiction."[9] Violence was both "ineluctable and unjustified, necessary and inexcusable".[10] Contrast this view with Hugo's vacillation which has nothing to do with the innocence of Hoederer (whom he deems to be "guilty" as a class traitor), but rather stems from his reliance upon him as a vicarious father figure. Thus, Hugo's scrupulosity is essentially self-interested, whereas Kaliayev's is altruistic and disinterested. In Camus' universe, revolutionary violence must be measured and contained, it has no right to be indiscriminate.

---

[7] "Ils vivent en effet sur le même paradoxe, unissant en eux le respect de la vie humaine en général et un mépris de leur propre vie, qui va jusqu'à la nostalgie du sacrifice suprême." Albert Camus, "Les Meurtriers délicats", in *Théâtre, Récits, Nouvelles*, ed. Roger Quilliot, Paris: Gallimard, Bibliothèque de la Pléiade, 1962: 1827–33 (1828). Henceforth cited TRN.

[8] Ibid.

[9] "Un si grand oubli de soi-même allié à un si grand souci de la vie des autres permet de supposer que ces meurtriers délicats ont vécu le destin révolté dans sa contradiction la plus extrême." TRN, 1831.

[10] "[…] le caractère inévitable de la violence, […]. Nécessaire et inexcusable, […]." TRN, 1831–32.

There are also parallels "after the event". Kaliayev is captured and convicted but, like Hugo, he has the chance to "cut a deal", and the terms are similar: renounce your assassination and live, or lay claim to it and die. Again, we have a *situation-limite* in both cases, each resolved by the death of the protagonist. But does this mean their motivations are the same? Hugo rejects Olga's offer of rehabilitation and faces the Party's hit squad because of a convoluted impulse to pay tribute to Hoederer by "giving him the death he deserved". This entails his own death, but it is also a betrayal of his comrades in the Party and, ironically, of the pragmatic precepts that Hoederer strove to teach him.

For his part, Kaliayev declines the "golden offer" made to him by the police chief, Skouratov—to save himself and his comrades by "choosing life" (including betrayal) for all of them—both because he stands by the justice of his action and because he is determined to pay for it with his own life.[11] As Camus writes: "Finally, in their minds, murder became identified with suicide. So, one life is paid for by another life. From this double sacrifice there arose an untainted moral value which was bound to serve the progress of justice."[12] In each case there is an admirable, if confused, element of self-sacrifice. However, again it is Kaliayev's motivation that is orientated towards the collective good, while Hugo's is slanted towards self-aggrandisement.

Freedom

Les Mains Sales

Freedom is an absolutely central theme in Sartre's thought and a key theme in Camus'. But if their protagonists find themselves in ever more limited situations in which they are more object than subject, does this mean their freedom is commensurately curtailed? As Hugo despairingly asks of Olga: "But what about *me*? What becomes of me in all of this? It's an assassination

---

[11] See Albert Camus, *Les Justes*, Paris: Gallimard, 1950, coll. Folio, 1973: 112–16. The 2007 impression is the reference in this article, henceforth cited LJ.

[12] "Finalement, le meurtre s'est identifié en eux avec le suicide. Une vie est alors payée par une autre vie. De ces deux holocaustes surgit une valeur intacte qui devait servir le progrès de la justice." TRN, 1832.

without an assassin."[13] Despite three years of reflection in prison, Hugo is still unable to explain his killing of Hoederer either as a deliberate act or as a crime of passion. Nor can he attribute it to orders from the Party: "With the best will in the world, what one does is never what the Party commands. [...] Orders abandon you beyond a certain point. The order stayed behind and I went forward alone and I killed alone and... I no longer even know why."[14] It can all be reduced to the random strokes of chance, "le hasard", fate took a hand: "Fate fired three shots, as it does in bad detective novels. With fate, you can start asking: 'What if...?'". [15] The circumstances were such that it is as if the act performed itself, with no conscious or purposeful agency.

Hugo never does discover why he killed Hoederer, and he feels ashamed that his motives were not what they *ought* to have been: "Because his policies were wrong, because he was lying to his comrades and putting the Party at risk".[16] So, he finds a rationale post-hoc: that of giving Hoederer the death he deserved, the death of a man who "dies for his ideas, dies for his politics, a man who is responsible for his death".[17] Hugo's refusal to be rehabilitated becomes a grandiloquent gesture in which, at last, he kills Hoederer deliberately, for the right reasons, and himself as well. But this is a strange kind of freedom, a retrospective justification which makes Hugo the political assassin he aspired to be. Therefore, it is an act performed in order to *be* rather than to *do*, what Sartre dismisses as a "gesture". Moreover, Sartre denounces suicide as "an absurdity which plunges my life into the absurd";[18]

---

[13] "Mais moi. *Moi*, là-dedans, qu'est-ce que je deviens? C'est un assassinat sans assassin." Jean-Paul. Sartre, *Les Mains sales*, Paris: Gallimard, 1948, coll. Folio, 1971: 234. The 1991 impression is the reference in this article, henceforth cited MS.

[14] "Avec la meilleure volonté du monde, ce qu'on fait, ce n'est jamais ce que le Parti vous commande. [...] Ça vous laisse tout seul, les ordres, à partir d'un certain moment. L'ordre était resté en arrière et je m'avançais tout seul et j'ai tué tout seul et... je ne sais même plus pourquoi." MS, 22.

[15] "Le hasard a tiré trois coups de feu, comme dans les mauvais romans policiers. Avec le hasard tu peux commencer les 'si' [...]." Ibid.Compare Camus' similar description of Meursault's murder of the young Arab man on the beach in *L'Étranger* (see TRN, 1168 and 1188).

[16] "[P]arce qu'il faisait de la mauvaise politique, parce qu'il mentait à ses camarades et parce qu'il risquait de pourrir le Parti." MS, 245.

[17] "Il meurt pour ses idées, pour sa politique; il est responsable de sa mort." MS, 246.

[18] "Le suicide est une absurdité qui fait sombrer ma vie dans l'absurde." Jean-Paul Sartre, *L'Être et le néant*, Paris: Gallimard, 1943: 624.

it is not a rational use of freedom. Thus, it would seem that Hugo is radically mistaken. Is the same true of Kaliayev?

Les Justes

Kaliayev's motivation is elaborated propter-hoc, not post-hoc. His commitment to the Organisation has been freely given, driven by ideological conviction, by the certainty that a cause worth killing for is also worth dying for: "Can one talk about terrorist action without taking part? [...] I know now that I would like to die on the spot, beside the Grand Duke. [...] Dying for the idea is the only way to rise to the level of the idea. It is the justification."[19] Kaliayev, like Hugo, tends to romanticise this scenario of murder and suicide combined, whilst Annenkov and Fedorov (much like Hoederer) deplore the implied self-regard and pointless waste of such an outcome: "You must try to get away. The Organisation needs you, you must save yourself."[20] "To kill yourself, you have to love yourself a lot. A true revolutionary cannot love himself."[21] And although he promises to "obey", Kaliayev remains free within the Party machine and capable of making his own decisions—specifically, *not* to throw his bomb at the Duke's carriage when he is accompanied by children—even though he subscribes in theory to the view that he is "not killing a man but killing the despotism he represents".[22]

This manifestation of Yanek's freedom gives rise to a discussion which has numerous resonances with various dialogues in Sartre's play. First he insists that he was not "cowardly" in failing to complete his task, but that the very sight of the children in effect "rendered him incapable" of doing so.[23] This ambivalent claim to responsibility is confused by his shifting the onus for

---

[19] "Peut-on parler de l'action terroriste sans y prendre part? [...] Et je sais maintenant que je voudrais périr sur place, à côté du grand-duc. [...] Mourir pour l'idée, c'est la seule façon d'être à la hauteur de l'idée. C'est la justification." LJ, 38.

[20] "Il faudra essayer de fuir. L'Organisation a besoin de toi, tu dois te préserver." Boria Annenkov, LJ, 31.

[21] "Pour se suicider il faut beaucoup s'aimer. Un vrai révolutionnaire ne peut pas s'aimer." Stepan Fedorov, LJ, 32.

[22] "Ce n'est pas lui que je tue. Je tue le despotisme." LJ, 42.

[23] See LJ, 55.

judging the rightness of his decision on to his comrades: "I came back because I thought I owed you an explanation, that you were my only judges, that you would tell me whether I was right or wrong, and that you could not be mistaken."[24] He insists that, once *they* have pronounced, *he* will obey, ambushing the carriage on its return journey, *even if* the children are still in it. Fedorov—an ideological hardliner, like Louis in Sartre's play—objects that the Organisation had already given him orders, which he then disobeyed. Yanek retorts: "I didn't have orders to murder children."[25] Fedorov—this time echoing Olga in *Les Mains sales*—maintains that *he* could shoot a child "if the Organisation ordered [him] to do so".[26] Kaliayev does not say this explicitly, but his experience is (like Hugo's) that "orders abandon you beyond a certain point". Like Abraham in Kierkegaard's parables of *Fear and Trembling*, both men learn that obedience to an order is still one's own decision.

In both plays, the question is the extent to which the individual remains autonomous in the context of a collective, and whether assertions of personal freedom are just intellectual gestures which harm the common interest. Hugo's murder of Hoederer is foolish, and subsequently his virtual suicide serves no purpose besides bolstering his sense of moral integrity. For his part, Yanek appears to reconcile subjective self-determination with the exigencies of the political cause when he succeeds in assassinating the Duke and embraces the mortal consequences, eschewing the deal offered by the police chief, Skouratov. By also rejecting the invitations to repentance of the Duke's widow, he too has a sense of dying with his moral integrity intact: "If I were not to die, then I would be a murderer."[27] Yet the Duchess sees this self-sacrificial gesture of atonement as an ethical sidestep: "You ought to live and consent to being a murderer. Did you not kill him? Only God can justify you."[28] And his comrades—even his beloved Dora—are inclined to agree with the Duchess: "I want Yanek to live", says Fedorov, "We need men like

---

[24] "Je suis revenu parce que je pensais que je vous devais des comptes, que vous étiez mes seuls juges, que vous me diriez si j'avais tort ou raison, que vous ne pouviez pas vous tromper." LJ, 56.

[25] "[L'Organisation] ne m'avait pas demandé d'assassiner des enfants." Ibid.

[26] "Je le pourrais si l'Organisation le commandait." LJ, 58.

[27] "Si je ne mourais pas, c'est alors que je serais un meurtrier." LJ, 119.

[28] "Tu dois vivre et consentir à être un meurtrier. Ne l'as-tu pas tué? Dieu te justifiera." Ibid.

him".[29] Dora adds: "If the only solution is death, then we are not on the right track. The right track is the one that leads to life, to the sunlight."[30] In short, they fear that Yanek's death will be, like Hugo's, in vain. Thus, neither hero retains his freedom to the end, since death is the antithesis of freedom. For both, the political act is freely accomplished but that freedom is finally extinguished in death. Should we conclude that politics demands the loss of individual freedom in order, paradoxically, to affirm its transcendent value? We can shed some light on this problematic by considering secondary characters.

Secondary characters

The parallels between these plays extend beyond the main protagonists. Hoederer and Louis, Jessica and Olga in *Les Mains sales*, and Annenkov, Fedorov, Dora, and even Alexis in *Les Justes*, all play their parts in the social, political, moral and philosophical contexts in which the heroes trace their trajectories. Hoederer and Louis are "of the same species: hard men", says Hugo—but they are also different: Hoederer is above all pragmatic, Louis above all ideological; Hoederer insists upon the Party's gaining access to power, and Louis upon orthodoxy. The result is a fratricidal conflict, setting Louis and the ideologues (including Olga and Hugo) against the political Party boss, Hoederer. Annenkov resembles Hoederer inasmuch as he is rational, pragmatic, devoted to the cause, ready to take risks, but also to accept a secondary role as circumstances may dictate. Unlike Hoederer, he has the loyalty of *all* his comrades, not only of a breakaway faction. Fedorov is almost a replica of Louis in terms of ideological rigour and political discipline. Yet he also matches Hugo in relentless intellectual dogma: "Nothing is forbidden that can serve our cause", he asserts, "There are no limits".[31] Anyone who thinks otherwise does not believe in the Revolution. This sort of fanaticism enables Camus to show up, by contrast, the "delicacy" of Kaliayev, not as a weakness but as a strength, much as Hoederer's moderate pragmatism contrasts favourably with Hugo's extravagant fanaticism.

---

[29] "Je souhaite que Yanek vive. Nous avons besoin d'hommes comme lui." LJ, 134.

[30] "Si la seule solution est la mort, nous ne sommes pas sur la bonne voie. La bonne voie est celle qui mène à la vie, au soleil." LJ, 135.

[31] "Rien n'est défendu de ce qui peut servir notre cause. [...] Il n'y a pas de limites." LJ, 61, 62.

In both plays the female characters are crucial. Jessica interrogates Hugo, tests his incoherent ideas, and reveals that his political commitment is a product of bourgeois intellectual neuroses, not of any ethical convictions. It is she who realises he is fascinated by Hoederer and understands why, whilst he is in denial about it himself. However, her weakness for game-playing is the undoing of them all, and her charade as the *femme fatale* triggers Hoederer's overdue assassination. Olga is a foil to Jessica, mature and serious versus immature and frivolous. There is a powerful attraction between her and Hugo, but she puts the cause before her feelings for him. In part, she loves him like a child, seeing his flaws and immaturity, including the stupidity of his marriage to Jessica and his infatuation with Hoederer. Yet she fails to persuade him to re-join the Party—a failure of advocacy or of love?

Dora is unquestionably in love with Yanek, although their rather dry and academic argument about what is meant by love makes us doubt whether he reciprocates her feelings. Nevertheless, she is, like Olga, on the side of the pragmatists in the Organisation, even if she has more sympathy with his moral scruples than the others. Indeed she argues with Fedorov in favour of a humane exigency to spare innocence and build the revolution on principles that are more akin to the humanist values of Yanek than to the dogmatism of Fedorov. Thus, whereas Olga (like Hoederer) wants to make Hugo understand that he has to get his hands dirty, Dora is in tune with Yanek's desire to safeguard his "purity" and understands why he sees his own death as a necessary expiation. And this brings us to the question of means and ends.

Means and ends

Does the end justify the means? And are Sartre and Camus equally clear or equally ambiguous on the subject? Sartre seems to uphold the position of Hoederer, namely that—in order to attain power, to win the class war—"All means are good so long as they are effective."[32] Yet the exponent of this view is killed by an unstable bourgeois intellectual who disagrees with him politically but is emotionally fascinated by him. Moreover that event takes place in conditions so laden with multiple meanings that Hugo's motivation

---

[32] "Tous les moyens sont bons quand ils sont efficaces." MS, 197.

remains opaque even to him forever after. What are we to infer from this semiotic plurality? If we reject Sartre's precautionary claims that he was "not taking sides",[33] I suggest one of two things. *Either*, Sartre wanted to affirm that political assassination is justifiable, because we know that Hoederer himself would have sanctioned it. If one believes the end justifies the means, then one has to respect the logic of the principle. Besides, this tactical elimination of Hoederer does not prevent the Party from adopting his strategy in due course, which demonstrates that the means employed (his assassination) have in fact led to the desired end, namely a pragmatic politics of compromise, exactly as Hoederer had envisaged. *Or*, Sartre wanted to affirm the position of Hugo who sacrifices his own life both in order to vindicate his moral stance and to justify the death of Hoederer. There is something admirable in Hugo's martyrdom. It symbolises an ethical perspective which transcends merely political questions, asserting an absolute value above the relative.

This second possibility seems to me to summarise the position of Camus, for whom Kaliayev's heroism is never in doubt and is finally admired by all his comrades, including even the hostile Fedorov. Dora dreams of dying the same death, even to the point of hanging by the same rope, betraying a romantic side which does not sit easily with her hitherto realistic outlook. Annenkov tries to dissuade her from these morbid musings—"You know very well we don't want any women in the front line"[34]—urging her to focus on the cause (just as Olga does with Hugo in *Les Mains sales*). Annenkov argues it is collective aims that matter, not the personal objectives of existential reconstruction which characterise Hugo's and Yanek's brief revolutionary careers, and their premature deaths.

For, even if all means are acceptable, it does not follow that they must include the death of the agent. Pragmatists in both plays say the activist's first duty is to serve the cause, and that this is best done by staying alive. The individual must be modest. On this much, at least, Sartre and Camus appear to agree: that there is some virtue in reserving the individual's right to dissent from the consensus when that is either morally or politically unacceptable. This is what Hoederer does when he negotiates with the Pentagon and the

---

[33] See Contat and Rybalka, op. cit., 178–80.

[34] "Tu sais bien que nous ne voulons pas de femmes au premier rang." LJ, 149.

Prince against his colleagues' better judgment. It is also what Yanek does when he "disobeys orders" by refusing to throw his bomb at the carriage with its child passengers. Authentic self-direction need not be over-ridden by collective commitment. If the end justifies the means for Sartre, those means confer no special rights upon the agent, but equally they do not curtail his freedom. And if the end does *not* always justify the means for Camus, the agent is still entitled to compensate for those means by exacting a redemptive moral toll upon himself.

Conclusion

I claimed at the outset that Camus "responded" to *Les Mains sales* twenty-one months after the premiere of Sartre's play. In fact, there is no explicit evidence that *Les Justes* was conceived as a riposte—it was already planned as the theatrical element of Camus' "triptych of revolt"—although there are several circumstantial and inter-textual clues.[35] We know—from an account given by Sartre himself, and recorded by Contat and Rybalka—that Camus saw one of the dress rehearsals of *Les Mains sales* and found it "excellent", but that he "disapproved of one detail":

> Camus had attended one of the last rehearsals with me (he had not yet read the text), and at the end, as we were walking back together, he said to me: "It's excellent, but there is one detail I disapprove of. Why does Hugo say: 'I don't love men for what they are but for what they ought to be'? And why does Hoederer reply: 'Whereas I love them for what they are.'? In my opinion, that should have been the other way around." In other words, he really believed that Hugo loved men for what they are, given that he did not want to lie to them, whereas Hoederer, on the contrary, became in his eyes a dogmatic communist who considered men for what they ought to be and deceived them in the name of an ideal. This is exactly the opposite of what I was trying to say.[36]

---

[35] Sandra Teroni has explored these in her article: "Les 'meurtriers délicats' face au réalisme politique", in *Etudes sartriennes, VIII*, "Sartre: une écriture en acte", RITM 24, Université Paris X, 2001: 91–102.

[36] "Camus avait assisté avec moi à l'une des dernières répétitions (il n'avait pas encore lu le texte), et à la fin, en me raccompagnant, il me dit: 'C'est excellent, mais il y a un détail que je n'approuve pas. Pourquoi Hugo dit-il: « Je n'aime pas les hommes pour ce qu'ils sont, mais

It is not clear whether Sartre tried to correct Camus' radical misconstruction of his (Sartre's) intentions.[37] Perhaps that was saved up for the coruscating review that Francis Jeanson would pen of *L'Homme révolté*, or the devastating retort that Sartre would write to Camus' famous letter on the subject.[38] But it is interesting that Camus should mis-identify the humanism of Hoederer as that of the youthful idealist, and wrongly associate Hugo's inflexible ideology with the ageing pragmatist, Hoederer. We might be tempted to conclude that Camus was not really paying attention, except that he was by no means the last critic to make this confusion, to the obvious consternation of Sartre and Beauvoir.

Almost two years later, they in turn saw the preview of *Les Justes*, an event of so little significance that Beauvoir devotes only ten lines to it in the 686 pages of *La Force des choses*:

> Camus [...] looked tired the evening of the preview of *Les Justes*, but the warmth of his welcome recalled the best days of our friendship. Beautifully acted, the play seemed to us academic. He accepted with a smiling and sceptical simplicity the handshakes and the compliments. Rosemonde Gérard—bent over, crumpled and all dolled-up—hurried over to him: "I like that better than *Les Mains sales*", she said, not having noticed Sartre, at whom Camus

---

pour ce qu'ils devraient être », et pourquoi Hoederer lui répond-il: « Et moi, je les aime pour ce qu'ils sont. »? Selon moi, cela aurait dû être le contraire.' En d'autres mots, il croyait en vérité que Hugo aimait les hommes pour ce qu'ils sont, étant donné qu'il ne voulait pas leur mentir, alors que Hoederer, au contraire, devenait à ses yeux un communiste dogmatique qui considérait les hommes pour ce qu'ils devraient être et qui les trompait au nom d'un idéal. C'est exactement le contraire de ce que je voulais dire." Sartre, cited by Contat and Rybalka, op. cit., 184.

[37] Teroni argues that Sartre, having read the essay "Les meurtriers délicats", uses some lines of dialogue in *Les Mains sales* to mock Camus' narrative of the 1905 Russian anarchists and his appraisal of their ethics.

[38] For a summary account of this terminal argument between Camus and Sartre, see Contat and Rybalka, op. cit., 249–51. Ronald Aronson has treated this notorious episode exhaustively in his excellent volume, *Camus & Sartre: The Story of a Friendship and the Quarrel that Ended It*, Chicago: University of Chicago Press, 2004, notably in Chapter 7, "The Explosion": 131–54.

flashed a conspiratorial smile, saying: "Two birds with one stone!" because he did not like to be taken for an imitator of Sartre.[39]

Leaving aside the catty remark about Mme Gérard—who, at the age of 78, might well be "bent over" and "crumpled", if not "dolled up"—to describe any work of art as "academic" is quite insulting, since it means "closely following conventional rules with frigidity or pretension".[40] It seems safe to assume that this terse dismissal summarises Sartre's view as well as Beauvoir's. No doubt the romantic attitudes of the poet Kaliayev would have seemed to him as naïve as those of the bourgeois intellectual Hugo, and the underlying political philosophy as unsophisticated as that of *L'Homme révolté*. For, Yanek is explicitly vindicated by his author whilst Hugo is implicitly condemned by his.

Lastly, Hugo's surname is Barine, a common noun from the Russian meaning "lord or master".[41] We note that "*barine*" is also the familiar epithet by which Foka (fellow inmate and hangman) ironically addresses Kaliayev in Act IV, eight times in as many pages. Given what Camus thought of Sartre's Hugo Barine, and that he must have known Sartre's opinion of him, it is possible that he was deliberately provoking Sartre by implicitly yoking the two protagonists together in this way. The same thought occurs when we notice that Fedorov, Yanek's severest critic, is replacing a comrade called Schweitzer, returning from exile in Switzerland, where "people are at least free".[42] According to "Les Meurtriers délicats", there was indeed a

---

[39] "Camus […] avait l'air très fatigué la nuit de la générale des *Justes*; mais la chaleur de son accueil ressuscita les meilleurs jours de notre amitié. Parfaitement jouée, la pièce nous parut académique. Il accueillit avec une simplicité souriante et sceptique les serrements de main et les compliments. Rosemonde Gérard, bossue, fripée, fanfreluchée s'est précipitée vers lui: 'J'aime mieux ça que *les Mains sales*', dit-elle, n'ayant pas aperçu Sartre à qui Camus adressa un sourire complice en disant: 'D'une pierre deux coups!' car il n'aimait pas qu'on le prît pour une émule de Sartre." Simone de Beauvoir, *La Force des choses*. Paris: Gallimard, 1963: 214–15. Rosemonde Gérard (1871–1953) was a poet, a playwright and the widow of Edmond Rostand, the author of (inter alia) *Cyrano de Bergerac*. I am indebted to Heather Johnson for pointing out that Beauvoir actually has more to say about the appearance of Mme Gérard than about Camus' play.

[40] "Qui suit étroitement les règles conventionnelles, avec froideur ou prétention." *Le Petit Robert, 1*: 10.

[41] See http://fr.wiktionary.org/wiki/barine.

[42] See LJ, 20 and 17, respectively.

Schweitzer in this faction, just as there was a Kaliayev, yet these are the only two names that Camus has not changed. Given that his ten-year relationship with Sartre encompassed the period in which Sartre moved into an apartment with his mother, Mme Mancy, in 1946, it is quite likely Camus knew that Mme Mancy's maiden name was Schweitzer. This is speculation, but it gains credence when we consider that Camus used his own mother's maiden name for the unsavoury neighbour, Raymond Sintès, of his protagonist Meursault in *L'Étranger*. Suppose Camus' severe and amoral ideologue, Fedorov (the Schweitzer substitute) is a conscious caricature of the attitude he attributed to Sartre (rightly or wrongly) in his mis-reading of *Les Mains sales*? And suppose this fact was not lost on Sartre and Beauvoir, who had so little to say about Camus' play when they saw it? Whether or not that is the case, there is *prima facie* evidence that the dialogue between Sartre and Camus, conducted through these parallel plays, turned out to be the opening exchange of a polemic that would culminate in their confrontation over *L'Homme révolté*, and the end of their friendship.

'My sensibility must speak, not cry out...': Form and feeling in the making of Camus' *L'Envers et l'Endroit*[1]

By Nicholas Padfield

Introduction

In Patricia Duncker's 2002 novel *The Deadly Space Between*, the narrator, the eighteen year-old A-level student, Tobias, finds himself in a Soho restaurant talking about Camus to the enigmatic Roehm, (possibly his mother's lover):

> Camus made me think, but he wasn't moving. You don't feel his books. You think about them. But this one made me so sad. Really sad. Sad enough to cry. *Le Premier Homme* is about his childhood in Algeria, his mother, his poor neighbourhood, the life of those times. Like a lost world. There are so many worlds you can never get back. Some worlds you can only find again in memories. He was like me, he was brought up by women in a woman's household. And so he was closer to women. He never had a father, and I didn't either. At least Catherine Camus could remember him. Some of the scenes are so vivid, that I can taste them now: killing the hen for Christmas, the children mixing poisons, the old Arabs in their cafés. They're just ordinary poor lives. But he describes them with such passion. I revised my opinion of Camus as a result of reading that book. I'll read every other account of childhood and test it against what he wrote. It's like a glimpse into his workshop...All his notes, sketches, the illegible words in brackets – I loved all the loose ends, the rawness of an unfinished book. It was like touching how he thought, how he worked.

[1] I gratefully acknowledge the help of my supervisor, Edmund Smyth, and of my friends, Victor Burgess and Geoff Medland, in the writing of this paper. Errors are, of course, my own.

> Catherine Camus said that he would have edited out all these
> passionate, personal feelings because he was so private and reserved.
> Well, if he'd have done that, then I'm glad he never finished the
> book...[2]

Tobias' registering of the 'rawness' of an unfinished book picks up
authentically on the words used by Catherine Camus to end the 'Editor's
Note' to the English translation of *The First Man*:

> Finally, it is obvious that my father would never have published this
> manuscript as it is, first for the simple reason that he had not
> completed it, but also because he was a very reserved man and would
> no doubt have masked his own feelings far more in its final version.
> But it seems to me...that one can most clearly hear my father's voice in
> this text because of its very rawness.[3]

Tobias' sense of 'touching how he thought, how he worked' on reading
Camus' last, posthumously published work is something which the reader of
his very first publication, *L'Envers et l'Endroit*, is likely to recognise and,
quite possibly, to share. Camus famously refused its republication until 1958,
and then in his Preface explained his reluctance: 'I reject nothing of what
these essays express but their form has always seemed clumsy to me.'[4] This
formal clumsiness, (one might say 'rawness'), is understandable, he claims,
in the work of such a youthful writer because 'at twenty-two, unless one is a
genius, one scarcely knows how to write' (5). And yet, the mature Camus
reflects on the profound significance of the content of these early writings in
his work as a whole: 'there is more genuine love in these clumsy pages than
in all those which have followed.' (5). He explains that he is more aware of
the 'clumsiness' of *L'Envers et l'Endroit* than of that of his other works
because it allows some of his deepest feelings to emerge. Later in the Preface
he remarks: 'clumsiness and disorder reveal too much of the secrets closest
to our hearts.' (13). A distinction is being made between considerations of

---

[2] Patricia Duncker, *The Deadly Space Between* (London: Picador, 2002) p. 54

[3] Albert Camus, *The First Man* (London : Penguin Classics, 2001) pp. vi-vii

[4] Albert Camus, "Betwixt and Between" in *Lyrical and Critical*, trans. Philip Thody
(London:Hamish Hamilton, 1967) All references to *L'Envers et l'Endroit* in this essay are
taken from this edition pages 5-47.

form and the emotional source which demands to find expression. Camus goes at some length to describe the importance of this source in the life and work of the artist:

> Each artist thus keeps in his heart of hearts a single stream which, so long as he is alive, feeds what he is and what he says...I myself know that my stream is in *L'Envers et l'Endroit*, in this world of poverty and sunlight in which I lived for so long...(6).

It is to this world that Camus is proud to have borne faithful witness in his first, published work:

> ...I can indeed confess that it has, for me, considerable value as testimony. I say for me since it is in my presence that it bears witness, and from me that it demands a fidelity whose depth and difficulties I alone can see. (5).

It was not immediately obvious to the young Camus that 'this world of poverty and sunlight' was suitable material for his own writing. When he was of a similar age to the fictional Tobias, and at a similar stage of his education, he also found a book which seemed to speak to him directly because it mirrored some of the particularities of his own experience. Jean Grenier, Camus' philosophy teacher at the Grand lycée de garçons d'Alger, recognising the talent of his seventeen year-old student, and knowing something of his family circumstances, loaned him the recently published first novel of his friend, André de Richard. This was *La Douleur*, a story set in a small provincial village during the First World War, which evoked the desolation of a widow, Thérèse Delombre and her young son, Georges, isolated by the death in action of the husband and father. Although its merits were recognised by a *jury littéraire* which included Mauriac, Bernanos and Julien Green, the novel provoked something of a scandal because it recounted the woman's sexual relationship with a German prisoner of war.[5] What is likely to have interested Camus most, however, is the depiction of the relationship between the abandoned mother and the son, particularly the intensity and complexity of the son's feelings towards his mother. Like Camus, de Richard was an *orphelin de guerre*, his father, like Camus' having

---

[5] See Introduction to André de Richaud, *La Douleur* (Paris : Grasset, 1931)

been killed during the early years of the war, and it is not surprising that the world depicted in the novel should have struck a chord of recognition in the young Camus. Certainly, he acknowledged that the novel had a profound effect upon him:

> ...I have never forgotten his fine book, which was the first to speak to me of what I knew : a mother, poverty, beautiful skies. I read it in one night, in the time-honored fashion, and, on awakening, endowed with a strange, new sensation of liberty, I advanced hesitantly into an unknown land. I had just learned that books did not merely distract you or help you to forget. My obstinate silences, that vague yet supreme suffering, the extraordinariness of the world, the nobility of my kith and kin, their poverty, in other words my secrets, could all be written about...[6]

La Douleur spoke to him of a world he recognised and, further, opened up the possibility that this world could be written about, that his own experience of it could legitimately form the material for his own first attempts at writing. His own silences, the inchoate nature of his own sufferings, his most secret feelings, the paradoxes of his family life could be the source of what he was going to find it possible to say.

But how might all this be said? How could these 'raw' experiences be fashioned into writing? What might be the appropriate literary forms? Clearly, the mature Camus of the Preface believes the 'gaucheries' of *L'Envers et l'Endroit* to be largely a matter of form. He acknowledges that the work of art must first of all make use of urgent emotion – what he recognises as 'my disorder, the violence of certain instincts, the graceless abandon into which I can cast myself'. (12). But, like Baudelaire who extolled the formal constraints of the sonnet form in rendering the emotion more intense[7], Camus believes that these 'dark forces of the soul' must be

---

[6] Albert Camus , "Rencontres avec André Gide" in Albert Camus, *Œuvres complètes* (Paris: Gallimard, Bibliothèque de la Pléiade,2006) III p. 881. Throughout this essay, passages quoted from the French are my translation, unless an English-language source is cited in the notes. Camus' inclusion of 'poverty' among those things about which the book spoke to him is intriguing. The social milieu of *La Douleur* is middle-class.

[7] 'Because the form is constraining, the idea shoots out more intensely.' Baudelaire *Lettre à Armand Fraise* 19 février 1860, quoted in *Vocabulaire pour la dissertation* (Paris : Larrousse, 1992) p.274

channelled; they must be made use of, 'but not without canalizing them, surrounding them with dykes, so that their tide also rises'. (12-13). He suggests that in his mature work the 'dykes' have perhaps been raised too high, and that this has led to a certain 'stiffness' for which he criticises himself. However, the opposite is true of his youthful writings. Hence, his reservations are artistic, just as, he explains, other people might have moral or religious objections. He is, on the one hand, 'a child of free nature', and, on the other, 'slave, and an admiring one to a severe artistic tradition'. (12). He seems to be debating with himself the extent to which, in the creation of a work of art, the rawness of experience must necessarily undergo a transformation. He yearns to discover an equivalence between who he is and what he says, and declares that, if this should ever come to be, the work he would create would resemble, in one way or another *L'Envers et l'Endroit*:

> It is simply that on the day when a balance is established between what I am and what I say, perhaps on that day, and I scarcely dare write it, I shall be able to compose the work of which I dream. What I have tried to say here is that in one way or another it will be like *L'Envers et l'Endroit* and that it will speak of a certain form of love. (13).

The present study seeks to examine how these issues are at play in Camus' earliest work in order to understand something of the ways in which, whether maladroitly or not, the raw material of personal experience is transposed into writing. How do considerations of form feature in the notes he was making during 1935 and 1936 in the first of his *Cahiers*? How does his voracious reading during this period (of Gide, for example) impact on his thinking about the craft of writing? And how significant in the development of this thinking is the intensive study of philosophy he was undertaking at this time? In considering these questions, the meanings of key terms – '*silence*', '*indifférence*', '*lucidité*', '*amour*' – are explored, and an attempt is made to understand what Camus means when he speaks in the 1958 Preface of 'the admirable silence of a mother and the effort of a man to rediscover a justice or a love which matches that silence.' (p.13) The main focus is on *L'Envers et l'Endroit*, but this is read in conjunction with the various notes and sketches which preceded its publication. These are now most readily accessible in the first two volumes of the new *Pléiade* edition of the *Œuvres Complètes* published in 2006 under the direction of Jacqueline Lévi-Valensi, and include *Les Voix du quartier pauvre* and the reconstituted *Louis Raingeard* which are printed as appendices to *L'Envers et l'Endroit* in Volume I, the *Premier Écrits 1932-1936* (including *Notes de Lecture* and *La Maison mauresque*) which can be found among the *Écrits Posthumes* in the same volume, and the first two *Cahiers* of the *Carnets 1935-1948* which appear in Volume II.

Early writings

The earliest experiments which reflect the attempt to balance *témoignage*, 'bearing witness', and what Camus sees as the necessary detachment of the writer in the search for appropriate forms, were worked on during a tumultuous period. Camus' biographers (for example, Olivier Todd[8], Roger Grenier[9], Herbert Lottman[10]) chronicle the vicissitudes of the young Camus' life in the seven years leading up to the publication of *L'Envers et l'Endroit* on May 10th 1937. What is of interest in terms of his development as a writer is the character of his educational experience and of his more general reading during these years. In 1930, Camus passed the first part of his baccalauréat and began sudying in the *classe de philosphie* under Jean Grenier, but at the same time the first attack of the tuberculosis which was going to mark these years meant a prolonged absence. He recommenced the following year and, in 1932, passed the baccalauréat and entered the *classe préparatoire* for the École normale supérieure. However, a recurrence of tuberculosis prevented him from pursuing his ambitions towards *agrégation* and he transferred his studies to the Faculté de Lettres in Alger. In 1935 he was duly awarded his licence in philosophy, and in May 1936, his Diplôme d'études supérieures for a dissertation entitled *Métaphysique chrétienne et néoplatonisme*. During this period he also joined and left the communist party, founded the Théâtre duTravail, worked as a clerk for a shipbroker and at the Préfecture, travelled in the Balearic Islands and in Germany, Austria, Czechoslovakia and Italy, left the family home to live, first, with his uncle and then with his brother, married and separated from Simone Hié and, before his illness, played football for Racing universitaire d'Alger. In the 1958 Preface Camus tells us that *L'Envers et l'Endroit* was written in the middle of this tumultuous period : 'The essays collected in this volume were written in 1935 and 1936 (I was 22 at the time) and published a year later, in Algeria, in a very limited edition.' (5). At the same time, then, that he was registering profound changes in his personal life – menacing illness, death (his grandmother's and

---

[8] OlivierTodd, *Albert Camus, une vie* (Paris : Gallimard, 1996)

[9] Roger Grenier, *Albert Camus :Soleil et ombre* (Paris : Gallimard, 1987)

[10] Herbert R. Lottman, *Albert Camus, a biography* (London: Weidenfeld and Nicolson, 1979)

the real prospect of his own), love, marriage, separation, political engagement, travel – he was undergoing a rigorous academic training in the domaine of philosophy, and had discovered, within himself, the conviction that he wished to be a writer.

The *Notes de Lecture* which Camus wrote in April 1933 give an insight into his preoccupations as he made his first tentative steps in his chosen *métier*. Almost immediately he castigates himself for allowing his emotional intensity to spill over into his writing. In a way which prefigures some of what we have noted in the Preface to *L'Envers et l'Endroit*, written twenty-seven years later in 1958, he argues with himself that he must subjugate his feelings, mask them under a cooler, more ironic detachment in order to let his writing do the work in engaging the reader's sympathetic attention:

> I would have to learn to master my sensibility, too prone to overflow. To conceal it under the irony and coolness I believed myself to be master of. I must come down to earth…My sensibility should speak, not cry out. It should do this because I want to write so that it can be felt in my work, not in life.[11]

One way of attempting a greater objectivity can be seen in the writing he was doing at this time. Having just finished *La Maison mauresque*[12], he notes 'I made every effort not to let my present sufferings appear'[13]. In an effort to avoid the directly autobiographical, he has sought a 'formula' in the external world which recalls T.S. Eliot's notion of the 'objective correlative'. In his 1919 essay on *Hamlet* Eliot wrote:

> The only way of expressing emotion in the form of art is by finding an 'objective correlative'; in other words, a set of objects, a situation, a chain of events which shall be the formula of that *particular* emotion; such that when the external facts, which must terminate in sensory experience, are given, the emotion is immediately evoked.[14]

---

[11] *Notes de Lecture, Œuvres complètes* I p. 955

[12] *Œuvres complètes* I pp. 967-975

[13] *Notes de Lecture* Op. Cit. p. 955

[14] T.S.Eliot, *Selected Essays* (London : Faber and Faber, 1932) p. 145

In these short, meditative prose poems, Camus seems to be searching for just this – 'I want to write so that (my sensibility) can be felt in my work... '. Here, he seeks to construct a symbolic representation of contradictory emotions through the 'correspondances' he discerns, in a Baudelairean sense, between the different parts of the house and different emotional registers:

> ...those fine and fleeting emotions one experiences on a first visit to a Moorish house I wanted to expand into 'correspondances'. I wanted to build a house of emotions. Here it is. In it, blue shadows and sunny courtyards succeed each other. The same question presents itself in the shade and in the sunlight.[15]

The binary oppositions characteristic of Camus' way of thinking about the world at this time, evidenced by his choice of *L'Envers et l'Endroit* as the title of his first published book[16], are clearly reflected in the evocative prose of these short pieces. Here the 'blue shadows' are contrasted with the 'sunny courtyards', 'shade' with 'sunlight'. In the second piece, 'L'Entrée'[17], the narrator moves onto the terrace which overlooks the Arab town and the sea. As evening approaches, the violent colours of the day gradually recede, but the accompanying stillness is contradicted by the brutal movement of the houses as they jostle steeply down towards the sea. A fleeting harmony is achieved as the calm serenity of the sea joins that of the sky which momentarily defeats the efforts of the town to disturb this tranquillity. But, as night covers the sky, the narrator is again disturbed when he registers the conflict between the bright lights of a steamship and the darkness of the waters. The conflict of these two elements, light and water, gives rise to an emotion of *inquiétude*, here best considered as a state of agitation, of instability:

> My agitation then returned as I was looking at this primordial mixture of water and of light where one wasn't able to say if the water was

---

[15] *La Maison mauresque,* Op. Cit. p. 967

[16] These oppositions are lost somewhat in the English translation, *Betwixt and Between,* but more evident in the American version, *The Wrong Side and the Right Side.* See Albert Camus, *Lyrical and Critical Essays,* ed. Philip Thody, trans. Ellen Conroy Kennedy (New York: Vintage Books, 1968)

[17] 'L'Entrée' *La Maison mauresque* Op. Cit. p. 967

blending with the light or if the light was drowning the water. Anxiety once more in the face of the conflict of two elements.[18]

The impersonality which Camus is seeking is achieved here through the displacement of the source of the emotion from the personal circumstances of the narrator to the detail of the seascape which constitutes the external reality being described. In this procedure the narrator becomes the anonymous conduit for registering the emotion provoked by the objective natural phenomena. The binary character of the successive oppositions is made explicit in a remarkable sentence which emphasises the brutality of the elemental discordance and explains the resultant feeling of disquiet: 'A binary rhythm, full of dread, a cruel and tyrannical jazz, without nostalgia, in front of the water and the light, the town and the sky, always...'[19] In contrast, the instability of this conflict gives way, in the third of these pieces, 'La Tombée de lumière'[20], to an evocation of stillness and silence as the narrator recalls the movement from shadow into the sudden brilliance of sunlight. The elemental warmth of the sun strips away 'false sentimentality' so that all else is forgotten in the 'single sensation of invading warmth'. Later in the same piece, the narrator finds himself, close to midday, in a small Muslim cemetery surrounded by fig trees. Here, all is silence and peace, and, again, human sentimentality, 'love of the pathetic' which has too often guided the narrator, is set against the 'plenitude of indifference' to be found in 'this silent abode'. This association of silence with an unmoveable indifference which is beyond the falseness of human sentiment anticipates what Camus is going to be writing later in *L'Envers et l'Endroit* about the 'indifference' and the 'admirable silence' of *cette mère étrange*.

At the time of this early experiment in the prose-poem genre, it is André Gide who most seems to influence Camus. He is the writer who is referred to most often in the *Notes de Lecture*. The young Gide, recovering, himself, from tuberculosis, had visited North Africa in 1893 and 1895 and had published *Les Nourritures terrestres* in 1897. In his preface to the 1927

---

[18] Ibid I p 968

[19] Ibid I p.968

[20] 'La Tombée de lumière' *La Maison mauresque* Op. Cit. p. 970

edition of this 'manifesto of Dionysian individualism'[21] Gide explains the context of its first appearance:

> *Les Nourritures terrestres* is the book, if not of a sick man, then at least of a convalescent, someone healed – of someone who has been ill. There is in its very lyricism, the excess of a person who embraces life like something he has almost lost.[22]

The parallels with Camus' own situation in 1933 are obvious. The narrator in *Les Nourritures terrestres* exhorts Nathanël to give himself up to a life of individualistic pleasure and sensuous enjoyment : 'Don't separate God from happiness, and invest all your happiness in the moment'[23]. But at 16, when Camus first encountered the book, before he was ill, it made little impact. He recalls that 'those exhortations seemed obscure to me. I stumbled before this hymn to Nature's bounty. In Alger, at 16, I was saturated with these riches.'[24] He was no Northern protestant discovering the world of the Mediterranean for the first time; he was already there. At that age he needed no urging towards physical enjoyment. However, his first debilitating attack of tuberculosis led to his isolation from the physical world. He recounts how 'a fortunate illness had taken me away from my beaches and my pleasures'. He subsequently reads 'all of Gide's work' and comes once more upon *Les Nourritures terrestres*. This time he experiences the 'shaking up so often described', but for him this was not to do with the sensuous enjoyment of life but with Gide's advocation of *dénuement*, which for Gide meant a stripping back to the essential rather than material deprivation: 'Well before Gide himself had confirmed this interpretation, I learned to read in *Les Nourritures Terrestres* the gospel of *dénuement* which I needed.' For Camus at this time, *dénuement* was not a desirable optional alternative to bourgeois materialism, but the living reality of the *pauvreté* which surrounded him. But to have this 'deprivation' extolled as a necessary prerequisite to 'happiness' would have confirmed the attitude to poverty he was later to describe in the 1958 Preface to *L'Envers et l'Endroit* : 'Poverty...was never a misfortune for me: it was radiant with sunlight' (6). It seems likely that the

---

[21] Pascal Bruckner, 'Happiness' in Lawrence D. Kritzman (ed.) *The Columbia History of Twentieth Century French Thought* (New York: Columbia University Press, 2006) p.243

[22] André Gide, *Les Nourritures Terrestres* (Paris : Gallimard, 1969) p. 11

[23] Ibid p. 31

[24] 'Rencontres avec André Gide' in *Œuvres complètes* III p.881

Gide of *Les Nourritures terrestres* was in Camus' mind as he wrote *La maison mauresque*. The deployment of the narrator, the description of the particularities of place, the evocation of emotion are characteristic of both works. Here, for example, is an extract from the opening of Part II of Book Four of *Les Nourritures terrestres*:

> The monumental terrace where we stood (the escalators led us there) overlooked the whole town and seemed, above the dense foliage, an immense vessel at her mooring ; sometimes she seemed to move towards the town. That summer I would sometimes climb to the highest point of this imaginary ship to enjoy, after the tumult of the streets, the contemplative calm of the evening.[25]

Of course, it can be argued that Gide's is an altogether more mature and assured achievement, evident in the success of the extended image of the imaginary ship, but the narrative and descriptive procedures he finds here provide a useful model for the 19 year-old Camus.

There is no doubt that Gide was a considerable influence in Camus' early development as a writer. In the *Notes de lecture* he made in April 1933 he castigates himself for the banality of his thoughts on Gide:

> Read all my notes on Gide. Appallingly banal. Puerile commonplaces. I was furious at the mediocrity of my own thought while contemplating the deep admiration I have for Gide.[26]

Here he articulates a familiar discrepancy between the profundity of his feeling and the adequacy of its form of expression, and shows himself, even at this early stage, to be an inheritor of that 'severe artistic tradition' that he mentions in the 1958 Preface. Elsewhere in the *Notes de Lecture* he refers to the characteristic tensions in Gide between the ascetic and the sensuous – what Michel Winock calls 'the two poles of his personality, his moral being and his hedonism'[27]. Camus talks of Gide's need to 'reconcile his lucidity

---

[25] André Gide, *Les Nourritures Terrestres* (Paris : Gallimard, 1969) p. 82

[26] *Notes de Lecture, Œuvres complètes* I p. 956

[27] Michel Winock, *Le Siècle des intellectuels* (2nd edition, Éditions du Seuil, 1999)

with his passion'[28]. This kind of opposition is reflected in the distinctions Camus is exploring at this time in *Cahier I* between the intellectual and the physical, between 'culture' and 'will', and between philosophy and literature. In May 1936, he notes:

> Against relapse and weakness : effort – Beware the demon:
> culture –the body
> the will – work (Phil.) ...
> Philosphical work : the absurd
> Literary work : strength, love and death under the sign of conquest
> Mingle the two genres while respecting each one's particular tone.
> Write, one day, a book that will give the meaning...[29]

These tensions and contradictions are at the centre of his thinking at the time of his writing of *L'Envers et l'Endroit*. Here, he is expressing a wish to bring together the 'literary' and the 'philosophical', to mix the two genres while respecting a certain particularity of tone. Whatever the questions about form, he makes explicit what it is that he wants to say. His first entry in *Cahier I* begins:

What I mean:

> That one can have – without romanticism – nostalgia for a lost poverty. A certain number of years lived in poverty is sufficient to create a sensibility. In this particular case, the strange feeling that a son has for his mother constitutes *his entire sensibility*. The way in which this sensibility shows itself in the most diverse contexts is sufficiently explained by the latent material memory of childhood (a glue that sticks to the soul).[30]

These are the things he feels it imperative to say. In an argument he seems to be having with himself, he is concerned about restraining the pressure of his own sensibility, and yet, paradoxically, he is insistent that he wishes to express the truth of his own experience: 'the work of art is a confession, I

---

[28] *Œuvres complètes* I p.958

[29] *Œuvres complètes* II p.809

[30] Ibid. p.795

must bear witness'. Despite what he has said earlier about irony and detatchment, he is insisting that the writing he wishes to produce will be confessional, a bearing of faithful witness to the love he finds in the reality of his own family life, and in the complexity of a son's 'bizarre' attachment to his mother amidst the poverty of Belcourt. He insists that 'it is in that life of poverty, among those people, unassuming or conceited, that I have most surely experienced what seems to me to be the true meaning of life'[31].

Two other of Camus' early writing projects reflect this struggle between the urge for autobiographical self-expression and the search for an appropriate form. It is in *Les Voix du quartier pauvre* [32], which Camus completed in 1934 after a second attack of tuberculosis, that the poor, working-class area of Belcourt and the detail of the family circumstances of his childhood, especially the mother-son relationship, are most visibly present in this early work. Indeed, if the posthumously-published and unfinished *The First Man* is excluded from consideration, it can be argued that this is the most directly autobiographical of all his writing. The first of the 'Voices', 'the voice of the woman who did not think' re-appears almost unchanged in 'Between Yes and No' in *L'Envers et l'Endroit*. Similarly the second and fourth voices, 'the voice of the man who was born in order to die' and 'the voice of the sick old woman left at home by people going to a cinema' are reproduced as two of the sections in 'Irony'. However, the third voice, 'the voice (of the woman) who was uplifted by music', does not appear in the later publication. As Roger Grenier points out 'on rewriting, Camus did not dare reveal all'[33]. Whatever the reason, the third voice includes the portrait of the mother's brother 'deaf, dumb, nasty and stupid' with whom she lives partly out of pity, partly out of fear and who prevents her from pursuing her relationship with the man she loves:

> It is, of course, out of pity that she lived with him. It was also out of fear. If only he had allowed her to live as she wished to. But he prevented her from seeing the man whom she loved.[34]

---

[31] Ibid. p. 795

[32] *Les Voix du quartier pauvre* in *Œuvres complètes* I pp. 75-86

[33] Roger Grenier, *Albert Camus: Soleil et ombre* (Paris : Gallimard, 1987) p. 27

[34] *Œuvres complètes* I p.81

The poignancy of the woman's situation is evoked when, after 'a dreadful brawl', she goes to see her son 'to weep':

> What was to be done really? Her misfortune was inescapable. She was too frightened of her brother to leave him. She hated him too much to forget. He would kill her one day, that was sure. She had said all this in a gloomy voice.[35]

It seems that it is in the rawness of the expression of emotion, here, that Camus is touching 'the true meaning of life' and the reality of his own experience. The 'intellectual' or 'philosophical' element which he is also seeking to include in his notion of what constitutes a 'work of art' is something subsequent to the directness of this expression. How this element might be incorporated, how to 'mingle the two genres', is something with which he will continue to experiment in these early writings.

Finally, dating from the same period 1934-1936 as *Les Voix du quqrtier pauvre* are the manuscript sketches of a 'novel of an autobiographical inspiration'[36], *Louis Raingeard*. Here again, although this time in the form of narrative, Camus works intensively at re-creating the quality of the childhood experience which, although aged only 22, he senses is already lost to him. In one passage, 'nostalgia for a lost poverty' and the symbol of the mother, for the narrator, as something which 'slumbered in the depths of his soul', as the source of 'his whole sensibility', is given vivid expression:

> Certainly he had made his life away from his mother...He was too proud not to recognise his intelligence, but that counted as nothing compared to what he felt so profoundly. Something was slumbering in the depths of his soul that was formed of the aroma of that infinite poverty...it was there, his whole sensibility...and he knew precisely everything which made (this) sensibility: it was that day when he had understood that he was born of his mother, and that she only rarely

---

[35] Ibid. p.81

[36] Ibid. p.1224

took to thinking. He was intelligent, as they say. And what separated him from her was precisely his intelligence.[37]

Education and new perspectives afforded by literature have led to the narrator's estrangement from the context which had nurtured him. The sense of loss is real and profound as is the recognition that it is inevitable. For Camus himself, it is this desire to re-connect with what has been lost, or to acknowledge the profound significance of his exile from it, which lies behind what he says in the 1958 Preface about 'the admirable silence of a mother and the effort of a man to rediscover a justice or a love which matches this silence'.

Structures of Feeling in *L'Envers et l'Endroit*

It is, of course, impossible to separate completely considerations of form and those of feeling, the structure of a work of art from its emotional content. Nevertheless, this section seeks to map the contours of feeling which reveal themselves in the five essays which make up *L'Envers et l'Endroit*. The polarisation implicit in the title is reflected in the thematic material of the essays which Camus deploys so that feelings of exile, isolation, fear and anguish are played against a counter-current of emotion which conveys the joys of a passionate engagement in life's abundance. As Peter Dunwoodie points out 'Camus strains to express the interdependence of the two poles...their inextricable and essential links; and they are to be read not alternately but simultaneously.'[38] The oppositional flow is complicated by the stance of the narrator, which varies from one of ironic detachment or reflective distance to one of much closer identification with the characters and their emotional engagement. There is also a temporal factor which impacts on the way feeling is structured, where past experience, particularly of childhood, is recalled and seen to have profound significance in the present. Above all, this relates to the feelings of a son towards his mother, and, in Camus' case, the recognition that what binds mother and son (which might be called love) is something elemental which renders futile human gesture and utterance, and might also be called 'indifference'.

---

[37] *Œuvres complètes* I p.90

[38] Peter Dunwoodie, *Camus : L'Envers et l'Endroit and L'Exil et le Royaume* (London : Grant and Cutler, 1985) p.12

In the first of the essays, 'Irony', the emotional tone is set with the references to suffering, illness and death in the second sentence: 'She was suffering from an illness that had almost killed her'. (15). The narration begins in the first person, but 'I' is used only in the very first sentence, and the narrator subsequently assumes the role of the detached, sometimes ironic observer. It is through the characters of the young man and the old woman that feelings are conveyed. From his ironic distance, the narrator can comment on the young man's naiveté: '...the young man...was of the opinion that being a burden on other people was better than dying. But that proved only one thing: that he had doubtless never been a burden on anybody.' (15). This ironic tone contrasts with the intensity and directness with which the young man's emotional reactions are conveyed : 'The young man listened to all this with an immense and unfamiliar pain that hurt his chest.' (16). The violence and rawness of the young man's emotion seem something beyond his control in the same way as the 'violence of certain instincts' for which Camus, the writer, criticises himself in the Preface. When the old lady holds on to his hand to prevent him leaving: 'He felt confronted by the most atrocious suffering he had ever known : that of a sick old woman left at home by people going to a cinema.' (40). The function of the young man as focaliser is to allow two different perspectives ; that of his naïve vulnerability 'without dykes', and that of the more worldly, more distant narrator. It is tempting to view this difference of perspective as reflecting, respectively, that of the twenty-two year old Camus, the writer, and that of his younger, emotional self. A further shift in perspective is afforded at the end of this section when the young man's sensitivity – he 'could not get rid of his feelings of remorse', as, from the street, he observes the light in the old lady's room go out - is contrasted with the self-comforting rationalisation of the daughter, who remarks: 'She always turns the light off when she's by herself. She likes to sit in the dark.' (17).

The irony of the daughter's indifferent refusal to recognise the reality that terrifies her mother is echoed in the 'the irony of the glances and the sudden mockery' (18) of the young men's reactions to the anecdotes of the old man in the next section. Again, the narrator is distanced from the young men and offers a detached commentary: 'Young men don't know that experience is a defeat and that we must lose everything to win a little knowledge.' (18). The old man has suffered during his life but chooses not to recount his sufferings : 'What do the sufferings of an old man matter when life absorbs you completely?' (18). Abandoned by the young men, the old man is once again alone. And in solitude there is only the reminder of imminent death: 'He was condemned to silence and loneliness. He was being told he would soon be dead.' (18). It is better for him to walk the streets than to return to the isolation of his bedroom to face the terrible prospect of death. The latter is conveyed in the image of 'a man in a light-coloured suit' who enters the old man's bedroom, sits facing him and sighs gently while, 'the latch clicks to behind him'. (19). This evocation of the *au-delà* recalls the tradition of the *fantastique* in French literature. In Villiers' *L'Intersigne,* for example, the narrator sees 'opposite me...upright...a form tall and dark...the breath of the other-world envelopped the visitor.'[39] Just as the paralysed old woman in the first section is half in and half out of this world - 'She only had half of herself in this world while the other half was already foreign to her' (15). – so the old man is already moving beyond earthly reality, as is emphasised in the repetition of the wife's unwittingly ironic remark: 'He's in the moon.'[40]

The third section of 'Irony' depicts a family of five dominated by the figure of the grandmother. The almost mute son and the infirm mother who 'thought with difficulty' are background figures, and what is recounted is focalised through the character of the younger of the two grandchildren. The autobiographical reflections are obvious. As in the two previous sections, an old person is going to die. This time, however, fear and solitude are replaced, in the case of the grandmother, by an insistence on including her family in every detail of her physical decline, even to the extent of requiring her grandchildren to assist her in carrying out her bodily functions. The emotional focus is not on the grandmother, but on the younger grandson's reactions. When his grandmother, in front of visitors and in the presence of his mother, obliges him to say that he loves his grandmother more than his mother, he experiences 'in his heart, a great upsurge of love for his ever silent mother.' (21). From the perspective of the two grandchildren 'who were at the age of absolute judgements, she was nothing but a fraud' (21), evidenced by her pretence at busyness at the arrival of visitors.[41] At her death the younger grandson can feel no sadness, cannot weep because he

---

[39] Villiers de l'Isle Adam, *Contes cruels* (Paris : Gallimard, 1983) p. 272

[40] The *Pléiade* editors note (I p.1220) that, according to Lucien Camus, this expression 'could have been used by Camus' own mother.'

[41] cf. the behaviour of M.Vinteuil in a celebrated passage of Proust's *Du côté de chez Swann* (Paris: Flammarion, 1987) p. 222. In a letter to Jean Grenier (25 August 1932) Camus expresses his admiration for Proust: '...very often you finish reading him with a touch of resentment. You have come across so many things that you have felt yourself. Everything has been said. There is nothing more to say.', Albert Camus and Jean Grenier, *Correspondances 1932-1960* (Paris : Gallimard, 1981) p. 13

cannot escape from the idea that he has just witnessed 'the last and most monstrous of this woman's performances' (22).

In the second essay, 'Between Yes and No', three recollected episodes of encounters between son and mother – 'images' in the mind of the narrator – are recounted in the third person, linked by meditative passages in the first person. There are temporal shifts between the now of the narrator's situation, sitting alone in an Arab café at evening, and the recollected past. A more tender nostalgia is evoked by the essay's Proustian opening: 'If it is true that the only paradises are those that we have lost...' (23). [42] For Anne-Marie Amiot, this quest for the 'lost paradise of childhood' is essentially a Romantic one and she invokes the 'romantic experiences of sensual memory related by Chateaubriand, Nerval, Baudelaire and Proust'.[43] Indeed, the narrator begins by describing how, like Proust's madeleine, a single detail – 'the smell of a room that has been shut up too long, the particular sound of a footstep on the road' (23) – can trigger the recollection of what has been loved. It is only love that can return us to our true selves. In this essay, the recollection is of primal significance to the narrator, 'For what has remained untouched in those hours which I am bringing back from the depths of forgetfulness is the memory of a pure emotion, a moment suspended in eternity.' (23). Alone in the Arab café as night descends, the narrator hears in the distant sound of the sea 'the peace and indifference of immortal things'. Out of this indifference is born a sort of secret song which transports him back in time: 'And I am home again. I think of a child living in a poor district.' (24). At this point the narration switches to the third person ; what is recounted is once again, as in 'Irony', focalised through the child. Precisely the same words are used to describe the mother: 'She was an invalid, had difficulty in thinking.' (25). When she is alone, her silence is 'a grief without repair'. If the child should enter and find her thus, he is frightened. He is beginning to 'feel a lot of things', though he is hardly aware of his own existence. He feels pity for his mother and does not know whether this is love. She has never caressed him 'for she wouldn't know how'. He stays looking at her and feels himself estranged though conscious of her pain. She is unaware of his presence because she is deaf. This is the

---

[42] cf. '...the true paradises are the paradises we have lost', Marcel Proust, *À la recherche du temps perdu* (Paris : Gallimard, Bibliothèque de la Pléiade, IV) p.449

[43] A.Amiot, 'Un romantisme corrigé, *Entre oui et non*' Europe.Revue de littérature mensuelle 77 :846 (October 1999) p.86

pivotal moment of pure emotion, suspended in time: 'this silence marks a pause, an immensely long moment. Because he is vaguely aware of this, the child thinks that the upsurge of feeling in him is love for his mother.' (25-26). As night thickens in the Arab café, the narrator reverts to the first person as he reflects on 'the indifference of this strange mother. The only thing that can serve as a measure for it is the immense solitude of the world.' (26). The 'upsurge of feeling in him' is a surge of awareness transcendent of time, which the child recognises as love for his mother. In this equation, 'his mother' is identified with 'the world', and 'indifference' is seen as something which these two profoundly important presences share, in the sense that the life that they are giving the child is beyond gratitude or human gesture; it is something primal, something which simply *is*. It is surely going too far to suggest, as does Edward J. Hughes, that 'the twenty-two-year-old Camus who authors this intimate portrait can draw only negative conclusions from the failing relationship', and that 'emotional negativity' clouds the portrait of the mother.[44]

Hughes' emphasis on negativity seems also to be contradicted in the depiction of a second incident from later in the son's life, when the mother sends for him after she has been brutally attacked by a stranger. Here it is tenderness and pity which are being evoked. The mother is lying in her bed when the narrator arrives and the doctor advises him not to leave her. He lies beside her in her suffering, registering her pain and agitation. Eventually, he falls asleep 'not without taking with him the tender and despairing image of a solitude for two.' (27). Later, much later he says, he appreciates the significance of this moment: 'this moment when he had felt the ties which attached him to his mother. As if she were the immense pity of his heart, spread out around him, made flesh...' The links which bind him to his mother are elemental, beyond the superficialities of gesture or utterance. This can only be expressed in an image. And it is the image, 'the tender and despairing image' which he carries away with him. As David H. Walker says in his discussion of *The First Man*: 'the image is the vocabulary of that

[44] Edward J. Hughes, 'Autobiographical soundings in *L'Envers et l'Endroit*' in Edward J. Hughes (ed.) *The Cambridge Companion to Camus* (Cambridge: Cambridge University Press, 2007) pp. 42-43

language of silence connecting the narrator to the crucial enigma of the mother.'[45]

In another shift of narrative stance, the first person resumes in a meditative passage in which the narrator reflects that 'there is a dangerous virtue in the word simplicity' (27), dangerous because, from a certain point of view, one might wish to die because there is nothing more significant in life than the fact of death. In his most profound experience of the world it is the simplicity of this which is overwhelming: '...every time that it seemed to me as if I had grasped the deep meaning of the world, it is its simplicity that has always overwhelmed me.' (28). The identification of the narrator with the son is acknowledged in the shift to the personal pronoun 'my' in the phrase which exemplifies this primordial simplicity: 'My mother, that evening, and her strange indifference.' A starker image is recalled as he remembers the 'demented flame' in the eyes of a cat who has half consumed the last dead kitten of her litter, and he reflects that 'when we are stripped down to a certain point, nothing leads anywhere anymore, hope and despair are equally groundless, and the whole of life can be summed up in an image.' (28). On this evening, it is the image of his childhood – 'a certain childhood' – which comes back to him, from which he can draw a 'lesson of love and poverty.' It is a moment suspended in time 'like a pause between yes and no'; 'hope' or 'disgust with life' are for another time.

A third encounter between the now grown-up son and the mother is recounted, once more in the third person. The son asks his mother whether he resembles his father, killed at the Marne. But he speaks without conviction: 'No memory, no emotion. Doubtless someone quite ordinary.' (29). It is a matter of fact and therein lies the simplicity. To the narrator it seems that 'the whole absurd simplicity of the world' (30) takes refuge in that room. But how can he separate that room from the deserted café in which he now sits? As he leaves and looks for a last time at the lights of the bay, it is not the hope of better days which comes to him but 'a serene and primitive indifference to everything and to myself.' He concludes: 'Yes, everything is simple. It is men who complicate things.' In stressing the need

---

[45] David H. Walker 'Knowing the place for the first time ?' in Peter Dunwoodie and Edward J. Hughes, *Constructing Memories: Camus, Algeria and 'Le Premier Homme'* (Stirling, Scotland: Stirling French Publications, 1998) p. 13

for 'lucidity', he aligns himself with those 'who prefer to look their fate in the eye.'

In the next essay, 'Iron in the Soul', there is a directness and coherence about the narrative which may derive from the fact that Camus wrote this account of visits to Prague and Vicenza almost immediately after his own visits to those cities. According to Olivier Todd, these took place in July, 1936.[46] It seems, then, that 'Iron in the Soul' is a much more direct transmission of experience than is to be found in the successive reworkings of the material of 'Irony' and 'Between Yes and No'. This time the narrative voice is consistently first person and undisguised, and it is difficult for the reader to avoid identifying the 'I' of the narrative with Camus himself. The geographical space between Prague and Vicenza, between the cold North of Central Europe and the warm South of the Mediterranean, maps symbolically a division between two emotional extremes. On the one hand, the narrator experiences the pain of solitude, alienation and stark self-confrontation in Prague; on the other hand, he finds solace and self-forgetfulness in the populous and abundant life of Vicenza. Both poles are given concrete exemplification. In Prague, the narrator's experience of the normal disorientation of being a stranger in an unfamiliar town – not knowing the way round, the barrier of language – intensifies into a more acute discomfort as the narrative tense shifts from past to present: 'My anxiety, still rather vague a few moments ago, fixes itself on this one point. I feel uneasy. I feel hungry and empty.' (31). This anxiety is given physical manifestation in his reaction to the food, dominated by the flavour of cumin. He fears being sick in the restaurant, surrounded by people. But his more profound fear is psychological; he fears being alone in his room at the hotel 'without money or enthusiasm, reduced to myself and to my poverty-stricken thoughts.' (32). The immediacy of the experience is given emphasis by quoting what the narrator has written down in the isolation of his bedroom, though he acknowledges that he has written merely as a means of getting to sleep: when the 'curtain of habits' is lifted and the 'comfortable loom' of familiar words and gestures is absent, man is left face to face with himself. 'I defy him to be happy', he comments (34). Yet, he argues, this experience is in itself illuminating:

---

[46] Olivier Todd, *Albert Camus, une vie* (Paris:Gallimard,1996) p.153

A great gulf widens between him and things. The world's music finds its way more easily into this less solid heart. As he is finally stripped bare, the slightest solitary tree becomes the most tender and fragile of images. (34).

Once more complexity resolves into the simplicity of an image. Here, the tender and fragile image of the isolated tree recalls the evocation of 'what we love' in the opening of 'Between Yes and No': ('We love the gentleness of certain gestures, the way a tree fits into a landscape.'). (23). The nostalgic tone, here, the comforting image conjured from memory, is brutally contrasted with the present reality which confronts the narrator when he views through a half-open door another image, this time projected by the light onto a cold, blue wall, the shadow of a corpse that has lain unheeded in the anonymous hotel room for days. Ironically, the light is 'a real living light' emphasising the absolute simplicity of the death - 'He was dead. Alone in his room.' – conveyed in two, short monosyllabic sentences. (35). The narrator's alienation has reached an insupportable extreme, expressed in the insistent repetition of his exclamation 'I couldn't go on'. (36).

Light is once more evoked in the introduction of the contrasting theme. A sense of life's abundance and recuperative power is heralded by the appearance of light as the narrator is en route for Venice: 'A light was coming to birth. I now know what it was: I was ready for happiness.' (36). The happiness materialises in Vicenza, its immediacy conveyed with a shift of tense to the present: 'I breathe in the only happiness I can attain...I spend the whole day walking about...Every person I meet, every scent on this street, is a pretext for my measureless love.' (37). However, this happiness does not derive simply from the escape from solitude. The shadow of the dead man in Prague is not forgotten in the vibrant sunshine of Vicenza. Just as the narrator has learned to understand his love for the world of poverty of his childhood, so he has glimpsed 'the lesson of the sun and of the countries which witnessed my birth.' (38). Sun and shadow, life and death, Vicenza and Prague – for Camus, of course, they co-exist. 'Both are dear to me, and I cannot separate my love for light and life from the secret attachment I bear for the experience of despair that I have tried to describe.' (39). For what the 'fullness without tears', the 'joyless peace' which his experience of Italy has brought him is an 'anguish' which both is and is not the anguish of Prague. It is an anguish which accepts absolutely the certainty of death while relishing the generous abundance of what life offers. In the indifference of the beautiful landscape of Northern Italy there is 'no promise of immortality', but what can revive his soul is the sensual apprehension of life's riches:

'eyes to see Vicenza', 'hands to touch the grapes', 'flesh to feel the night's caress on the road (from) Monte Berico...'(39). The emotional extremes represented by Prague and Vicenza are thus not simple binary oppositions. As Geneviève Henrot demonstrates, an element of the one exists in the other: 'an enclave of the kingdom in the lands of exile, and a shard of exile at the heart of the kingdom ; in the 'no' an aspiration to 'yes', in the shadow of 'yes' a memory of 'no'.[47]

The fourth essay, 'Love of Life' has the least enigmatic title of the collection. It continues the evocation of plenitude which concluded 'Iron in the Soul' and features another voyage, this time to the Balearic Islands, undertaken in 1935, a year before the journey to Prague. The opening situates the narrator in another café at evening, on this occasion in Parma, where the café is teeming with life. He reflects that without cafés, travel would be difficult, because they allow the stranger to overcome his isolation. They offer 'a place where, in the evenings, we try to rub shoulders with other men, enable us to mime in familiar gestures the man we were at home, and who, seen from a distance, is so like a stranger' (41). The dense crowd are gathered to enjoy the performance of a voluptuous dance by a woman with 'the face of a young girl, but carved out of a mountain of flesh.' (40). Her sensual movement mimes 'the act of love with her whole body'. (41). At the same time she is 'sticky with sweat'. The narrator/observer sees in this another image of contradiction: 'an ignoble and exalting image of life, with despair in her empty eyes and thick sweat on her belly...' (41). The physical enjoyment of life is once more juxtaposed with its necessary corollary – the sweat, the empty eyes, the absence of hope which constitute mortality. For the narrator, the experience of this paradox is at its most vivid and intense in the countries of the Mediterranean: 'And never perhaps has any country, except the Mediterranean, taken me so far from myself and yet so near.' (42).

In contrast to the frenzy of the scene in the café, the empty district around the cathedral and the little Gothic cloister of San Francisco afford the narrator the space for reflection. In the silence he observes the flight of pigeons and hears the occasional clanking of a chained metal cup against the stone sides of a well. In a moment of lucidity he recognises the essential transitoriness of this scene: 'In an hour, a minute, a second, now perhaps, everything could

---

[47] G.Henrot, 'Bouillonnements et tourbillons : configurations thématiques dans *La mort dans l'âme* d'A.Camus' <u>Studi francesi</u> 38.112 (1994) p.60

collapse.' (42). And yet, the world would continue 'modest, ironic and discreet'. He experiences a sense of equilibrium, yet this is 'coloured by all the apprehension of its own end.' (43). The world is indifferent, yet offers abundance, above all the countries of the Mediterranean. However, for the narrator, this is not because the Mediterranean landscape – 'the language of these countries' – responds to his questions, or answers his concerns, but because it renders them useless and irrelevant. That is what is meant by 'indifference'. Love of life and knowledge of the inevitability of its ending are co-existent: 'There is no love of life without despair of life.' (43).

The final essay resumes the title of the whole collection, 'Betwixt and Between'. It begins with an anecdote. An old woman used a small legacy which came to her late in life to buy her own tomb. Work was carried out to prepare it and she took pleasure in visiting it to view progress. On completion she continued to visit it each Sunday. She would enter the tomb where 'confronting what she was and what she would become...she effortlessly pierced the secret designs of Providence.' (45). One Toussaint, arriving late, she found that violets had been placed at the door of the tomb by passers by believing the tomb to be occupied and unremembered. The anecdote is recounted like an exemplary fable, rather than a transcription of authentic, lived experience. The narration is neutral and anonymous; there is none of the personal involvement that has been noted in the earlier essays.

It serves, however, to introduce a personal commentary: 'And now I think of these things again.' (46). The shift to the 'I' marks a transition to the present time and the particularities of place, 'the garden...these few branches...the light.' The effects of light and shadow, of cloud hiding and then revealing the sun, lead the narrator to exclaim: 'one light coming to birth, and I am filled with a confused and whirling joy'. (46). What is important is to seize the moment, to enter into the 'play of foliage and of light.' Other things – 'other men and the graves they purchase' – are for another time. It is another of those suspended moments – 'today is a resting place, and my heart goes off in search of itself' – that were noted in 'Between Yes and No'. The only anxiety is the feeling of inevitability that this 'impalpable moment' will slip through his fingers like quicksilver. It will end, inevitably, like life itself. But for the moment, he exclaims, '...my whole kingdom is of this world.' (47).

In its juxtaposition of the story of the woman who turns her back on the world and prepares her own tomb, with the thoughts of the man who reflects on his devouring love of life, the essay re-states some of the conflicting currents, representing the *envers* and the *endroit* of the world, which have run through the collection. What else is re-stated is that this is not, for Camus, a matter of choice:

> I do not want to choose between these two sides of the world, and I do not like a choice to be made…Great courage still consists of gazing steadfastly at the light as on death. (47).

The Problem of Form

Analysis of the formal concerns raised by Camus in relation to *L'Envers et l'Endroit* requires consideration of questions of genre, temporality and narrative voice, as Camus experiments with different ways of telling in the five pieces which make up the collection. There is a secondary set of questions relating to the overall structure and coherence of the work. This section sets out to consider, firstly, some of the narrative methods Camus uses, especially his use of first and third person narration, and the different functions which can be attributed to his use of 'I' in these essays, bearing in mind what has been noted earlier about his desire to seek a greater anonymity in his writing. Secondly, the ways in which the five constituent parts which make up *L'Envers et l'Endroit* are linked together, and the extent to which they make a coherent whole are discussed. Finally, consideration is given to whether it was the undisguised subjectivity of the writing or the overall structure of the collection which was most exercising Camus when he spoke, in the 1958 Preface, of the 'maladroitness' of the work.

I: Seeking a Voice

A matter of weeks after the publication of *L'Envers et l'Endroit* in May 1937, Camus was already expressing concern about its lack of objectivity. In a letter to his close friend, Jean de Maisonseul[48], on July 8 1937, he says that the newspaper reviews of his book have left him with nothing to complain about, that the welcome it has received is more than he had hoped for. However, he agrees with his friend that the work has been too personal: 'I

---

[48] The *Pléiade* editors point out (*Œuvres Complètes* I p.1227) that, in 1937, Jean de Maisonseul (1912-1999) was 'already an old friend'. They had been classmates in 1932.

agree with you, Jean: one should have stayed in the background...'[49] He attributes this problem to his lack of skill – 'I lack craft' – and to his youthfulness and love of life – 'it's my youth and my love of life that prevents me from... being objective'. Nevertheless, he feels he has touched 'the true sense of the world', and explains that he has allowed himself to write with all his passion – 'to tell all with all my passion – to go all the way' – while acknowledging the 'weakness' of the consequent lack of objectivity. He goes on to say that one day he will write a 'work of art', 'a creation', but he insists that he will be saying the same things, and the only developments will be formal ones – 'It will be the same things that I will say, and my whole progress, I'm afraid, will be in the form – which I would like to be more impersonal.'

In *L'Envers et l'Endroit*, Camus, despite himself, cannot hide himself. He clearly does not set out to be 'autobiographical', but he has learned (for example, from de Richard) that his own experience (of poverty, for example) could provide suitable material for his writing. He also has a strong sense of loyalty to the world into which he was born and wishes to bear witness to the truth of it, for his writing to be a *témoignage*. At the same time, and paradoxically, he wants to distance himself from a too direct expression of his own sensibility, to construct a work of art which engages the emotional response of the reader through the artifice of the writer. The tensions inherent in this paradox can be explored through an examination of the various constructions and projections of the self to be found in these essays. In doing so, it is particularly helpful to bear in mind Gérard Genette's distinction between 'mood' and 'voice', a distinction between the question *'who is the character whose point of view orients the narrative perspective?* and the very different question *who is the narrator?* – or, more simply, the question *who sees?* and the question *who speaks?*'[50]

In 'Iron in the Soul', for example, the 'I' of the first person narrative which recounts the contrasting personal experience of Prague and Vicenza is the same 'I' who is able to modulate seamlessly into a philosophical reflection on what has been experienced. As was noted in the previous section, the voyage Camus himself made, and his shaping of it into writing were

---

[49] The letter can be found in *Œuvres Complètes* I pp. 97-98

[50] Gérard Genette, *Narrative Discourse*. Translated by Jane E. Lewin (Ithaca, New York : Cornell University Press, 1980) p.186

contemporaneous, and there is a directness in this transmission of experience. There is no attempt to 'stay in the background', to disguise a possible identification between narrator and author. The same is true of 'Love of Life', the other *récit de voyage* in the collection, where the 'I' recounts a visit to the Balearic Islands which Camus had visited in 1935. Here, the 'I'/narrator is the observer of the sensual dance in the crowded café, and, later, the solitary presence in the cloisters of San Francesco who absorbs the stillness and the silence of the moment and reflects on its transitory nature. In these two essays, the narrator, the central character and the philosophical commentator form a unified construction which, in the mind of the reader, constitutes an idea of the writer, that is to say, of Camus himself.

In two of the earlier essays, 'Irony' and 'Between Yes and No', the personal involvement of the narrator in the story and his philosophical distancing from it are less clear-cut. The dualities inherent in this simultaneous detachment and engagement were in the forefont of Camus' mind at the time of writing these essays. His thinking can be traced in the pages of the *Carnets* in the entries he was making in 1936 and 1937. In May, 1936, he is exhorting himself not to 'detach myself from the world…to commit myself fully'.[51] A little later he writes:

> Intellectual? Yes. And never deny it. Intellectual = he who splits himself in two. I like that. I am happy to be both. 'Can they be combined?' That's a practical question. You have to make the effort.[52]

Right at the outset of his career he is aware of the issue, for the writer, of 'multiple selves', of what T.S. Eliot calls that 'dedoublement of the personality against which the subject struggles'.[53] For Camus, it is necessary for the writer to be both intellectually detached and emotionally and physically engaged. He accepts that this involves a double rôle, a kind of splitting in two, but sees this as a practical problem which needs to be addressed. For Jacqueline Lévi-Valensi, this *dédoublement* is recognised by Camus in his choice of 'Irony' as the title of the first piece in the collection,

---

[51] *Œuvres Complètes* II p.808

[52] Ibid. p.810

[53] T.S. Eliot, *The Criterion* XII p.469 (He is talking about Jules Laforgue's use of irony.)

because 'the practice of writing and the practice of irony derive from the same movement of the mind which splits in two, situates itself at one and the same time both within its object and outside it...'.[54] It is the practice of irony which allows Camus, from a philosophical point of view, as we saw in the last chapter, to maintain his lucidity, to gaze 'steadfastly at the light as on death'. As a writer, the *dédoublement* requires, in the more fictional, less autobiographical parts of the collection, a more complex deployment of narrative voice. In the first episode of 'Irony', very substantially a reproduction of 'the voice of the sick old lady people left at home to go to a cinema' from *Les Voix du quartier pauvre*, he changes the original text and introduces a narrative 'I' into what had been a third person narration. This is accompanied by the fictional device of a non-specific temporal marker – 'two years ago'. The new text reads: 'Two years ago I knew an old woman'. (p.15) Later, another imprecise temporal marker – 'that particular day' – is used to introduce the second paragraph. In the next episode, 'I' is again introduced when the meanderings of the old man are being described: 'He walks along, turns at the corner of the street, stumbles and almost falls. I have seen him'. (19). In his use of these novelistic mechanisms to lend an impression of authenticity and immediacy, Camus might be said to be practising his versatility as a writer – the *métier* which, in his letter to Jean de Maisonseul he explains that he lacks. However, it is also an important way of identifying himself with the *quartier pauvre* in which he grew up, and of presenting his writing as in some ways a personal testimony. Hence the philosopher who offers the aphorisms of the concluding paragraph of 'Irony' – 'Death for us all, but his own death to each' (22) – is also both the ironic narrator of the events recounted, and one who has walked the streets and heard the voices of Belcourt, the working-class area of Alger where Camus was born.

The 'I' that introduces 'Between Yes and No' seeks to establish a much more direct contact with the reader. The tone is intimate, almost confessional : 'I can find a name for this tender and inhuman feeling which inhabits me today', 'I am remembering', 'I am back at home', 'those hours which I am bringing back', 'Only this memory is true in me and I always discover it too late'. (p.23) The repeated use of first person pronouns – 'I', 'me', 'myself' – insist that this is an intense and personal communication which is being made

---

[54] Jacqueline Lévi-Valensi, *Albert Camus ou la naissance d'un romancier* (Paris : Gallimard, 2006) p.360

as though for a single reader only. When the first person plural is used it is to make a generalising statement about the human condition that we as individuals might share in solidarity: 'We love the gentleness of certain gestures...' It is the hour and place for such intimacies – 'In this Moorish café...It is already night'. The scene is set for the narrator's memories to return and for a significant, personal experience to be communicated – 'the memory of a pure emotion, a moment suspended in eternity.'

However, at this point in the narration, in what seems to be a dissociative strategy, the character of 'a child living in a poor district' (24) is introduced whose point of view, to use Genette's terminology, 'orients the narrative perspective', thereby, ostensibly, moving it away from the narrator. Hence we may say that it is the child 'who sees' and the narrator 'who speaks'. However, a complication arises in this, the most profoundly personal part of *L'Envers et l'Endroit*, because the child is a projection of the narrator's younger self, an identification which is rendered explicit, as we saw earlier, when the narrator switches back to the first person to acknowledge 'My mother, that evening, and her strange indifference'. (28). This is a sudden, deliberate fracture of the prevailing narrative mode. At this significant moment, Camus seems driven to break the *pacte de lecture* in order to bear personal testimony and yet, at the same time, before and after this moment, he feels the need to exercise his craft as a writer in order to establish a narrative distance. This hesitation between a directly autobiographical representation of the experience and a fictional narrative, recalls Catherine Camus' remarks on *The First Man* which were noted in the Introduction: 'he was a very reserved man and would no doubt have masked his own feelings far more in its final version'. The instinct to 'mask his feelings' seems to be present in this, his earliest published work, for, despite all he says about the lack of objectivity in his writing, it is clear that he is here seeking to set the narrator at some distance from the experience. After the moment of personal identification, the next scene between mother and son is recounted with, it seems, deliberate artificiality, in conventional, third-person story-telling mode: 'And thus it was that not long ago, in a house in an old part of the town, a son went to see his mother'. (28). Here, there are no particularities of place ('a house', 'an old part'), or time ('not long ago') or person ('a son', 'his mother'). It is as though a too close intimacy has been checked, and, although the narrative goes on to present another intimate scene between mother and son, the hesitation between proximity and distance on the part of the narrator remains a stylistic feature of this essay. Camus' remark in his letter to Jean de Maisonseul that he felt he could allow himself to 'tell all with all my passion' seems, in this respect, wide of the mark.

Edward J. Hughes sums this up admirably when he says that 'the raw exposure given to kith and kin in *L'Envers et l'Endroit* signals a complex and often reluctant autobiographer.'[55]

In this, his earliest, published writing, it is tempting to think of Camus as experimenting with different ways of telling as though it were part of his apprenticeship to his chosen *métier*. His varied deployment of narrative voice in the collection has stylistic consequences for his choice of tenses. In 'Irony', for example, the point in time of the act of narration is implicitly the present: this is the tense of the concluding reflection –'None of this fits together?' (22) – and it is from this present that the narrator looks back to the past. In the first episode, as we have seen, the intervention of the narrator – 'I knew an old woman' (15) – is in the *passé composé* and, hence, temporally close to the present of the narration. Having established a notional moment in the past – 'that particular day' – when the events occurred, the narrative tense is largely the pluperfect – 'The guests had risen from the table to go and wash their hands...' (16), 'Every one else had kissed her', 'He had given her a...handshake' (17). However, at the climax of the episode, when the young man looks up and sees the light in the old lady's room extinguish, the drama of the moment is captured in the *passé simple*: 'He looked up at the lighted window, a great dead eye in the silent house. The eye closed.' (17). In 'Between Yes and No', in contrast, the present tense is used both for the reflection of the narrator in the Arab café, and for the recollected events of the past: 'If the child comes in at this moment, he sees the thin shape with its bony shoulders and stops: he is afraid'. (25). Here, the drama and poignancy of the moment is made all the more immediate by the use of the present tense.

In these various ways, Camus can be seen to be practising his writerly craft across a number of different genres, seeking appropriate forms of expression for philosophical reflection, personal reminiscence and accounts of the experience of travel. Elements of fiction, autobiography, philosophy and *récit de voyage* can all be identified in the collection, and this diversity of genre, in itself, constitutes another formal problem for Camus; that of the overall structure and coherence of the work.

---

[55] Edward J. Hughes, Op. Cit. p.49

II: 'A hidden reasoning which unifies...': the problem of cohesion

Finding a noun which satisfactorily describes the ensemble of the five constituent parts of *L'Envers et l'Endroit* has proved difficult. So far in this essay we have used, rather loosely, the term 'collection' or its French equivalent *recueil* to refer to the whole of the work, rather than the five individual pieces. A satisfactory term for these 'pieces' seems equally elusive. Philip Thody, the English translator of *L'Envers et l'Endroit*, calls them 'lyrical essays', which seems to acknowledge their hybridity, at least with regard to their personal and philosophical dimensions.[56] Camus, himself, refers to them as *essais*, though Jacqueline Lévi-Valensi suggests that he uses the term 'in its current usage as "attempt" rather than in its purely literary sense'.[57] If she is correct, he views them therefore as attempts, in keeping with his immaturity, rather than finished products. For the 'whole' of what is to become *L'Envers et l'Endroit*, Camus uses, at an early stage in its genesis, the term 'book'. In March, 1936, in the *Carnets*, he notes 'My book. I must think about it constantly'.[58] However, as Jacqueline Lévi-Valensi points out, 'it is impossible to specify what form Camus envisaged for it'.[59] She goes on to suggest that he may have had in mind simply an 'alternating structure' between 'reflections' and 'stories', thus mixing the 'essay' and the 'narrative'. The problem of form was already an issue for Camus. In the *Carnets* for May, 1937 can be found the sketch of a *Projet de Préface pour l'Envers et l'Endroit* which was not included in the publication. Here he describes the essays, in a typically self-deprecating manner, as rough attempts: 'In the way they are presented, these essays are, for many people, lacking in shape.'[60] But he goes on to ask the reader to recognise a progression in the overall structure:

> For those who will take these pages for what they really are : 'essays', the only thing I would ask of them is to follow the progression therein.

---

[56] Philip Thody, *Albert Camus :Lyrical and Critical* (London: Hamish Hamilton, 1967)

[57] Jacqueline Lévi-Valensi, *Albert Camus ou la naissance d'un romancier* (Paris : Gallimard, 2006) p.357

[58] *Œuvres complètes* II p.806

[59] Op. cit. p. 353

[60] *Œuvres complètes* II p. 815

> From the first page to the last they will perhaps sense a hidden
> reasoning which unifies them...[61]

He hopes, then, that his readers, as they read from the first to the last page of
his 'book', will sense *une démarche sourde* which will give the work its
cohesion. '*Démarche sourde*', in this context, might best be translated as a
hidden or implicit process of thought or reasoning, and it seems to be the
philosopher in Camus, rather than the creative artist, who is making this
claim.

Critics have largely focused on the interplay of antithetical themes in
commenting on the overall structure of the work. The *Pléiade* editors see
Camus' organisation of the previously written material, and that specifically
written for the collection, as establishing 'a progression and a circularity
while emphasising the coexistence of opposites'.[62]   They discern this
coexistence of opposites in the titles of 'Between Yes and No' and, the last
essay, 'L'Envers et l'Endroit', and in the juxtaposition of the third and fourth
essays, 'Iron in the Soul' and 'Love of Life'. They also note that 'Iron in the
Soul', itself, consists of 'two antithetical accounts', those of Prague and
Vicenza. The process of organising his material has evidently moved Camus
away from his original notion of a simple alternating structure towards a
more complex 'coexistence'. Peter Dunwoodie, similarly, emphasises the
simultaneous presence of polar opposites:

> Oscillating between positive and negative, joy and anguish,
> identification and detachment, Camus strains to express the
> interdependence of two poles, *envers* and *endroit*, their inextricable
> and essential links; and they are to be read not alternately but
> simultaneously.[63]

Dunwoodie's use of the word 'strains' suggests that the effort involved in
bringing these oppositions into play may not have been wholly successful.

---

[61] Ibid. p. 815-816

[62] *Œuvres complètes* I p. 1214

[63] Peter Dunwoodie, *Camus : L'Envers et l'Endroit and L'Exil et le Royaume* (London : Grant
and Cutler, 1985) p.12

But generally, commentators on *L'Envers et l'Endroit* have been more generous in their estimation of the book than Camus himself. Jacqueline Lévi-Valensi, for example, sees the progression through the five essays as a voyage of discovery: 'The whole of the collection corresponds...to a dramatized vision of the stages traversed by the human being in the exploration not of his psychological reality or his individual subjectivity, but of his place in the world.'[64]   Similarly, for Agnès Spiquel, the collection represents 'a sort of spiritual itinerary' from the ironic observations of the first essay, through the repatriated soul which reconnects in the 'interval of a moment' with the memory of a 'lost paradise', through the double experience of 'desolation' and 'ecstasy' in 'Iron in the Soul', and the essential link between 'love' and 'despair' in 'Love of Life', to the concluding 'refusal to choose' between the two versions proposed by the title in the last essay, 'L'Envers et l'Endroit', which she sees as as indissociable as the recto and verso of a page.[65]   There is a suggestion here that there is a dynamism and an evolution running through the work, corresponding with what Camus wanted his readers to recognise when, in the *Projet de Préface*, he asks that they should 'follow the progression'.

A less generous estimation of the coherence of *L'Envers et l'Endroit* might suggest that there is something more pragmatic in Camus' bringing together of this material for publication as the second book to appear in the *Méditerranéennes* series published in Alger by Edmond Charlot. Camus clearly took great pains to try and link his disparate material into a coherent form. As we know from his meticulous planning of his later work, such coherence was important to him. His conception of his work in terms of 'cycles' of three discrete, yet linked, works consisting of novel, philosophical essay and play, first seen in the 'cycle of the Absurd' with *The Stranger*, *The Myth of Sisyphus* and *Caligula*, clearly separates out into distinct entities, work in some of the genres with which he is simultaneously grappling in *L'Envers et l'Endroit*. The heterogeneous nature of the five essays reflects the fact that they were written at different times and with different ends in view. Talking of 'the difficulties of the genesis of *L'Envers et l'Endroit*', Jacqueline Lévi-Valensi emphasises this when she remarks that 'presentation

---

[64] Jacqueline Lévi-Valensi, *Albert Camus ou la naissance d'un romancier* (Paris : Gallimard, 2006) p.451

[65] Agnès Spiquel, 'L'Envers et l'Endroit, recueil' in Jeanyves Guérin (ed.) *Dictionnaire Albert Camus* (Paris : Éditions Robert Laffont, 2009) p. 256

as a collection had not been anticipated by Camus originally'.[66] If there is a 'spiritual journey' to be traced through the collection, it is perhaps in the subjectivity of the author rather than in the constructed the work of art. In this early work we can discern to some extent how the later distinction between 'literary work' and 'philosophical work' came to be important. For in trying to combine the two in *L'Envers et l'Endroit*, he runs into the formal problems which cause him to consider, later in his career, this early work 'maladroit'.

Conclusion

'It's like a glimpse into his workshop,' Tobias, Patricia Duncker's narrator, is quoted as saying in the introduction to this essay. He is, of course, referring to the unfinished *The First Man,* but reading the early writing of Camus up to and including the publication of *L'Envers et l'Endroit* offers a similar insight into the young writer's ways of working. 'All his notes and sketches,' says Tobias enthusiastically, and, indeed, it is in the various drafts and early versions of *L'Envers et l'Endroit* that we can see Camus experimenting both with the content – 'what I mean' – and the form of what will become the 'work of art'. But, for Camus, *L'Envers et l'Endroit* does not represent that finished work of art because, as we have seen, he is dissatisfied with its form: 'I reject nothing of what these essays express, but their form has always seemed clumsy to me', he says in the 1958 Preface. (5). We have seen that the formal problems which confronted Camus at the time of writing *L'Envers et l'Endroit* were complex. There was the tension between the impulse to 'tell all' and a contrary impulse to establish a writerly detachment, to construct a work of art that would 'speak', rather than to let his sensibility cry out: 'My sensibility should speak, not cry out...' as he says in the *Notes de Lecture*.[67] These contrary impulses led him to experiment with a variety of ways of using narrative voice, particularly his deployment of 'I' as a piece of novelistic rhetoric, or for the expression of personal testimony, or, in a universalising sense, for the articulation of a philosophical point of view.

In his letter to Jean de Maisonseul he is defensive about the subjectivity of his writing while acknowledging that it was necessary for a writer to

---

[66] Op. cit. p. 353

[67] *Œuvres complètes* I p.957

maintain a greater reserve. A year after publication, he was writing in the *Carnets*: 'the true work of art is that which tells least'[68]. It can be argued that Camus never in his later work got anywhere near the kind of self-exposure to be found in an essay like 'Between Yes and No'. Indeed, critics have noted a certain taciturnity as a feature of Camus' later novels. Dominique Rabaté, for example, notes that a 'desire for conciseness can be seen in each of his novels which must stay faithful to a sort of vow of silence.'[69] She goes on to remark that Camus' characters 'hesitate between a loquaciousness (which cannot hide the flaws which their discourse seeks, in fact, to conceal) and a reserve close to silence.' She is perhaps thinking of a character like Clamence in *The Fall* as an example of an elusive, masking loquacity, and of Meursault in *The Stranger* as an example of a character who utters, without revealing anything of an interior, psychological self.

We have noted, while recognising a thematic unity, a further set of formal problems relating to the disparate nature and the generic mixture of the material which constitutes *L'Envers et l'Endroit*. A consequence seems to be that Camus organises his subsequent work with a deliberate and scrupulous regard for generic distinctiveness: literary work, philosophical work, theatrical work.

In studying these earliest writings of Camus, we discern, then, a series of oppositions. As well as the thematic oppositions implicit in the title *L'Envers et l'Endroit* - between the bleakness of man's mortality and the ironic exuberance of life's abundance – there are contrary impulses which clearly exercised Camus as a young writer: engagement versus detachment, self-revelation versus ironic distance, autobiography versus fiction, *témoignage* versus philosophy, the Gidean conflict between the ascetic and the hedonistic. There are also a son's separation from his mother, and that search for an equivalence between 'who he is' and 'what he says'. Further study might show the ways in which these dualities play out in Camus' later work, and thus lead to a fuller understanding of why, for Camus, *L'Envers et l'Endroit*, whatever its formal shortcomings, represents, in his own words, 'that single stream in the life of the artist which nourishes all that he is and all that he says.'

---

[68] *Œuvres complètes* II p. 862

[69] Dominique Rabaté, 'Roman' in Jeanyves Guérin (ed.) *Dictionnaire Albert Camus* (Paris : Éditions Robert Laffont, 2009) p. 802

Works Cited

Amiot, A. "Un romantisme corrigé, 'Entre oui et non'". Europe. Revue de littérature   mensuelle (numéro spécial consacré à Albert Camus) 77:846 (octobre 1999) pp. 76-89.

Bruckner, Pascal. 'Happiness' in Kritzman, Lawrence D. (ed), *The Columbia History of Twentieth Century French Thought* (New York: Columbia University Press, 2006)

Camus, Albert. *Œuvres complètes* (Paris : Gallimard, Bibliothèque de la Pléiade, 4 volumes : Volumes I and II, 2006 ; Volumes III and IV, 2008)

Camus, Albert and Grenier, Jean. *Correspondance 1932-1960* (Paris : Gallimard, 1981) de l'Isle-Adam, Villiers. *Contes cruels* (Paris : Gallimard, 1983) de Richard, André. *La Douleur* (Paris: Grasset, 1931)

Duncker, Patricia. *The Deadly Space Between* (London: Picador, 2002)

Dunwoodie, Peter. *Camus : 'L'Envers et l'Endroit' and 'L'Exil et le Royaume'* (London :   Grant and Cutler, 1985)

Eliot, T.S. *Selected Essays* (London: Faber and Faber 1932)

Genette, Gérard. *Narrative Discourse*. Translated by Jane E. Lewin (Ithaca, New York :   Cornell University Press, 1980)

Gide, André. *Les Nourritures terrestres* (Paris: Gallimard, 1969)

Grenier, Roger. *Albert Camus : Soleil et ombre* (Paris : Gallimard, 1987)

Guérin, Jeanyves. (ed), *Dictionnaire Albert Camus* (Paris : Robert Laffont, 2009)

Henrot, G. "Bouillonnements et tourbillons. Configurations thématiques dans 'La mort dans l'âme' d'A.Camus." Studi francesi 38.112 (1994) pp.45-60.

Hughes, Edward J. "Autobiographical Soundings in *L'Envers et l'Endroit.*" E.J. Hughes [ed.], *The Cambridge Companion to Camus* (Cambridge : Cambridge University Press, 2007) pp. 39-49.

Lévi-Valensi, Jacqueline. *Albert Camus ou la naissance d'un romancier* (Paris : Gallimard, 2006)

Lottman, Herbert R. *Albert Camus, a biography* (London: Weidenfeld and Nicolson, 1979)

Proust, Marcel. *Du côté de chez Swann* (Paris : GF Flammarion, 1987)

Thody, Philip. *Albert Camus :Lyrical and Critical* (London: Hamish Hamilton, 1967)

Todd, Olivier. *Albert Camus, une vie* (Paris : Gallimard, 1996)

Walker, David H.'Knowing the place for the first time ?' in Peter Dunwoodie and Edward J. Hughes, *Constructing memories: Camus, Algeria and 'Le Premier Homme'* (Stirling, Scotland: Stirling French publications, 1998) pp. 9-20

Winock, Michel. *Le Siècle des intellectuels* (2nd edition, Éditions du Seuil, 1997)

Aestheticizing a Bacillus: Disease and Destiny in Albert Camus' *The Plague*

By Patrick Reilly

What is the novel, in fact, if not the universe where action finds its form, where the final words are said, the human being abandoned to the other human beings, where everything bears the mark of destiny.

— Albert Camus, *The Rebel*

Most plague texts have their genesis in fact. Albert Camus' *The Plague* (la Peste) is no exception. Therefore, to study the aesthetics of plague literature—or more particularly, the aesthetic constructs of destiny in plague literature—is to examine the process by which the factual reality of plague is first perceived and then translated by an author into a literary reality. A process that begins in perception—and indeed, the ancient Greeks defined aesthetics as perception—thus ends in representation; the plague text re-presents plague's fact.

Set in the coastal city of Oran in Algeria in the unspecified year of 194–, the genesis of Camus' *The Plague,* published in postwar 1947, in all likelihood lies in the outbreak of bubonic plague in Oran in the 1940s. Some students of Camus, however, attribute the genesis of the novel less specifically and believe it to be a fictive composite based on several epidemics that darkened the history of Algeria, a principal one being the cholera epidemic that killed a large percentage of Oran's population in 1849, following the French colonization. Oran and its environs had in fact suffered numerous epidemics by the time Camus published his novel. A research report by the Center for Disease Control and Prevention shows that Oran was decimated by plague in 1556 and in 1678, whereas outbreaks of plague after European colonization—185 cases in 1921, 76 in 1931, 95 in 1944—fell far short of the epidemic described in the novel.

Although Camus locates the novel in the French colony of Algeria in North Africa, the city of Oran feels essentially European, and all of Camus' central characters are of European descent. The geography fixes a distance between the colony and France, between North Africa and Europe, at the same time that the cultural disposition of the populace obliterates it. Oran is perhaps less significant as the city in which a plague appears than as any city in which plague may appear. In Oran it does what in any city it might: It arrives, no one knows from where. Its cause is impossible to ascertain, its etiology remaining unclear, its course impossible to predict or explain. Indiscriminately it kills by the hundreds, for days, weeks, months. Death tolls rise until the bacillus begins to grow attenuated. Until the pestilence itself seems to die. For, mysteriously, it goes away. Yet it will no doubt return again, because in the story of the pestilence in Oran, as in any tale of plague, there can be no "final victory [*victoire definitive*]," but rather "only the record of what had to be done, and what assuredly would have to be done again" (271), as the novel's narrator and journal-writer, the physician and atheist Dr. Rieux, who knows his Lucretius and Thucydides,[1] notes at the close of the novel. Like the mythic dragon's teeth of Thebes, the plague is always in the earth.

Camus' *The Plague,* then, like Defoe's *Journal of a Plague Year,* to which it owes some artistic debt, offers a realistically detailed chronicle of the plague in Oran; but concealed, and revealed, in that chronicle is a tale that invests the plague with a larger, more universal, mythic significance. Thus the novel can be read both literally, in concrete terms of a specific plague, and symbolically, in abstract terms of a mythic plague; and in between, the novel no doubt offers possibilities that can be read metaphorically, in the figurative terms of a political or social plague, for instance.[2] Importantly, though, for the narrator, the 194– bubonic outbreak in Oran stands in the moment of the

---

[1] Thucydides in his *History of the Peloponnesian War* chronicles the progress of the plague that originated in Ethiopia and that in 430 BCE decimated Athens; Lucretius concludes his *De Rerum Natura* with a grim account of the great plague of Athens, which derives much of its detail (but not its moral attitude) from Thucydides. Early in his narrative Rieux recalls especially the image of "the plague-fires of which Lucretius tells, which the Athenians kindled on the seashore" and where after nightfall the living brought their dead (38).

[2] As Lev Braun asserts in *Witness of Decline,* "the beleaguered city of Oran is an obvious allegory of the Resistance in occupied Europe [as Camus himself confirmed in *Lyrical and Critical Essays* (339)]. . . . In a broader sense, the plague is the war, or Nazism (or any totalitarian government), or, generally speaking, any kind of social or political upheaval" (85).

novel as an epidemiological apogee in the long, still unfinished history of plague. In that sense, the plague narrative can perhaps be most clearly read, as Susan Sontag suggests in *AIDS as Metaphor,* as an epitome: "Camus in not protesting anything, not corruption or tyranny, not even morality. The plague is no more or less than an exemplary event, the irruption of death that gives life its seriousness. His use of plague is more epitome than metaphor, is detached, stoic, aware—it is not about bringing judgment" (59-60). And in that sense, as Germaine Brée points out in *Camus, The Plague* is very unlike Defoe's *Journal* (and numerous other works in the library of Camus' authorial mind), in which pestilence is deemed "to be the punishment meted out by God as a consequence of man's collective sinfulness" (119).

The "event" as it evolves in the narrative is of course shaped by the narrator's vision, but that does not preclude the introduction of contrary perspectives on the progress of the plague. The narrator is not about "bringing judgment" any more than is Camus. Neither is he deaf to voices that might regard the plague with less stoic detachment than he, and in the course of the narrative emerge (at least) two distinct, contrary constructs by which to view the plague and its destiny: one, that of Dr. Rieux, which brings scientific observation to bear upon its depiction of plague; the other, Father Paneloux's, which seeks out a theological rationale to explain the cause for the terror that has befallen the city of Oran. More insistently than do the plague texts of Defoe and Manzoni, Camus' *The Plague* founds its argument in the dichotomy between science and religion, out of which arise numerous corollaries of duality, like reason and faith, empiricism and metaphysics, epidemiology and dogma, humanism and Christianity.[3] More modern, and more relevant in its empirical approach to the problem at hand, though Rieux's scientific perspective may be than Paneloux's metaphysical one, both constructs will in the end prove to be contrarily aesthetic. Out of their contrariety and their conjunction—out of the intellectual conflict between the

---

[3] The principle of duality characterizes Camus' work from the outset of his career, notes Cruickshank: "The Mediterranean duality at the basis of Camus' thought strikes one immediately in his earliest published work, *L'envers et l'endroit.* The title itself suggests a dualism with its reference to the right and wrong side of a piece of material. The image also emphasizes the close relatedness of the two terms of his experience . . . In each instance happiness and suffering intensify each other. The acuteness of Camus' reaction to each is due to the fact of their contrasting coexistence . . . The contrast between youth and age, life and death, pleasure and fear is maintained throughout *L'ironie*" (25-26). See also Germaine Brée's critical biography *Camus* (119).

earthly, humanist practitioner of medicine and the tortured medievalist priest who would save mankind's soul—emerges the novel's aesthetic construct of destiny. Philosophically and psychologically, the linear-thinking metaphysician is pitted against the mythopoeic sensibility of an empiricist who has perceived in history the cyclical nature of plague and observed firsthand, as an epidemiologist, its effects in the world it inhabits—and who, in the end, in his role as narrator, asserts what he can now fully imagine: As inevitable as its destiny is the certainty of the plague's eternal return.[4]

Ultimately in Camus' multilayered narrative the plague defines and is defined by every narrative detail, every novelistic turn of event, every intellectual posture, every disposition of character, every ambiguity and every metaphor. Yet, at the same time, plague defies the constructs that would contain or explain it; its full reality lies always beyond the intelligence and imagination of its interpreters. Camus acknowledges (as does his narrator) the inadequacy of the human intellect, be its perspective scientific or metaphysical, in its attempts to make comprehensible a thing that is in itself incomprehensible or, equally frightening, a thing that in itself simply is. For Camus (and the narrator), plague assumes its own destiny. It is. And when it isn't it will be again.

In *The Plague* Camus' Dr. Rieux serves a dual purpose. A man of science and a doctor dedicated to tending the sick and the dying, he is the protagonist of the plague narrative. He is also the narrator of the tale, however, as he discloses at the end of the novel when he prepares to turn the entries in his journal (as well as those in the diaries of his friend, the plague victim Tarrou) into a chronicle of the plague in Oran, which, of course, is essentially the eye-witness account the reader has just read. In this, Camus acknowledges his debt to Defoe, who used a similar device in *Journal of a Plague Year,* by which H. F. presents the events in London as if they were unfolding before him at the very time he was recording them, thus to heighten with immediacy the illusion of reality. Like Defoe's self-effacing H. F., too, Camus' narratorial Rieux incorporates scientific detail, like statistics in regard to day-

---

[4] Braun observes that Camus in several passages of *The Rebel* "accepts the Greek conception of a cyclical or undulatory process in history" and that "[o]ccasionally he seems to borrow Nietzsche's conception of the 'eternal recurrence of the same'" (144). Similar observations might be drawn from the Camusian narrator's views of history in *The Plague.*

to-day fatalities, to lend further authenticity to the horror that has been visited upon the citizens of Oran.

Apparently scientific, then—a realistic, empirical account of the plague's progress in Oran—Dr. Rieux's journal, or chronicle as it becomes, is equally, and perhaps more so, aesthetic: a construct that artfully orders what are supposedly the known facts of the plague in the face of what remains terrifyingly unknown about the plague's course—its destiny, if you will—as Rieux daily strives to prevent the spread of the epidemic, treat its victims, and seek a cure. So it is that the doctor as chronicler makes aesthetic choices; after all, he does not know everything about plague or about the plague in Oran, nor does he record everything about plague that he knows (he does not presume to be writing anything like a definitive tome).

The narrative in fact begins quite modestly by describing "this very ordinary town of Oran, which is merely a large French port on the Algerian coast, headquarters of the Prefect of a French 'Department'" (5). The very ordinariness of Oran, however, magnifies all the more the horror to come; the doctor-chronicler is also a skillful narrator. Recording a sequence of mostly quotidian events, he reserves his revelation of "their somewhat extraordinary character" (5) until the opening of the second chapter when the unnerving first sign of a potential bubonic catastrophe appears: "When leaving his surgery on the morning of April 16, Rieux felt something soft under his foot. It was a dead rat [*un rat mort*] lying in the middle of the landing" (7). Destiny in the very ordinary town of Oran is indeed about take an extraordinary turn.

Bubonic plague narratives previous to the twentieth century hardly mention dead rats at all—live rats scuttle when Renzo returns to his destroyed home in the concluding pages of *The Betrothed,* but no dead ones appear either in Manzoni's text or in that of his primary source, Ripamonte's *History of Milan;* they appear neither dead nor alive in Defoe—but in *The Plague* from the outset they are conspicuous. There is the one under Rieux's foot, then two more, followed by four and five and ten, twenty . . . Eventually eight thousand dead rats will be recorded. By the 1940s the connection between dead rats and bubonic plague was a long-established matter of scientific knowledge. "Those rats died of plague," concludes Rieux's colleague, Dr. Castel. "Or of something extremely like it," he adds, and ominously predicts, "And they've loosed on the town tens of thousands of fleas [*des dizaines des milliers de puces*] which will spread the infection in geometrical progression unless it's checked in time" (58). That an individual's destiny may be altered, or determined, by a bacteria-bearing flea that has lately abandoned the dying rat it infected is a premise as distasteful as it is horrifying, to doctors as well as the townspeople of Oran. Yet the public response to a possible outbreak of plague in Oran is neither immediate nor unified. What may be but a few isolated cases is no cause for alarm, the cry of epidemic is premature, and this is the twentieth century after all: The citizens of Oran retreat into denial, as if by not speaking the word "plague"—and no one is, except for Rieux— the reality that it represents can be escaped.

Denial can only disguise fear. Rieux, a doctor and a scientist, confronts it. He cannot doubt the fearful telltale signs of plague that he clearly recognizes; and however inadequately he may be able to identify the cause of its outbreak at this particular time in this particular place, he is acutely aware of its history and its effects. First in his journal, then in his chronicle, and ultimately as the narrator in and of the novel *La peste,* the doctor recounts the events he witnesses firsthand in Oran and ponders in an historical context their calamitous effects. By Rieux's estimate, plague has afflicted humankind "some thirty" times in centuries past and claimed the lives of "one hundred million people" (36). In light of such numbers, Rieux finds it difficult to imagine the world's history as a construct for human destiny by which the human spirit is evolving progressively toward a glorious realization of its elemental freedom. Indeed, in his rumination on plague history—or on plagues as history—and human freedom, Rieux may have in the ironic frame of his mind the Hegelian view of history as a dialectical progression out of whose heteronomous impulses is continually developing an ideal of human freedom.[5] As Rieux contemplates the townsfolk who have not "given a thought to anything like plague, which rules out any future, cancels journeys, silences the exchange of views"—which truncates time, appropriates space, stifles human intercourse, obliterates individual choice—he remarks: "They

---

[5] In Hegel's view of history as a dialectical progression, "world history is thus the unfolding of the Spirit [*Geist*] in time, as nature is the unfolding of Idea in space" until the Spirit recognizes its own essential freedom. For Camus, however, the "approach to the problem of man's conflict with the order of things," Braun states, "is in no way dialectical; it is clearly dualistic. Camus' novelty is that his is a horizontal dualism, ruling out any higher ontological status for human aspirations or achievements. Between the two poles of the conflict there is no movement, no oscillation as in Kierkegaard's sense, since Camus insists that both incompatible aspects of the human situation be kept in mind as a precondition of genuine revolt" (132).

fancied themselves free, and no one will ever be free so long as there are pestilences" (36).

Even before the "whole series of fantastic possibilities out of keeping with that grey-and-yellow town under his eyes" begin to unfold," the "old pictures of the plague," the history of pestilence, its visitations repeated again and again—and now—unsettle Rieux's scientific equanimity:

> Athens, a charnel-house reeking to heaven and deserted even by the birds. Chinese towns cluttered up with victims silent in their agony; the convicts at Marseilles piling rotting corpses into pits; the building of the Great Wall in Provence to fend off the furious plague wind; [Jaffa and its hideous beggars;] the damp, putrefying pallets stuck to the mud floor at the Constantinople lazar-house, where the patients were hauled up from their beds with hooks; the carnival of masked doctors at the Black Death; men and women copulating in the cemeteries of Milan; cartloads of dead bodies rumbling through London's ghoul-haunted darkness—nights and days filled always and everywhere with the eternal cry of human pain. (38)[6]

Far more so than the plague texts of Defoe, Manzoni, and Mann, Camus' *The Plague* is informed by narratives of prior pestilences, both ancient and modern, from Greek myths to modern-day chronicles, from biblical tales to accounts of the actual plague of Athens, the Black Death in London and Milan and Marseilles, the great plague of China. Gleaned from Rieux's medical texts and histories—and sourced in Camus' *Notebooks*[7]—the

---

[6] *"Athènes empestée et désertée par les oiseaux, les villes chinoises repliés d'agonisants silencieux, les gagnards de Marseille empilant dans des trous les corps dégoulinants, la construction en Pronvence du grand mur qui devait arrêter le vent furieux de la peste, Jaffa et sis hideux méndicants, les lits humides et pouris collés á la terre battue de l'hôpital de Constantinople, les malades tirés avec des crochets, le carnaval des médicins masqués pendant la Peste noire, les accouplements des vivants dans les cimetières de Milan, les charretes de morts dans Londres épouvanté, et les jours remplis, partout et toujours, du cri interminable des homes"*(43).

[7] Germaine Brée provides in a footnote Camus' reading list in preparation for the composition of *The Plague*. "Camus, as he started work on his novel, listed in his *Notebook*s: Thucydides: *History of the Peloponnesian War*; Boccaccio: *The Plague of Florence* (no doubt in the *Decameron*); Manzoni: *The Betrothed*; Daniel Defoe: *Journal of the Plague Year*; H. de Manfred and Jack London, each with a note 'The Scarlet Plague.' And he lists innumerable others, including memoirs by Mathurin Marais; accounts by Michelet, Pushkin, Charles Nicole and others; history, statistics, and symptoms culled from the works of doctors such as Antonin

plagues proceed across the stage of the narrator's mind and the pages of his narrative: from the plague of Constantinople, where ten thousand died in a single day, to the plague in Canton, where the bubonic plague bacillus was first identified—in 1894, by Alexandre Yersin (thus the name *bacillus Yersinia pestis* for the pathogen)—and where forty thousand rats died before their fleas massively infected the populace, to, just seventy years later, the plague in Oran.

A bacillus, then, has been insinuating itself into the aesthetic of human destiny for hundreds upon hundreds of years. Not until the Swiss-French physician and bacteriologist Yersin's discovery late in the nineteenth century, however, was science able to isolate the pathogen for bubonic plague and classify the conditions under which it operates. So it is that Rieux as well as Dr. Castel knows that the bubonic bacillus is carried by infected fleas living on—and eventually killing—rats, which they then abandon for another warm-blooded animal: the human. In the face of bubonic plague the modern scientist has at least one advantage over his counterparts from the Middle Ages to the Industrial Age; in dead rats he has a sure signpost to catastrophe. Having made the connection between the dead rats and bubonic plague, Rieux and his colleagues know what to expect: the fevers, the buboes, the infected lymph nodes—the symptoms the same as those of the victims in Defoe's London and Manzoni's Milan. Regarding the bacillus itself, though, Rieux does perceive a notable difference, one that elicits further unease and dread: The bacillus has apparently mutated. "I am bound to add that there are specific modifications which don't quite tally with the classical description of the plague bacillus" (46), Rieux observes.

Rieux's observation casts the science regarding plague not into doubt but into flux. As the bacillus mutates, the science changes. The how of plague is not fixed, and the why of it—in 194–, in Oran—is as elusive and mysterious as was the cause of the plague of Athens to Thucydides. Famine has not befallen the land, and the country does not appear to be at war, which frequently facilitated the transmission of plague geographically in the past. (One of the Four Horsemen of the Apocalypse, Plague in most narratives is

---

Proust; passages from the Bible (particularly as he stated in his second version and admonished himself for the 'use the Bible') and principally from *Deuteronomy*, *Leviticus*, *Exodus*, *Jeremiah*, and *Ezekiel*" (120). Styling and punctuation are as they appear in Brée's text.

contingent on either War or Famine, or both.) Neither is an original carrier, a patient zero, named, as is often the case in plague literature and was the case in both Defoe's *Journal* and Manzoni's *Betrothed;* nor do other factors that commonly contribute to the outbreak and spreading of plague, like climatological extremes or urban overcrowding, assume significance in the account of the narrator. In any case, of more concern to the narrator than any speculative why or even the scientific how is the empirical what of the plague in Oran.

Empirical observation and modern epidemiology afford Rieux a construct by which to present the threat of the plague and to forecast the destiny of—and his hope for—the community. However, his empirical evidence proves to be suspect and his knowledge of epidemiology unconvincing to the town elders. Oran's Prefect is likewise reluctant to come to terms with the possible reality of an epidemic when Rieux and his colleagues press him to convene a "health committee [*commission sanitaire*]" (45), although the health committee itself will be reluctant to call for drastic measures in a situation that is not yet apparently drastic. Why declare an emergency, the Prefect reasons, as will the committee, when this disease has not even been proved to be contagious. In response, Rieux the empiricist would hardly cast himself as a prophet, but he would exercise, and recommend, foresight on the basis of scientific evidence: "The point isn't whether the measures provided for in the code are rigorous, but whether they are needful to prevent the death of half the population" (47).

Not a prophet, an empiricist for sure, a chronicler and a doctor, a student of history and a man of science, Rieux brings his knowledge of the historical past to bear upon his observations of the current outbreak of disease in Oran. To that knowledge, historical and scientific, he adds imagination. Rieux imagines fully what might be—and soon proves to be—the consequence of the ignorance and denial that insulate the Prefect, the health committee, and the community at large from a timely confrontation with destiny, a destiny that Rieux deems to be inevitable. The empiricist is also a fatalist; but his is a fatalism that demands not surrender to an abstract principle but action in spite of it. Rieux's foresight benefits from hindsight, as his perception of the present is prefaced by his familiarity with the past, and his empiricism is wedded to his imagination. Rieux embraces all the contraries that spur him into action. All serve to define, and determine, Rieux's conception and construction of himself as, primarily, a medical practitioner actively committed to Oran's battle against a bacillus, and in that commitment he perceives and pursues his personal destiny in the face of plague. The fatalist in Rieux does not submit to fate; rather, he combats it.

However confounding in its inexplicability the why of the plague may be to Rieux's informed scientific mind, Rieux as a medical practitioner soldiers on against absurd odds. An anti-bubonic serum has been developed, but at the moment it is unavailable in Oran, apparently because no one expected the plague to return. Until serum can be transported from Paris to "the colony," Rieux can only attempt to administer to the plague's symptomatic effects: "stupor and extreme prostration, buboes, intense thirst, delirium, dark blotches on the body, internal dilatation . . . The pulse becomes fluttering, dicrotic and intermittent, and death ensues as the result of the slightest movement . . ." (37). In its medical objectivity, Rieux's description, which in its stylistic mode is not unlike that of cholera's effects as they are detailed by Mann's narrator in *Death in Venice,* all the more conjures the bubonic horrors of the disease when its advance is unchecked by serum or cure. Still, there is no guarantee that the serum when it is delivered will prevail over the bacillus or halt the course of the contagion. In fact, it won't; but from the outset Rieux is philosophically skeptical of the efficacy of serums in that he believes plague inheres with a lifespan of its own and, with or without serum, it will fulfill its own bacillary destiny—and for a time appropriate the destiny of Oran: "If, as was most likely, it died out, all would be well. If not, one would know it anyhow for what it was and what steps should be taken for coping with, and finally overcoming, it" (39). On empirical grounds, too, Rieux doubts the benefits of the serum, given that the bacillus, by his observation, appears to have mutated since its last invasion of Oran. The "specific modifications" to the "classical" bacillus that Rieux detects only add to the confusion of health officials and their ability confidently to predict the course the plague will take. The scientifically determined cause of bubonic plague, then, is in itself proving to be protean, incomplete, yet to be fully comprehended.

The same might be said of its history, and destiny. As Rieux presents it, the destiny of plague is played out in history. So it is that plague, for Rieux, can only be comprehended in terms of the past, which, as yet, to his scientific mind, has yielded no cause for the pestilence as history has recorded it. Destiny is thus defined historically by the plague's effects, more of which are yet to be evidenced as they will continue to evolve in the future that history has yet to write. Beyond history, then, destiny is a blank, for like history it is always in the process of being written, which does not prevent it from being divined, however falsely, inaccurately, or prejudicially. But Rieux is not a diviner, prophet, or seer. He is a scientist; he allows the facts of the present case to speak for themselves and the facts as he presents them are descriptive, not predictive or even prescriptive, for the facts even now, in light of a protean bacillus, fail to reveal a fixed cause. (Besides, the bacillus explains only the scientific how, not the more speculative why.) Ignorance of cause of course does not equal absence of cause. Nor do Rieux's facts preclude fiction; for his history of plague's evident effects as well as his chronicle of them in Oran is shaped by his perception of plague's apparent destiny, and as such his scientific discourse, which strives for bald objectivity, is an aesthetic construct colored inevitably by his imagination and subjectivity: none of which casts into doubt his integrity as a scientist and humanist.

The humanist embraces his personal destiny as a medical practitioner. Tellingly, in his historical survey of plague, for all the variations it may present in terms of time and place, and whatever its toll on the civilizations it has threatened, however it may have been presumed to be prevented or explained, however various its effects, in every case of plague from ancient times to modern one element has remained demonstrably the same: that of human suffering, or as Rieux states it, "the eternal cry of human pain [*(le) cri interminable des hommes*]" (38). In that cry the humanist in Rieux hears the call not for speculative scientific or metaphysical explanations, not for hows or whys, but for a what, for action. A window affords Rieux a view of everyday life in Oran, of the "certitude" that lies in the familiar and quotidian, before the city lies in the grip of the plague: "There lay certitude; there, in the daily round. All the rest hung on mere threads and trivial contingencies; you couldn't waste your time on it. The thing was to do your job as it should be done" (39). Whatever faults Rieux may find with the Oranians—their bourgeois attitudes, their materialism, their unexplored values and incurious minds (or as Camus says of them in *Noces,* "On the boulevard in Oran one does not raise the problem of being and one is not concerned with the road to perfection" [59])—he finds in them fellow human beings as well. His job is clear to him; he will minister to their human pain. That job, for the humanist Rieux, is equivalent to a moral obligation.

Rieux can find no empirical evidence to support any argument that places human destiny—or the morality on which the religious, like Paneloux, for instance, often deem it to be contingent—in divine hands. Toward the end of his philosophical work *The Rebel (L'homme révolté)*, Camus posits that "the rebel rejects divinity in order to share in the struggles and destiny of all men" (306). So does Rieux; as he tells God's earthly intermediary Paneloux, who views the plague as a divine punishment visited upon the world for crimes known and unknown: "There are times when the only feeling I have is one of mad revolt" (192). Furthermore, for Camus' rebel, revolt is one of the "essential dimensions" of being human.[8] Neither the Hegelian revolt of the slave against the master nor the Marxist revolt of the proletarian against the ruling class, Camus' is a metaphysical revolt against the conditions of life defined by the idea of divine justice. Rieux's rejection of the divine, though, does not equal a Luciferian *non serviam,* for while the atheist Dr. Rieux will not serve God, he will serve humanity—he will participate fully in "the destiny of all men." He is in fact compelled to serve his fellow human beings. Because God won't.

In a God-absent universe humankind perforce has to take responsibility for its destiny. Cruickshank observes that "there is underlying tolerance to be felt in [Camus'] atheism which sees human solutions as the natural answer to human problems" (38). Rieux's friend Tarrou finds the conjunction of philosophical atheism and humanist behavior initially contradictory: "Why do you yourself show such devotion, considering you don't believe in God?" Tarrou asks, and Rieux responds "that if he had believed in an all-powerful God he would have ceased caring for the sick and leave it to Him. But no one in the world believes in a God of that sort" (114). What Rieux believes he continually asserts in terms of his role as a humanist and physician, as when he quite simply states, and again restates, what he perceives to be his personal destiny, "There are sick people and they need curing" (114). In his genuine fellow feeling and ministrant impulses, Rieux indeed might exemplify the "heroic humanism" or at least prefigure the rebel-hero in Camus' construction of humanitarian ethics whereby, in Braun's words, "the sense of universal brotherhood [is] coupled with the demand for happiness through a passionate and tragic existence" (118).[9]

Like Camus' truly absurd yet absurdly happy Sisyphus, Rieux refuses to give in to the never-ending possibility of defeat. As Rieux notes, "Everyone

---

[8] See Herbert Read's Foreword to Camus' *The Rebel* (viii).

[9] Enlarging on the "humanitarian ethics [in *The Rebel*] toward which Camus had been groping since his early works," Lev Braun writes: "It is tragic humanism and heroic humanism too, in a world where nothing is given or explained, where every bit of happiness has to be wrenched from a harsh fate and every value created in darkness and suffering as a source of order in an absurd world. In this perspective, life becomes indeed meaningful" (118).

knows that pestilence has a way of recurring in the world" (35). Plague seems always to have been—from Homer to Lucretius to Procopius to Yersin, from Thucydides to Mann, from the Bible to Defoe to Manzoni—and always about to be again, "yet," says Rieux, "somehow we find it hard to believe in ones that crash down on our heads from a blue sky. There have been as many plagues as wars in history; yet always plagues and wars take people equally by surprise" (35). Even as the plague abates and Oran again settles into its comfortable bourgeois existence, Rieux imagines in markedly aesthetic terms the resurgence of a horror borne by some pestiferous bacillus:

> And, indeed, as he listened to the cries of joy rising from the town, Rieux remembered that such joy is always imperiled. He knew what those jubilant crowds did not know but would have learned from books: that the plague bacillus never dies or disappears for good; that it can lie dormant for years and years in furniture and linen-chests; that it bides its time in bedrooms, cellars, trunks and book-shelves; and that perhaps the day would come when, for the bane and the enlightening of men, it roused up its rats again, and sent them forth to die in a happy city. (272)[10]

If the poetic imagination of the man of science evidences itself in this lyrically executed coda at the end of the novel, the vision that it metaphorically and metonymically presents restates the one certainty Rieux has gleaned from his experience: Plague is. As it has been it will be again. No destiny is secure.

---

[10] *"Écoutant, en effet, les cris d'allégresse qui montaient de la ville, Rieux se souvenait que cette allégresse était toujours menacée. Car il savait ce que cette foule en joie ignorait, et qu'on peut lire dans les livres, que le bacilli de la peste ne meurt ni ne disparaît jamais, qu'il peut rester pendant des dizaines d'années endormi dans les chambers, les caves, les malles, les mouchoirs et les paperasses, et que, peut-être, le jour viendrait où, pour le malheur et l'enseignement des hommes, la peste revéillerait ses rats et les enverrait mourir dans une cité heureuse"* (279).

Works Cited

Braun, Lev. *Witness of Decline, Albert Camus: Moralist of the Absurd.* Rutherford: Fairleigh Dickinson University Press, 1974.

Brée, Germaine. *Camus.* New Brunswick: Rutgers University Press, 1961.

_____, Ed. *Camus: A Collection of Critical Essays.* Englewood Cliffs, N.J.: Prentice Hall, Inc., 1962.

Camus, Albert. *La peste.* Paris: Gallimard, 1947.

_____. *L'envers et l'endoit.* Paris: Gallimard, 1947.

_____. *L'Homme révolté.* Paris: Gallimard. 1951.

_____. Lyrical and Critical Essays. Ed. Philip Thody. New York: Alfred A. Knopt, 1969.

_____. "L'ironie". *L'envers et l'endroit.* Paris: Gallimard, 1958.

_____.*The Plague, the Fall, Exile and the Kingdom*, Trans. Stuart Gilbert. New York: The Everyman Library, Alfred A. Knopf, 2004.

_____. *The Rebel.* Trans. Anthony Bower. New York: Vintage Books, 1956.

Cruickshank, John. *Albert Camus and the Literature of Revolt.* London: Oxford University Press,   1959.

Defoe, Daniel. *A Journal of the Plague Year: Written by a citizen who continued all the while in London.* New York: Barnes and Noble Books, 2004 (1722).

Hegel, George Friedrich. *Introduction to the Philosophy of History.* Trans. Leo Rauch.Cambridge: Hackett Publishing Company, 1988.

Holy Bible, The: Containing the Old and New Testament; Authorized King James Version. New York: Oxford University Press, (Pilgrim Edition) 1952.

Kierkegaard, Soren. *Kierkegaard's Writings*. Trans. & Ed. H.V. & E.H. Hong. Princeton: Princeton University Press, 1978.

Lucretius Carus, Titus. "On the Plague at Athens" (Book 6) *The Way things are: The De rerum natura of Titus Lucretius Carus*. Trans. Rolfe Humphries. Bloomington: Indiana University Press, 1968.

Mann, Thomas. *Death in Venice*. Trans. David Luke. Death in Venice, Tonio Kroger and Other Writings. New York: Continuum, The German Library, 2003.

Manzoni, Alessandro. *The Betrothed*. Trans. Andrew Colquhoun. New York: E. P. Dutton & Co. Inc., 1961 (1951).

Nietzsche, Friedrich Wilhelm. *Thus spake Zarathustra*. Trans. Thomas Common. New York: The Modern Library, 1950.

Ripamonte, Giuseppe. *De peste Mediolani quae fuit anno 1630*. Milan: 1640.

Sontag, Susan. *AIDS as Metaphor*. New York: Farrar, Straus & Giroux, 1989.

Thucydides. "The Plague of Athens" (Chapter 47). *The Peloponnesian War*. Trans. C. F. Smith. Cambridge: Loeb Classical Library, Cambridge University Press, 2001.

'Némesis veille...': An Attempt to Understand Camus' Unfinished Essay

By Luke Richardson

On January the 4th 1960, shortly before 2pm, a car carrying Albert Camus crashed just outside the town of Villeblevin in Northern France. Camus was killed instantly. His friend Michael Gallimard, who had been driving, would die later in hospital. The world reacted with understandable shock and sadness at the sudden death of one of the pre-eminent literary figures of the Twentieth Century – a death, many observed, so senseless and absurd that it would perhaps not have been out of place in one of Camus' own novels. Debris from the crash was scattered over five hundred meters. Police collected from near the car a small, black leather valise, caked in mud, which was identified as belonging to the accident's famous victim and was returned to his widow. Inside were a French translation of Shakespeare's *Othello*, a translation of Nietzsche's *Die fröliche Wissenschaft*, a notebook and around one hundred and fifty pages of a manuscript for a unfinished novel, *Le Premier Homme*.[1]

Camus' death provides a problematic challenge to those who set out to study his work. In some cases the tone of his later works, his diminished output and his increasing political isolation over the issues of Algeria and the Sartre polemic are neatly formulated into a narrative of decline that can only end with his death. For others his death was tragic and incongruous but perhaps fitting for a man who spent so long pondering the nature of death and the absurd, and too spared him the pain of witnessing the culmination of the Algerian War. In reality, after a nearly six year period of debilitating writer's block following the publication of *L'Homme révolté* in 1951, Camus was, by late 1959, experiencing something of a creative renaissance. His novel *La Chute* had been published to considerable acclaim (even from Sartre) a few years earlier, he had been granted the artistic directorship of a Parisian

---

[1] Camus (2008c: 261ff).

theatre (the reason for his trip to Paris that day and perhaps for his interest in *Othello*) and he had begun his autobiographical novel *Le Premier Homme* which, according to his notes and plans, seems to have been his most ambitious fictional undertaking to date. The novel, even in its nascent state, also seems to offer, as David Carroll argues, Camus' most comprehensive engagement with the idea of French Algeria, the colonial legacy and the potential for independence.[2] Camus' life was cut short at a moment of extreme creative activity that followed nearly half a decade of silence. The tragedy of his death lies as much in the works that he would not live to create as in simply its absurdity or abruptness. Yet these incomplete works and lines of thought that are suddenly extinguished provide a tantalising problem for Camus scholars. How far can we attempt to study what his incomplete works would have come to mean and how far can this only ever be speculation? *Le Premier Homme* has clearly provided a rich source of material for critical attempts to explore the development of Camus' literary style. However, for an exploration of the development of his thought, another document found in the valise is potentially of even greater interest: the notebook. Camus' notebooks (which begin in the late 1930s) documented a lifetime of ideas, sketches for novels and plays and quotations. The notebook marked 'number nine', recovered from the roadside near Villeblevin, was no different except that the projects he took notations for would never come to fruition. Published now in the third volume of the collected *Carnets*, notebook nine does not only give insights into the creation of *Le Premier Homme* but also seemingly the beginning of another book-length essay to follow on from *Le Mythe de Sisyphe* in 1942 and *L'Homme révolté* in 1951. Once again, Camus would return to the world of ancient Greek myth to provide his model for the work that would have been titled *The Myth of Nemesis*. This paper will attempt a brief discussion of what we can establish about this essay and the direction of Camus' thought in the late 1950s and why attempting to understand Camus' unfinished work remains vitally important. A study of his notebooks, as well as his previous works, reveals that perhaps the dominant figure of Camus' final days was not Jaques Cormery but in fact the Greek goddess of vengeance.

Firstly, it is important to provide an outline of what the notebooks contain about the Nemesis essay. Unlike *Le Premier Homme*, a work that can be described as "unfinished", *Nemesis* was barely begun. We have a collection

---

[2] Carroll (2007).

of notations that begin with 'Nemesis' or 'For Nemesis' as well as a handful of references to the goddess in *L'Été* and *L'Homme révolté*. However, Camus notes clearly show the central place he gave to the project and more important that he was beginning a new 'cycle' of works around this theme. Camus distilled his work into three distinct stages: 'I. The myth of Sisyphus (Absurd) – II. The myth of Prometheus (Revolt) – III. The myth of Nemesis.'[3] The grouping together of *L'Étranger*, *Le Mythe de Sisyphe* and *Caligula* as the 'Absurd' cycle and *La Peste*, *Les Justes* and *L'Homme révolté* as the cycle of 'Revolt' was not done retrospectively but rather were carefully planned triumvirates of a novel, a play and a companion essay to explore his themes. In each case Camus categorised these 'cycles' by their adherence to a Greek myth. Nemesis was to prove the same: 'Before the third stage: short stories for "A Hero for Our Times." Themes of judgement and exile. The third stage is Love: The First Man, Don Faust. The myth of Nemesis'.[4] "A Hero for Our Times" had been a working title for *La Chute*, which had begun life as a short story, around the same time as the other works grouped together in *L'Exil et le Royaume*, but which had grown to the length of a short novel. *La Chute* was less a planned exercise than a spontaneous creation which took on something of a life of its own and helped Camus to break the writers block which he so vividly described in the contemporaneous short story 'Jonas'. It seems *La Chute* did not form part of one of Camus' "cycles", rather, having rediscovered pleasure in his literary output, he once again returned to thought of a third cycle on the theme of "Love", with a novel *Le Premier Homme*, a play *Don Faust* and an essay *Nemesis*. We know virtually nothing about his plans for *Don Faust* beyond the title and a few notations suggesting that it was indeed planned as a synthesis of the Don Juan myth (which had so fascinated him in *Le Mythe de Sisyphe*) and the legend of Faust but Camus left virtually no further clues. The number of references and notes to Nemesis do however allow us to begin to establish an idea of the proposed essay's content.

The figure of Nemesis, the mythical Goddess of vengeance, mother of Clytemnestra and Helen, occupied an important position in Camus' thought long before the late 1950s. As early as 1947 he wrote 'Nemesis: The goddess of measure. All those who have overstepped the limit will be piteously

---

[3] Camus (1965b: 257).

[4] Camus (2008c: 157).

destroyed'.[5] The myth also appears substantially in *L'Homme révolté* and the earlier essay 'L'Exil d'Hélène' as demonstrable of the idea of "limits" or "moderation". One of Camus' primary critiques of modern Europe in his early 1950s' essays was that it had become ideologically totalitarian. This description extended beyond simply the dictatorships of Germany and Russia but was a more general affliction of thought across the ideological spectrum: 'Our Europe…eager for the conquest of totality, is the daughter of excess.'[6] In seeking a 'future Empire of reason…it pushes back the eternal limits'.[7] The result of the ideological totality was the disasters of Twentieth Century conflict, embodied by the mythical Goddess: 'Nemesis is watching, goddess of moderation [la mesure] not of vengeance. All those who go beyond the limit are by her piteously chastised'.[8] Orme (and Warren) have pointed out the difficulty of translating the sense of what Camus means by 'la mesure' into English.[9] Moderation is a perfectly correct translation (and is used by Philip Thody) however the sense of the word 'moderation' in English, suggesting Protestant ideas of self-control or personal restraint, is not what Camus meant here. Its usage in French commonly suggests an inviolable and invisible limit that the word 'mesure' only implies, for example 'cela passe toute mesure' or 'il a depassé la mesure'. Camus had very little interest in moderation in the sense of personal abstinence or temperance. Not only do these ideas go against the earlier writings of *Noces* and their visceral enjoyment of nature which although not openly hedonistic, are certainly an immediate and unapologetically sensual pleasure, but also Camus of course practised little moderation in aspects of his personal life.[10] What Camus instead was specifically interested in is the idea of a *limit*, a limit which should not, and indeed cannot, be crossed without incurring consequences. Twentieth Century Europe had crossed the *limit* of ideology. The Enlightenment had pronounced the dictatorship of Reason and History which in turn had enslaved humankind. He juxtaposed modern ideological corruption with the perfect example of the ancient Greeks, a common rhetorical trope for Camus (and something which I have discussed in the

---

[5] Camus (1965b: 156).

[6] '…est fille de démesure.' (O.C.III: 597). [Nb. Camus' works are cited from the *Œuvres completes*, translations are my own.]

[7] O.C.III: 597

[8] 'Némésis veille, déesse de la mesure, non de la vengeance' (O.C.III: 597).

[9] Orme (2007: 177ff) for his discussion of Nemesis. Cf. Vigileno (2007).

[10] Cf. Woelfel (1987).

---

past): 'The Greeks who for centuries questioned what was just would not understand anything of our idea of justice. Equity, for them, supposes a limit while our entire continent is convulsed in the search for a justice that it wants to be total'.[11] Justice that proclaimed itself absolute could never be truly just. To put this more plainly, Camus cites the ancient philosopher Heraclitus: 'presumption: regression of progress'.[12] It was not only the ideological totality of post-Enlightenment Europe that concerned Camus but also its sense of history. History too proclaimed itself absolute: the Marxist and Hegelian forms of history both placed moral value at the end of the historical process therefore negating the present: 'For the Greeks, values were pre-existent in every action and marked out by exact limits. Modern philosophy places its values at the end of action. They are not, but they become; and we shall know them completely only at the end of history. When they disappear, limits do as well'.[13] The sense of limits was violated by the principles of history and by the sense of total justice and this had led to the disasters afflicting modern Europe: 'The Greeks never said that limit could not be crossed. They said that it existed and that one who dared to exceed it would be struck down without mercy. Nothing in the history of today can contradict.'[14] It's important to understand that this 'being struck down', or the corrective vengeance of Nemesis, is certainly not superstitious as in a divine intervention or a Karmic correction or simply wishful thinking that wrong doers will be undone eventually. Rather for Camus, acts of violating natural limits contained the seeds of destruction within them. If history was total and only judged at its end, then any act could be called moral if it contributed towards this end, even if it were the murder of thousands. If justice is absolute and justice rules that all your enemies are unjust could this include soldiers, civilians, children? This ideological immoderation and the rise of total war and military technology presented the ultimate and perhaps final symbol of Nemesis: the atomic weapon. 'Men', Camus wrote, 'have finally become equals with God, but only in his cruelty'.[15] He once more cites Heraclitus, 'excess is a fire' and wrote in *L'Homme révolté*: that the concept of limits '...was symbolized by Nemesis, the goddess of moderation and the implacable enemy of the immoderate. A process of thought, which

---

[11] O.C.III: 597-8. For more see Richardson (2011) and Richardson (2012).

[12] O.C.III: 597-8.

[13] O.C.III: 597-9.

[14] O.C.III: 600.

[15] Camus (1965b: 101).

wanted to take into account the contemporary contradictions of rebellion, should seek its inspiration from this goddess'.[16]

It seems evident that the essay on *Nemesis* would have been a continuation of these ideas. Camus' ideas tended to build upon each other rather than offering radical departures and changes in direction. Realising that the Absurd could only be 'a point of departure', *L'Homme révolté* effectively stated that while a Sisyphean struggle against the Absurd did not intrinsically provide a source of ethical justice, the realisation that one should not kill oneself ultimately provided a moral imperative that one should not kill others. Equally, we can think about the *Nemesis* essay building on the philosophy of *L'Homme révolté* and potentially setting out to answer some of its critics. There are few notes in notebook nine that are definitively marked as for the essay and what exists is often cryptic and opaque. Nevertheless there does seem to be an evident expansion of the themes of limits from his earlier essays: 'Nemesis: Thoughts centred on the history of those who despise time the most, its effects, its edifices, and its civilisations. History for them is what destroys'.[17] Again history, or a Marxist or Hegelian sense of historicism, is singled out for criticism. 'Nemesis: Profound complicity of Marxism and Christianity (to develop). That is why I am against both'.[18] This is an idea which features strongly in *L'Homme révolté* too but on which Camus was evidently keen to expand. For him, Christianity fundamentally transgressed the idea of a limit to ideology. By its very nature it pronounced itself absolute and equally deferred the present to an imagined future. There is certainly nothing in Camus' last notebook which backs up the sometimes mooted theory that he was softening his opposition to Christianity or perhaps even on the verge of undergoing a monumental conversion.[19] If anything, *Nemesis* would have made this opposition clearer. Camus fundamentally privileged ? an understanding and an embrace of the human condition, even in its contradictions and absurdities. 'Nemesis: Drunkenness of the soul and body is not madness, but comfort and numbness, true madness blazes atop interminable lucidity'.[20] While drunkenness of the body is a straightforward

---

[16] O.C.III: 315

[17] Camus (2008c: 175).

[18] Camus (2008: 192).

[19] For example Mumma (2005).

[20] Camus (2008: 32).

enough concept, I think it is not unreasonable to consider "drunkenness of the soul", providing impassiveness and false comfort instead of true understanding, as another critique of religion.

Camus' writing, in note forms, is obviously vague and difficult to follow. In no case is this truer than in the longest single section of writing on *Nemesis* and the last, completed just a few weeks before his death. A few excerpts are 'Black Horse, white horse, a single hand controls the two passions. At breakneck speed the race is joyous', 'Equally hard, equally soft, the slope, the slope of day. But at the summit? A single mountain', 'Behind the cross, the devil. Leave them together. Your empty altar is elsewhere'. In these notations he is actually aping the style of another philosopher, the oft-cited Heraclitus, who was becoming a greater and greater influence on his thought. Heraclitus, known to Timon of Philus as 'riddler' or to Cicero as 'the obscure one', was so called due to the sometimes impenetrably cryptic nature of what survives of his writing.[21] Camus had already cited Heraclitus in both 'L'Exil d'Hélène' and *L'Homme révolté* when talking about Nemesis so it seems entirely in keeping that the pre-Socratic philosopher would have played a significant role in the finished essay and in this passage seemingly a significant role in Camus' style. Whether Camus would have included this kind of Hericlitian prose in the finished essay or whether this was a kind of writing exercise is of course unknowable. What we can say is that these examples each provide a vignette of equilibrium; two things that appear radically different in fact are the same. There is no totality between white horse and black horse, in fact both impulses stem from the same place. Equally political left and right, Communism and Fascism, ancient and modern too come from the same place, are "a single mountain". The limit that should not be transgressed left ? so generally defined in his previous essays, here stems from the fundamental equilibrium of humanism. Proclaiming ideological totality in the face of such equilibrium is naturally fruitless. Here, in his last entry on the theme of Nemesis, do we see a notable expansion and continuation of his previous works.

This third cycle is not the cycle of 'moderation' or 'measure' but rather the cycle of love. What can Camus have meant by that? It is unlikely that he meant simply Romantic love. Certainly very little in *Le Premier Homme* could support that conclusion. It is far more likely is the sense of love for the

---

[21] Cf. Bakalis (2005) under Heraclitus.

earth, love for the humanity and love for the equilibrium within both of these. Camus' fidelity to the earth and embrace of the present moment is a major theme of his earliest works. A reformulation of these ideas, combined of course with a call for a return to the thought of the Greeks, constituted the ending of *L'Homme révolté*', 'La Pensée de Midi', often criticised for its perceived vagueness and referred to dismissively by Sartre as 'what you call, I think, "Mediterranean measure"'. It seems quite natural that Camus would offer a response to these criticisms in his next works. Certainly the sensual adoration of nature's beauty remained strong in *Le Premier Homme* with an added element that the nameless and faceless figures of *Noces* have been replaced by his friends and family: 'I wanted to speak of those I love and of that only. Intense joy'.[22] Love has become all encompassing, not only a love of the earth but a love of humanity. Yet there remained an equilibrium even within this: 'Nemesis: Sometimes loves kills with no justification other than itself. There is even a limit when loving a person amounts to killing all others. In certain ways, there is no love without personal and absolute guilt. But this guilt is solitary'.[23] This guilt is the guilt of realising that even in the embrace of the present and the rejection of history and the deferred rewards of Christianity, one may still fear death: '[Man] is afraid of himself and for himself, refusing then his condition. And his first concern is to seek a justification which relieves a little of the weight of his guilt. Since one must be guilty, at least one is not guilty alone'.[24] Even in guilt Camus saw a sense of universal fraternity. The only way to conquer the ideological totalitarianism that had taken modern Europe to the edge, was through love: recognising the joys of the earth and of humanity and realising that against these death was not to be feared but rather the natural and necessary limit which has to exist in all things.

To discuss the direction of Camus' argument further would cross into outright speculation. Everything I have said so far has attempted to base itself on his notes or previous works. There clearly is not much of his argument that can be developed and the work, fascinating as it may be in prospect, is ultimately lost. What has the purpose of this discussion been then? Hopefully it has highlighted a few important points about Camus' late thought. Firstly, there is his continuing intellectual relationship with

---

[22] Camus (2001: 250).

[23] Camus (2008b: 65).

[24] Camus (2008b: 65).

Nietzsche. Camus' understanding of Heraclitus, and pre-Socratic philosophy more generally, was heavily filtered though Nietzsche as indeed was Camus' understanding more generally of Greek culture. Ancient Greece was a kind of intellectual interface with Nietzsche where Camus could engage with his thought and extrapolate and expand what he agreed with, without openly stating that he was doing so. Nietzsche first wrote that the Greeks had a sense of 'measure' or 'moderation'.[25] Nietzsche used ancient Greece to critique the excesses of modern culture. Nietzsche too wrote extensively about Heraclitus (see Joshua Robert-Gibson). Similarly Greece undoubtedly continued to fascinate Camus. Choosing a mythic exemplar, like Sisyphus and Prometheus, to articulate his philosophy gave him the artistic freedom and simultaneous critical distance that he clearly found so creatively rewarding in his essays.[26] Warren argues that rather than 'limits' or 'moderation' a better sense of what Camus meant by 'la mesure' was the Greek concept 'sosphrosyne', a complex concept to translate into English but which ultimately means, as the Delphic Oracle proclaimed, 'nothing in excess', moderation, control and recognition of limitations.[27] For Sophocles, the "divine retribution" of Nemesis was not vengeful but rather the ultimate act of unification. Perhaps most importantly, *Nemesis* gives us more of a basis to understand Camus' other works and more generally his state of mind in the last years of his life. As stated, *Le Premier Homme* arguably began to articulate a literary response to the Algerian situation. Perhaps the most apparent case of this is Cormery's meeting with the French farmer, the one 'they hate in Paris' and who will die where he lives rather than move to Algiers. Over an anisette the farmer tells Cormery: "'Besides us, you know who are the only ones who can understand it", "The Arabs.", "Exactly. We were made to understand each other. Fools and brutes like us, but with the same blood of men.'" Settlers, the colonized population: for Camus both the same mountain. The coarse farmer provides a realisation of the fundamental equilibrium of humanity disturbed by the totalitarian ideologies of the French government and the FLN. Equally, in his short story 'L'Hôte', human companionship and mutual understanding between Daru and the guest are made impossible by the extremism that surrounds them. Camus' positions on Algeria, his calls for a civil truce and cessation of violence and his criticism of French and Algerian nationalists alike tally perfectly with the kind of

---

[25] Cf. van Tongeren (2002).

[26] Cf. Brée (1976).

[27] Orme (2007: 177ff.)

philosophy of equilibrium and conciliation he was writing in his final days. The question perhaps remains did his philosophy fit his time or did his pain at seeing the country of his birth torn apart and perhaps ultimately of realising the untenable position of France as a colonial oppressor lead to a philosophy which called for love and reconciliation?

This is perhaps even clearer in the case of European politics. Camus' weariness with partisan politics was palpable in the last years of his life. He wrote in his notebooks of 'This Left that I belong to, in spite of me and in spite of it.' [28] The continuing fallout from his polemic with Sartre as well as the increased scrutiny bought on by the Nobel Prize win and the Algerian War had left him exhausted. Again in his notebooks he wrote in 1959 'Television broadcast. I cannot "appear" now without causing reactions. Remember, repeat to myself, that I must eliminate all unproductive polemic.'[29] Again, *Nemesis* and its calls for ideological moderation and the recognition of continuity between peoples, even those of opposed views, seems a natural and understandable reaction to this climate. *La Chute* has been read as a critique of Sartre and left wing intellectuals. Perhaps rather it can be seen more generally as a critique of ideology that pronounced itself total. There is little moderation or doubt in Clamance. Just as Caligula is arguably the anti-Sisyphus, perhaps Clamence is the anti-Nemesis?[30]

Perhaps the most striking thing about the notes for Camus' *Nemesis* essay is the continuity they offer with *L'Homme révolté* and his earlier thought. There is no sudden departure and many of the themes and ideas that preoccupied him continue to do so. Of course, to a degree the fragmentary nature of the work means that any discussion of it remains speculative. It may have altered or radically shifted in direction from the early notes. Yet the fragments leave an image of a writer who, although creatively more fulfilled than perhaps at any time in his mature life, still struggled to articulate a sense of his personal philosophy in regards to the polemically charged intellectual environment in which he existed. Unlike *L'Homme révolté* however, *Nemesis* seems to have made this culture itself a point of interrogation and the subject of a critical discussion. Whatever the flaws in a finished essay may have been, we are

---

[28] Camus (2008c: 252).

[29] Camus (2008c: 247).

[30] Caligula as the Anti-Sisyphus see Richardson (2012).

undoubtedly poorer that it was never completed as, if nothing else, the prospect of how Camus would have finished the work as the situation in Algeria continued to deteriorate would have been a fascinating one. Perhaps while *L'Homme révolté* was without doubt a flawed work, Camus' critique of Communism was far ahead of its time and looks increasingly prescient today in comparison to the writings of Sartre and other left wing intellectuals on the same subject. Camus' ideas of a limit, which humanity's arrogance and the rise of technology combined to violate with disastrous consequences, potentially looks equally prescient with regards to modern problems like anthropogenic climate change or the perils of unchecked capitalism. Camus' voice would be one missing from these debates and many others that followed. In this context the fragments of *Nemesis* remain an equally unsatisfying and tragic postscript to the work of one of the Twentieth Century's most complex intellectuals.

Bibliography

N. Bakalis, *Handbook of Greek Philosophy: From Thales to the Stoics Analysis and Fragments* (Bloomington: Trafford Publishing, 2006).

G. Brée, 'Avatars of Prometheus: A Shifting Camusian Image' in *Mythology in French Literature* ed. P. Crant. University of South Carolina French Literature Series 3 (1976) pp. 138-148.

A. Camus, *Notebooks 1935 – 1942* (trans. by P. Thody) (New York: The Modern Library, 1965a)

A. Camus, *Notebooks 1942 – 1951* (trans. by J. O'Brien) (New York: Alfred A. Knopf, 1965b)

A. Camus, *The First Man* (trans. By D. Hapgood) (Harlow: Penguin, 2001).

A. Camus, *Œuvres complètes, tome 1 : 1931 – 1944,* Bibliothèque de la Pléiade, R. Gay-Crosier (ed.) (Paris: Gallimard. 2006a) (O.C.I).

A. Camus, *Œuvres complètes, tome 2 : 1944 – 1948,* Bibliothèque de la Pléiade, R. Gay-Crosier (ed.) (Paris: Gallimard, 2006b) (O.C.II).

A. Camus, *Œuvres complètes, tome 3 : 1949 – 1956,* Bibliothèque de la Pléiade, R. Gay-Crosier (ed.) (Paris: Gallimard, 2008a) (O.C.III).

A. Camus, *Œuvres complètes, tome 4 : 1957 – 1959,* Bibliothèque de la Pléiade, R. Gay-Crosier (ed.) (Paris: Gallimard, 2008b) (O.C.IV).

A. Camus, *Notebooks 1951 – 1959* (trans. by R. Bloom) (Chicago: Ivan R. Dee, 2008c).

D. Carroll, *Camus, the Algerian: Colonialism, Terror, Justice* (New York: Columbia University Press, 2007).

H. Mumma, *Albert Camus and the Minister* (Brewster MA: Paraclete Press, 2005).

M. Orme, *The Development of Albert Camus' Concern for Social and Political Justice* (Florham: Farleigh Dixon, 2007).

L. Richardson, 'Sisyphus and Caesar: The Opposition of Greece and Rome in Albert Camus' Absurd Cycle' in *Classical Receptions Journal* 4.1 (2012) pp. 66-89.

L. Richardson, 'Camus the Athenian' in *The Journal of Camus Studies* (2011) pp. 132-144.

P. van Tongeren, 'Nietzsche's Greek Measure' in *The Journal of Nietzsche Studies* 24 (2002) pp. 5-24.

L. Viglieno, 'Némésis, Déesse inspiratrice du dernier Camus?' A. Fosty (ed.), *Albert Camus et la Grèce* (Aix-en-Provence: Écritures du Sud, 2007) pp. 49-66.

J. Woelfel, *Albert Camus on the Sacred and the Secular* (Lanham: University Press of America, 1987).

Camus' Sense of the Sacred

By Ron Srigley

Introduction

> The best and simplest hypothesis is, in effect, to postulate God. God is like democracy: the least corrupt and therefore the best of all possible solutions.

> — Jean Baudrillard, "This is the Fourth World War"

Camus' analysis of modernity was carried out in stages or cycles. Those cycles are familiar to all scholars of Camus' work. They are the famous cycles of the absurd, rebellion, and love.[1] As I have argued elsewhere, those cycles, far from being autobiographical and denoting a straightforward movement of improvement, chart a gradual descent into the darkest ambitions of the age in an effort to discover their true character.[2] In *The Rebel*, the essay for the cycle of rebellion, Camus identifies the feature of modernity that most clearly distinguishes it from other historical periods: murder. This does not mean that other epochs did not commit murder. Clearly they did. But for Camus there is something about modern murderers that distinguishes them from those of the ancient world: modern murderers claim to be and appear to many as innocent.[3] The problem here is not merely the ease with which moderns kill (though that is always something worth keeping in mind), but that they consider doing so, even on an extraordinary scale, reasonable, justified, and even good.[4] This is different. The ancients

---

[1] Albert Camus, *Notebooks 1942-1951*, trans. Justin O'Brien (New York: Paragon House, 1991).

[2] Ron Srigley, *Albert Camus' Critique of Modernity* (Columbia: University of Missouri Press, 2011).

[3] Albert Camus, *The Rebel*, trans. Anthony Bower (New York: Vintage Books, 1991), 4.

[4] In *The Rebel* Camus says that modern murderers imagine themselves "philanthropists" (4).

would kill if they deemed it necessary. But it would never occur to them that mass murder was justified. This is why Camus argues that confronted with this violence "the conscience could remain firm and the judgement clear." Not so in the modern context, because moderns use philosophy and even morality to justify murder. "Slave camps under the flag of freedom, massacres justified by philanthropy or a taste for the super human, in one sense cripple judgement."[5] This is not merely a problem of obfuscation or euphemistic language, which exist in all ages. For Camus the difficulty is that we experience such things as justified. Understanding and critically assessing this odd inversion of our moral world is the "strange challenge" posed by our age.[6]

Camus argues that the disjunction between things and our experience of them that encourage modern homicide is a disposition characteristic of the age as a whole and not just of regimes that commit murder on a grand scale. In liberal democratic regimes also we see people and yet do not see them. We perceive their form and movement but their meaning or substance eludes us. We have mined the human condition for all its features – social, psychological, and biological. The genetic, demographic, economic, morphological and political aspects of human life are known to us in a detail unimaginable in previous historical epochs. Yet for all our knowledge we have trouble coming up with a good reason why murdering people on mass should be avoided, why uploading our consciousness into a computer might take some of the enjoyment out of life, or why doing something slow, like reading a book, might yield greater insight into the world than a computer word pattern search of several daily newspapers.

The excesses of modernity are for Camus due to a loss of a "sense of the sacred."[7] The meaning of this term will become clearer as the analysis unfolds, but for now we can say that the great barrier to its contemporary articulation is the predominance of distinctively Christian patterns of meaning that tend to be accepted as much by critics as by the religious thinkers who endorse them as paradigmatic of speech about the divine.

---

[5] Albert Camus, *The Rebel*, 4. Albert Camus, *Essais*, (Paris: Gallimard, 1965), 413.

[6] Ibid.

[7] Albert Camus, *Lyrical and Critical Essays*, trans. Ellen Conroy Kennedy and ed. Philip Thody (New York: Vintage Books, 1970), 364.

Camus himself was tempted on occasion. But only on occasion, and only tempted. He acknowledged Christianity's resistance to the contemporary blood lust and was grateful for the manner in which that resistance "sanctified the value of life."[8] Yet he came to believe that the value of this resistance had been compromised fundamentally by the tradition's apocalyptic aspirations, against which not even its own notion of a "spiritual nature" proved an effective barrier.[9] Camus would express this complex assessment of Christianity and his own sense of the sacred in a number of nuanced and sometimes paradoxical ways: "Secret of my universe: imagine God without the immortality of the soul."[10] "The Greeks made allowances for the divine. But *the divine was not everything.*"[11] "I often read that I am atheistic; I hear people speak of my atheism. Yet these words say nothing to me; for me they have no meaning. I do not believe in God *and* I am not an atheist."[12]

In light of such ambiguities commentators have adopted a number of different interpretative strategies. The most common one is to place Camus on one or the other side of the debate, but with reservations. For instance, Jean Onimus acknowledges a sense of "primal mystery" in Camus' works, an "intuition that things are more than themselves and that a living presence is revealed through them."[13] Yet he also asserts that Camus' refusal of Christianity left him with a "stagnant universe, a benighted chaos where human folly blazes."[14] Bernard Murchland, more conciliatory but less circumspect, claims that "the development of [Camus'] work must, if it

---

[8] Albert Camus, *The Rebel*, 279.

[9] Albert Camus, "Helen's Exile" in *Lyrical and Critical Essays*, 151. Christianity resisted the modern effort for transform nature by insisting on a "spiritual nature." However, the notion of such a nature is only one element with Christianity. There are also its apocalyptic ambitions, in which nature is subordinate to history and to the desire for totality. A similar mixture of approbation and critique can be found in Camus' essay, "The Unbeliever and Christians" in *Resistance, Rebellion, and Death*, trans. Justin O'Brien (New York: Vintage Books, 1974), 69-74.

[10] Albert Camus, *Notebooks 1942-1951*, 12.

[11] Ibid., 128.

[12] Albert Camus, *Notebooks 1951-1959*, trans. Ryan Bloom (Chicago: Ivan R.Dee, 2008), 112.

[13] Jean Onimus, *Albert Camus and Christianity*, trans. Emmett Parker (Alabama: University of Alabama, 1970), 13.

[14] Ibid., 105-6.

continues, ultimately culminate in some spiritual position." As evidence for the assertion he suggests that Camus' novel *The Fall* might signal "the dark night before the coming of grace."[15] Among modern interpreters is David Sprintzen. Unlike Onimus and Murchland, Sprintzen applauds Camus' rejection of "transcendent absolutes." However, he also claims that Camus' "ill-defined and sometimes substantialized conception of human nature" prevents him from embracing modernity's principal achievement and the most obvious consequence of his own repudiation of transcendent reality – the "historicization of nature."[16]

My analysis departs from these interpretations in several ways. Though the antitheses these commentators identify in Camus' books exist and therefore justify their respective readings in some measure, I think a potentially more fruitful approach is to accept the ambiguities as they stand and to puzzle over their meaning. Camus' disbelief in God coupled with his denial of the appellation atheist suggests to me a more subtle account than one that ascribes to him a failure to affirm unambiguously one or the other term of an opposition he explicitly rejects. Of course, one *Notebook* entry does not an argument make. Nonetheless, I think there is sufficient evidence in the corpus to support the claim that Camus considered the debate between Christians and moderns to be a non-starter and the apocalyptic ambitions of both accounts to be highly problematic.

I begin my analysis with a discussion of Camus' critique of modernity, particularly its emphasis on the notion of quantity and the consequences of that emphasis for the question of meaning. Then I explore the manner in which that emphasis is derived from Christianity's radical separation of sacred and profane reality and the peculiar nature of its pursuit of perfection. I conclude with a brief sketch of Camus' sense of the sacred and an account of how it supersedes the limitations of both Christianity and modernity.

---

[15] Bernard Murchland, "The Dark Night Before the Coming of Grace" in *Camus: A Collection of Critical Essays*, ed. Germaine Brée (New Jersey: Prentice-Hall, Inc., 1962), 63.

[16] Sprintzen, David. *Camus: A Critical Examination* (Philadelphia: Temple University Press, 1988), 44, 275-278.

Modern Civilization and the Reign of Quantity

Camus argues that the brutality of modernity is due to its abandonment of the "vertical civilization of quality" in favour of a "horizontal civilization of quantity."[17] By vertical civilization he means one in which a preoccupation with quality or substance is a significant consideration in both public and private affairs. By horizontal civilization he means the modern Western world, beginning with Columbus' conquest of the Americas and continuing into our contemporary technological society's conquest of human and non-human nature.[18]

For Camus these conquests are not merely an expression of the natural desire to acquire common to all civilizations and peoples. They signal rather a new relationship to reality in which meaning is experienced not as present but as elsewhere or yet to come. The brutality of such a civilization stems from this change of meaning and not from its conquests understood as the acquisition of territory in the traditional sense, though these conquests were certainly brutal.[19] If meaning is confined to the future absolutely, then the deprivations of the present are also absolute. Lagging behind historically or politically or even philosophically in that conquest does not merely disadvantage one competitively, but damns one to meaninglessness. However, since utter meaninglessness is not endurable (when anyone says it is, watch carefully – consolations are on their way), one must somehow supply the missing meaning oneself. But how can this be done? Meaning cannot be found in experience because experience is tied relationally to what is present. It must therefore be found in the impulse of acquisition itself, and the engine of that impulse is the will. Because the will is unguided by reason or meaning, its most complete expression is the most powerful one. As Camus argues in *The Rebel*, meaning then becomes "power" or more precisely a lust for power whose most complete expression is "frenzy."[20] Frenzy is power at its height, unfocused and completely unrestrained. Its excesses fill up the present while

---

[17] Albert Camus, *Notebooks 1951-1959*, 73.

[18] Ibid., 74; *The Rebel*, 215-ff; *Lyrical and Critical Essays*, 139. In *Notebooks 1951-1959* the next entry begins: "In a civilization such as ours..."

[19] For a compelling, early account of both forms of brutality, see Bartolomé de las Casas, *A Short Account of the Destruction of the Indies*, trans. & ed. Nigel Griffin (London: Penguin Books, 1992).

[20] Albert Camus, *The Rebel*, 225.

simultaneously blurring all sense of time or temporal progression, thus creating a momentary sense of completion – an eternal present, if you will. But this sense of completion cannot last so long as history has not achieved its predicted end. In order for the illusion of meaning to be preserved the will must therefore expend itself constantly in new acquisitions with no concern for order, object, or proportion. The world and its inhabitants become mere occasions for the expression of one's power. Camus characterizes the resulting form of life as "an enormous, brutal orgy" in which objects and events mix indiscriminately and in complete disregard of their nature.[21]

In the early and mid-twentieth century this frenzied lust for meaning was extremely violent. That violence was the consequence of a confrontation between an old world of quality and a new world of quality and pure efficiency. Camus offers us a graphic image of the latter world in his novel *The Plague*. As the ill and the dead from the plague multiply, the citizens of Oran becoming increasingly efficient in their treatment of them.[22] Those who fall ill are immediately separated from their family and loved ones to be interned in mass camps where their fate is inevitably to die alone. As to the dead, as the bodies pile up, the methods of internment become more and more efficient, leading first to perfunctory funerals, then to the elimination of funerals altogether in favour of mass graves, and finally to the crematorium. Yet so imperious is the human desire to lament and to resist this efficient handling of those lost to them that, despite official warnings and armed patrols, the citizens of Oran line the tracks leading to the crematorium to throw flowers on the bodies of the nameless dead.[23]

One of the profound insights of *The Plague* is that although the camps and burial practices developed by the city's officials are indeed very efficient means of dealing with the plague victims, they also lead the Oranians to commit great moral evils. This is something Rieux and his friends finally come to understand. As a consequence they begin to change their practices.

---

[21] Ibid.

[22] The description of the manner in which Rieux and the town officials determine to respond to the epidemic in this regard is found in Part Three of the novel. Albert Camus, *The Plague*, trans. Stuart Gilbert (London: Penguin Books, 1960), 138-152.

[23] "The residents in this area soon learnt what was going on. And, though the cliffs were patrolled night and day, little groups of people contrived to thread their way unseen between the rocks and would toss flowers into the open trailers as the trams went by." Ibid., 147.

By the end of the story Rieux will refuse to allow Tarrou to be sent to the camp, preferring instead to care for him in his own home, in flagrant disregard of the rules.[24] Though such a decision increases the risk of death and the spreading contagion, it heals Rieux of the moral contagion of efficiency and of the spiritual death it entails.

Twentieth century totalitarian regimes understand reality in a way similar to the Oranians, though their policies are more actively violent than those of the latter. Totalitarians treat substantial or qualitative realities (people) as if they were mere quantities (numbers or matter) in order to cleanse the world of the naturally deficient and sick. The result is a frenzied or total violence. Western liberal democracies are more like Oranian society in both thought and practice.[25] Though fully committed to the principles of quantity and efficiency, we discourage violence as a means of carrying it out domestically. In our time the transition from a qualitative to a quantitative civilization is nearing completion, which can be seen in the principled exclusion of all questions of meaning from public discussion, whether of health, education, economics, or the weather, in favour of purely quantitative measures of meaning and productivity. For instance, the exclusion of questions about real wealth during the sub-prime mortgage debacle in the United States is mirrored in rise of credentialing as the final goal of university education. In both cases commodity values (GPAs, tuition, housing prices) rise as real values drop through the floor.[26] In the United States alone education is a trillion dollar industry, and its mavens know how to juke the stats as effectively as any Wall Street broker.[27] Anyone who walks into a university classroom today can feel that change in her bones. We are simply no longer concerned with quality of the education we offer our students or the real cultivation of their intellectual abilities – we are concerned with numbers and with the illusion of quality they create statistically.

---

[24] Tarrou himself comments: "it's the first time I've known you to do the injection without ordering the patient off the isolation ward." Ibid., 230.

[25] As with Orwell's setting of *Nineteen Eighty-Four* in the United Kingdom, Camus' setting of *The Plague* in Oran (that is to say, the West) was not accidental.

[26] One of the best analyses of the subprime mortgage crisis can be found in Michael Lewis, "The End", *Portfolio Magazine*, December 2008.

[27] Richard Arum & Josipa Roksa, *Academically Adrift: Limited Learning on College Campuses* (Chicago: University of Chicago Press, 2010).

Though these contexts may seem quite remote from the excesses of contemporary totalitarianism, it is the same principle at work in both of them. As Camus says in *The Rebel*, "to ensure man's empire over the world, it is necessary to supress in the world and in man everything that escapes the Empire, everything that does not come under the reign of quantity: and this is an endless undertaking."[28] The mastery of the human and non-human nature rests on the "reign of quantity." Anywhere it becomes the guiding ethos in public and private affairs, substantial questions of meaning or quality must be suppressed.

We have set aside the burdens and responsibilities of substantial reality in favour of the alluring dream of virtual reality – an avatar in which the former survives only as appearance whose manipulation is carried out with keystrokes rather than weapons and is potentially infinite.[29] What twentieth century totalitarian would not be envious? It is as if our entire world is being "uploaded" into cyber space. Politically and experientially the frenzy is still there, but it has become benign. One can witness it in the manic acquisitions made at the newest Apple Store. For us, too, the deprivations of the present drive us to the future as a means of securing meaning. But our frenzied consumers expend their will only in the acquisition of money and the salvation it affords them through the purchase of the latest sacraments on offer from Steve Jobs and company. There is a high cost to be paid here also – lives lost in an endless accumulation of wealth, the emotional wasteland of the bourgeois, obsessive work alternating with obsessive screen watching, periodic vacations to ward of the creeping sense of meaninglessness, and the willing handing over of an entire generation of children to a technology industry that is anything but benign. But at least we are not killing one another. Apple employees are armed not with automatic weapons but wireless cash registers. You cannot even get a real receipt anymore. It is an ideal transaction that even the reality of paper, with its potential for waste, would render unholy.[30] But at least our dreams are no longer troubled by the

---

[28] Albert Camus, *The Rebel*, 234.

[29] For a compelling discussion of this change, see Jean Baudrillard, *The Perfect Crime*, trans. Chris Turner (London: Verso Books, 1996).

[30] The ethic of productivity and the notion of efficiency that underlie the quantitative principle require that there be as little waste in the system as possible. See Jean Baudrillard, *The Transparency of Evil: Essays on Extreme Phenomena*, trans. Chris Turner (London: Verso Books, 1993).

final apocalypse sought by the previous century. We now believe the malleability of human nature to be infinite so there will never be a final solution.[31] And why would anyone want one so long as the machines keep running and the dividends keep accumulating? Perhaps there is always something to be thankful for.

What caused this transition from a vertical to a horizontal civilization? How did modernity come to abandon so completely the concern with quality that had defined all previous societies in favour of a desire for a quantitative mastery of reality? The desire for completion that animates modernity's most apocalyptic ambitions is not itself the cause of these excesses. That desire is natural and universally human. All people long for completion and suffer its absence. These are the vertical movements toward quality that Camus claims animate all civilizations. But modernity has come into an inheritance in this regard. Its understanding of these movements was so thoroughly imbued with Christian sentiments and formulations that even the Renaissance, that great restoration of Classical culture, philosophy, and science was in the end more Christian and Roman than Greek. Moderns acquired from Christianity both an impetus and framework for their dream of perfection in which God in the traditional sense played no part. How the Christian notion of divinity encouraged and abetted such an ambition is what we must now consider.

Christianity and the Desire for Perfection

In Christianity substance is God or the other world.[32] God is the perfection that human beings seek in their desire for completion. Because the world has substance only derivatively from God, the denial of God entails a loss of meaning which is absolute.[33] This is the essence of the Christian teaching and

---

[31] In *The Rebel* Camus argues that this notion of "infinite malleability" is one of modernity's primary ambitions.

[32] Cf. Dostoevsky, *The Brothers Karamazov*, trans. Constance Garnett (New York: W. W. Norton & Company, 1976). In his account of the teachings of the Christian faith, Zosima tells his listeners that if that feeling [of contact with other mysterious worlds] grows weak or is destroyed in you, the heavenly growth will die away in you. Then you will be indifferent to life and even grow to hate it" (299-300).

[33] Cf. Søren Kierkegaard: "Nature, the totality of created things, is the work of God. And yet God is not there." And again: "Nature is, indeed, the work of God, but only the handiwork is present, not God." Søren Kierkegaard, *Concluding Unscientific Postscript,* trans. David Swenson and Walter Lowrie (Princeton: Princeton University Press, 1941), 218-220.

the basis of its critique of modernity. According to Christianity, moderns deny God but mask the meaninglessness to which that denial commits them with surrogate forms of perfection. However, because these surrogate perfections deny substance, they cannot provide meaning but only excitement, the satisfactions of which are often intense but always fleeting.

Despite its elevated language, there is much that is sensible in the Christian teaching. Like the ancients, Christians identify their highest aspirations with what is most beautiful in life and place that reality in the other world so as to preserve it the machinations of mortals. Thus does it provide a source of meaning and a measure of conduct that is free from human folly and cunning. The existence of perfection is affirmed while allowing our natural desire to criticize to flourish, but without the danger of that criticism leading to despair or nihilistic destruction. Jean Baudrillard's remark in the epigraph to this analysis is apropos: God is our best bet because he affirms our desire for perfection while absolving us the responsibility to achieve it. The same salutary ambiguity is evident in Samuel Beckett's play, *Waiting for Godot*. Vladimir and Estragon wait for Godot, however neither of them wants him to arrive.[34] And they have good reason for their reticence. Given what little they know about him from their various encounters, should Godot arrive the character he would most closely resemble is Pozzo, with his whip.[35]

Interpreted in this way the Christian teaching is recognizably related to the philosophy of the ancient Greeks and the older messianic teachings of Judaism in which the Messiah's coming is affirmed but never desired.[36] But there are also important differences, the most significant of which is the way in which Christians distinguish between God and world and the implications

---

[34] Samuel Beckett, *Waiting for Godot*, trans. Samuel Beckett (New York: Grove Press, 1982).

[35] Paul Corey, *Messiahs and Machiavellians: Depicting Evil in the Modern Theatre* (Notre Dame: Notre Dame Press, 2008).

[36] Derrida's messianicity without messianism is an effective reformulation of that ancient teaching. "The Messiah might also be the one I expect even while I do not want him to come...That is why the man who addressed the Messiah said, 'When will you come?' That is a way to say, well as long as I speak to you, as long as I ask you that question, 'When will you come?,' at least you are not coming. And that is the condition for me to go one asking questions and living. So there is some ambiguity in the messianic structure. We wait for something we would like not to wait for." Jacques Derrida, *Deconstruction in a Nutshell: A Conversation with Jacques Derrida*, ed. John Caputo (New York: Fordham University Press, 1997), 24-25.

of that distinction for Christianity's apocalyptic ambitions. The comparison with *Waiting for Godot* is illuminating in this respect. If meaning resides solely with God, then the world has no meaning at all. This is the reason for Camus' assertion in *The Rebel* that it was Christianity that first "emptied the world of its substance."[37] Christians reject that argument, of course. They claim that though God is meaning and meaning is transcendent, God is also present in the world through the incarnation and sacraments. But this does not resolve the problem, because dogmas and rituals are not reality but a "conglomeration of symbols."[38] They are words, not experiences. To say that God can be experienced only if one first believes a series of propositions that cannot be experienced is simply not the same thing as experiencing something immediately and directly, including God.

The desire for perfection always involves a measure of "elsewhereness" in order to account for the imperiousness of the experience and the fact that it is never completely fulfilled. This elsewhereness is also evident in the Christian apocalyptic literature, and there is nothing wrong with it per se. One might question the quality of the stories as stories, but that is a different matter. Nonetheless, with the development of these stories, something important had changed.[39] The distinction between transcendence and immanence became so acute in the Christian tradition that the apocalyptic narrative tended to have the opposite effect of what it did in the traditional ancient literature of this type. Rather than encouraging people to cultivate virtue and pursue perfection in all of their affairs, the apocalyptic narratives actually compromised those ambitions. In Christianity the desire for perfection ceased to be a story about moral improvement and instead became a personal and political program to secure one's own salvation and to defeat one's enemies, the achievement of which eclipsed all ethical considerations.[40] But saving yourself and achieving victory are simply not the same things as becoming

---

[37] Albert Camus, *The Rebel*, 190.

[38] Ibid.

[39] In *Cosmos, Chaos, and the World to Come*, Norman Cohn argues that the Christian apocalypticism, though perhaps the most developed form of the teaching, has antecedents in Zoroastrianism. Normal Cohn, *Cosmos, Chaos, and the World to Come: The Ancient Roots of Apocalyptic Faith* (New Haven: Yale University Press, 1995).

[40] This argument was made by Zdravko Planinc during a lecture entitle "Utopia/Dystopia, Perfection/ Imperfection: Ancients and Moderns" delivered at the University of Prince Edward Island on November 5, 2012.

virtuous in the classical sense. Indeed, for a writer such as Plato virtue often requires foregoing salvation understood as self-preservation in order to fulfill its demands.[41] Eternal salvation is in this sense a kind of desperate self-interest magnified and religiously justified.[42]

Once that change had occurred all the distortions inherent in the narrative that would normally amount to nothing (they are just stories after all) began to have very serious philosophical and political implications, most of which were exacerbated significantly by the tendency of Christians to act publically on the basis of the Church's most sectarian teachings.[43] The most capable minds within the tradition understood the meaning of the transition and attempted to limit its potential damage by creating doctrinal and ecclesiastical hedges around the most extreme of its apocalyptic aspirations. This was the work of the early councils and patristic writers such as Origen and Augustine.[44] However, once the apocalyptic ambitions began to seem realizable and gain credibility in certain wings of the Church, there was no way to silence them completely. And the situation became even more acute in the modern period. Modern apocalyptic thinkers retained the worst elements of the tradition, including the Christian tendency for poor storytelling. This is not idiosyncratic. As Camus says in "The Future of Tragedy," the reason apocalyptic stories make for bad literature is that they are melodramatic.[45] One side of the confrontation is good, the other completely evil, and the bulk of the story is merely a matter of ensuring that everyone gets her just deserts. But these literary problems pale by comparison to the real political consequences of the teachings. Modern

---

[41] To give only one example, in book 1 of the *Republic* Socrates "defeats" Thrasymachus's argument, thereby saving himself, but claims that his victory is empty because it has not taught him what real justice is. Plato, *Republic*, trans. Allan Bloom (New York: Basic Books, 1968), 354a-c.

[42] *The Fall* is perhaps Camus' most penetrating analysis of this aspect of the Christian teaching. Jean-Baptiste Clemance's obsession with immortality in the sense of a future life is an expression of his self-love. See chapter 3 of Ron Srigley, *Albert Camus' Critique of Modernity*, "Modernity in Its Fullest Expression."

[43] Norman Cohn's *The Pursuit of the Millennium* offers a colourful and disturbing account of such actions. Norman Cohn, *The Pursuit of the Millennium: Revolutionary Millenarians and the Mystical Anarchists of the Middle Ages* (London: Pimlico, 2004).

[44] See books 20-22 of Augustine, *City of God*, trans. Gerald G. Walsh (New York: Doubleday, Image Books, 1958).

[45] Albert Camus, *Lyrical and Critical* Essays, 301-2.

sectarianism is more violent and brutal than the worst excesses of the Church. There are many reasons for this, but one of the most important is the fact that the ancient, non-apocalyptic account of perfection had been completely eclipsed by the Church over the course of centuries and therefore there existed no living tradition to appeal to or fall back on when the physical violence threatened to become apocalyptic. People simply felt that way about reality and about other people.

Camus' Sense of the Sacred

Camus understood clearly the character of his time and attempted to respond to it carefully in his writing. He also wanted to express faithfully his own experience of the sacred and explain how it might help to overcome the excesses of Christianity and modernity. His solution is as simple as it is elegant and becomes perfectly clear if you only think about it for a moment. In Christian and modern accounts the price of permanent perfection in the future is absolute deprivation in the present. One could also say that present deprivation is the necessary condition for future perfection. Camus describes this experience in *The Fall*, in which Jean-Baptiste Clemance uses the torments of the "little ease" to distort and exploit natural feelings of guilt in order to justify and encourage excessive desires for salvation and innocence.[46] As Nietzsche argues in the *Antichrist*, in this regard Christianity requires sickness as much as the Greeks required health.[47]

Camus longs for perfection too and even identifies it with the sacred or God. But he reverses the terms of the Christian account and argues that divinity is present in deprivation too. For him the sacred is an experience of fulfillment or completion and it is always experienced in the present.[48] Deprivation lies in the future and is consummated in death. These two divinities preside over our coming and going and both of them come from "deep within the earth."[49]

---

[46] Albert Camus, *The Fall*, trans. Justin O'Brien (New York: Vintage International, 1991), 109-118.

[47] Friedrich Nietzsche, *Twilight of the Idols/The Anti-Christ*, trans. R. J. Hollingdale (London: Penguin Books, 1990).

[48] Albert Camus, *Lyrical and Critical Essays*, 71, 102, 70.

[49] Ibid., 72, 170, 328.

This does not mean Camus accepts death easily or thinks its deprivations only apparent. He does not. "Creating conscious deaths," the task of his early essay "The Wind at Djemila," "is to diminish the distance that separates us from the world and to accept a consummation without joy, alert to the rapturous images of a world forever lost."[50] Camus' account is classical because it acknowledges that eternal perfection is unattainable, not because it is absent, but rather because it *does not last*. The argument here is not that death prevents the realization of perfection because it has no sequel. That is to say, the problem is not that there is no afterlife in which reality will be restored or redeemed. Rather, it is the stronger claim that the world is so perfectly suited to human life, so rich in sound, colour, and taste and so full of meaning, that a better arrangement *cannot be imagined*. "What is strange about finding on earth the unity Plotinus longed for?" Camus asks incredulously. Or again: "If I obstinately refuse all the 'later ons' of this world, it is because I have no desire to give up my present wealth. I do not want to believe that death is a gateway to another life. For me, it is a closed door. Everything I am offered seeks to deliver man from the weight of his own life. But as I watch the great birds flying heavily through the sky at Djemila, it is precisely a certain weight of life I ask for and obtain."[51] Life is its meaning. Or in another idiom, the world is "divine."[52]

As I noted at the beginning of this discussion, Camus distinguishes between the sacred and a future life. He affirms the former and denies the latter. The formulation seems to suggest a important though qualified agreement with Christianity. Camus believes in God and desires the perfection entailed by that belief, but refuses or is unable to believe in its achievement. He is thus left with tragedy rather than redemption. This is Camus as pagan and proto-typical Christian. He acknowledges sin, desires salvation, but cannot accept grace. There is, however, another way of interpreting the remark, one that moves in the opposite direction. Camus' denial of a future life is not a repudiation of immortality but of perfection in the Christian sense. Christian perfection is not immortality but the apocalypse. The primary feature of the apocalypse is not deathlessness but a change of reality. The apocalypse is driven by ethics or the need for a final improvement that goes by the name of redemption.

---

[50] Ibid., 78.

[51] Ibid., 76.

[52] Ibid., 7.

Camus recognizes the deficiencies of life and the correlative need for ethics but he also knows there is something that "transcends ethics" and its nagging complaint about the world.[53] He does not know what to call this something, however. He stutters to describe it because he does not want ethics to compromise this experience of transcendence or for the experience to compromise ethics. The language he settles on suggests a darker, more mysterious order in which all things are included and whose refusal is the ground from which arise the most unyielding denials of transcendence and the most dangerous and apocalyptic demands.[54] Camus rejects both excesses in order to embrace the "unchanging" mysterious order. This is the divine object of his desire, participation in which provides the only context in which the experience of immorality makes sense.[55] Herein lies Camus' divinity, his immortality, and his opposition to the Christian desire for perfection in a future life.

There is an awareness of the sacred or transcendence in all of Camus' writings, from *The Myth of Sisyphus* to *The First Man*. I would go so far as to say that there is not a book or essay in the entire corpus that is not somehow concerned with exploring the human confrontation with this reality. And there are gods too – "the sun, the night, the sea."[56] These are the cosmic divinities common to all civilizations. But Camus also claims to experience the sacred in things that are far less obviously transcendent. He speaks of it as lying buried in a "valley of olive trees," or as whispering through the silent ruins of North Africa, or as shining forth in the asphodels of spring and in the odor of crushed mastic bulbs.[57] This not poetic excess. Camus claims that the "mystery" he experiences and which draws him is actually *in* such things. This is tantamount to saying that the sacred is not merely apparent in the visible world but that the visible itself partakes of the sacred in an essential way. Here the traditional categories of transcendence and immanence blur and lose their pre-eminence as analytic tools for speaking about divinity. They give way to cosmology in which the sacred has no discernible borders in human experience or the natural world and is therefore present to us all in

---

[53] "Return to Tipasa" in ibid., 170.

[54] Ibid., 171.

[55] Albert Camus, "Preface to *The Wrong Side and the Right Side*" in ibid., 7.

[56] Albert Camus, *Lyrical and Critical Essays*, 328.

[57] Ibid., 170, 102, 68.

ways we have been told for millennia it is not. In such formulations we find good reasons to be cheerful and to begin again to explore the world as it is given to us.

Bibliography

Arum, Richard & Roksa, Josipa. *Academically Adrift: Limited Learning on College Campuses*. Chicago: University of Chicago Press, 2010.

Baudrillard, Jean. *The Perfect Crime*. Trans. Chris Turner. London: Verso Books, 1996.

_____. *The Transparency of Evil: Essays on Extreme Phenomena*. Trans. Chris Turner. London: Verso Books, 1993.

Beckett, Samuel. *Waiting for Godot*. Trans. Samuel Beckett. New York: Grove Press, 1982.

Camus, Albert. *Essais*. Paris: Gallimard, 1965.

_____. *The Fall*. Trans. Justin O'Brien. New York: Vintage International, 1991.

_____. *Lyrical and Critical Essays*. Trans. Ellen Conroy Kennedy. Ed. Philip Thody. New York: Vintage Books, 1970.

_____. *Notebooks 1942-1951*. Trans. Justin O'Brien. New York: Paragon House, 1991.

_____. *Notebooks 1951-1959*. Trans. Ryan Bloom. Chicago: Ivan R. Dee, 2008.

_____. *The Rebel*. Trans. Anthony Bower. New York: Vintage Books, 1991.

Cohn, Normal. *Cosmos, Chaos, and the World to Come: The Ancient Roots of Apocalyptic Faith*. New Haven: Yale University Press, 1995.

_____. *The Pursuit of the Millennium: Revolutionary Millenarians and the Mystical Anarchists of the Middle Ages*. London: Pimlico, 2004.

Corey, Paul. *Messiahs and Machiavellians: Depicting Evil in the Modern Theatre*. Notre Dame: Notre Dame Press, 2008.

Derrida, Jacques. *Deconstruction in a Nutshell: A Conversation with Jacques Derrida*. Ed. John Caputo. New York: Fordham University Press, 1997.

Dostoevsky, Fyodor. *The Brothers Karamazov*. Trans. Constance Garnett. New York: W. W. Norton & Company, 1976.

Kierkegaard, Søren. *Concluding Unscientific Postscript.* Trans. David Swenson and Walter Lowrie. Princeton: Princeton University Press, 1941.

Lewis, Michael. "The End." *Portfolio Magazine*. December 2008.

Murchland, Bernard. "The Dark Night Before the Coming of Grace." In *Camus: A Collection of Critical Essays*. Ed. Germaine Brée. New Jersey: Prentice-Hall, Inc., 1962.

Nietzsche, Friedrich. *Twilight of the Idols/The Anti-Christ*. Trans. R. J. Hollingdale. London: Penguin Books, 1990.

Onimus, Jean. *Albert Camus and Christianity*. Trans. Emmett Parker. Alabama: University of Alabama, 1970.

Planinc, Zdravko. "Utopia/Dystopia, Perfection/ Imperfection: Ancients and Moderns." Lecture delivered at the University of Prince Edward Island, November 5, 2012.

Plato, *Republic*. Trans. Allan Bloom. New York: Basic Books, 1968.

Sprintzen, David. *Camus: A Critical Examination*. Philadelphia: Temple University Press, 1988.

Srigley, Ron. *Albert Camus' Critique of Modernity* (Columbia: University of Missouri Press, 2011.

Journal of Camus Studies – Manuscript Submission Guidelines

Mission & Scope:

The *Journal of Camus Studies* is designed to provide an interdisciplinary forum for conversation about the life and work of Albert Camus. The *Journal of Camus Studies* was founded in 2008 as the *Journal of the Albert Camus Society* by Simon Lea. The inaugural volume represented the work of international authors exploring the life and work of Camus from a variety of philosophical and theoretical perspectives. In 2010, Peter Francev was appointed General Editor in an effort to focus more intentionally on reaching an academic audience. The goal of the journal is to provide an international and interdisciplinary resource for those interested in furthering the work and thought of Albert Camus and his contemporaries.

Manuscripts:

Abstracts: Prior to manuscript submission, authors are asked to submit the following: full contact information along with a brief, one-paragraph biography detailing current affiliation, research interests and recent publications, as well as an abstract of no more than 250 words.

Manuscript Preparation: Manuscripts should be no longer than 10,000 words (text and notes). The entire paper must be double-spaced, with one-inch margins and 12-point font, in MS Word. Both the paper and notes must conform to the *MLA Style Manual and Guide to Scholarly Publishing*, 3rd edition. They must avoid sexist and ethnic biases. Also, manuscripts must not be under consideration by another publication. Along with the manuscript, the author must prepare a separate file as a cover letter. This file will include a history of the manuscript, whether it is derived from an M.A. or Ph.D. thesis with the advisor's name, whether it has been presented at a conference, or other pertinent information about its development. Authors are encouraged to submit all materials using MS Word to the General Editor who, then, will forward the materials to the review committee.

Review Process:

The *Journal of Camus Studies* follows a policy of blind, peer review; please ensure that the main body of the manuscript contains no identifying remarks. All comments by reviewers are confidential and shall not be published. Final judgment with regard to publication is made by the General Editor.

When the editor receives a submission, the manuscript will undergo a peer review. At least, two reviewers will provide evaluative comments for each submission. On the basis of this review, the manuscript may be unconditionally rejected, conditionally accepted, or unconditionally accepted for publication. Each submitter will be provided with the peer review statements and may respond to the comments, ask questions, or seek clarification as desired. Evaluations, typically, will be complete within 6-8 weeks. Standard evaluation forms are used by the reviewers. If a particular reviewer cannot complete a review within a timely manner, the editor will seek an alternative, qualified reviewer. Sometimes the opinion of a reviewer is important enough that the editor must wait a little longer.

Conference Announcements and Book Reviews:

Announcements and correspondence regarding conferences, panels, papers, and other news of interest should be sent to the Editor, *Journal of Camus Studies*, at the address given below.

Books to be reviewed will be reviewed as long as they are relevant to the life and times of Albert Camus. Books should be sent to the Editor, *Journal of Camus Studies*, at the address given below.

Professor Peter Francev
General Editor, *Journal of Camus Studies*

Dept. of English
Mount San Antonio College
1100 N. Grand Ave
Walnut, California 91789-1399

pfrancev@mtsac.edu